082
REF

HOPWOOD HALL
COLLEGE

...URCE CENTRE

Collins

Quotations

HarperCollins Publishers
Westerhill Road
Bishopbriggs
Glasgow
G64 2QT

This Edition 2013

Reprint 10 9 8 7 6 5 4 3 2 1 0

© HarperCollins Publishers 2004, 2013

ISBN 978-0-00-793590-1

Collins® is a registered trademark of
HarperCollins Publishers Limited

www.collinslanguage.com

A catalogue record for this book is
available from the British Library

Typeset by Davidson Publishing
Solutions

Printed in Great Britain by Clays Ltd,
St Ives plc

INTRODUCTION

'By necessity, by proclivity, and by delight, we all quote,' wrote Emerson over a century ago, and dictionaries of quotations continue to fascinate, entertain and inform in equal measure. In this edition of *Collins Quotations* the reader will find old favourites from classical authors and the great poets and playwrights alongside observation on contemporary life from today's authors, artists, sports personalities, television shows, villains and politicians. This results in a very mixed bag that includes the disgraced entrepreneur Nicholas van Hoogstraten on incarceration: 'When they put me away in 1968, it was nothing. When I was freed I was five times richer, a hundred times more intelligent and a thousand times more dangerous'; Tariq Ali on September 11: 'September 11 and its aftermath have shown that the whole world is the United States empire'; and Giles, the urbane English watcher in *Buffy the Vampire Slayer* on American football: 'I just think it's rather odd that a nation that prides itself on its virility should feel compelled to strap on forty pounds of protective gear just to play rugby.'

The quotations in this selection are presented thematically for ease of reference. Within each subject the entries are arranged alphabetically by author. Quotations from languages other than English appear in English translation, unless they are sufficiently well known to be familiar to the reader in their original language. Writers of speeches will find the thematic arrangement of immense value, and those readers who wish to find quotes from specific authors can easily do so by consulting the index of sources. In those few instances where there are quotations by two authors of the same name, dates of birth and death have been included in the index to differentiate them.

Every care has been taken to verify the quotations, and where the source cannot be identified with certainty, the quote appears as an attribution. We welcome letters from readers and if anyone can add to our knowledge of sources, or indeed wishes to send in favourite quotations for inclusion in a later edition, we would be delighted to hear from them.

CONTENTS

ABSENCE

ASHFORD, Daisy (1881–1972)
My life will be sour grapes and ashes without you.

[*The Young Visiters* (1919)]

BEHAN, Brendan (1923–1964)
When I came back to Dublin, I was courtmartialled in my absence and sentenced to death in my absence, so I said they could shoot me in my absence.

[*The Hostage* (1958)]

CLOUGH, Arthur Hugh (1819–1861)
That out of sight is out of mind
Is true of most we leave behind.

[*Songs in Absence* (1849)]

LA ROCHEFOUCAULD (1613–1680)
Absence diminishes mediocre passions and increases great ones, as the wind extinguishes candles and kindles fire.

[*Maximes*, (1678)]

See **SEPARATION**

ACCIDENTS

COREN, Alan (1938–2007)
The Act of God designation on all insurance policies; which means, roughly, that you cannot be insured for the accidents that are most likely to happen to you.

[*The Lady from Stalingrad Museum* (1977)]

GRAHAM, Harry (1874–1936)
'There's been an accident!' they said,
'Your servant's cut in half; he's dead!'
'Indeed!' said Mr Jones, 'and please
Send me the half that's got my keys.'

[*Ruthless Rhymes for Heartless Homes* (1899)]

PUNCH
What is better than presence of mind in a railway accident? Absence of body.

[1849]

SIMPSON, N.F. (1919–2011)
Knocked down a doctor? With an ambulance? How could she? It's a contradiction in terms!

[*One-Way Pendulum* (1960)]

WILKES, John (1727–1797)
The chapter of accidents is the longest chapter in the book.

[Attr.]

ACTING

ASTOR, Mary (1906–1987)
A painter paints, a musician plays, a writer writes – but a movie actor waits.

[*A Life on Film* (1967)]

BANKHEAD, Tallulah (1903–1968)
Acting is a form of confusion.

[*Tallulah* (1952)]

CUSACK, John (1966–)
Acting should be like punk in the best way. It should be a full-on expression of self – only without the broken bottles.

[*Uncut*, August 2000]

DAVIS, Bette (1908–1989)
Without wonder and insight, acting is just a trade. With it, it becomes creation.

[*The Lonely Life* (1962)]

FONDA, Jane (1937–)
You spend all your life trying to do something they put people in asylums for.

[*Halliwell's Filmgoer's Book of Quotes* (1973)]

GARLAND, Judy (1922–1969)
I was born at the age of 12 on a Metro-Goldwyn-Mayer lot.

[*The Observer*, February 1951]

GIELGUD, Sir John (1904–2000)
Being another character is more interesting than being yourself.

[Attr.]

HULL, Josephine (1886–1957)
Playing Shakespeare is very tiring. You never get to sit down, unless you're a King.

[In Cooper and Hartman, *Violets and Vinegar* (1980)]

LUNT, Alfred (1892–1977)
(On acting)
Speak in a loud clear voice and try not to bump into the furniture.

[In Halliwell, *Filmgoer's Book of Quotes* (1973)]

RICHARDSON, Sir Ralph (1902–1983)
The art of acting consists in keeping people from coughing.

[*The Observer*]

The most precious things in speech are pauses.

[Attr.]

RUSSELL, Rosalind (1911–1976)
Acting is standing up naked and turning around slowly.

[*Life Is a Banquet* (1977)]

SHAKESPEARE, William (1564–1616)
(On the power of acting)
He would drown the stage with tears,
And cleave the general ear with horrid speech;
Make mad the guilty, and appal the free,
Confound the ignorant, and amaze indeed
The very faculties of eyes and ears.
[*Hamlet*, II.ii]

SHERIDAN, Richard Brinsley (1751–1816)
I wish, sir, you would practise this without me. I can't stay dying here all night.
[*The Critic* (1779)]

SMITH, Will (1968–)
I'm not always comfortable with subtle.
[*The Sunday Times*, February 2001]

See **ACTORS, THEATRE**

ACTION

AMIEL, Henri-Frédéric (1821–1881)
Action is but coarsened thought – thought become concrete, obscure, and unconscious.
[*Journal*, 1850]

BEERBOHM, Sir Max (1872–1956)
Anything that is worth doing has been done frequently. Things hitherto undone should be given, I suspect, a wide berth.
[*Mainly on the Air* (1946)]

CANETTI, Elias (1905–1994)
Whatever their activity is, the active think they are better.
[*The Human Province* (1969)]

CARLYLE, Thomas (1795–1881)
The end of man is an Action and not a Thought, though it were the noblest.
[*Sartor Resartus* (1834)]

CHESTERFIELD, Lord (1694–1773)
It is an undoubted truth, that the less one has to do, the less time one finds to do it in. One yawns, one procrastinates, one can do it when one will, and therefore one seldom does it at all.
[Letter]

CONFUCIUS (c.550–c.478 BC)
Chi Wen Tzu always thought three times before taking action. Twice would have been quite enough.
[*Analects*]

DE GAULLE, Charles (1890–1970)
Deliberation is the work of many men. Action, of one alone.
[*War Memoirs*]

ELIOT, George (1819–1880)
Our deeds determine us, as much as we determine our needs.
[*Adam Bede* (1859)]

FLETCHER, John (1579–1625)
Deeds, not words shall speak me.
[*The Lover's Progress* (1647)]

HUXLEY, T.H. (1825–1895)
The great end of life is not knowledge but action.
[*Science and Culture* (1877)]

JOWETT, Benjamin (1817–1893)
The way to get things done is not to mind who gets the credit for doing them.
[Attr.]

KEMPIS, Thomas á (c.1380–1471)
Truly, when the day of judgement comes, it will not be a question of what we have read, but what we have done.
[*De Imitatione Christi* (1892)]

LA ROCHEFOUCAULD (1613–1680)
We would often be ashamed of our finest actions if the world could see the motives behind them.
[*Maximes* (1678)]

SHAW, George Bernard (1856–1950)
Activity is the only road to knowledge.
[*Man and Superman* (1903)]

SPINOZA, Baruch (1632–1677)
I have taken great care not to laugh at human actions, not to weep at them, nor to hate them, but to understand them.
[*Tractatus Politicus* (1677)]

SZASZ, Thomas (1920–2012)
Men are rewarded and punished not for what they do, but rather for how their acts are defined. This is why men are more interested in better justifying themselves than in better behaving themselves.
[*The Second Sin* (1973)]

ACTORS

ANONYMOUS
(On a performance of Cleopatra by Sarah Bernhardt)
How different, how very different from the home life of our own dear Queen!
[Remark]
Totus mundus agit histrionem. The whole world plays the actor.
[Motto of Globe playhouse]

BENCHLEY, Robert (1889-1945)
(Suggesting an epitaph for an actress)
She sleeps alone at last.
[Attr.]

BRANDO, Marlon (1924-2004)
An actor's a guy who, if you ain't talking about him, ain't listening.
[*The Observer*, 1956]

COLERIDGE, Samuel Taylor (1772-1834)
(Of Edmund Kean)
To see him act is like reading Shakespeare by flashes of lightning.
[*Table Talk* (1835)]

COWARD, Sir Noël (1899-1973)
(Comment on a child star, in a long-winded play)
Two things should be cut: the second act and the child's throat.
[In Richards, *The Wit of Noël Coward*]

DILLER, Phyllis (1917-1974)
(Of Arnold Schwarzenegger)
He has so many muscles that he has to make an appointment to move his fingers.
[Attr.]

DUNDY, Elaine (1927-2008)
The question actors most often get asked is how they can bear saying the same things over and over again night after night, but God knows the answer to that is, don't we all anyway; might as well get paid for it.
[*The Dud Avocado* (1958)]

FIELD, Eugene (1850-1895)
(Of Creston Clarke as King Lear)
He played the King as though under momentary apprehension that someone else was about to play the ace.
[Attr.]

FORD, John (1895-1973)
It is easier to get an actor to be a cowboy than to get a cowboy to be an actor.
[Attr.]

HITCHCOCK, Alfred (1899-1980)
I deny that I ever said that actors are cattle. What I said was, 'Actors should be treated like cattle'.
[Attr.]
Nobody can really like an actor.
[*The New Yorker*, 1992]

HOPPER, Hedda (1890-1966)
At one time I thought he wanted to be an actor. He had certain qualifications, including no money and a total lack of responsibility.
[*From Under My Hat* (1953)]

JOHNSON, Samuel (1709-1784)
Players, Sir! I look upon them as no better than creatures set upon tables and joint stools to make faces and produce laughter, like dancing dogs.
[In Boswell, *The Life of Samuel Johnson* (1791)]

KAUFMAN, George S. (1889-1961)
(On Raymond Massey's interpretation of Abraham Lincoln)
Massey won't be satisfied until somebody assassinates him.
[In Meredith, *George S. Kaufman and the Algonquin Round Table* (1974)]

LANCHESTER, Elsa (1902-1986)
(Of Maureen O'Hara)
She looked as though butter wouldn't melt in her mouth – or anywhere else.
[Attr.]

LEVANT, Oscar (1906-1972)
Romance on the High Seas was Doris Day's first picture; that was before she became a virgin.
[*Memoirs of an Amnesiac* (1965)]

MALOUF, David (1934-)
Actors don't pretend to be other people; they become themselves by finding other people inside them.
[*Harland's Half Acre* (1984)]

OLIVIER, Laurence (Baron) (1907-1989)
(To Dustin Hoffman, who had stayed up all night to play a character in the film Marathon Man (1976) who had stayed up all night)
Why not try acting? It's much easier.

PARKER, Dorothy (1893-1967)
(Remark on a performance by Katherine Hepburn)
She ran the whole gamut of the emotions from A to B.
[In Carey, *Katherine Hepburn* (1985)]
Scratch an actor and you'll find an actress.
[Attr.]

WILLIAMSON, Nicol (1938-2011)
(Of Sean Connery)
Guys like him and Caine talk about acting as if they knew what it was.
[Interview, Daily *Mail*, 1996]

WINCHELL, Walter (1897-1972)
(Referring to a show starring Earl Carroll)
I saw it at a disadvantage – the curtain was up.
[In Whiteman, *Come to Judgement*]

See **ACTING, THEATRE**

ADDICTION

BANKHEAD, Tallulah (1903–1968)
Cocaine isn't habit-forming. I know, because I've been taking it for years.

[Attr.]

BURROUGHS, William S. (1914–1999)
Junk is the ideal product ... the ultimate merchandise. No sales talk necessary. The client will crawl through a sewer and beg to buy.

[*Naked Lunch* (1959)]

JUNG, Carl Gustav (1875–1961)
Every form of addiction is a bad thing, irrespective of whether it is to alcohol, morphine or idealism.

[*Memories, Dreams, Thoughts* (1962)]

ADULTERY

ARCHER, Mary (1944–)
By the time I discovered it, it was in the past – wives are not the first to find out about these matters.

[*The Sunday Times*, July 2001]

AUSTEN, Jane (1775–1817)
I am proud to say that I have a very good eye at an Adultress, for tho' repeatedly assured that another in the same party was the She, I fixed upon the right one from the first.

[Letter to Cassandra Austen, 1801]

BENCHLEY, Robert (1889–1945)
(Comment on an office shared with Dorothy Parker)
One cubic foot less of space and it would have constituted adultery.

[Attr.]

BURCHILL, Julie (1960–)
(Reply to comments by ex-husband Tony Parsons)
I did not leave him due to his infidelity ... but because of my own flagrant adultery and because I was simply very, very bored with him.

[*The Guardian*, July 2001]

BYRON, Lord (1788–1824)
What men call gallantry, and gods adultery, Is much more common where the climate's sultry.

[*Don Juan* (1824)]

Merely innocent flirtation. Not quite adultery, but adulteration.

[*Don Juan* (1824)]

CARTER, Jimmy (1924–)
I've looked on a lot of women with lust. I've committed adultery in my heart many times. God recognizes I will do this and forgives me.

[Interview with *Playboy*, 1976]

HUXLEY, Aldous (1894–1963)
There are few who would not rather be taken in adultery than in provincialism.

[*Antic Hay* (1923)]

MAUGHAM, William Somerset (1874–1965)
You know, of course, that the Tasmanians, who never committed adultery, are now extinct.

[*The Bread-Winner*]

RICHELIEU, Duc de (1766–1822)
(On discovering his wife with her lover)
Madame, you must really be more careful. Suppose it had been someone else who found you like this.

[In Wallechinsky, *The Book of Lists* (1977)]

SHAKESPEARE, William (1564–1616)
Adultery?
Thou shalt not die. Die for adultery? No.
The wren goes to't, and the small gilded fly
Does lecher in my sight.
Let copulation thrive.

[*King Lear*, IV.vi]

See **MARRIAGE, SEX**

ADULTS

BEAUVOIR, Simone de (1908–1986)
What is an adult? A child blown up by age.

[*The Woman Destroyed* (1969)]

HARRIS, Sydney J. (1917–1986)
We have not passed that subtle line between childhood and adulthood until we move from the passive voice to the active voice – that is, until we have stopped saying 'It got lost', and say, 'I lost it'.

[Attr.]

MILLAY, Edna St Vincent (1892–1950)
Was it for this I uttered prayers, And sobbed and cursed and kicked the stairs, That now, domestic as a plate, I should retire at half-past eight?

['Grown-up' (1920)]

ROSTAND, Jean (1894–1977)
To be an adult is to be alone.

[*Thoughts of a Biologist* (1939)]

SHAKESPEARE, William (1564–1616)
Your lordship, though not clean past your youth, hath yet some smack of age in you, some relish of the saltness of time.
[*Henry IV, Part 2*, I.ii]

SZASZ, Thomas (1920–2012)
A child becomes an adult when he realizes that he has a right not only to be right but also to be wrong.
[*The Second Sin* (1973)]

ADVERTISING

ALLEN, Fred (1894–1957)
An advertising agency is 85 per cent confusion and 15 per cent commission.
[*Treadmill to Oblivion* 1954]

DOUGLAS, Norman (1868–1952)
You can tell the ideals of a nation by its advertisements.
[*South Wind* (1917)]

FITZGERALD, Zelda (1900–1948)
We grew up founding our dreams on the infinite promise of American advertising. I still believe that one can learn to play the piano by mail and that mud will give you a perfect complexion.
[*Save Me the Waltz* (1932)]

HUXLEY, Aldous (1894–1963)
It is far easier to write ten passably effective Sonnets, good enough to take in the not too inquiring critic, than one effective advertisement that will take in a few thousand of the uncritical buying public.
[*On the Margin* (1923)]

JEFFERSON, Thomas (1743–1826)
Advertisements contain the only truths to be relied on in a newspaper.
[Letter, 1819]

JOHNSON, Samuel (1709–1784)
Promise, large promise, is the soul of an advertisement.
[*The Idler* (1758–1760)]

LAHR, John (1941–)
Society drives people crazy with lust and calls it advertising.
[*The Guardian*, August 1989]

LEACOCK, Stephen (1869–1944)
Advertising may be described as the science of arresting the human intelligence long enough to get money from it.
[In Prochow, *The Public Speaker's Treasure Chest*]

LEVERHULME, Viscount (1851–1925)
Half the money I spend on advertising is wasted, and the trouble is I don't know which half.
[In Ogilvy, *Confessions of an Advertising Man* (1963)]

MCLUHAN, Marshall (1911–1980)
Ads are the cave art of the twentieth century.
[*Culture Is Our Business* (1970)]

NASH, Ogden (1902–1971)
Beneath this slab
John Brown is stowed.
He watched the ads,
And not the road.
['Lather as You Go' (1942)]

ADVICE

BIERCE, Ambrose (1842–c.1914)
Advice: The smallest current coin.
[*The Cynic's Word Book* (1906)]

BISMARCK, Prince Otto von (1815–1898)
To youth I have but three words of counsel
– work, work, work.
[Attr.]

BURTON, Robert (1577–1640)
Who cannot give good counsel? 'tis cheap, it costs them nothing.
[*Anatomy of Melancholy* (1621)]

EDWARD VIII (later Duke of Windsor) (1894–1972)
Perhaps one of the only positive pieces of advice that I was ever given was that supplied by an old courtier who observed: 'Only two rules really count. Never miss an opportunity to relieve yourself; never miss a chance to sit down and rest your feet.'
[*A King's Story* (1951)]

EMERSON, Ralph Waldo (1803–1882)
It was a high counsel that I once heard given to a young person, – 'Always do what you are afraid to do.'
[*Essays, First Series* (1841)]

HARRIS, George (1844–1922)
(In his address to students at the beginning of a new academic year)
I intended to give you some advice but now I remember how much is left over from last year unused.
[In Braude, *Braude's Second Encyclopedia* (1957)]

LA ROCHEFOUCAULD (1613–1680)
One gives nothing so generously as advice.
[*Maximes* (1678)]

STEINBECK, John (1902–1968)
No one wants advice – only corroboration.
[Attr.]

THOREAU, Henry David (1817–1862)
I have lived some thirty years on this planet, and I have yet to hear the first syllable of valuable or even earnest advice from my seniors.
[*Walden* (1854)]

AGE

ADAMS, John Quincy (1767–1848)
I inhabit a weak, frail, decayed tenement; battered by the winds and broken in on by the storms, and, from all I can learn, the landlord does not intend to repair.
[Attr.]

ADENAUER, Konrad (1876–1967)
(To his doctor)
I haven't asked you to make me young again. All I want is to go on getting older.
[Attr.]

AGNEW, Spiro T. (1918–1996)
The lessons of the past are ignored and obliterated in a contemporary antagonism known as the generation gap.
[*New York Times*, October 1969]

ALLEN, Dave (1936–2005)
I still think of myself as I was 25 years ago. Then I look in a mirror and see an old bastard and I realise it's me.
[*The Independent*, 1993]

ALLEN, Woody (1935–)
I recently turned sixty. Practically a third of my life is over.
[*The Observer Review*, 1996]

BAINBRIDGE, Beryl (1934–2010)
The older one becomes the quicker the present fades into sepia and the past looms up in glorious technicolour.
[*The Observer*, 1998]

BARUCH, Bernard M. (1870–1965)
I will never be an old man. To me, old age is always fifteen years older than I am.
[*The Observer*, 1955]

BENNY, Jack (1894–1974)
Age is strictly a case of mind over matter. If you don't mind, it doesn't matter.
[*New York Times*, February 1974]

BINYON, Laurence (1869–1943)
They shall grow not old, as we that are left grow old:
Age shall not weary them, nor the years condemn.
At the going down of the sun and in the morning
We will remember them.
['For the Fallen' (1914)]

BLAKE, Eubie (1883–1983)
(He died five days after his hundredth birthday)
If I'd known I was gonna live this long, I'd have taken better care of myself.
[*The Observer*, 1983]

BRENAN, Gerald (1894–1987)
Old age takes away from us what we have inherited and gives us what we have earned.
[*Thoughts in a Dry Season* (1978)]

BYRON, Lord (1788–1824)
Years steal Fire from the mind as vigour from the limb;
And life's enchanted cup but sparkles near the brim.
[*Childe Harold's Pilgrimage* (1818)]

CAMPBELL, Joseph (1879–1944)
As a white candle
In a holy place,
So is the beauty
Of an aged face.
['The Old Woman' (1913)]

CHEVALIER, Maurice (1888–1972)
I prefer old age to the alternative.
[Attr.]

COLLINS, Mortimer (1827–1876)
A man is as old as he's feeling, A woman as old as she looks.
['The Unknown Quantity']

COMPTON-BURNETT, Dame Ivy (1884–1969)
(Describing a certain woman's age)
Pushing forty? She's clinging on to it for dear life.
[Attr.]

DAY, Doris (1924–)
The really frightening thing about middle age is the knowledge that you'll grow out of it.
[A. E. Hotchner *Doris Day: Her Own Story* (1976)]

DEPARDIEU, Gérard (1948–)
At twenty you have many desires which hide the truth, but beyond forty there are only real and fragile truths – your abilities and your failings.
[*The Daily Mail*, 1991]

DEWEY, John (1859-1952)
It is strange that the one thing that every person looks forward to, namely old age, is the one thing for which no preparation is made.
[Attr.]

DISRAELI, Benjamin (1804-1881)
When a man fell into his anecdotage it was a sign for him to retire from the world.
[*Lottair* (1870)]

ELIZABETH (the Queen Mother) (1900-2002)
Is it just me, or are pensioners getting younger these days?
[*The Sunday Times*, July 2001]

ESTIENNE, Henri (1531-1598)
If only youth knew; if only age could.
[*Les Prémices* (1594)]

FRANKLIN, Benjamin (1706-1790)
At twenty years of age, the will reigns; at thirty, the wit; and at forty, the judgement.
[*Poor Richard's Almanac* (1741)]

GONNE, Maud (1865-1953)
Oh how you hate old age – well so do I ... but I, who am more a rebel against man than you, rebel less against nature, and accept the inevitable and go with it gently into the unknown.
[Letter to W.B. Yeats]

HALL, Sir Peter (1930-)
We do not necessarily improve with age: for better or worse we become more like ourselves.
[*The Observer*, 1988]

HILTON, James (1900-1954)
Anno domini ... that's the most fatal complaint of all, in the end.
[*Goodbye, Mr Chips* (1934)]

HOLMES, Oliver Wendell (Jr) (1841-1935)
(At the age of 86, on seeing a pretty girl) Oh, to be seventy again!
[In Fadiman, *The American Treasury*]

HOPE, Bob (1903-2003)
I don't generally feel anything until noon, then it's time for my nap.
[*International Herald Tribune*, 1990]

IRVING, Washington (1783-1859)
Whenever a man's friends begin to compliment him about looking young, he may be sure that they think he is growing old.
[*Bracebridge Hall* (1822)]

MARX, Groucho (1895-1977)
Age is not a particularly interesting subject. Anyone can get old. All you have to do is live long enough.
[*Groucho and Me* 1959]

NASH, Ogden (1902-1971)
Do you think my mind is maturing late, Or simply rotted early?
['Lines on Facing Forty' (1942)]

ORWELL, George (1903-1950)
At 50, everyone has the face he deserves.
[*Notebook*, 1949]

PATTISON, Ian (1950-)
Rab C. Nesbitt: I hate middle age. Too young for the bowling green, too old for Ecstasy.
[*Rab C. Nesbitt*, television series]

PITKIN, William B. (1878-1953)
Life Begins at Forty.
[Title of book, 1932]

POWELL, Anthony (1905-2000)
Growing old is like being increasingly penalized for a crime you haven't committed.
[*A Dance to the Music of Time* (1973)]

REAGAN, Ronald (1911-2004)
I am delighted to be with you. In fact, at my age, I am delighted to be anywhere.
[Speech at the Oxford Union, 1992]

RUBINSTEIN, Helena (c.1872-1965)
I have always felt that a woman has a right to treat the subject of her age with ambiguity until, perhaps, she passes into the realm of over ninety. Then it is better she be candid with herself and with the world.
[*My Life for Beauty* (1965)]

SANTAYANA, George (1863-1952)
The young man who has not wept is a savage, and the old man who will not laugh is a fool.
[*Dialogues in Limbo* (1925)]

SEXTON, Anne (1928-1974)
In a dream you are never eighty.
['Old' (1962)]

SHAKESPEARE, William (1564-1616)
Unregarded age in corners thrown.
[*As You Like It*, II.iii]
Age, I do abhor thee; youth, I do adore thee.
[*The Passionate Pilgrim*, xii]

SHAW, George Bernard (1856-1950)
Old men are dangerous: it doesn't matter to them what is going to happen to the world.
[*Heartbreak House* (1919)]

SMITH, Logan Pearsall (1865–1946)
There is more felicity on the far side of
baldness than young men can possibly
imagine.
['Last Words' (1933)]

SOLON (c.638–c.559 BC)
I grow old ever learning many things.
[In Bergk (ed.) *Poetae Lyrici Graeci*]

SPARK, Muriel (1918–2006)
Being over seventy is like being engaged in a
war. All our friends are going or gone and we
survive amongst the dead and the dying as on
a battlefield.
[*Memento Mori*]

THOMAS, Dylan (1914–1953)
Do not go gentle into that good night,
Old age should burn and rave at close of day;
Rage, rage against the dying of the light.
['Do Not Go Gentle into that Good Night'
(1952)]

TROTSKY, Leon (1879–1940)
Old age is the most unexpected of all the
things that happen to a man.
[*Diary in Exile*, 8 May 1935]

TUCKER, Sophie (1884–1966)
(Asked, when 80, the secret of longevity)
Keep breathing.
[Attr.]

WALL, Max (1908–1990)
To me Adler will always be Jung.
[Telegram to Larry Adler on his 60th birthday]

WALPOLE, Horace (1717–1797)
Old age is no such uncomfortable thing if one
gives oneself up to it with a good grace, and
doesn't drag it about 'To midnight dances and
the public show'.
[Letter, 1774]

WEBB, Sidney (1859–1947)
Old people are always absorbed in something,
usually themselves; we prefer to be absorbed
in the Soviet Union.
[Attr.]

WHITE, Patrick (1912–1990)
The aged are usually tougher and more
calculating than the young, provided they
keep enough of their wits about them. How
could they have lived so long if there weren't
steel buried inside them?
[*The Eye of the Storm* (1973)]

WHITMAN, Walt (1819–1892)
Women sit or move to and fro, some old,
some young.
The young are beautiful – but the old are
more beautiful than the young.
['Beautiful Women' (1871)]

WILDE, Oscar (1854–1900)
One should never trust a woman who tells
one her real age. A woman who would tell
one that would tell one anything.
[*A Woman of No Importance* (1893)]
Mrs Allonby: I delight in men over seventy.
They always offer one the devotion of a lifetime.
[*A Woman of No Importance* (1893)]
The old believe everything: the middle-aged
suspect everything: the young know everything.
[*The Chameleon*, 1894]

WILLIAMS, William Carlos (1883–1963)
In old age
the mind
casts off
rebelliously
an eagle
from its crag.
[*Paterson* (1946–1958)]

WODEHOUSE, P.G. (1881–1975)
He was either a man of about a hundred and
fifty who was rather young for his years or a
man of about a hundred and ten who had
been aged by trouble.
[In Usborne, *Wodehouse at Work to the End*
(1976)]

WORDSWORTH, William (1770–1850)
The wiser mind
Mourns less for what age takes away
Than what it leaves behind.
['The Fountain' (1800)]

YEATS, W.B. (1865–1939)
I thought no more was needed
Youth to prolong
Than dumb-bell and foil
To keep the body young.
O who could have foretold
That the heart grows old?
['A Song' 1918]

See **LONGEVITY, MATURITY, YOUTH**

AGA KHAN III (1877-1957)
(Justifying his liking for alcohol)
I'm so holy that when I touch wine, it turns into water.
[Attr. in Compton Miller, *Who's Really Who* (1983)]

ALDRICH, Henry (1647-1710)
If all be true that I do think,
There are five reasons we should drink;
Good wine – a friend – or being dry –
Or lest we should be by and by –
Or any other reason why.
['Five Reasons for Drinking' (1689)]

ANONYMOUS
Hath wine an oblivious power?
Can it pluck out the sting from the brain?
The draught might beguile for an hour,
But still leaves behind it the pain.
['Farewell to England'; sometimes attr. to Byron]

(Menu translation)
Our wines leave you nothing to hope for.
[*The Times*, 1999]

BECON, Thomas (1512-1567)
For when the wine is in, the wit is out.
[*Catechism* (1560)]

BEHAN, Brendan (1923-1964)
I only take a drink on two occasions – when I'm thirsty and when I'm not.
[In McCann, *The Wit of Brendan Behan*]

BENCHLEY, Robert (1889-1945)
(Reply when asked if he realised that drinking was a slow death)
So who's in a hurry?
[Attr.]

BURNS, Robert (1759-1796)
Freedom and whisky gang thegither,
Tak aff your dram!
['The Author's Earnest Cry and Prayer' (1786)]

BURTON, Robert (1577-1640)
I may not here omit those two main plagues, and common dotages of human kind, wine and women, which have infatuated and besotted myriads of people. They go commonly together.
[*Anatomy of Melancholy* (1621)]

CHANDLER, Raymond (1888-1959)
Alcohol is like love: the first kiss is magic, the second is intimate, the third is routine. After that you just take the girl's clothes off.
[*The Long Good-bye* (1953)]

CHURCHILL, Sir Winston (1874-1965)
(Said at lunch with an Arab leader whose religion forbade smoking and alcohol)
I must point out that my rule of life prescribed as an absolutely sacred rite smoking cigars and also the drinking of alcohol before, after, and if need be during all meals and in the intervals between them.
[*Triumph and Tragedy*]

CONNOLLY, Billy (1942-)
A well-balanced person has a drink in each hand.
[*Gullible's Travels*]

COOPER, Derek (1925-)
(Highland saying)
One whisky is all right; two is too much; three is too few.
[*A Taste of Scotch* (1989)]

COPE, Wendy (1945-)
All you need is love, love or, failing that, alcohol.
[Variation on a Lennon and McCartney song]

DE QUINCEY, Thomas (1785-1859)
It is most absurdly said, in popular language, of any man, that he is disguised in liquor; for, on the contrary, most men are disguised by sobriety.
[*Confessions of an English Opium Eater* (1822)]

DIBDIN, Charles (1745-1814)
Then trust me, there's nothing like drinking
So pleasant on this side the grave;
It keeps the unhappy from thinking,
And makes e'en the valiant more brave.
['Nothing like Grog']

DICKENS, Charles (1812-1870)
Bring in the bottled lightning, a clean tumbler, and a corkscrew.
[*Nicholas Nickleby* (1839)]

DOM PERIGNON (c.1638-1715)
(On discovering champagne)
Come quickly, I am tasting stars!

DUNNE, Finley Peter (1867-1936)
There is wan thing an' on'y wan thing to be said in favour iv dhrink, an' that is that it has caused manny a lady to be loved that otherwise might've died single.
[*Mr Dooley Says* (1910)]

FARQUHAR, George (1678-1707)
I have fed purely upon ale; I have eat my ale, drank my ale, and I always sleep upon ale.
[*The Beaux' Stratagem* (1707)]

FITZGERALD, Edward (1809–1883)
Drink! for you know not whence you came,
nor why:
Drink! for you know not why you go, nor
where.
[*The Rubáiyát of Omar Khayyám* (1879)]

FITZGERALD, F. Scott (1896–1940)
First you take a drink, then the drink takes a
drink, then the drink takes you.
[In Jules Feiffer, *Ackroyd*]

FLOYD, Keith (1943–2009)
All my life I have been a very thirsty person.
[*The Sunday Times*, FEBRUARY 2001]

LLOYD GEORGE, David (1863–1945)
(To a deputation of ship owners urging a
campaign for prohibition during the First
World War)
We are fighting Germany, Austria, and drink,
and so far as I can see the greatest of these
deadly foes is drink.
[Speech, 1915]

MAP, Walter (c.1140–c.1209)
If die I must, let me die drinking in an inn.
[*De Nugis Curialium* (1182)]

MARTIN, Dean (1917–1995)
I feel sorry for people who don't drink. When
they wake up in the morning, that's the best
they are going to feel all day.
[Attr.]

MARX, Groucho (1895–1977)
I was T.T. until prohibition.
[Attr.]

MENCKEN, H.L. (1880–1956)
I've made it a rule never to drink by daylight
and never to refuse a drink after dark.
[*New York Post*, 1945]

NASH, Ogden (1902–1971)
Candy
Is dandy
But liquor
Is quicker.
['Reflections on Ice-Breaking' (1931)]

O'SULLIVAN, John L. (1813–1895)
(Of whisky)
A torchlight procession marching down your
throat.
[Attr.]

OSLER, Sir William (1849–1919)
(His description of alcohol)
Milk of the elderly.
[*The Globe and Mail*, 1988]

PASCAL, Blaise (1623–1662)
Too much and too little wine. Give him none,
he cannot find truth; give him too much, the
same.
[*Pensées*, 1670]

PEACOCK, Thomas Love (1785–1866)
There are two reasons for drinking; one is,
when you are thirsty, to cure it; the other,
when you are not thirsty, to prevent it ...
Prevention is better than cure.
[*Melincourt* (1817)]

PLINY THE ELDER (AD 23–79)
In vino Veritas. Wine brings out the truth!
[*Historia Naturalis*]

RABELAIS, François (c.1494–c.1553)
I drink for the thirst to come.
[*Gargantua* (1534)]

SHAW, George Bernard (1856–1950)
I'm only a beer teetotaller, not a champagne
teetotaller.
[*Candida* (1898)]

TARKINGTON, Booth (1869–1946)
There are two things that will be believed of
any man whatsoever, and one of them is that
he has taken to drink.
[*Penrod* (1914)]

THATCHER, Denis (1915–2003)
(Reply to someone who asked if he had a
drinking problem.)
Yes, there's never enough.
[*Daily Mail*, 1996]

THOMAS, Dylan (1914–1953)
An alcoholic is someone you don't like who
drinks as much as you do.
[Attr.]

THURBER, James (1894–1961)
It's a naïve domestic Burgundy, without any
breeding, but I think you'll be amused by its
presumption.
[Cartoon caption in *The New Yorker*, 1937]

WILDE, Oscar (1854–1900)
I have made an important discovery ... that
alcohol, taken in sufficient quantities,
produces all the effects of intoxication.
[Attr.]

WODEHOUSE, P.G. (1881–1975)
It was my Uncle George who discovered that
alcohol was a food well in advance of modern
medical thought.
[*The Inimitable Jeeves* (1923)]

WRIGHT, Ian (1963-)
(On his Arsenal teammate's alcoholism)
It took a lot of bottle for Tony [Adams] to own up.

AMBITION

BERNIERES, Louis de (1954-)
The trouble with fulfilling your ambitions is you think you will be transformed into some sort of archangel and you're not. You still have to wash your socks.
[*The Times*, February 1999]

BROWNING, Robert (1812-1889)
'Tis not what man does which exalts him, but what a man would do!
['Saul' (1855)]

BURKE, Edmund (1729-1797)
Well is it known that ambition can creep as well as soar.
[*Third Letter ... on the Proposals for Peace with the Regicide Directory of France* (1797)]

CAESAR, Gaius Julius (c.102-44 BC)
I would rather be the first man here (in Gaul) than second in Rome.
[Attr. in Plutarch, *Lives*]

CONRAD, Joseph (1857-1924)
All ambitions are lawful except those which climb upward on the miseries or credulities of mankind.
[*A Personal Record* (1912)]

DALI, Salvador (1904-1989)
At the age of six I wanted to be a cook. At seven I wanted to be Napoleon. And my ambition has been growing steadily ever since.
[*The Secret Life of Salvador Dali* (1948)]

GILBERT, W.S. (1836-1911)
If you wish in this world to advance
Your merits you're bound to enhance,
You must stir it and stump it,
And blow your own trumpet,
Or, trust me, you haven't a chance!
[*Ruddigore* (1887)]

HERBERT, George (1593-1633)
Who aimeth at the sky
Shoots higher much than he that means a tree.
[*The Temple* (1633)]

KENEALLY, Thomas (1935-)
It's only when you abandon your ambitions that they become possible.
[*Australian*, 1983]

RALEIGH, Sir Walter (c.1552-1618)
(Written on a window-pane, and referring to his ambitions at the court of Elizabeth I)
Fain would I climb, yet fear I to fall.
[Attr.]

SHAKESPEARE, William (1564-1616)
I charge thee, fling away ambition:
By that sin fell the angels. How can man then,
The image of his Maker, hope to win by it?
[*Henry VIII*, III.ii]
'Tis a common proof
That lowliness is young ambition's ladder,
Whereto the climber-upward turns his face;
But when he once attains the upmost round,
He then unto the ladder turns his back,
Looks in the clouds, scorning the base degrees
By which he did ascend.
[*Julius Caesar*, II.i]
I have no spur
To prick the sides of my intent, but only
Vaulting ambition, which o'er-leaps itself,
And falls on th' other.
[*Macbeth*, I.vii]

SHAW, George Bernard (1856-1950)
The Gospel of Getting On.
[*Mrs Warren's Profession* (1898)]

WAGNER, Jane (1927-)
All my life I always wanted to be somebody. Now I see that I should have been more specific.
[Attr.]

WEBSTER, Daniel (1782-1852)
(On being advised not to join the overcrowded legal profession)
There is always room at the top.
[Attr.]

AMERICA

ALI, Tariq (1943-)
September 11 and its aftermath have shown that the whole world is the United States empire.
[*The Guardian*, January 2002]

ANONYMOUS
(On GIs in Britain)
Overpaid, overfed, oversexed, and over here.
[Remark during World War II]
A man went looking for America and couldn't find it anywhere.
[Advertisement for the film *Easy Rider*, 1969]

AUDEN, W.H. (1907-1973)
God bless the U.S.A., so large, so friendly, and so rich.

['On the Circuit']

AYKROYD, Dan (1952-)
What the American public doesn't know is what makes it the American public.

[*Tommy Boy*, film, 1995]

BAUDRILLARD, Jean (1929-2007)
The microwave, the waste disposal, the orgasmic elasticity of the carpets, this soft resort-style civilization irresistibly evokes the end of the world.

[*America* (1986)]

BURROUGHS, William S. (1914-1999)
America is not a young land: it is old and dirty and evil before the settlers, before the Indians. The evil is there waiting.

[*Naked Lunch* (1959)]

CLEMENCEAU, Georges (1841-1929)
America is the only nation in history which miraculously has gone directly from barbarism to degeneration without the usual interval of civilization.

[Attr.]

COOLIDGE, Calvin (1872-1933)
The business of America is business.

[Speech, 1925]

DÍAZ, Porfirio (1830-1915)
Poor Mexico, so far from God and so near to the United States!

[Attr.]

EDWARD VIII (later Duke of Windsor) (1894-1972)
The thing that impresses me most about America is the way parents obey their children.

[In *Look*, 1957]

EISENHOWER, Dwight D. (1890-1969)
Whatever America hopes to bring to pass in this world must first come to pass in the heart of America.

[Inaugural address, 1953]

EMERSON, Ralph Waldo (1803-1882)
America is a country of young men.

[*Society and Solitude* (1870)]
The Americans have little faith. They rely on the power of a dollar.

[Lecture, 1841, 'Man the Reformer']

FITZGERALD, F. Scott (1896-1940)
Americans, while willing, even eager, to be serfs, have always been obstinate about being peasantry.

[*The Great Gatsby* (1926)]

FORD, Gerald R. (1913-2006)
(Referring to his own appointment as President)
I guess it proves that in America anyone can be President.

[In Reeves, *A Ford Not a Lincoln*]

FREUD, Sigmund (1856-1939)
Yes, America is gigantic, but a gigantic mistake.

[Peter Gay *Freud: A Life for Our Time* (1988)]

FUENTES, Carlos (1928-2012)
What America does best is to understand itself. What it does worst is to understand others.

[*Time*, 1986]

JOHNSON, Samuel (1709-1784)
I am willing to love all mankind, except an American.

[In Boswell, *The Life of Samuel Johnson* (1791)]

KENNEDY, John F. (1917-1963)
The United States has to move very fast to even stand still.

[*The Observer*, 1963]
And so, my fellow Americans: ask not what your country can do for you – ask what you can do for your country. My fellow citizens of he world: ask not what America will do for you, but what together we can do for the freedom of man.

[Inaugural address, 1961]

MCCARTHY, Senator Joseph (1908-1957)
McCarthyism is Americanism with its sleeves rolled.

[Speech, 1952]

MENCKEN, H.L. (1880-1956)
No one ever went broke underestimating the intelligence of the American people.

[Attr.]

MINIFIE, James M. (1900-1974)
The United States is the glory, jest, and terror of mankind.

[In Purdy (ed.), *The New Romans* (1988)]

ROOSEVELT, Eleanor (1884-1962)
I think if the people of this country can be reached with the truth, their judgment will be in favour of the many, as against the privileged few.
[Ladies' Home Journal]

ROOSEVELT, Theodore (1858-1919)
There can be no fifty-fifty Americanism in this country. There is room here for only hundred per cent Americanism, only for those who are Americans and nothing else.
[Speech, 1918]

STAPLEDON, Olaf (1886-1950)
That strange blend of the commercial traveller, the missionary, and the barbarian conqueror, which was the American abroad.
[Last and First Men (1930)]

STEIN, Gertrude (1874-1946)
In the United States there is more space where nobody is than where anybody is. That is what makes America what it is.
[The Geographical History of America (1936)]

TALLEYRAND, Charles-Maurice de (1754-1838)
I found there a country with thirty-two religions and only one sauce.
[In Pedrazzini, Autant en apportent les mots]

TOYNBEE, Arnold (1889-1975)
America is a large, friendly dog in a very small room. Ever time it wags its tail it knocks over a chair.
[Broadcast news summary, 1954]

VIDAL, Gore (1925-2012)
The land of the dull and the home of the literal.
[Reflections upon a Sinking Ship (1969)]

WELLS, H.G. (1866-1946)
Every time Europe looks across the Atlantic to see the American eagle, it observes only the rear end of an ostrich.
[America]

WILDE, Oscar (1854-1900)
The youth of America is their oldest tradition. It has been going on now for three hundred years.
[A Woman of No Importance (1893)]

WILSON, Woodrow (1856-1924)
America is the only idealistic nation in the world.
[Speech, 1919]

ZANGWILL, Israel (1864-1926)
America is God's Crucible, the great Melting-Pot where all the races of Europe are melting and re-forming!
[The Melting Pot (1908)]

ANARCHY

ANONYMOUS
Anarchy may not be the best form of government, but it's better than no government at all.

BENNETT, Alan (1934-)
We started off trying to set up a small anarchist community, but people wouldn't obey the rules.
[Getting On (1972)]

See **GOVERNMENT, POLITICS**

ANGER

BACON, Francis (1561-1626)
Anger makes dull men witty, but it keeps them poor.
['Apophthegms' (1679)]

**THE BIBLE
(King James Version)**
A soft answer turneth away wrath.
[Proverbs, 15:1]
Be ye angry, and sin not; let not the sun go down upon your wrath.
[Ephesians, 4:26]

BLAKE, William (1757-1827)
The tygers of wrath are wiser than the horses of instruction.
[The Marriage of Heaven and Hell (c. 1790-1793)]

CONGREVE, William (1670-1729)
Heav'n has no rage, like love to hatred turned, Nor Hell a fury, like a woman scorn'd.
[The Mourning Bride (1697)]

CONNOLLY, Cyril (1903-1974)
There is no fury like an ex-wife searching for a new lover.
[The Unquiet Grave (1944)]

DILLER, Phyllis (1917-1974)
Never go to bed mad. Stay up and fight.
[Phyllis Diller's Housekeeping Hints]

DRYDEN, John (1631-1700)
Beware the fury of a patient man.
[Absalom and Achitophel (1681)]

FULLER, Thomas (1608–1661)
Anger is one of the sinews of the soul; he that wants it hath a maimed mind.
[*The Holy State and the Profane State* (1642)]

HALIFAX, Lord (1633–1695)
Anger is never without an Argument, but seldom with a good one.
[*Thoughts and Reflections* (1750)]

HAZLITT, William (1778–1830)
Spleen can subsist on any kind of food.
['On Wit and Humour' (1819)]

IRVING, Washington (1783–1859)
A tart temper never mellows with age, and a sharp tongue is the only edged tool that grows keener with constant use.
['Rip Van Winkle' (1820)]

SHAW, George Bernard (1856–1950)
Beware of the man who does not return your blow: he neither forgives you nor allows you to forgive yourself.
[*Man and Superman* (1903)]

SIDNEY, Sir Philip (1554–1586)
O heavenly Foole, thy most kisse worthy face
Anger invests with such a lovely grace,
That Anger's selfe I needes must kisse againe.
[*Astrophel and Stella* (1591)]

SPYRI, Johanna (1827–1901)
Anger has overpowered him, and driven him to a revenge which was rather a stupid one, I must acknowledge, but anger makes us all stupid.
[*Heidi* (1880)]

TWAIN, Mark (1835–1910)
When angry count four; when very angry swear.
[*Pudd'nhead Wilson's Calendar* (1894)]

ANIMALS

BLAKE, William (1757–1827)
Tyger Tyger, burning bright In the forests of the night: What immortal hand or eye Could frame thy fearful symmetry?
['The Tyger' (1794)]

BUSH, George W. (1946–)
(On a dispute between farmers with irrigation rights and native Americans with fishing rights)
I know the human being and the fish can coexist peacefully.
[Speech, 2000]

CANETTI, Elias (1905–1994)
Whenever you observe an animal closely, you have the feeling that a person sitting inside is making fun of you.
[*The Human Province*]

ELIOT, George (1819–1880)
Animals are such agreeable friends – they ask no questions, they pass no criticisms.
[*Scenes of Clerical Life* (1858)]

FLEMING, Ian (1908–1964)
A horse is dangerous at both ends and uncomfortable in the middle.
[*The Sunday Times*, October 1966]

FOYLE, Christina (1911–1999)
Animals are always loyal and love you, whereas with children you never know where you are.
[*The Times*, 1993]

FROUDE, James Anthony (1818–1894)
Wild animals never kill for sport. Man is the only one to whom the torture and death of his fellow creatures is amusing in itself.
[*Oceana, or England and her Colonies* (1886)]

GOLDSMITH, Oliver (c.1728–1774)
Brutes never meet in bloody fray, Nor cut each other's throats, for pay.
['Logicians Refuted' (1759)]

PEACOCK, Thomas Love (1785–1866)
Nothing can be more obvious than that all animals were created solely and exclusively for the use of man.
[*Headlong Hall* (1816)]

SHAKESPEARE, William (1564–1616)
No beast so fierce but knows some touch of pity.
[*Richard III*, I.ii]

SOLZHENITSYN, Alexander (1918–2008)
Nowadays we don't think much of a man's love for an animal; we mock people who are attached to cats. But if we stop loving animals, aren't we bound to stop loving humans too?
[*Cancer Ward* (1968)]

SPENCER, Herbert (1820–1903)
People are beginning to see that the first requisite to success in life, is to be a good animal.
[*Education* (1861)]

VOLTAIRE (1694–1778)
There are two things for which animals are to be envied: they know nothing of future evils, or of what people say about them.
[Letter, 1739]

SELLAR, Walter (1898-1951) and YEATMAN, Robert Julian (1897-1968)
To confess that you are totally ignorant about the Horse, is social suicide: you will be despised by everybody, especially the horse.
[*Horse Nonsense* (1933)]

See **CATS, DOGS**

APPEARANCE

AESOP (6th century BC)
It is not only fine feathers that make fine birds.
[*Fables*]

BROWN, James (1933-2006)
Hair is the first thing. And teeth the second. Hair and teeth. A man got those two things he's got it all.
[*The Godfather of Soul* (1986)]

DICKENS, Charles (1812-1870)
He might have brought an action against his countenance for libel, and won heavy damages.
[*Oliver Twist* (1838)]

SARTRE, Jean-Paul (1905-1980)
Things are entirely what they appear to be and behind them ... there is nothing.
[*La Nausée*, (1938)]

WILDE, Oscar (1854-1900)
It is only shallow people who do not judge by appearances.
[*The Picture of Dorian Gray* (1891)]

WINDSOR (Duchess of (Wallis Simpson)) (1896-1986)
One can never be too thin or too rich.
[Attr.]

See **BEAUTY, VANITY**

ARCHITECTURE

BACON, Francis (1561-1626)
Houses are built to live in and not to look on; therefore let use be preferred before uniformity, except where both may be had.
[*Essays* (1625)]

BENTLEY, Edmund Clerihew (1875-1956)
Sir Christopher Wren
Said, 'I am going to dine with some men.
If anybody calls
Say I am designing St Paul's.'
[*Biography for Beginnners*]

GOETHE (1749-1832)
I [call] architecture a kind of petrified music.
[*Gespräche mit Eckermann*, 1829]

LE CORBUSIER (1887-1965)
A house is a machine for living in.
[*Vers une architecture* (1923)]

LETTE, Kathy (1958-)
Inner-city council estates make you believe the world was really built in six days.
[*Mad Cows* (1996)]

LEVIN, Bernard (1928-2004)
What has happened to architecture since the second world war that the only passers-by who can contemplate it without pain are those equipped with a white stick and a dog?
[*The Times* 1983]

MIES VAN DER ROHE, Ludwig (1886-1969)
Less is more.
[*New York Herald Tribune*, 1959]

WRIGHT, Frank Lloyd (1869-1959)
The physician can bury his mistakes, but the architect can only advise his client to plant vines.
[*New York Times Magazine*, 1953]

See **ART**

ARGUMENT

ADDISON, Joseph (1672-1719)
Our disputants put me in mind of the skuttle fish, that when he is unable to extricate himself, blackens all the water about him, till he becomes invisible.
[*The Spectator*, 1712]

ANONYMOUS
This is a rotten argument, but it should be good enough for their lordships on a hot summer afternoon.
[Annotation in ministerial brief]

BILLINGS, Josh (1818-1885)
Thrice is he armed that hath his quarrel just,
But four times he who gets his blow in fust.
[*Josh Billings, his Sayings* (1865)]

FERGUSSON, Sir James (1832-1907)
I have heard many arguments which influenced my opinion, but never one which influenced my vote.
[Attr.]

GAY, John (1685-1732)
Those, who in quarrels interpose,
Must often wipe a bloody nose.
[*Fables* (1727)]

HERBERT, George (1593-1633)
Be calm in arguing; for fiercenesse makes
Errour a fault, and truth discourtesie.
[*The Temple* (1633)]

INGE, William Ralph (1860–1954)
It takes in reality only one to make a quarrel.
It is useless for the sheep to pass resolutions
in favour of vegetarianism while the wolf
remains of a different opinion.
[Outspoken Essays (1919)]

JOHNSON, Samuel (1709–1784)
I dogmatize and am contradicted, and in this
conflict of opinions and sentiments I find
delight.
[In Sir John Hawkins, *Life of Samuel Johnson*
(1787)]

LA ROCHEFOUCAULD (1613–1680)
Quarrels would not last long if the fault were
on one side only.
[Maximes (1678)]

LOWELL, James Russell (1819–1891)
There is no good in arguing with the
inevitable. The only argument available with
an east wind is to put on your overcoat.
[Democrcy and Other Addresses (1887)]

POTTER, Stephen (1900–1969)
(A blocking phrase for conversation)
'Yes, but not in the South', with slight
adjustments will do for any argument about
any place, if not about any person.
[Lifemanship (1950)]

ROSTAND, Jean (1894–1977)
A married couple are well suited when both
partners usually feel the need for a quarrel at
the same time.
[Le Mariage]

YEATS, W.B. (1865–1939)
We make out of the quarrel with others,
rhetoric; but of the quarrel with ourselves,
poetry.
['Anima Hominis' (1917)]

**AILESBURY, Maria (Marchioness of)
(d.1893)**
My dear, my dear, you never know when any
beautiful young lady may not blossom into a
Duchess!
[In Portland, *Men, Women, and Things* (1937)]

BURKE, Edmund (1729–1797)
Nobility is a graceful ornament to the civil
order. It is the Corinthian capital of polished
society.
[Reflections on the Revolution in France...
(1790)]

CHARLES (Prince of Wales) (1948–)
The one advantage about marrying a princess
– or someone from a royal family – is that
they do know what happens.
[Attr.]

HOPE, Anthony (1863–1933)
'Bourgeois,' I observed, 'is an epithet which
the riff-raff apply to what is respectable, and
the aristocracy to what is decent.'
[The Dolly Dialogues (1894)]

LÉVIS, Duc de (1764–1830)
(Noblesse oblige.)
Nobility has its obligations.
[Maximes et réflexions (1812)]

LLOYD GEORGE, David (1863–1945)
A fully equipped duke costs as much to keep
up as two Dreadnoughts; and dukes are just
as great a terror and they last longer.
[Speech, 1909]

MACHIAVELLI (1469–1527)
For titles do not reflect honour on men, but
rather men on their titles.
[Dei Discorsi]

MANNERS, Lord (1818–1906)
Let wealth and commerce, laws and learning die,
But leave us still our old nobility!
[England's Trust (1841)]

MILL, John Stuart (1806–1873)
Persons require to possess a title, or some
other badge of rank, or of the consideration of
people of rank, to be able to indulge
somewhat in the luxury of doing as they like
without detriment to their estimation.
[On Liberty (1859)]

MITFORD, Nancy (1904–1973)
An aristocracy in a republic is like a chicken
whose head had been cut off: it may run
about in a lively way, but in fact it is dead.
[Noblesse Oblige (1956)]

MOSLEY, Charles (1948–)
Did you know that a peer condemned to
death had the right to be hanged with a silken
cord? A bit like insisting that the electric chair
had to be Chippendale.
[The Observer, 1999]

NORTHCLIFFE, Lord (1865–1922)
When I want a peerage, I shall buy one like an
honest man.
[Attr.]

PEARSON, Hesketh (1887–1964)
There is no stronger craving in the world than
that of the rich for titles, except that of the
titled for riches.
[Attr.]

SEITZ, Raymond (1940–)
In the British aristocracy, the gene pool has always had a shallow end.
[*The Observer*, 1998]

SHAW, George Bernard (1856–1950)
Titles distinguish the mediocre, embarrass the superior, and are disgraced by the inferior.
[*Man and Superman* (1903)]

TENNYSON, Alfred (Lord) (1809–1892)
Kind hearts are more than coronets,
And simple faith than Norman blood.
['Lady Clara Vere de Vere' (c. 1835)]

THACKERAY, William Makepeace (1811–1863)
Nothing like blood, sir, in hosses, dawgs, and men.
[*Vanity Fair* (1848)]

WELLINGTON (Duke of) (1769–1852)
I believe I forgot to tell you I was made a Duke.
[In a letter to his nephew, 1814]

WOOLF, Virginia (1882–1941)
Those comfortably padded lunatic asylums which are known, euphemistically, as the stately homes of England.
[*The Common Reader* (1925)]

See **CLASS**

THE ARMY

ANONYMOUS
(Definition of NAAFI)
Where you can eat dirt cheap.
[In Frank Muir, *A Kentish Lad* (1997)]

BAXTER, James K. (1926–1972)
The boy who volunteered at seventeen
At twenty-three is heavy on the booze.
['Returned Soldier' (1946)]

BRODSKY, Joseph (1940–1996)
It is the army that finally makes a citizen of you; without it, you still have a chance, however slim, to remain a human being.
['Less Than One' (1986)]

CHURCHILL, Sir Winston (1874–1965)
You may take the most gallant sailor, the most intrepid airman, or the most audacious soldier, put them at a table together – what do you get? The sum of their fears.
[In Macmillan, *The Blast of War*]

FREDERICK THE GREAT (1712–1786)
An army, like a serpent, goes on its belly.
[Attr.]

GERRY, Elbridge (1744–1814)
A standing army is like a standing member: an excellent assurance of domestic tranquillity but a dangerous temptation to foreign adventure.
[The *Observer*, 1998]

GREEN, Michael (1927–)
Fortunately, the army has had much practice in ignoring impossible instructions.
[*The Boy Who Shot Down an Airship* (1988)]

HELLER, Joseph (1923–1999)
I had examined myself pretty thoroughly and discovered that I was unfit for military service.
[*Catch-22* (1961)]

HOFFMANN, Max (1869–1927)
(Of the British army in World War I)
Ludendorff: The English soldiers fight like lions. Hoffman: True. But don't we know that they are lions led by donkeys.
[In Falkenhayn, *Memoirs*]

HULL, General Sir Richard (1907–1989)
National Service did the country a lot of good but it darned near killed the army.
[Attr.]

KISSINGER, Henry (1923–)
The conventional army loses if it does not win. The guerilla wins if he does not lose.
['Foreign Affairs', XIII (1969)]

MARLBOROUGH (Duke of) (1650–1722)
No soldier can fight unless he is properly fed on beef and beer.
[Attr.]

MILLIGAN, Spike (1918–2002)
The Army works like this: if a man dies when you hang him, keep hanging him until he gets used to it.
[Attr.]

PATTON, General George S. (1885–1945)
Untutored courage is useless in the face of educated bullets.
[*Cavalry Journal*, 1922]

SASSOON, Siegfried (1886–1967)
Soldiers are citizens of death's gray land,
Drawing no dividend from time's tomorrows...
['Dreamers' (1917)]

SHAKESPEARE, William (1564–1616)
That in the captain's but a choleric word
Which in the soldier is flat blasphemy.
[*Measure For Measure*, II.ii]

SHAW, George Bernard (1856–1950)
You can always tell an old soldier by the
inside of his holsters and cartridge boxes. The
young ones carry pistols and cartridges: the
old ones, grub.
[*Arms and the Man* (1898)]

TOLSTOY, Leo (1828–1910)
The chief attraction of military service has
been and will remain this compulsory and
irreproachable idleness.
[*War and Peace* (1868–1869)]

TRUMAN, Harry S. (1884–1972)
(Of General MacArthur)
I didn't fire him because he was a dumb son
of a bitch, although he was, but that's not
against the law for generals. If it was, half to
three-quarters of them would be in gaol.
[In Miller, *Plain Speaking* (1974)]

TUCHOLSKY, Kurt (1890–1935)
The French soldier is a civilian in disguise, the
German civilian is a soldier in disguise.
['Ocean of Pain' (1973)]

USTINOV, Sir Peter (1921–2004)
As for being a General, well, at the age of four
with paper hats and wooden swords we're all
Generals. Only some of us never grow out of it.
[*Romanoff and Juliet* (1956)]

WILDE, Lady Jane (1826–1896)
There's a proud array of soldiers – what do
they round your door?
They guard our master's granaries from the
thin hands of the poor.
['The Famine Years']

See **WAR, WEAPONS**

ART

ALBERT (Prince Consort) (1819–1861)
The works of art, by being publicly exhibited
and offered for sale, are becoming articles of
trade, following as such the unreasoning laws
of markets and fashion; and public and even
private patronage is swayed by their
tyrannical influence.
[Speech to the Royal Academy, May 1851]

ALEXANDER, Hilary (1818–1895)
To the accountants, a true work of art is an
investment that hangs on the wall.
[*Sunday Telegraph*, 1993]

ANONYMOUS
We would prefer to see the Royal Opera
House run by a philistine with the requisite
financial acumen than by the succession of
opera and ballet lovers who have brought a
great and valuable institution to its knees.
[Select Committe Report into the
Royal Opera House, 1997]

ANOUILH, Jean (1910–1987)
Life is very nice, but it has no shape. It is the
purpose of art to give it shape.
[*The Rehearsal* (1950)]

ARTAUD, Antonin (1896–1948)
No one has ever written, painted, sculpted,
modelled, built or invented except literally to
get out of hell.
[In Lewis Wolpert, *Malignant Sadness* (1999)]

BACON, Francis (1909–1993)
The job of the artist is always to deepen the
mystery.
[*Sunday Telegraph*, 1964]

BEAVERBROOK, Lord (1879–1964)
Buy old masters. They fetch a better price
than old mistresses.
[Attr.]

BING, Rudolf (1902–1997)
It is so much worse to be a mediocre artist
than to be a mediocre post office clerk.
[*5000 Nights at the Opera* (1972)]

BLAKE, William (1757–1827)
When Sr Joshua Reynolds died
All Nature was degraded:
The King dropd a tear into the Queens Ear:
And all his Pictures Faded.
[Annotations to Sir Joshua Reynolds' Works
(c. 1808)]

BOWEN, Elizabeth (1899–1973)
Art is the only thing that can go on mattering
once it has stopped hurting.
[*The Heat of the Day* (1949)]

BRAQUE, Georges (1882–1963)
Art is meant to disturb, science reassures.
[*Day and Night, Notebooks* (1952)]

CHEKHOV, Anton (1860–1904)
The artist may not be a judge of his
characters, only a dispassionate witness.
[Attr.]

CHESTERTON, G.K. (1874–1936)
The artistic temperament is a disease that
afflicts amateurs.
[*Heretics* (1905)]

CONNOLLY, Cyril (1903–1974)
There is no more sombre enemy of good art than the pram in the hall.
[*Enemies of Promise* (1938)]

CONRAD, Joseph (1857–1924)
A work that aspires, however humbly, to the condition of art should carry its justification in every line.
[*The Nigger of the Narcissus* (1897)]

CONSTANT, Benjamin (1767–1834)
Art for art's sake, without a purpose; every purpose distorts the true nature of art. But art achieves a purpose which it does not have.
[*Journal intime*, 1804]

DEBUSSY, Claude (1862–1918)
Art is the most beautiful of all lies.
[*Monsieur Croche, antidilettante*]

DEGAS, Edgar (1834–1917)
Art is vice. You don't marry it legitimately, you rape it.
[In Paul Lafond, *Degas* (1918)]

DEMARCO, Richard (1930–)
Art is for everyone – paint, like a piece of music, is the most international thing I know.
[Attr.]

ELLIS, Havelock (1859–1939)
Every artist writes his own autobiography.
[*The New Spirit* (1890)]

EMERSON, Ralph Waldo (1803–1882)
Art is a jealous mistress, and, if a man have a genius for painting, poetry, music, architecture, or philosophy, he makes a bad husband and an ill provider.
[*Conduct of Life* (1860)]

EYRE, Sir Richard (1943–)
I would like to see the good in art made popular and the popular made good.
[BBC radio interview, 1998]

FADIMAN, Clifton (1904–1999)
(Of Gertrude Stein)
I encountered the mama of dada again.
[*Appreciations* (1955)]

GAUGUIN, Paul (1848–1903)
Art is either a plagiarist or a revolutionist.
[In Huneker, *Pathos of Distance* (1913)]

GEORGE I (1660–1727)
I hate all Boets and Bainters.
[In Campbell, *Lives of the Chief Justices* (1849)]

GOETHE (1749–1832)
Classicism I call health, and romanticism disease.
[*Gespräche mit Eckermann*, 1829]

HERBERT, Sir A.P. (1890–1971)
A highbrow is the kind of person who looks at a sausage and thinks of Picasso.
[Attr.]

HERSHAW, William (1957–)
(On Damien Hirst's entry for the Turner Prize for contemporary art)
A coo and a cauf Cut in hauf.
[*The Cowdenbeath Man*]

HIRST, Damien (1965–)
(On winning the Turner Prize)
It's amazing what you can do with an E in A-level art, twisted imagination and a chainsaw.
[*The Observer*, 1995]

INGRES, J.A.D. (1780–1867)
Drawing is the true test of art.
[*Pensées d'Ingres* (1922)]

KENNEDY, John F. (1917–1963)
In free society art is not a weapon ... Artists are not engineers of the soul.
[Speech, 1963]

KLEE, Paul (1879–1940)
Art does not reproduce what is visible; it makes things visible.
['Creative Credo' (1920)]

KRAUS, Karl (1874–1936)
The only person who is an artist is the one that can make a puzzle out of the solution.
[*By Night* (1919)]

MAYAKOVSKY, Vladimir (1893–1930)
Art is not a mirror to reflect the world, but a hammer with which to shape it.
[*The Guardian*, 1974]

MOORE, George (1852–1933)
Art must be parochial in the beginning to be cosmopolitan in the end.
[*Hail and Farewell: Ave* (1911)]

MOSES, Grandma (1860–1961)
(Of painting)
I don't advise any one to take it up as a business proposition, unless they really have talent, and are crippled so as to deprive them of physical labor.
[Attr.]

MURDOCH, Iris (1919–1999)
All art deals with the absurd and aims at the simple. Good art speaks truth, indeed is truth, perhaps the only truth.
[*The Black Prince* (1989)]

PATER, Walter (1839–1894)
All art constantly aspires towards the condition of music.
[*Studies in the History of the Renaissance* (1873)]

PICASSO, Pablo (1881–1973)
(Remark made at an exhibition of children's drawings)
When I was their age, I could draw like Raphael, but it took me a lifetime to learn to draw like them.
[In Penrose, *Picasso: His Life and Work* (1958)]

RENOIR, Pierre Auguste (1841–1919)
(On why he still painted although he had arthritis of his hands)
The pain passes, but the beauty remains.
[Attr.]

RÜCKRIEM, Ulrich (1938–)
People don't want art, they want football.
[*Scala*, 1992]

RUSKIN, John (1819–1900)
Fine art is that in which the hand, the head, and the heart of man go together.
[*The Two Paths* (1859)]
(Of one of Whistler's works)
I have seen, and heard, much of Cockney impudence before now; but never expected to hear a coxcomb ask two hundred guineas for flinging a pot of paint in the public's face.
[*Fors Clavigera*, Letter 79, 1877]

SAATCHI, Charles (1943–)
Ninety per cent of the art I buy will probably be worthless in ten years' time.
[*The Observer*, 1997]

SAND, George (1804–1876)
Art is not a study of positive reality; it is a search for ideal truth.
[*The Devil's Pond* (1846)]

SARGENT, John Singer (1856–1925)
Every time I paint a portrait I lose a friend.
[In Bentley and Esar, *Treasury of Humorous Quotations* (1951)]

SPALDING, Julian (1948–)
The professional art world is becoming a conspiracy against the public.
[*The Daily Mail*, 1996]

STOPPARD, Tom (1937–)
What is an artist? For every thousand people there's nine hundred doing the work, ninety doing well, nine doing good, and one lucky bastard who's the artist.
[*Travesties* (1975)]

TOLSTOY, Leo (1828–1910)
Art is a human activity which has as its purpose the transmission to others of the highest and best feelings to which men have risen.
[*What is Art?* (1898)]

USTINOV, Sir Peter (1921–2004)
If Botticelli were alive today he'd be working for Vogue.
[*The Observer*, 1962]

VIDAL, Gore (1925–2012)
He will lie even when it is inconvenient, the sign of the true artist.
[*Two Sisters* (1970)]

WHISTLER, James McNeill (1834–1903)
(Replying to the question 'For two days' labour, you ask two hundred guineas?')
No, I ask it for the knowledge of a lifetime.
[In Seitz, *Whistler Stories* (1913)]

WILDE, Oscar (1854–1900)
All art is quite useless.
[*The Picture of Dorian Gray* (1891)]

WYLLIE, George (1921–2012)
Public art is art that the public can't avoid.
[Attr.]

See **NATURE**

BACON, Francis (1561–1626)
I had rather believe all the fables in the legend, and the Talmud, and the Alcoran, than that this universal frame is without a mind.
[*Essays* (1625)]

BUCHAN, John (1875–1940)
An atheist is a man who has no invisible means of support.
[Attr.]

BUÑUEL, Luis (1900–1983)
I am still an atheist, thank God.
[Attr.]

BURKE, Edmund (1729–1797)
Man is by his constitution a religious animal; ... atheism is against, not only our reason, but our instincts.
[*Reflections on the Revolution in France...* (1790)]

CUMMINGS, William Thomas (1903–1945)
There are no atheists in the foxholes.
[In Romulo, *I Saw the Fall gof the Philippines* (1943)]

DIDEROT, Denis (1713-1784)
See this egg. It is with this that one overturns all the schools of theology and all the temples on earth.
[*Le Rêve de d'Alembert* (1769)]

ORWELL, George (1903-1950)
He was an embittered atheist (the sort of atheist who does not so much disbelieve in God as personally dislike Him).
[*Down and Out in Paris and London* (1933)]

OTWAY, Thomas (1652-1685)
These are rogues that pretend to be of a religion now! Well, all I say is, honest atheism for my money.
[*The Atheist* (1683)]

ROSSETTI, Dante Gabriel (1828-1882)
The worst moment for the atheist is when he is really thankful and has nobody to thank.
[Attr.]

SARTRE, Jean-Paul (1905-1980)
She didn't believe in anything; only her scepticism kept her from being an atheist.
[*Words* (1964)]

TURGENEV, Ivan (1818-1883)
The courage to believe in nothing.
[*Fathers and Sons* (1862)]

YOUNG, Edward (1683-1765)
By Night an Atheist half believes a God.
[*Night-Thoughts on Life, Death and Immortality*]

See **GOD, RELIGION**

BEAUTY

BACON, Francis (1561-1626)
There is no excellent beauty, that hath not some strangeness in the proportion.
[*Essays* (1625)]

BLAKE, William (1757-1827)
Exuberance is Beauty.
['Proverbs of Hell' (1793)]

BUCK, Pearl S. (1892-1973)
It is better to be first with an ugly woman than the hundredth with a beauty.
[*The Good Earth* (1931)]

BURCHILL, Julie (1960-)
It has been said that a pretty face is a passport. But it's not, it's a visa, and it runs out fast.
[*Mail on Sunday* 1988]

BYRON, Lord (1788-1824)
She walks in beauty, like the night
Of cloudless climes and starry skies;
And all that's best of dark and bright
Meet in her aspect and her eyes.
['She Walks in Beauty' (1815)]

CONFUCIUS (c.550-c.478 BC)
Everything has its beauty but not everyone sees it.
[*Analects*]

CONGREVE, William (1670-1729)
Beauty is the lover's gift.
[*The Way of the World* (1700)]

CONSTABLE, John (1776-1837)
There is nothing ugly; I never saw an ugly thing in my life: for let the form of an object be what it may, – light, shade, and perspective will always make it beautiful.
[In C.R. Leslie, *Memoirs of the Life of John Constable* (1843)]

COUSIN, Victor (1792-1867)
There must be religion for religion's sake, morality for morality's sake, as there is art for art's sake … the beautiful cannot be the way to what is useful, nor to what is good, nor to what is holy; it leads only to itself.
[Lecture, 1818]

DRYDEN, John (1631-1700)
When beauty fires the blood, how love exalts the mind.
[*Cymon and Iphigenia* (1700)]

ELLIS, Havelock (1859-1939)
The absence of flaw in beauty is itself a flaw.
[*Impressions and Comments* (1914)]

EMERSON, Ralph Waldo (1803-1882)
Though we travel the world over to find the beautiful we must carry it with us or we find it not.
[*Essays, First Series* (1841)]

FRENCH, Dawn (1957-)
If I were alive in Rubens's time, I'd be celebrated as a model. Kate Moss would be used as a paint brush.
[*Sunday Times*, 2006]

GAINSBOURG, Serge (1928-1991)
Ugliness is, in a way, superior to beauty because it lasts.
[*The Scotsman*, 1998]

HUGO, Victor (1802-1885)
Beauty is as useful as usefulness. Maybe more so.
[*Les Misérables* (1862)]

HUME, David (1711–1776)
Beauty is no quality in things themselves: It
exists merely in the mind which contemplates
them; and each mind perceives a different
beauty.
[*Essays, Moral, Political, and Literary* (1742)]

KEATS, John (1795–1821)
A thing of beauty is a joy for ever: Its
loveliness increases; it will never Pass into
nothingness; but still will keep A bower quiet
for us, and a sleep Full of sweet dreams, and
health, and quiet breathing.
['Endymion' (1818)]

MOLIÈRE (1622–1673)
The beauty of a face is a frail rnament, a
passing flower, a moment's brightness
belonging only to the skin.
[*Les Femmes savantes* (1672)]

MORTIMER, Sir John (1923–2009)
Beauty is handed out as undemocratically as
inherited peerages, and beautiful people have
done nothing to deserve their astonishing
reward.
[*The Observer*, 1999]

RUSKIN, John (1819–1900)
Remember that the most beautiful things in
the world are the most useless; peacocks and
lilies for instance.
[*The Stones of Venice* (1851)]

RUSSELL, Bertrand (1872–1970)
Mathematics, rightly viewed, possesses not
only truth, but supreme beauty –a beauty
cold and austere, like that of sculpture.
[*Mysticism and Logic* (1918)]

SAKI (1870–1916)
I always say beauty is only sin deep.
['Reginald's Choir Treat' (1904)]

SAPPHO (fl. 7th–6th centuries BC)
Beauty endures for only as long as it can be
seen; goodness, beautiful today, will remain
so tomorrow.
[In Nairn Attallah, *Women* (1987)]

TOLSTOY, Leo (1828–1910)
It is amazing how complete is the delusion
that beauty is goodness.
[*The Kreutzer Sonata* (1890)]

VIRGIL (70–19 BC)
O beautiful boy, do not put too much trust in
your beauty.
[*Eclogues*, II, line 17]

WOLLSTONECRAFT, Mary (1759–1797)
Taught from their infancy that beauty is
woman's sceptre, the mind shapes itself to
the body, and roaming round its gilt cage,
only seeks to adorn its prison.
[*A Vindication of the Rights of Woman* (1792)]

See **APPEARANCE**

BED

BENJAMIN, Walter (1892–1940)
Books and bimbos can be taken to bed.
[*One-way street*, 1928]

HERBERT, George (1593–1633)
When boyes go first to bed, They step into
their voluntarie graves.
[*The Temple* (1633)]

HUXLEY, Aldous (1894–1963)
'Bed,' as the Italian proverb succinctly puts it,
'is the poor man's opera.'
[*Heaven and Hell* (1956)]

JOHNSON, Samuel (1709–1784)
I have, all my life long, been lying till noon;
yet I tell all young men, and tell them with
great sincerity, that nobody who does not rise
early will ever do any good.
[In Boswell, *Journal of a Tour to the Hebrides*
(1785)]

LAUDER, Sir Harry (1870–1950)
O! it's nice to get up in the mornin',
But it's nicer to stay in bed.
[Song, 1913]

PEPYS, Samuel (1633–1703)
And mighty proud I am (and ought to be
thankful to God Almighty) that I am able to
have a spare bed for my friends.
[*Diary*, August 1666]

THURBER, James (1894–1961)
Early to rise and early to bed makes a male
healthy and wealthy and dead.
[*The New Yorker*, 1939]

See **IDLENESS AND UNEMPLOYMENT,
SLEEP**

BELIEF

AMIEL, Henri-Frédéric (1821–1881)
A belief is not true because it is useful.
[*Journal*, 1876]

BAGEHOT, Walter (1826–1877)
So long as there are earnest believers in the world, they will always wish to punish opinions, even if their judgement tells them it is unwise, and their conscience that it is wrong.
[*Literary Studies* (1879)]

**THE BIBLE
(King James Version)**
Lord, I believe; help thou mine unbelief.
[*Mark*, 9:24]
Blessed are they that have not seen, and yet have believed.
[*John*, 20:29]
Faith is the substance of things hoped for, the evidence of things not seen.
[*Hebrews*, 11:1]
Faith without works is dead.
[*James*, 2:20]

BUCK, Pearl S. (1892–1973)
I feel no need for any other faith than my faith in human beings.
[*I Believe* (1939)]

CAESAR, Gaius Julius (c.102–44 BC)
Men generally believe what they wish.
[*De Bello Gallico*]

CARROLL, Lewis (1832–1898)
If you'll believe in me, I'll believe in you.
[*Through the Looking-Glass* (1872)]

CHESTERTON, G.K. (1874–1936)
Reason is itself a matter of faith. It is an act of faith to assert that our thoughts have any relation to reality at all.
[*Orthodoxy* (1908)]

COWARD, Sir Noël (1899–1973)
Life without faith is an arid business.
[*Blithe Spirit* (1941)]

FRANK, Anne (1929–1945)
In spite of everything I still believe that people are good at heart.
[*The Diary of Anne Frank* (1947)]

FREUD, Sigmund (1856–1939)
The more the fruits of knowledge become accessible to men, the more widespread is the decline of religious belief.
[*The Future of an Illusion* (1927)]

GRANT, George (1918–1988)
We listen to others to discover what we ourselves believe.
[*CBC Times*, 1959]

JENKINS, David (1925–)
As I get older I seem to believe less and less and yet to believe what I do believe more and more.
[*The Observer*, 1988]

JOWETT, Benjamin (1817–1893)
My dear child, you must believe in God in spite of what the clergy tells you.
[In M. Asquith, *Autobiography* (1922)]

KANT, Immanuel (1724–1804)
There is only one (true) religion; but there can be many different kinds of belief.
[*Religion within the Boundaries of Mere Reason* (1793)]

MENCKEN, H.L. (1880–1956)
Faith may be defined briefly as an illogical belief in the occurrence of the improbable.
[*Prejudices* (1927)]

ORWELL, George (1903–1950)
Doublethink means the power of holding two contradictory beliefs in one's mind simultaneously, and accepting both of them.
[*Nineteen Eighty-Four* (1949)]

RUSSELL, Bertrand (1872–1970)
It is undesirable to believe a proposition when there is no ground whatever for supposing it true.
[*Sceptical Essays* (1928)]
(On being asked if he would be willing to die for his beliefs)
Of course not. After all, I may be wrong.
[Attr.]

STORR, Dr Anthony (1920–2001)
One man's faith is another man's delusion.
[*Feet of Clay* (1996)]

TURGENEV, Ivan (1818–1883)
The courage to believe in nothing.
[*Fathers and Sons* (1862)]

VALÉRY, Paul (1871–1945)
What has always been believed by everyone, everywhere, will most likely turn out to be false.
[*Moralities*, 1932]

VOLTAIRE (1694–1778)
Faith consists in believing what reason does not believe ... It is not enough that a thing may be possible for it to be believed.
[*Questions sur l'Encyclopédie* (1770–1772)]

See **FAITH, RELIGION**

BENEFACTORS

BAGEHOT, Walter (1826-1877)
The most melancholy of human reflections, perhaps, is that, on the whole, it is a question whether the benevolence of mankind does most good or harm.
[*Physics and Politics* (1872)]

COMPTON-BURNETT, Dame Ivy (1884-1969)
At any time you might act for my good. When people do that, it kills something precious between them.
[*Manservant and Maidservant* (1947)]

CONNOLLY, Billy (1942-)
(Of Andrew Carnegie)
It was said that he gave money away as silently as a waiter falling down a flight of stairs with a tray of glasses.
[*Gullible's Travels*]

CREIGHTON, Mandell (1843-1901)
No people do so much harm as those who go about doing good.
[*The Life and Letters of Mandell Creighton* (1904)]

GILBERT, W.S. (1836-1911)
I love my fellow creatures – I do all the good I can –
Yet everybody says I'm such a disagreeable man!
[*Princess Ida* (1884)]

GOLDSMITH, Oliver (c.1728-1774)
And learn the luxury of doing good.
['The Traveller' (1764)]

JOHNSON, Samuel (1709-1784)
Patron. Commonly a wretch who supports with insolence, and is paid with flattery.
[*A Dictionary of the English Language* (1755)]

MACHIAVELLI (1469-1527)
It is the nature of men to be bound by the benefits they confer as much as by those they receive.
[*The Prince* (1532)]

TITUS VESPASIANUS (AD 39-81)
Recalling once after dinner that he had done nothing to help anyone all that day, he gave voice to that memorable and praiseworthy remark: 'Friends, I have lost a day.'
[In Suetonius, *Lives of the Caesars*]

WORDSWORTH, William (1770-1850)
On that best portion of a good man's life;
His little, nameless, unremembered acts
Of kindness and of love.
['Lines composed a few miles above Tintern Abbey' (1798)]

See **GOODNESS**

BIOGRAPHY

AMIS, Martin (1949-)
To be more interested in the writer than the writing is just eternal human vulgarity.
[*The Observer Review*, 1996]

ARBUTHNOT, John (1667-1735)
One of the new terrors of death.
[In Carruthers, *Life of Pope* (1857)]

BENTLEY, Edmund Clerihew (1875-1956)
The art of Biography
Is different from Geography.
Geography is about Maps,
But Biography is about chaps.
[*Biography for Beginners* (1905)]

CARLYLE, Thomas (1795-1881)
A well-written Life is almost as rare as a well-spent one.
[*Critical and Miscellaneous Essays* (1839)]

CRISP, Quentin (1908-1999)
An autobiography is an obituary in serial form with the last instalment missing.
[*The Naked Civil Servant* (1968)]

DAVIES, Robertson (1913-1995)
Biography at its best is a form of fiction.
[*The Lyre of Orpheus* (1988)]

DISRAELI, Benjamin (1804-1881)
Read no history: nothing but biography, for that is life without theory.
[*Contarini Fleming* (1832)]

EMERSON, Ralph Waldo (1803-1882)
There is properly no history; only biography.
[*Essays, First Series* (1841)]

FRYE, Northrop (1912-1991)
There's only one story, the story of your life.
[In Ayre, *Northrop Frye: A Biography* (1989)]

GRANT, Cary (1904-1986)
Nobody is ever truthful about his own life. There are always ambiguities.
[*The Observer*, 1981]

GUEDALLA, Philip (1889-1944)
Biography, like big-game hunting, is one of the recognized forms of sport, and it is as unfair as only sport can be.
[*Supers and Supermen* (1920)]

JOHNSON, Samuel (1709-1784)
Nobody can write the life of a man, but those who have eat and drunk and lived in social intercourse with him.
[In Boswell, *The Life of Samuel Johnson* (1791)]

SALINGER, J.D. (1919-2010)
If you really want to hear about it, the first thing you'll probably want to know is where I was born and what my lousy childhood was like, and how my parents were occupied and all before they had me, and all that David Copperfield kind of crap.
[*The Catcher in the Rye* (1951)]

TROLLOPE, Anthony (1815-1882)
In these days a man is nobody unless his biography is kept so far posted up that it may be ready for the national breakfast-table on the morning after his demise.
[*Doctor Thorne* (1858)]

WEST, Dame Rebecca (1892-1983)
Just how difficult it is to write biography can be reckoned by anybody who sits down and considers just how many people know the real truth about his or her love affairs.
[*Vogue*, 1952]

WILDE, Oscar (1854-1900)
Every great man has his disciples, but it is always Judas who writes the biography.
[Attr.]

BIRTH

ACKERLEY, J.R. (1896-1967)
I was born in 1896, and my parents were married in 1919.
[*My Father and Myself* (1968)]

APPLETON, Nicole (1974-)
It was easier than having a tattoo.
[*The Sunday Times*, July 2001]

BHAGAVADGITA
For that which is born death is certain, and for the dead birth is certain. Therefore grieve not over that which is unavoidable.
[Ch. II]

CALDERÓN DE LA BARCA, Pedro (1600-1681)
For man's greatest offence is to have been born.
[*Life is a Dream* (1636)]

CONGREVE, William (1670-1729)
I came upstairs into the world; for I was born in a cellar.
[*Love for Love* (1695)]

FROMM, Erich (1900-1980)
Man's main task in life is to give birth to himself.
[*Man for Himself*]

LETTE, Kathy (1958-)
Childbirth was the moment of truth in my life. Suddenly you realise that you are having the greatest love affair of your life (but you also realise that God's a bloke).
[*The Observer*, June 1999]

MADONNA (1958-)
I'm not interested in being Wonder Woman in the delivery room. Give me drugs.

MITCHELL, Margaret (1900-1949)
Death and taxes and childbirth! There's never any convenient time for any of them.
[*Gone With The Wind* (1936)]

WISDOM, Sir Norman (1918-2010)
I was born in very sorry circumstances. My mother was sorry and my father was sorry as well.
[*The Observer*, 1998]

See **PREGNANCY**

BOOKS

AUDEN, W.H. (1907-1973)
Some books are undeservedly forgotten; none are undeservedly remembered.
[*The Dyer's Hand* (1963)]

BACON, Francis (1561-1626)
Some books are to be tasted, others to be swallowed, and some few to be chewed and digested; that is, some books are to be read only in parts; others to be read but not curiously; and some few to be read wholly, and with diligence and attention.
['Of Studies' (1625)]

BARNES, Julian (1946-)
Books say: she did this because. Life says: she did this. Books are where things are explained to you; life is where things aren't.
[*Flaubert's Parrot* (1984)]

BELLOC, Hilaire (1870-1953)
When I am dead, I hope it may be said:
'His sins were scarlet, but his books were read.'
[*Sonnets and Verse* (1923)]

BRADBURY, Ray (1920-2012)
You don't have to burn books to destroy a culture. Just get people to stop reading them.
[*Reader's Digest*, January 1994]

BRODSKY, Joseph (1940-1996)
There are worse crimes than burning books.
One of them is not reading them.
[Remark, 1991]

BURGESS, Anthony (1917-1993)
The possession of a book becomes a
substitute for reading it.
[*New York Times Book Review*]

BYRON, Lord (1788-1824)
'Tis pleasant, sure, to see one's name in print;
A Book's a Book, altho' there is nothing in't.
[*English Bards and Scotch Reviewers* (1809)]

CHANDLER, Raymond (1888-1959)
If my books had been any worse I should not
have been invited to Hollywood, and ... if they
had been any better, I should not have come.
[Letter to C.W. Morton, 1945]

DAVIES, Robertson (1913-1995)
A truly great book should be read in youth,
again in maturity, and once more in old age,
as a fine building should be seen by morning
light, at noon, and by moonlight.
[In Grant, *The Enthusiasms of
Robertson Davies*]

DESCARTES, René (1596-1650)
The reading of all good books is like a
conversation with the finest men of past
centuries.
[*Discours de la Méthode* (1637)]

DIODORUS SICULUS (c.1st century BC)
(Inscription over library door in Alexandria)
Medicine for the soul.
[*History*]

EVANS, Dame Edith (1888-1976)
(On being told that Nancy Mitford had been
lent a villa to enable her to finish a book)
Oh really. What exactly is she reading?
[Attr.]

FORSTER, E.M. (1879-1970)
I suggest that the only books that influence
us are those for which we are ready, and
which have gone a little farther down our
particular path than we have yet got
ourselves.
[*Two Cheers for Democracy* (1951)]

FRYE, Northrop (1912-1991)
The book is the world's most patient medium.
[*The Scholar in Society*, film, 1984]

FULLER, Thomas (1608-1661)
Learning hath gained most by those books by
which the printers have lost.
[*The Holy State and the Profane State* (1642)]

**GLOUCESTER, William (Duke of)
(1743-1805)**
Another damned, thick, square book. Always
scribble, scribble, scribble! Eh! Mr. Gibbon?
[In Henry Best, *Personal and Literary
Memorials* (1829)]

GOLDSMITH, Oliver (c.1728-1774)
A book may be amusing with numerous
errors, or it may be very dull without a single
absurdity.
[*The Vicar of Wakefield* (1766)]

HEINE, Heinrich (1797-1856)
It is there, where they Burn books, that
eventually they burn people too.
[*Almansor: A Tragedy* (1821)]

HORACE (65-8 BC)
You can destroy what you haven't published;
the word once out cannot be recalled.
[*Ars Poetica*]

HUXLEY, Aldous (1894-1963)
The proper study of mankind is books.
[*Crome Yellow* (1921)]

KAFKA, Franz (1883-1924)
I think you should only read those books
which bite and sting you.
[Letter to Oskar Pollak, 1904]
... a book must be the axe for the frozen sea
within us.
[Letter to Oskar Pollak, 1904]

KORAN
Every age hath its book.
[Chapter 13]

LAING, R.D. (1927-1989)
Few books today are forgivable.
[*The Politics of Experience* (1967)]

LARKIN, Philip (1922-1985)
Get stewed: Books are a load of crap.
['A Study of Reading Habits' (1964)]

LICHTENBERG, Georg (1742-1799)
There can hardly be a stranger commodity in
the world than books. Printed by people who
don't understand them; sold by people who
don't understand them; bound, criticized and
read by people who don't understand them,
and now even written by people who don't
understand them.
[A Doctrine of Scattered Occasions]

MACAULAY, Dame Rose (1881-1958)
It was a book to kill time for those who like it
better dead.
[Attr.]

MADONNA (1958-)
Everyone probably thinks that I'm a raving nymphomaniac, that I have an insatiable sexual appetite, when the truth is I'd rather read a book.
[*Q Magazine*, June 1991]

MARX, Groucho (1890-1977)
I did toy with the idea of doing a cook-book ... I think a lot of people who hate literature but love fried eggs would buy it if the price was right.
[*Groucho and Me* (1959)]

MAUGHAM, William Somerset (1874-1965)
There is an impression abroad that everyone had it in him to write one book; but if by this is implied a good book the impression is false.
[*The Summing Up* (1938)]

POWELL, Anthony (1905-2000)
Books Do Furnish a Room.
[*Title of novel*, 1971]

ROGERS, Samuel (1763-1855)
When a new book is published, read an old one.
[Attr.]

SAMUEL, Lord (1870-1963)
A library is thought in cold storage.
[*A Book of Quotations* (1947)]

SMITH, Logan Pearsall (1865-1946)
A best-seller is the gilded tomb of a mediocre talent.
[*Afterthoughts* (1931)]

STEVENSON, Robert Louis (1850-1894)
Books are good enough in their own way, but they are a mighty bloodless substitute for life.
[*Virginibus Puerisque* (1881)]

TUPPER, Martin (1810-1889)
A good book is the best of friends, the same today and for ever.
[*Proverbial Philosophy* (1838)]

WAUGH, Evelyn (1903-1966)
Particularly against books the Home Secretary is. If we can't stamp out literature in the country, we can at least stop it being brought in from outside.
[*Vile Bodies* (1930)]

WESLEY, John (1703-1791)
Beware you be not swallowed up in books! An ounce of love is worth a pound of knowledge.
[In Southey, *Life of Wesley* (1820)]

WEST, Dame Rebecca (1892-1983)
God forbid that any book should be banned. The practice is as indefensible as infanticide.
[*The Strange Necessity* (1928)]

WILDE, Oscar (1854-1900)
There is no such thing as a moral or an immoral book. Books are well written, or badly written. That is all.
[*The Picture of Dorian Gray* (1891)]

WODEHOUSE, P.G. (1881-1975)
(Dedication)
To my daughter Leonora without whose never-failing sympathy and encouragement this book would have been finished in half the time.
[*The Heart of a Goof* (1926)]

See **CENSORSHIP, CRITICISM, FICTION, LITERATURE, PUBLISHING, READING, WRITERS, WRITING**

BOREDOM

AUSTIN, Warren Robinson (1877-1962)
(On being asked if he found long debates at the UN tiring)
It is better for aged diplomats to be bored than for young men to die.
[Attr.]

BIERCE, Ambrose (1842-c.1914)
Bore: A person who talks when you wish him to listen.
[*The Cynic's Word Book* (1906)]

BRIDIE, James (1888-1951)
Boredom is a sign of satisfied ignorance, blunted apprehension, crass sympathies, dull understanding, feeble powers of attention and irreclaimable weakness of character.
[*Mr Bolfry* (1943)]

BRYSON, Bill (1951-)
I mused for a few moments on the question of which was worse, to lead a life so boring that you are easily enchanted or a life so full of stimulus that you are easily bored.
[*The Lost Continent* (1989)]

BYRON, Lord (1788-1824)
Society is now one polish'd horde, Form'd of two mighty tribes, the Bores and Bored.
[*Don Juan* (1819-1824)]

CHESTERTON, G.K. (1874-1936)
There is no such thing on earth as an uninteresting subject; the only thing that can exist is an uninterested person.
[*Heretics* (1905)]

DE VRIES, Peter (1910–1993)
I wanted to be bored to death, as good a way
to go as any.
[Comfort me with Apples (1956)]

FREUD, Sir Clement (1924–2009)
If you resolve to give up smoking, drinking
and loving, you don't actually live longer; it
just seems longer.
[The Observer, 1964]

GAUTIER, Théophile (1811–1872)
Sooner barbarity than boredom.
[Attr.]

JERROLD, Douglas William (1803–1857)
(Remark to a small thin man who was boring
him)
Sir, you are like a pin, but without either its
head or its point.
[Attr.]

LA ROCHEFOUCAULD (1613–1680)
We are almost always bored by the very
people whom we are not allowed to find
boring.
[Maximes, (1678)]

SHAKESPEARE, William (1564–1616)
Life is as tedious as a twice-told tale
Vexing the dull ear of a drowsy man.
[King John, III.iv]

TAYLOR, Bert Leston (1866–1921)
A bore is a man who, when you ask him how
he is, tells you.
[The So-Called Human Race (1922)]

THOMAS, Dylan (1914–1953)
Dylan talked copiously, then stopped.
'Somebody's boring me,' he said, 'I think
it's me.'
[In Heppenstall, *Four Absentees* (1960)]

UPDIKE, John (1932–2009)
A healthy male adult bore consumes one and
a half times his own weight in other people's
patience.
[Assorted Prose (1965)]

VOLTAIRE (1694–1778)
The secret of being boring is to say
everything.
[Discours en vers sur l'homme (1737)]

BRITAIN

ACHESON, Dean (1893–1971)
Great Britain ... has lost an Empire and not yet
found a role.
[Speech, 1962]

ATTLEE, Clement (1883–1967)
I think the British have the distinction above
all other nations of being able to put new
wine into old bottles without bursting them.
[Hansard, 1950]

BULLOCK, Alan (Baron) (1914–2004)
The people Hitler never understood, and
whose actions continued to exasperate him
to the end of his life, were the British.
[Hitler, A Study in Tyranny (1952)]

CAMP, William (1926–2002)
What annoys me about Britain is the rugged
will to lose.
[Attr.]

CASSON, Sir Hugh (1910–1999)
The British love permanence more than they
love beauty.
[The Observer, 1964]

EDMOND, James (1859–1933)
I had been told by Jimmy Edmond in Australia
that there were only three things against
living in Britain: the place, the climate and the
people.
[In Low, *Low Autobiography*]

HARLECH, Lord (1918–1985)
In the end it may well be that Britain will be
honoured by historians more for the way she
disposed of an empire than for the way in
which she acquired it.
[New York Times, 1962]

THOMSON, James (1700–1748)
'Rule, Britannia, rule the waves;
Britons never will be slaves.'
[Alfred: A Masque (1740)]

See **ENGLAND, IRELAND, PATRIOTISM,
SCOTLAND**

BUREAUCRACY

ACHESON, Dean (1893–1971)
A memorandum is written not to inform the
reader but to protect the writer.
[Attr.]

ADENAUER, Konrad (1876–1967)
There's nothing which cannot be made a
mess of again by officials.
[Der Spiegel, 1975]

ALLEN, Fred (1894–1956)
A conference is a gathering of important
people who singly can do nothing, but
together can decide that nothing can be
done.
[Attr.]

ANONYMOUS
A committee is a cul-de-sac down which
ideas are lured and then quietly strangled.
[*New Scientist*, 1973]
A camel is a horse designed by a committee.

BERLE, Milton (1908-2002)
Committee – a group of men who keep
minutes and waste hours.
[Attr.]

GOWERS, Sir Ernest (1880-1966)
It is not easy nowadays to remember
anything so contrary to all appearances as
that officials are the servants of the public;
and the official must try not to foster the
illusion that it is the other way round.
[*Plain Words*]

HUXLEY, Aldous (1894-1963)
Official dignity tends to increase in inverse
ratio to the importance of the country in
which the office is held.
[*Beyond the Mexique Bay* (1934)]

MCCARTHY, Mary (1912-1989)
Bureaucracy, the rule of no one, has become
the modern form of despotism.
[*The New Yorker*, 1958]

SAMPSON, Anthony (1926-2004)
(Of the Civil Service)
Members rise from CMG (known sometimes
in Whitehall as 'Call Me God') to the KCMG
('Kindly Call Me God') to ... the GCMG ('God
Calls Me God').
[*The Anatomy of Britain* (1962)]

SAMUEL, Lord (1870-1963)
(Referring to the Civil Service)
A difficulty for every solution.
[Attr.]

SANTAYANA, George (1863-1952)
The working of great institutions is mainly the
result of a vast mass of routine, petty malice,
self interest, carelessness, and sheer mistake.
Only a residual fraction is thought.
[*The Crime of Galileo*]

THOMAS, Gwyn (1913-1981)
My life's been a meeting, Dad, one long
meeting. Even on the few committees I don't
yet belong to, the agenda winks at me when I
pass.
[*The Keep* (1961)]

TREE, Sir Herbert Beerbohm (1853-1917)
A committee should consist of three men,
two of whom are absent.
[In Pearson, *Beerbohm Tree*]

VIDAL, Gore (1925-2012)
There is something about a bureaucrat that
does not like a poem.
[*Sex, Death and Money* (1968)]

BUSINESS

ANONYMOUS
A Company for carrying on an undertaking
of Great Advantage, but no one to know what
it is.
[*The South Sea Company Prospectus*]

AUSTEN, Jane (1775-1817)
Business, you know, may bring money, but
friendship hardly ever does.
[*Emma* (1816)]

BALZAC, Honoré de (1799-1850)
Generous people make bad shopkeepers.
[*Illusions perdues* (1843)]

BARNUM, Phineas T. (1810-1891)
Every crowd has a silver lining.
[Attr.]

BARTON, Bruce (1886-1967)
Jesus picked up twelve men from the bottom
ranks of business and forged them into an
organization that conquered the world.
[*The Man Nobody Knows: A Discovery of the
Real Jesus*]

BETJEMAN, Sir John (1906-1984)
You ask me what it is I do. Well actually, you
know,
I'm partly a liaison man and partly P.R.O.
Essentially I integrate the current export drive
And basically I'm viable from ten o'clock till five.
['Executive' (1974)]

BUFFETT, Warren (1930-)
There was more misdirected compensation in
corporate America in the past five years as
there was in the hundred years before that.
[*The Guardian*, 2003]

COHEN, Sir Jack (1898-1979)
Pile it high, sell it cheap.
[Business motto]

DENNIS, C.J. (1876-1938)
It takes one hen to lay an egg, But seven men
to sell it.
['The Regimental Hen']

FORD, Henry (1863-1947)
A business that makes nothing but money is
a poor kind of business.
[Interview]

FRANKLIN, Benjamin (1706–1790)
No nation was ever ruined by trade.
[*Essays*]

GALBRAITH, J.K. (1908–2006)
The salary of the chief executive of the large corporation is not a market award for achievement. It is frequently in the nature of a warm personal gesture by the individual to himself.
[*Annals of an Abiding Liberal* (1980)]

GOLDWYN, Samuel (1882–1974)
Chaplin is no business man – all he knows is that he can't take anything less.
[Attr.]

GREENSPAN, Alan (1926–)
An infectious greed seemed to grip much of our business community of the late 1990s.
[*New York Times*, 2002]

MENCKEN, H.L. (1880–1956)
(Referring to the businessman)
He is the only man who is ever apologizing for his occupation.
[*Prejudices* (1927)]

NAPOLEON I (1769–1821)
England is a nation of shopkeepers.
[In O'Meara, *Napoleon in Exile* (1822)]

ONASSIS, Aristotle (1906–1975)
The secret of business is to know something that nobody else knows.
[*The Economist*, 1991]

PUZO, Mario (1920–1999)
He's a businessman. I'll make him an offer he can't refuse.
[*The Godfather* (1969)]

REVSON, Charles (1906–1975)
In the factory we make cosmetics. In the store we sell hope.
[In Tobias, *Fire and Ice* (1976)]

RODDICK, Anita (1942–2007)
I am still looking for the modern equivalent of those Quakers who ran successful businesses, made money because they offered honest products and treated their people decently ... This business creed, sadly, seems long forgotten.
[*Body and Soul* (1991)]

SHEEN, J. Fulton (1895–1979)
(Referring to his contract for a television appearance)
The big print giveth and the fine print taketh away.
[Attr.]

SMITH, Adam (1723–1790)
People of the same trade seldom meet together, even for merriment and diversion, but the conversation ends in a conspiracy against the public, or in some contrivance to raise prices.
[*Wealth of Nations* (1776)]

THURLOW, Edward (First Baron) (1731–1806)
Did you ever expect a corporation to have a conscience, when it has no soul to be damned, and no body to be kicked?
[Attr.]

WARHOL, Andy (c.1926–1987)
Being good in business is the most fascinating kind of art.
[*The Observer*, 1987]

YOUNG, Andrew (1932–)
Nothing is illegal if one hundred businessmen decide to do it.
[Attr.]

See **BUYING AND SELLING, CAPITALISM, ECONOMICS, MONEY AND WEALTH**

CANADA

CAPONE, Al (1899–1947)
I don't even know what street Canada is on.
[Attr.]

MAHY, Margaret (1936–2012)
Canadians are Americans with no Disneyland.
[*The Changeover* (1984)]

CAPITALISM

ANONYMOUS
Capitalism is the exploitation of man by man. Communism is the complete opposite.
[Described by Laurence J. Peter as a 'Polish proverb']

CONNOLLY, James (1868–1916)
Governments in a capitalist society are but committees of the rich to manage the affairs of the capitalist class.
[*Irish Worker*, 1914]

DENG XIAOPING (1904–1997)
(On whether China should adopt socialist or private enterprise policies)
It doesn't matter whether the cat is black or white, as long as it catches mice.
[Communist Youth League conference, 1962]

GALBRAITH, J.K. (1908–2006)
You must now speak always of the market system. The word 'capitalism', once the common reference, has acquired a deleterious Marxist sound.
[*The Observer*, 1998]

GONNE, Maud (1865–1953)
To me judges seem the well paid watch-dogs of Capitalism, making things safe and easy for the devil Mammon.
[Letter to W.B. Yeats]

HAMPTON, Christopher (1946–)
If I had to give a definition of capitalism I would say: the process whereby American girls turn into American women.
[*Savages* (1973)]

ILLICH, Ivan (1926–2002)
In a consumer society there are inevitably two kinds of slaves: the prisoners of addiction and the prisoners of envy.
[*Tools for Conviviality* (1973)]

KELLER, Helen (1880–1968)
Militarism ... is one of the chief bulwarks of capitalism, and the day that militarism is undermined, capitalism will fail.
[*The Story of My Life* (1902)]

KEYNES, John Maynard (1883–1946)
I think that Capitalism, wisely managed, can probably be made more efficient for attaining economic ends than any alternative system yet in sight, but that in itself it is in many ways extremely objectionable.
['The End of Laissez-Faire' (1926)]

LENIN, V.I. (1870–1924)
Under capitalism we have a state in the proper sense of the word, that is, a special machine for the suppression of one class by another.
[*The State and Revolution* (1917)]

MALCOLM X (1925–1965)
You show me a capitalist, I'll show you a bloodsucker.
[*Malcolm X Speaks*, 1965]

MARX, Karl (1818–1883)
Capitalist production creates, with the inexorability of a law of nature, its own negation.
[*Das Kapital* (1867)]

OBAMA, Barack (1961–)
(At a summit with the chief executives of the US's thirteen biggest banks during the financial crisis)
My administration is the only thing between you and the pitchforks.
[ABC News, 2009]

See **BUSINESS**

CATS

ARNOLD, Matthew (1822–1888)
Cruel, but composed and bland,
Dumb, inscrutable and grand,
So Tiberius might have sat,
Had Tiberius been a cat.
['Poor Matthias']

ELIOT, T.S. (1888–1965)
Macavity, Macavity, there's no one like Macavity,
There never was a Cat of such deceitfulness and suavity.
He always has an alibi, and one or two to spare:
At whatever time the deed took place –
MACAVITY WASN'T THERE!
['Macavity: the Mystery Cat', (1939)]

MONTAIGNE, Michel de (1533–1592)
When I play with my cat, who knows whether she isn't amusing herself with me more than I am with her?
[*Essais* (1580)]

ROWBOTHAM, David Harold (1924–2010)
Let some of the tranquillity of the cat
Curl into me.
['The Creature in the Chair']

SACKVILLE-WEST, Vita (1892–1962)
The greater cats with golden eyes
Stare out between the bars.
Deserts are there, and different skies,
And night with different stars.
[*The King's Daughter* (1929)]

SMITH, Stevie (1902–1971)
Oh I am a cat that likes to
Gallop about doing good.
['The Galloping Cat' (1972)]

TESSIMOND, A.S.J. (1902–1962)
Cats, no less liquid than their shadows,
Offer no angles to the wind.
They slip, diminished, neat, through loopholes
Less than themselves.
[*Cats* (1934)]

See **ANIMALS**

CAUTION

ANONYMOUS
Whatever you do, do it warily, and take
account of the end.
[Gesta Romanorum]

ARMSTRONG, Dr John (1709–1779)
Distrust yourself, and sleep before you fight.
'Tis not too late tomorrow to be brave.
[The Art of Preserving Health (1744)]

BELLOC, Hilaire (1870–1953)
And always keep a-hold of Nurse
For fear of finding something worse.
[Cautionary Tales (1907)]

DRYDEN, John (1631–1700)
But now the world's o'er stocked with
prudent men.
[The Medal (1682)]

LINCOLN, Abraham (1809–1865)
When you have got an elephant by the hind
leg, and he is trying to run away, it's best to
let him run.
[Remark, 1865]

CELEBRITY

ALLEN, Fred (1894–1956)
A celebrity is a person who works hard all his
life to become well known, and then wears
dark glasses to avoid being recognized.
*[Laurence Peter Quotations for Our Time
(1977)]*

JACKSON, Michael (1958–2009)
I was a veteran, before I was a teenager.

KISSINGER, Henry (1923–)
The nice thing about being a celebrity is that,
if you bore people, they think it's their fault.
[Attr.]

MENCKEN, H.L. (1880–1956)
A celebrity is one who is known to many
persons he is glad he doesn't know.

O'ROURKE, P.J. (1947–)
You can't shame or humiliate modern
celebrities. What used to be called shame and
humiliation is now called publicity.
[Give War a Chance (1992)]

UPDIKE, John (1932–2009)
Celebrity is a mask that eats into the face.
[Memoirs (1989)]

See **FAME, REPUTATION**

CENSORSHIP

BOROVOY, A. Alan (1932–)
It is usually better to permit a piece of trash
than to suppress a work of art.
[When Freedoms Collide (1988)]

CRONENBERG, David (1943–)
Censors tend to do what only psychotics do:
they confuse reality with illusion.
[Cronenberg on Cronenberg (1992)]

EMERSON, Ralph Waldo (1803–1882)
Every burned book enlightens the world.
[Attr.]

GORDIMER, Nadine (1923–)
Censorship is never over for those who have
experienced it. It is a brand on the
imagination that affects the individual who
has suffered it, forever.
[Lecture, June 1990]

GRIFFITH-JONES, Mervyn (1909–1979)
(At the trial of D.H. Lawrence's novel Lady
Chatterley's Lover)
Is it a book you would even wish your wife or
your servants to read?
[The Times, 1960]

PINTER, Harold (1930–2008)
(On the execution of Nigerian writer Ken
Saro-Wiwa)
Murder is the most brutal form of censorship.
[The Observer, 1995]
Censorship in the UK reveals a deeply
conservative country still in thrall to its strict
Protestant values.
[Index on Censorship, 1996]

RUSHDIE, Sir Salman (1946–)
Means of artistic expression that require large
quantities of finance and sophisticated
technology – films, plays, records – become,
by virtue of that dependence, easy to censor
and to control. But what one writer can make
in the solitude of one room is something no
power can easily destroy.
[Index on Censorship, 1996]

STROMME, Sigmund (1946–)
Strict censorship cannot be maintained
without terrorism.
[Index on Censorship, 1996]

See **BOOKS, PORNOGRAPHY**

CHANGE

ANONYMOUS
Change imposed is change opposed.
[Management slogan, Deloitte and Touche, 1999]

AURELIUS, Marcus (121–180)
The universe is change; life is what thinking makes of it.
[*Meditations*]

BACON, Francis (1561–1626)
That all things are changed, and that nothing really perishes, and that the sum of matter remains exactly the same, is sufficiently certain.
[*Thoughts on the Nature of Things* (1604)]

CONFUCIUS (c.550–c.478 BC)
They must often change who would be constant in happiness or wisdom.
[*Analects*]

HERACLITUS (c.540–c.480 BC)
You cannot step twice into the same river.
[In Plato, *Cratylus*]

HOOKER, Richard (c.1554–1600)
Change is not made without inconvenience, even from worse to better.
[In Johnson, *Dictionary of the English Language* (1755)]

IRVING, Washington (1783–1859)
There is a certain relief in change, even though it be from bad to worse; as I have found in travelling in a stage-coach, that it is often a comfort to shift one's position and be bruised in a new place.
[*Tales of a Traveller* (1824)]

KARR, Alphonse (1808–1890)
Plus ça change, plus c'est la même chose.
The more things change the more they remain the same.
[*Les Guêpes* (1849)]

LUCRETIUS (c.95–55 BC)
Some groups increase, others diminish, and in a short space the generations of living creatures are changed and like runners pass on the torch of life.
[*De Rerum Natura*]

MALCOLM X (1925–1965)
Usually when people are sad, they don't do anything. They just cry over their condition. But when they get angry, they bring about a change.
[*Malcolm X Speaks*, 1965]

SWIFT, Jonathan (1667–1745)
There is nothing in this world constant, but inconstancy.
[*A Critical Essay upon the Faculties of the Mind* (1709)]

THOREAU, Henry David (1817–1862)
Things do not change; we change.
[*Walden* (1854)]

TOFFLER, Alvin (1928–)
Future shock ... the shattering stress and disorientation that we induce in individuals by subjecting them to too much change in too short a time.
[*Future Shock* (1970)]

See **TIME**

CHARACTER

ELIOT, George (1819–1880)
'Character', says Novalis, in one of his questionable aphorisms – 'character is destiny.'
[*The Mill on the Floss* (1860)]

FRISCH, Max (1911–1991)
Every uniform corrupts one's character.
[*Diary*, 1948]

GOETHE (1749–1832)
Talent is formed in quiet retreat,
Character in the headlong rush of life.
[*Torquato Tasso* (1790)]

KARR, Alphonse (1808–1890)
Every man has three characters: that which he exhibits, that which he has, and that which he thinks he has.
[Attr.]

LINCOLN, Abraham (1809–1865)
Character is like a tree and reputation like its shadow. The shadow is what we think of it; the tree is the real thing.
[In Gross, *Lincoln's Own Stories*]

MURRAY, Les A. (1938–)
In the defiance of fashion is the beginning of character.
[*The Boy who Stole the Funeral* (1979)]

REAGAN, Ronald (1911–2004)
You can tell a lot about a fellow's character by the way he eats jelly beans.
[*Daily Mail*, 1981]

SIMPSON, O.J. (1947–)
The only thing that endures is character. Fame and wealth – all that is illusion. All that endures is character.
[*The Guardian*, 1995]

WILSON, Woodrow (1856-1924)
Character is a by-product; it is produced in
the great manufacture of daily duty.
[Speech, 1915]

See **REPUTATION**

CHARITY

BACON, Francis (1561-1626)
In charity there is no excess.
['Of Goodness, and Goodness of Nature'
(1625)]

BROWNE, Sir Thomas (1605-1682)
Charity begins at home, is the voice of the
world.
[*Religio Medici* (1643)]

CARNEGIE, Andrew (1835-1919)
Of every thousand dollars spent in so-called
charity today, it is probable that nine hundred
and fifty dollars is unwisely spent.
['Wealth' (1889)]

FULLER, Thomas (1608-1661)
He that feeds upon charity has a cold dinner
and no supper.
[Attr.]

POPE, Alexander (1688-1744)
In Faith and Hope the world will disagree,
But all Mankind's concern is Charity.
[*Essay on Man* (1733)]

ROUSSEAU, Jean-Jacques (1712-1778)
The feigned charity of the rich man is for him
no more than another luxury; he feeds the
poor as he feeds dogs and horses.
[Letter to M. Moulton]

SHERIDAN, Richard Brinsley (1751-1816)
Rowley: I believe there is no sentiment he has
more faith in than that 'charity begins at
home'. Sir Oliver Surface: And his, I presume,
is of that domestic sort which never stirs
abroad at all.
[*The School for Scandal* (1777)]

VOLTAIRE (1694-1778)
The man who leaves money to charity in his
will is only giving away what no longer
belongs to him.
[Letter, 1769]

See **BENEFACTORS, GENEROSITY**

CHARM

BARRIE, Sir J.M. (1860-1937)
(On charm)
It's a sort of bloom on a woman. If you have
it, you don't need to have anything else; and
if you don't have it, it doesn't much matter
what else you have.
[*What Every Woman Knows* (1908)]

BIERCE, Ambrose (1842-c.1914)
Please: To lay the foundation for a
superstructure of imposition.
[*The Enlarged Devil's Dictionary* (1961)]

CAMUS, Albert (1913-1960)
You know what charm is: a way of getting the
answer yes without having asked any clear
question.
[*The Fall* (1956)]

CONNOLLY, Cyril (1903-1974)
All charming people have something to
conceal, usually their total dependence on
the appreciation of others.
[*Enemies of Promise* (1938)]

FARQUHAR, George (1678-1707)
Charming women can true converts make,
We love the precepts for the teacher's sake.
[*The Constant Couple* (1699)]

LERNER, Alan Jay (1918-1986)
Oozing charm from every pore,
He oiled his way around the floor.
[*My Fair Lady* (1956)]

MACNALLY, Leonard (1752-1820)
On Richmond Hill there lives a lass,
More sweet than May day morn,
Whose charms all other maids surpass,
A rose without a thorn.
['The Lass of Richmond Hill' (1789)]

WAUGH, Evelyn (1903-1966)
Charm is the great English blight. It does
not exist outside these damp islands. It spots
and kills anything it touches. It kills love, it
kills art.
[*Brideshead Revisited* (1945)]

WILDE, Oscar (1854-1900)
It is absurd to divide people into good and
bad. People are either charming or tedious.
[*Lady Windermere's Fan*]

AMIS, Kingsley (1922–1995)
It was no wonder that people were so horrible
when they started life as children.
[*One Fat Englishman* (1963)]

AUDEN, W.H. (1907–1973)
Only those in the last stages of disease could
believe that children are true judges of
character.
[*The Orators* (1932)]

AUSTEN, Jane (1775–1817)
On every formal visit a child ought to be of
the party, by way of provision for discourse.
[*Sense and Sensibility* (1811)]

BACON, Francis (1561–1626)
Children sweeten labours, but they make
misfortunes more bitter.
[*Essays* (1625)]

BALDWIN, James (1924–1987)
Children have never been very good at
listening to their elders, but they have never
failed to imitate them. They must, they have
no other models.
[*Nobody Knows My Name* (1961)]

BOWEN, Elizabeth (1899–1973)
There is no end to the violations committed
by children on children, quietly talking alone.
[*The House in Paris* (1935)]

CARROLL, Lewis (1832–1898)
I am fond of children (except boys).
[Letter to Kathleen Eschwege, 1879]

FROST, Sir David (1939–)
Having one child makes you a parent; having
two you are a referee.
[*The Independent*, 1989]

GEORGE V (1865–1936)
My father was frightened of his mother. I was
frightened of my father, and I'm damned well
going to make sure that my children are
frightened of me.
[In R. Churchill, *Lord Derby* – 'King of
Lancashire' (1959)]

HARWOOD, Gwen (1920–1995)
'It's so sweet to hear their chatter, watch
them grow and thrive,'
she says to his departing smile. Then, nursing
the youngest child, sits staring at her feet.
To the wind she says, 'They have eaten me
alive.'
[*Poems* (1968)]

INGE, William Ralph (1860–1954)
The proper time to influence the character of
a child is about a hundred years before he is
born.
[*The Observer*, 1929]

JONSON, Ben (1572–1637)
Rest in soft peace, and, ask'd say here doth lye
Ben Jonson his best piece of poetrie.
['On My First Son' (1616)]

KNOX, Ronald (1888–1957)
`A loud noise at one end and no sense of
responsibility at the other.
[Attr.]

LEBOWITZ, Fran (1946–)
Remember that as a teenager you are at the
last stage in your life when you will be happy
to hear that the phone is for you.
[*Social Studies* (1981)]

MILLER, Alice (1923–2010)
Society chooses to disregard the
mistreatment of children, judging it to be
altogether normal because it is so
commonplace.
[*Pictures of a Childhood* (1986)]

MITFORD, Nancy (1904–1973)
I love children – especially when they cry, for
then someone takes them away.
[Attr.]

MONTAIGNE, Michel de (1533–1592)
It should be noted that children at play are
not merely playing; their games should be
seen as their most serious actions.
[*Essais* (1580)]

NASH, Ogden (1902–1971)
Children aren't happy with nothing to ignore,
And that's what parents were created for.
['The Parent' (1933)]

PAVESE, Cesare (1908–1950)
One stops being a child when one realizes
that telling one's trouble does not make it
better.
[*The Business of Living: Diaries 1935–50*

PLATH, Sylvia (1932–1963)
(On seeing her newborn baby)
What did my fingers do before they held him?
What did my heart do, with its love?
I have never seen a thing so clear.
His lids are like the lilac flower
And soft as a moth, his breath.
I shall not let go.
There is no guile or warp in him.
May he keep so.
['Three Women: A Poem for Three Voices' (1962)]

SPOCK, Dr Benjamin (1903-1998)
There are only two things a child will share willingly – communicable diseases and his mother's age.
[Attr.]

VIDAL, Gore (1925-2012)
Never have children, only grandchildren.
[*Two Sisters* (1970)]

WILDE, Oscar (1854-1900)
Children begin by loving their parents. After a time they judge them. Rarely, if ever, do they forgive them.
[*A Woman of No Importance* (1893)]

See **FAMILIES, PARENTS, YOUTH**

BRECHT, Bertolt (1898-1956)
In those days [our Lord] could demand that men love their neighbour, because they'd had enough to eat. Nowadays it's different.
[*Mother Courage and her Children* (1941)]

BRUCE, Lenny (1925-1966)
(Referring to the Crucifixion)
It was just one of those parties which got out of hand.
[*The Guardian*, 1979]

BUTLER, Samuel (1835-1902)
They would have been equally horrified at hearing the Christian religion doubted, and at seeing it practised.
[*The Way of All Flesh* (1903)]

CAEN, Herb (1916-1997)
The trouble with born-again Christians is that they are an even bigger pain the second time around.
[*San Francisco Chronicle*, 1981]

CARLYLE, Thomas (1795-1881)
If Jesus Christ were to come today, people would not even crucify him. They would ask him to dinner, and hear what he had to say, and make fun of it.
[In Wilson, *Carlyle at his Zenith* (1927)]

CHESTERTON, G.K. (1874-1936)
The Christian ideal has not been tried and found wanting. It has been found difficult; and left untried.
[*What's Wrong with the World* (1910)]

COLERIDGE, Samuel Taylor (1772-1834)
He who begins by loving Christianity better than Truth will proceed by loving his own sect or church better than Christianity, and end by loving himself better than all.
[*Aids to Reflection* (1825)]

DISRAELI, Benjamin (1804-1881)
A Protestant, if he wants aid or advice on any matter, can only go to his solicitor.
[*Lothair* (1870)]

ELLIS, Bob (1942-)
Show me a Wednesday wencher and a Sunday saint, and I'll show you a Roman Catholic.
[*The Legend of King O'Malley* (1974)]

FRANCE, Anatole (1844-1924)
Christianity has done a great deal for love by making a sin of it.
[*Le Jardin d'Epicure* (1894)]

LENNON, John (1940-1980)
We're more popular than Jesus Christ now. I don't know which will go first. Rock and roll or Christianity.
[*The Beatles Illustrated Lyrics*]

LUTHER, Martin (1483-1546)
Be a sinner and sin strongly, but believe and rejoice in Christ even more strongly.
[Letter to Melanchton]

MELVILLE, Herman (1819-1891)
Better sleep with a sober cannibal than a drunken Christian.
[*Moby Dick* (1851)]

MENCKEN, H.L. (1880-1956)
Puritanism: The haunting fear that someone, somewhere, may be happy.
[*A Mencken Chrestomathy* (1949)]

MONTESQUIEU, Charles (1689-1755)
No kingdom has ever had as many civil wars as the kingdom of Christ.
[*Lettres persanes* (1721)]

NIETZSCHE, Friedrich Wilhelm (1844-1900)
The Christian decision to find the world ugly and bad has made the world ugly and bad.
[*The Gay Science* (1887)]

PENN, William (1644-1718)
No pain, no palm; no thorns, no throne; no gall, no glory; no cross, no crown.
[*No Cross, No Crown* (1669)]

RUSSELL, Bertrand (1872-1970)
There's a Bible on that shelf there. But I keep it next to Voltaire – poison and antidote.
[In Harris, *Kenneth Harris Talking To:* (1971)]

SANTAYANA, George (1863-1952)
The Bible is literature, not dogma.
[Introduction to Spinoza's *Ethics*]

TEMPLE, William (1881-1944)
Christianity is the most materialistic of all
great religions.
[*Readings in St John's Gospel* (1939)]

TUTU, Archbishop Desmond (1931-)
For the Church in any country to retreat from
politics is nothing short of heresy. Christianity
is political or it is not Christianity.
[*The Observer*, 1994]

TWAIN, Mark (1835-1910)
Most people are bothered by those passages
in Scripture which they cannot understand;
but as for me, I always noticed that the
passages in Scripture which trouble me most
are those that I do understand.
[In Simcox, *Treasury of Quotations on
Christian Themes*]

YBARRA, Thomas Russell (1880-1971)
A Christian is a man who feels Repentance on
a Sunday
For what he did on Saturday
And is going to do on Monday.
['The Christian' (1909)]

ZANGWILL, Israel (1864-1926)
Scratch the Christian and you find the pagan
– spoiled.
[*Children of the Ghetto* (1892)]

See **RELIGION**

THE CHURCH

AMBROSE, Saint (c.340-397)
Where Peter is, there of necessity is the
Church.
[*Explanatio psalmi* 40]

ANDREWES, Bishop Lancelot (1555-1626)
The nearer the Church the further from God.
[*Sermon 15, Of the Nativity* (1629)]

AUGUSTINE, Saint (354-430)
Outside the church there is no salvation.
[*De Baptismo*]

BANCROFT, Richard (1544-1610)
Where Christ erecteth his Church, the devil in
the same churchyard will have his chapel.
[*Sermon*, 1588]

BELLOC, Hilaire (1870-1953)
I always like to associate with a lot of priests
because it makes me understand anti-clerical
things so well.
[Attr.]

**THE BIBLE
(King James Version)**
Thou art Peter, and upon this rock I will build
my church; and the gates of hell shall not
prevail against it.
[*Matthew*, 16:18]

BLAKE, William (1757-1827)
But if at the Church they would give us some
Ale,
And a pleasant fire our souls to regale:
We'd sing and we'd pray all the live-long day;
Nor ever once wish from the Church to stray.
[*Songs of Experience* (1794)]

D'ALPUGET, Blanche (1944-)
Convent girls never leave the church, they
just become feminists. I learned that in
Australia.
[*Turtle Beach* (1981)]

DEVLIN, Bernadette (1947-)
Among the best traitors Ireland has ever had,
Mother Church ranks at the very top, a
massive obstacle in the path to equality and
freedom.
[*The Price of My Soul*]

EMERSON, Ralph Waldo (1803-1882)
I like the silent church before the service
begins, better than any preaching.
[*Essays, First Series* (1841)]

SWIFT, Jonathan (1667-1745)
I never saw, heard, nor read, that the clergy
were beloved in any nation where Christianity
was the religion of the country. Nothing can
render them popular, but some degree of
persecution.
[*Thoughts on Religion* (1765)]

TEMPLE, William (1881-1944)
I believe in the Church, One Holy, Catholic
and Apostolic, and I regret that it nowhere
exists.
[Attr.]

TUCHOLSKY, Kurt (1890-1935)
What the church can't prevent, it blesses.
[*Scraps* (1973)]

WAUGH, Evelyn (1903-1966)
There is a species of person called a 'Modern
Churchman' who draws the full salary of a
beneficed clergyman and need not commit
himself to any religious belief.
[*Decline and Fall* (1928)]

See **RELIGION**

CINEMA

ALLEN, Woody (1935-)
My films are therapy for my debilitating depression. In institutions people weave baskets. I make films.
[*The Sunday Times*, 2001]

ALTMAN, Robert (1922-2006)
What's a cult? It just means not enough people to make a minority.
[*The Observer*, 1981]

BROWN, Geoff (1949-)
Dictators needed a talking cinema to twist nations round their fingers: remove the sound from Mussolini and you are left with a puffing bullfrog.
[*The Times*, 1992]

DISNEY, Walt (1901-1966)
Girls bored me - they still do. I love Mickey Mouse more than any woman I've ever known.
[In Wagner, *You Must Remember This*]

GODARD, Jean-Luc (1930-)
Of course a film should have a beginning, a middle and an end. But not necessarily in that order.
[Attr.]

Photography is truth. Cinema is truth twenty-four times a second.
[*Le Petit Soldat*, film, 1960]

GOLDWYN, Samuel (1882-1974)
Why should people go out and pay money to see bad films when they can stay at home and see bad television for nothing?
[*The Observer*, 1956]

GRIFFITH, D.W. (1874-1948)
(Said when directing an epic film)
Move those ten thousand horses a trifle to the right. And that mob out there, three feet forward.
[Attr.]

HITCHCOCK, Alfred (1899-1980)
The length of a film should be directly related to the endurance of the human bladder.
[In Simon Rose, *Classic Film Guide* (1995)]

JUNG, Carl Gustav (1875-1961)
The cinema, like the detective story, makes it possible to experience without danger all the excitement, passion and desire which must be repressed in a humanitarian ordering of life.
[Attr.]

LUCAS, George (1944-)
(On Star Wars)
I thought it was too wacky for the general public.

MARX, Groucho (1895-1977)
We in this industry know that behind every successful screenwriter stands a woman. And behind her stands his wife.
[Attr.]

MINGHELLA, Anthony (1954-2008)
(On winning an oscar for Best Director for The English Patient)
It's a great day for the Isle of Wight.
[*Scotland on Sunday*, 1999]

ROGERS, Will (1879-1935)
The movies are the only business where you can go out front and applaud yourself.
[In Halliwell, *Filmgoer's Book of Quotes* (1973)]

TRACY, Spencer (1900-1967)
(Defending his demand for equal billing with Katharine Hepburn)
This is a movie, not a lifeboat.
[Attr.]

See **HOLLYWOOD, SHOWBUSINESS**

CITIES

BURGON, John William (1813-1888)
Match me such marvel save in Eastern clime,
A rose-red city 'half as old as Time'!
['Petra' (1845)]

CAESAR, Augustus (63 BC-AD 14)
He so beautified the city that he justly boasted that he found it brick and left it marble.
[In Suetonius, *Lives of the Caesars*]

COLTON, Charles Caleb (c.1780-1832)
If you would be known, and not know, vegetate in a village; if you would know, and not be known, live in a city.
[*Lacon* (1820)]

COWPER, William (1731-1800)
God made the country, and man made the town.
[*The Task* (1785)]

KIPLING, Rudyard (1865-1936)
Cities and Thrones and Powers,
Stand in Time's eye,
Almost as long as flowers,
Which daily die:
But, as new buds put forth,
To glad new men,
Out of the spent and unconsidered Earth,
The Cities rise again.
['Cities and Thrones and Powers' (1906)]

MILTON, John (1608–1674)
Towred Cities please us then,
And the busie humm of men.
['L'Allegro' (1645)]

MORRIS, Charles (1745–1838)
A house is much more to my taste than a tree,
And for groves, oh! a good grove of chimneys
for me.
['Country and Town', 1840]

MORRIS, Desmond (1928–)
Clearly, then, the city is not a concrete jungle,
it is a human zoo.
[*The Human Zoo* (1969)]

AUSTEN, Jane (1775–1817)
Oh! who can ever be tired of Bath?
[*Northanger Abbey* (1818)]

CRAIG, Maurice James (1919–2011)
Red bricks in the suburbs, white horse on the
wall,
Eyetalian marbles in the City Hall:
O stranger from England, why stand so
aghast?
May the Lord in his mercy be kind to Belfast.
['Ballad to a traditional Refrain']

AUSTEN, Jane (1775–1817)
One has not great hopes from Birmingham.
I always say there is something direful in the
sound.
[*Emma* (1816)]

APPLETON, Thomas Gold (1812–1884)
A Boston man is the east wind made flesh.
[Attr.]

BOSSIDY, John Collins (1860–1928)
And this is good old Boston,
The home of the bean and the cod,
Where the Lowells talk only to Cabots,
And the Cabots talk only to God.
[Toast at Harvard dinner, 1910]

EMERSON, Ralph Waldo (1803–1882)
We say the cows laid out Boston. Well, there
are worse surveyors.
[*Conduct of Life* (1860)]

BAEDEKER, Karl (1801–1859)
Oxford is on the whole more attractive than
Cambridge to the ordinary visitor; and the
traveller is therefore recommended to visit
Cambridge first, or to omit it altogether if he
cannot visit both.
[*Baedeker's Great Britain* (1887)]

RAPHAEL, Frederic (1931–)
This is the city of perspiring dreams.
[*The Glittering Prizes* (1976)]

CAPONE, Al (1899–1947)
(Talking about suburban Chicago)
This is virgin territory for whorehouses.
[In Kenneth Allsop, *The Bootleggers* (1961)]

GARIOCH, Robert (1909–1981)
In simmer, whan aa sorts foregether
in Embro to the ploy,
fowk seek out friens to hae a blether,
or faes they'd fain annoy;
smorit wi British Railways' reek
frae Glesca or Glen Roy
or Wick, they come to hae a week
of cultivatit joy,
or three,
in Embro to the ploy.
[*Selected Poems* (1966)]

GOEBBELS, Joseph (1897–1945)
(Of Edinburgh)
enchanting ... it shall make a delightful
summer capital when we invade Britain.
[Attr.]

BRIDIE, James (1888–1951)
You must not look down on ... Glasgow which
gave the world the internal combustion
engine, political economy, antiseptic and
cerebral surgery, the balloon, the mariner's
compass, the theory of Latent Heat, Tobias
Smollett and James Bridie.
[Letter to St John Ervine]

CERNUDA, Luis (1902–1963)
(On leaving Glasgow, where he had lived from
1939 to 1943)
Rarely have I been so pleased to leave a place.
[*Chronicle of a book* (1958)]

MCGONAGALL, William (c.1830–1902)

Beautiful city of Glasgow, I now conclude my
muse,
And to write in praise of thee my pen does
not refuse;
And, without fear of contradiction, I will
venture to say
You are the second grandest city in Scotland
at the present day.

[*'Glasgow'* (1890)]

SMITH, Alexander (1830–1867)

City! I am true son of thine;
Ne'er dwelt I where great mornings shine
Around the bleating pens;
Ne'er by the rivulets I strayed,
And ne'er upon my childhood weighed
The silence of the glens.
Instead of shores where ocean beats,
I hear the ebb and flow of streets.
Thou hast my kith and kin:
My childhood, youth, and manhood brave;
Thou hast that unforgotten grave
Within thy central din.
A sacredness of love and death
Dwells in thy noise and smoky breath.

[*City Poems* (1857)]

CITIES: LONDON

AUSTEN, Jane (1775–1817)

Nobody is healthy in London. Nobody can be.

[*Emma* (1816)]

BLAKE, William (1757–1827)

I wander thro' each charter'd street,
Near where the charter'd Thames does flow
And mark in every face I meet
Marks of weakness, marks of woe.

[*'London'* (1794)]

BLÜCHER, Prince (1742–1819)

(Remark made on seeing London in June,
1814)
What junk!

[Attr.]

BRIDIE, James (1888–1951)

London! Pompous Ignorance sits enthroned
there and welcomes Pretentious Mediocrity
with flattery and gifts. Oh, dull and witless
city! Very hell for the restless, inquiring,
sensitive soul. Paradise for the snob, the
parasite and the prig; the pimp, the placeman
and the cheapjack.

[*The Anatomist* (1931)]

CHAMBERLAIN, Joseph (1836–1914)

Provided that the City of London remains as it
is at present, the clearing-house of the world,
any other nation may be its workshop.

[Speech, London, 1904]

COBBETT, William (1762–1835)

(Of London)
But what is to be the fate of the great wen of
all? The monster, called ... 'the metropolis of
the empire'?

[*'Rural Rides'*, 1822]

COLMAN, George (the Younger) (1762–1836)

Oh, London is a fine town,
A very famous city,
Where all the streets are paved with gold,
And all the maidens pretty.

[*The Heir at Law* (1797)]

DISRAELI, Benjamin (1804–1881)

London; a nation, not a city.

[*Lothair* (1870)]

DOYLE, Sir Arthur Conan (1859–1930)

London, that great cesspool into which all the
loungers of the Empire are irresistibly drained.

[*A Study in Scarlet* (1887)]

DUNBAR, William (c.1460–c.1525)

London, thou art the flower of cities all!
Gemme of all joy, jasper of jocunditie.

[*'London'* (1834)]

GIBBON, Edward (1737–1794)

Crowds without company, and dissipation
without pleasure.

[*Memoirs of My Life and Writings* (1796)]

JOHNSON, Samuel (1709–1784)

When a man is tired of London, he is tired of
life; for there is in London all that life can
afford.

[In Boswell, *The Life of Samuel Johnson* (1791)]

MEYNELL, Hugo (1727–1780)

The chief advantage of London is, that a man
is always so near his burrow.

[In Boswell, *The Life of Samuel Johnson* (1791)]

MORRIS, William (1834–1896)

Forget six counties overhung with smoke,
Forget the snorting steam and piston stroke,
Forget the spreading of the hideous town;
Think rather of the pack-horse on the down,
And dream of London, small and white and
clean,
The clear Thames bordered by its gardens green.

[*The Earthly Paradise* (1868–1870)]

SWIFT, Jonathan (1667–1745)
It is the folly of too many to mistake the echo of a London coffee house for the voice of the kingdom.
[*The Conduct of the Allies* (1711)]

WORDSWORTH, William (1770–1850)
Earth has not anything to show more fair;
Dull would he be of soul who could pass by
A sight so touching in its majesty:
This city now doth, like a garment, wear
The beauty of the morning; silent, bare,
Ships, towers, domes, theatres, and temples lie
Open unto the fields, and to the sky,
All bright and glittering in the smokeless air ...
Dear God! the very houses seem asleep;
And all that mighty heart is lying still!
['Sonnet composed upon Westminster Bridge' (1807)]

CITIES: MANCHESTER

BOLITHO, William (1890–1930)
The shortest way out of Manchester is notoriously a bottle of Gordon's gin.
[*The Treasury of Humorous Quotations*]

CITIES: MELBOURNE

BEVEN, Rodney Allan (1916–1982)
The people of Melbourne
Are frightfully well-born.
['Observation Sociologique']

BYGRAVES, Max (1922–2012)
I've always wanted to see a ghost town. You couldn't even get a parachute to open here after 10 p.m.
[*Melbourne Sun*, 1965]

JILLETT, Neil (1933–)
(A phrase wrongly attributed to Ava Gardner, who starred in the film On the Beach, adapted from Nevil Shute's novel of that name (1957))
On the Beach is a story about the end of the world, and Melbourne sure is the right place to film it.
[Attr.]

CITIES: NAPLES

GLADSTONE, William (1809–1898)
This is a negation of God erected into a system of government.
[*Letter to Lord Aberdeen*, 1851]

CITIES: NEW YORK

GILMAN, Charlotte Perkins (1860–1935)
New York ... that unnatural city where every one is an exile, none more so than the American.
[*The Living of Charlotte Perkins Gilman* (1935)]

KOCH, Ed (1924–2013)
Being a New Yorker is a state of mind. If, after living there for six months, you find that you walk faster, talk faster and think faster, you are a New Yorker.
[*The Observer*, 1999]

MCALLISTER, Ward (1827–1895)
There are only about four hundred people in New York society.
[Interview with Charles H. Crandall in the *New York Tribune*, 1888]

SIMON, Neil (1927–)
New York ... is not Mecca. It just smells like it.
[*California Suite* (1976)]

STOUT, Rex Todhunter (1886–1975)
I like to walk around Manhattan, catching glimpses of its wild life, the pigeons and cats and girls.
[*Three Witnesses*, 'When a Man Murders']

CITIES: PARIS

ELMS, Robert (1927–)
Paris is the paradise of the easily impressed – the universal provincial mind.
[In Julie Burchill, *Sex and Sensibility* (1992)]

HAMMERSTEIN II, Oscar (1895–1960)
The last time I saw Paris,
Her heart was warm and gay,
I heard the laughter of her heart
in ev'ry street café.
['The Last Time I Saw Paris', song, 1940, from *Lady Be Good*]

HEMINGWAY, Ernest (1898–1961)
If you are lucky enough to have lived in Paris as a young man, then wherever you go for the rest of your life, it stays with you, for Paris is a moveable feast.
[*A Moveable Feast* (1964)]

HENRI IV (1553–1610)
Paris is well worth a mass.
[Attr.]

KURTZ, Irma (1935–)
Cities are only human. And I had begun to see Paris for the bitch she is: a stunning transvestite – vain, narrow-minded and all false charm.
[*Daily Mail*, 1996]

CITIES: PHILADELPHIA

FIELDS, W.C. (1880–1946)
Last week, I went to Philadelphia, but it was closed.

[Attr.]

CITIES: PRAGUE

PROWSE, William Jeffrey (1836–1870)
Though the latitude's rather uncertain,
And the longitude also is vague,
The persons I pity who know not the city,
The beautiful city of Prague.

['The City of Prague']

CITIES: ROME

BURGESS, Anthony (1917–1993)
Rome's just a city like anywhere else. A vastly overrated city, I'd say. It trades on belief just as Stratford trades on Shakespeare.

[*Inside Mr Enderby* (1968)]

CLOUGH, Arthur Hugh (1819–1861)
Rome, believe me, my friend, is like its own Monte Testaceo, Merely a marvellous mass of broken and castaway wine-pots.

[*Amours de Voyage* (1858)]

HORACE (65–8 BC)
The smoke and wealth and noise of Rome.

[*Odes*]

CITIES: ST ANDREWS

LANG, Andrew (1844–1912)
St Andrews by the Northern Sea,
A haunted town it is to me!

['Almae Matres' (1884)]

CITIES: SYDNEY

SLESSOR, Kenneth (1901–1971)
(On Sydney's ferry-boats)
At sunset, when the Harbour is glazed with pebbles of gold and white, and the sun is burning out like a bushfire behind Balmain, the ferry-boats put on their lights. They turn into luminous water-beetles, filed with a gliding, sliding reflected glitter that bubbles on the water like phosphorus.

[*Bread and Wine* (1970)]

CITIES: VENICE

BENCHLEY, Robert (1889–1945)
(Telegram sent on arriving in Venice)
Streets flooded. Please advise.

[Attr.]

CAPOTE, Truman (1924–1984)
Venice is like eating an entire box of chocolate liqueurs in one go.

[*The Observer*, 1961]

MORRIS, Jan (1926–)
There's romance for you! There's the lust and dark wine of Venice! No wonder George Eliot's husband fell into the Grand Canal.

[*Venice* (1960)]

See **COUNTRY**

CIVILIZATION

ADDAMS, Jane (1860–1935)
Civilization is a method of living, an attitude of equal respect for all men.

[Speech, Honolulu, 1933]

ALCOTT, Bronson (1799–1888)
Civilization degrades the many to exalt the few.

[Table Talk (1877)]

ANONYMOUS
(Local resident on the opening of the first Russian McDonalds Restaurant, Moscow, 1990)
It's like the coming of civilization.

BAGEHOT, Walter (1826–1877)
The whole history of civilization is strewn with creeds and institutions which were invaluable at first, and deadly afterwards.

[*Physics and Politics* (1872)]

BATES, Daisy May (1863–1951)
The Australian native can withstand all the reverses of nature, fiendish droughts and sweeping floods, horrors of thirst and enforced starvation – but he cannot withstand civilisation.

[*The Passing of the Aborigines* ... (1938)]

DISRAELI, Benjamin (1804–1881)
Increased means and increased leisure are the two civilizers of man.

[Speech, Manchester, 1872]

GANDHI (1869–1948)
(When asked what he thought of Western civilization)
I think it would be an excellent idea.

[Attr.]

GARROD, Heathcote William (1878–1960)
(In response to criticism that, during World War I, he was not fighting to defend civilization)
Madam, I am the civilization they are fighting to defend.
[In Balsdon, *Oxford Now and Then* (1970)]

GAUGUIN, Paul (1848–1903)
Civilization is paralysis.
[In Cournos, *Modern Plutarch* (1928)]

HILLARY, Sir Edmund (1919–2008)
There is precious little in civilization to appeal to a Yeti.
[*The Observer*, 1960]

JAMES, William (1842–1910)
Our civilization is founded on the shambles, and every individual existence goes out in a lonely spasm of helpless agony.
[*Varieties of Religious Experience* (1902)]

KNOX, Ronald (1888–1957)
It is so stupid of modern civilization to have given up believing in the devil when he is the only explanation of it.
[Attr.]

MILL, John Stuart (1806–1873)
I am not aware that any community has a right to force another to be civilized.
[*On Liberty* (1859)]

PAGLIA, Camille (1947–)
If civilisation had been left in female hands, we would still be living in grass huts.
[*Sex, Art and American Culture: Essays* (1992)]

PARK, Mungo (1771–1806)
(Remark on finding a gibbet in an unexplored part of Africa)
The sight of it gave me infinite pleasure, as it proved that I was in a civilized society.
[Attr.]

ROGERS, Will (1879–1935)
You can't say civilization don't advance, however, for in every war they kill you a new way.
[*New York Times*, 1929]

TREVELYAN, G.M. (1876–1962)
Disinterested intellectual curiosity is the life blood of real civilization.
[*English Social History* (1942)]

YEATS, W.B. (1865–1939)
A civilisation is a struggle to keep self-control.
[*A Vision* (1925)]

See **CULTURE**

CLASS

ARNOLD, Matthew (1822–1888)
One has often wondered whether upon the whole earth there is anything so unintelligent, so unapt to perceive how the world is really going, as an ordinary young Englishman of our upper class.
[*Culture and Anarchy* (1869)]

BELLOC, Hilaire (1870–1953)
Like many of the Upper Class
He liked the Sound of Broken Glass.
[*New Cautionary Tales* (1930)]

BRENAN, Gerald (1894–1987)
Poets and painters are outside the class system, or rather they constitute a special class of their own, like the circus people and the gipsies.
[*Thoughts in a Dry Season* (1978)]

BROUGHAM, Lord Henry (1778–1868)
The great Unwashed.
[Attr.]

BURGESS, Anthony (1917–1993)
Without class differences, England would cease to be the living theatre it is.
[Remark, 1985]

CARTLAND, Barbara (1902–2000)
(When asked in a radio interview whether she thought that British class barriers had broken down)
Of course they have, or I wouldn't be sitting here talking to someone like you.
[In J. Cooper, *Class* (1979)]

CHELSEA, Jenny (Viscountess)
(Introducing a seminar on upper class behaviour)
So many people don't know how to behave at a shooting party.
[*The Observer*, 1998]

CLARK, Alan (1928–1999)
If you bed people of below-stairs class, they will go to the papers.
[*The Times*, 1999]

CURZON, Lord (1859–1925)
(On seeing some soldiers bathing)
I never knew the lower classes had such white skins.
[Attr.]

DOYLE, Roddy (1958–)
'You're working class, right?'
'We would be if there was any work.'
[*The Commitments*, film, 1991]

CLONING

EDWARD, Prince (1964–)
We are forever being told we have a rigid class structure. That's a load of codswallop.
[*Daily Mail*, 1996]

ELIZABETH (the Queen Mother) (1900–2002)
My favourite programme is 'Mrs Dale's Diary'. I try never to miss it because it is the only way of knowing what goes on in a middle-class family.
[Attr.]

ENGELS, Friedrich (1820–1895)
The history of all hitherto existing society is the history of class struggles.
[*The Communist Manifesto* (1848)]

LERNER, Alan Jay (1918–1986)
An Englishman's way of speaking absolutely classifies him.
[*My Fair Lady* (1956)]

MARX, Karl (1818–1883)
What I did that was new was prove ... that the class struggle necessarily leads to the dictatorship of the proletariat.
[Letter, 1852]

PARSONS, Tony (1953–)
The working class has come a long way in recent years, all of it downhill. They look like one big Manson family.
[*Arena*, 1989]

RATTIGAN, Terence (1911–1977)
You can be in the Horse Guards and still be common, dear.
[*Separate Tables* (1955)]

SCARGILL, Arthur (1941–)
(On John Prescott's description of himself as middle class)
I have little or no time for people who aspire to be members of the middle class.
[Remark at the launch of the Socialist Labour Party, 1996]

STANTON, Elizabeth Cady (1815–1902)
It is impossible for one class to appreciate the wrongs of another.
[In Anthony and Gage, *History of Woman Suffrage* (1881)]

THEROUX, Paul (1941–)
The ship follows Soviet custom: it is riddled with class distinctions so subtle, it takes a trained Marxist to appreciate them.
[*The Great Railway Bazaar* (1975)]

See **ARISTOCRACY, EQUALITY, SNOBBERY**

CLONING

ANONYMOUS
(After Scottish scientists pioneered the cloning of a sheep, Dolly.)
There'll never be another ewe? Don't count on it!
[News headline, 1997]

CLUBS

DICKENS, Charles (1812–1870)
(Of the House of Commons)
I think ... that it is the best club in London.
[*Our Mutual Friend* (1865)]

JOHNSON, Samuel (1709–1784)
Boswell is a very clubbable man.
[In Boswell, *The Life of Samuel Johnson* (1791)]

MARX, Groucho (1895–1977)
Please accept my resignation. I don't want to belong to any club that would have me as a member.
[*Groucho and Me* (1959)]

MORTIMER, Sir John (1923–2009)
One enlightened member said that in the past the Garrick Club excluded lunatics, gays and women: now the first two classes have been let in there's no conceivable reason to bar the third.
[Attr.]

WILDE, Oscar (1854–1900)
(Refusing to attend a function at a club whose members were hostile to him)
I should be like a lion in a cage of savage Daniels.
[Attr.]

See **BOREDOM**

COFFEE

CHELEBI, Katib (1609–1657)
Coffee is a cold dry food, suited to the ascetic life and sedative of lust.
[In G.L. Lewis (trans.), *The Balance of Truth* (1957)]

POPE, Alexander (1688–1744)
Coffee, which makes the politician wise,
And see through all things with his half-shut eyes.
[*The Rape of the Lock*, 1712]

THACKERAY, William Makepeace (1811–1863)
Why do they always put mud into coffee on board steamers? Why does the tea generally taste of boiled boots?
[The Kickleburys on the Rhine (1850)]

TWAIN, Mark (1835–1910)
The best coffee in Europe is Vienna coffee, compared to which all other coffee is fluid poverty.
[Greatly Exaggerated]

COMEDY

CHAPLIN, Charlie (1889–1977)
All I need to make a comedy is a park, a policeman and a pretty girl.
[My Autobiography (1964)]

FELDMAN, Marty (1933–1982)
Comedy, like sodomy, is an unnatural act.
[The Times, 1969]

MOLIÈRE (1622–1673)
It's a strange job, making decent people laugh.
[L'Ecole des Femmes (1662)]

PRIESTLEY, J.B. (1894–1984)
Comedy, we may say, is society protecting itself – with a smile.
[George Meredith (1926)]

COMMON SENSE

DESCARTES, René (1596–1650)
Common sense is the best distributed thing in the world, for we all think we possess a good share of it.
[Discours de la Méthode (1637)]

EINSTEIN, Albert (1879–1955)
Common sense is the collection of prejudices acquired by age eighteen.
[Attr.]

EMERSON, Ralph Waldo (1803–1882)
Nothing astonishes men so much as common-sense and plain dealing.
['Art' (1841)]

COMMUNISM

ATTLEE, Clement (1883–1967)
Russian Communism is the illegitimate child of Karl Marx and Catherine the Great.
[The Observer, 1956]

BEVAN, Aneurin (1897–1960)
(Of the Communist Party)
Its relationship to democratic institutions is that of the death watch beetle – it is not a Party, it is a conspiracy.
[Attr.]

ELLIOTT, Ebenezer (1781–1849)
What is a communist? One who hath yearnings
For equal division of unequal earnings.
[Epigram, 1850]

ENGELS, Friedrich (1820–1895)
A spectre is haunting Europe – the spectre of Communism.
[The Communist Manifesto (1848)]

KHRUSHCHEV, Nikita (1894–1971)
(On the possibility that the Soviet Union might one day reject communism)
Those who wait for that must wait until a shrimp learns to whistle.
[Attr.]

KISSINGER, Henry (1923–)
I don't see why we need to stand by and watch a country go Communist due to the irresponsibility of its people.
[Attr.]

LENIN, V.I. (1870–1924)
Communism is Soviet power plus the electrification of the whole country.
[Report at the Congress of Soviets, 1920]

MCCARTHY, Senator Joseph (1908–1957)
(Of an alleged communist)
It makes me sick, sick, sick way down inside.
[In Lewis, *The Fifties* (1978)]

MORLEY, Robert (1908–1992)
There's no such thing in Communist countries as a load of old cod's wallop, the cod's wallop is always fresh made.
[Punch, 1974]

PUTIN, Vladimir (1952–)
First and foremost it is worth acknowledging that the demise of the Soviet Union was the greatest geopolitcal catastrophe of the century.
[Speech, 2005]

ROGERS, Will (1879–1935)
Communism is like prohibition, it's a good idea but it won't work.
[Weekly Articles (1981)]

SMITH, F.E. (1872–1930)
(On Bolshevism)
Nature has no cure for this sort of madness, though I have known a legacy from a rich relative work wonders.

[*Law, Life and Letters* (1927)]

SOLZHENITSYN, Alexander (1918–2008)
For us in Russia, communism is a dead dog, while for many people in the West, it is still a living lion.

[*The Listener*, 1979]

YELTSIN, Boris (1931–2007)
Let's not talk about communism. Communism was just an idea, just pie in the sky.

[*The Independent*, 1989]

See **CAPITALISM, SOCIALISM**

THE BIBLE
(King James Version)
Blessed are the merciful: for they shall obtain mercy.

[*Matthew*, 5:7]

BURNS, Robert (1759–1796)
Then gently scan your brother man,
Still gentler sister woman;
Tho' they may gang a kennin wrang,
To step aside is human.

['Address to the Unco Guid' (1786)]

DALAI LAMA (1935–)
Compassion and love are not mere luxuries. As the source of both inner and external peace, they are fundamental to the continued survival of our species.

[*The Times*, June 1999]

ELIOT, George (1819–1880)
We hand folks over to God's mercy, and show none ourselves.

[*Adam Bede* (1859)]

GAY, John (1685–1732)
He best can pity who has felt the woe.

[*Dione* (1720)]

GIBBON, Edward (1737–1794)
Our sympathy is cold to the relation of distant misery.

[*Decline and Fall of the Roman Empire* (1788)]

LAZARUS, Emma (1849–1887)
Give me your tired, your poor,
Your huddled masses yearning to breathe free.
['The New Colossus' (1883); verse inscribed on the Statue of Liberty]

SHAKESPEARE, William (1564–1616)
The quality of mercy is not strain'd;
It droppeth as the gentle rain from heaven
Upon the place beneath. It is twice blest:
It blesseth him that gives and him that takes.

[*The Merchant of Venice*, IV.i]

WILDE, Oscar (1854–1900)
I can sympathize with everything, except suffering.

[*The Picture of Dorian Gray* (1891)]

COMPUTERS

ANDERSON, Jeremy S.
There are two major products that come out of Berkeley: LSD and UNIX. We don't believe this to be a coincidence.

AVISHAI, Bernard (1949–)
The danger from computers is not that they will eventually get as smart as men, but we will meanwhile agree to meet them halfway.

BERNERS-LEE, Sir Tim (1955–)
(On the internet)
There is great danger that it becomes a place where untruths start to spread more than truths.

[*The Guardian*, 2006]

BROOKER, Charlie (1971–)
Macs are glorified Fisher-Price activity centres for adults.

[*The Guardian*, 2007]

BUSH, Vannevar (1890–1974)
The world has arrived at an age of cheap complex devices of great reliability, and something is bound to come of it.

CRINGELY, Robert X. (1953–)
If the automobile had followed the same development cycle as the computer, a Rolls-Royce would today cost $100, get one million miles to the gallon, and explode once a year, killing everyone inside.

HAWKING, Stephen (1942–)
I think computer viruses should count as life. I think it says something about human nature that the only form of life we have created so far is purely destructive. We've created life in our own image.

KULAWIEC, Rich
Any sufficiently advanced bug is indistinguishable from a feature.

MINOR, Janet
I have a spelling checker
It came with my PC;
It plainly marks four my revue
Mistakes I cannot sea.
I've run this poem threw it,
I'm sure your pleased too no,
Its letter perfect in it's weigh,
My checker tolled me sew.

SEGAL, Erich (1937–2010)
The OED database is one of the wonders
of the modern world – to paraphrase
Christopher Marlowe, 'infinite riches in a
little ROM'.
[*The Times Literary Supplement*, 1992]

STOLL, Clifford (1951–)
Why is it drug addicts and computer
afficionados are both called users?

STROUSTRUP, Bjarne (1950–)
C makes it easy to shoot yourself in the foot.
C++ makes it harder, but when you do, it
blows away your whole leg.

WATSON, Thomas J. (1874–1956)
(The founder of IBM on the prospects for
desktop computers)
I think there's a world market for about five
computers.
[In Martin Moskovits *Science and Society*, 1995]

WOZNIAK, Steve (1950–)
Never trust a computer you can't throw out a
window.
See **INNOVATION, TECHNOLOGY**

CONSCIENCE

ANONYMOUS
Conscience is what hurts when everything
else feels so good.

HENDERSON, Arthur (1863–1935)
The plural of conscience is conspiracy.
[*The Independent*, 1992]

HOBBES, Thomas (1588–1679)
A man's conscience and his judgement is the
same thing, and as the judgement, so also
the conscience, may be erroneous.
[Attr.]

MENCKEN, H.L. (1880–1956)
Conscience is the inner voice that warns us
somebody may be looking.
[*A Mencken Chrestomathy* (1949)]

NASH, Ogden (1902–1971)
He who is ridden by a conscience
Worries about a lot of nonscience;
He without benefit of scruples
His fun and income soon quadruples.
['Reflection on the Fallibility of Nemesis'
(1940)]

SHAKESPEARE, William (1564–1616)
A peace above all earthly dignities,
A still and quiet conscience.
[*Henry VIII*, III.ii]

CONSUMER SOCIETY

BRYSON, Bill (1951–)
We used to build civilizations. Now we build
shopping malls.
[*Neither Here Nor There* (1991)]

GALBRAITH, J.K. (1908–2006)
In a community where public services have
failed to keep abreast of private consumption
things are very different. Here, in an
atmosphere of private opulence and public
squalor, the private goods have full sway.
[*The Affluent Society* (1958)]

GITLIN, Todd (1943–)
There is a misunderstanding by marketers in
our culture about what freedom of choice is.
In the market, it is equated with multiplying
choice. This is a misconception. If you have
infinite choice, people are reduced to
passivity.
[*New York Times*, 1990]

IACOCCA, Lee (1924–)
People want economy and they will pay any
price to get it.
[*New York Times*, 1974]

ILLICH, Ivan (1926–2002)
In both rich and poor nations consumption is
polarized while expectation is equalized.
[*Celebration of Awareness* (1970)]

JAMES, Clive (1939–)
The last stage of fitting the product to the
market is fitting the market to the product.
[*The Observer*, 1989]

LARKIN, Philip (1922–1985)
Recognising that if you haven't got the money
for something you can't have it – this is a
concept that's vanished for many years.
[Interview, *The Observer*, 1979]

MARCUSE, Herbert (1898-1979)
The people recognize themselves in their
commodities; they find their soul in their
automobile, hi-fi set, split-level home,
kitchen equipment.
[*One-Dimensional Man* (1964)]

NICHOLSON, Vivian (1936-)
(Reply when asked what she would do with
the £152,000 she won on the pools in 1961)
I'm going to spend, spend, spend, that's what
I'm going to do.
[In V. Nicholson and S. Smith, *I'm Going to
Spend, Spend, Spend*]

VEBLEN, Thorstein (1857-1929)
Conspicuous consumption of valuable goods
is a means of reputability to the gentleman of
leisure.
[*The Theory of the Leisure Class* (1899)]

See **CAPITALISM, GREED, MONEY AND
WEALTH, SHOPPING**

CONTEMPT

AUSTEN, Jane (1775-1817)
She was nothing more than a mere
good-tempered, civil and obliging young
woman; as such we could scarcely dislike her
– she was only an Object of Contempt.
[*Love and Freindship* (1791)]

BIERCE, Ambrose (1842-c.1914)
Contempt: The feeling of a prudent man for
an enemy who is too formidable safely to be
opposed.
[*The Enlarged Devil's Dictionary* (1961)]

**CHATEAUBRIAND, François-René
(1768-1848)**
One is not superior merely because one sees
the world in an odious light.
[Attr.]

CONGREVE, William (1670-1729)
A little disdain is not amiss; a little scorn is
alluring.
[*The Way of the World* (1700)]

ROOSEVELT, Theodore (1858-1919)
The poorest way to face life is to face it with a
sneer.
[Attr.]

SHAW, George Bernard (1856-1950)
I have never sneered in my life. Sneering
doesn't become either the human face or the
human soul.
[*Pygmalion* (1916)]

See **RIDICULE**

CONTRACEPTION

ADLER, Larry (1914-2001)
Vasectomy means not ever having to say
you're sorry.
[Attr.]

ALLEN, Woody (1935-)
I want to tell you a terrific story about oral
contraception. I asked this girl to sleep with
me and she said 'no'.
[Attr.]

MENCKEN, H.L. (1880-1956)
It is now quite lawful for a Catholic woman to
avoid pregnancy by a resort to mathematics,
though she is still forbidden to resort to
physics and chemistry.
[*Notebooks* (1956)]

MILLIGAN, Spike (1918-2002)
Contraceptives should be used on every
conceivable occasion.
[*The Last Goon Show of All*]

RUSSELL, Dora (1894-1986)
We want far better reasons for having
children than not knowing how to prevent
them.
[*Hypatia*]

THOMAS, Irene (1920-2001)
Protestant women may take the Pill. Roman
Catholic woman must keep taking The Tablet.
[*The Guardian*, 1990]

See **SEX**

CONVERSATION

BAGEHOT, Walter (1826-1877)
The habit of common and continuous speech
is a symptom of mental deficiency.
[*Literary Studies* (1879)]

BOSWELL, James (1740-1795)
Johnson: Well, we had a good talk. Boswell:
Yes, Sir; you tossed and gored several
persons.
[*The Life of Samuel Johnson* (1791)]

CONFUCIUS (c.550-c.478 BC)
For one word a man is often deemed to be
wise, and for one word he is often deemed to
be foolish. We should be careful indeed what
we say.
[*Analects*]

DISRAELI, Benjamin (1804-1881)
I grew intoxicated with my own eloquence.
[*Contarini Fleming* (1832)]

DRYDEN, John (1631–1700)
But far more numerous was the herd of such
Who think too little and who talk too much.
[*Absalom and Achitophel* (1681)]

HALIFAX, Lord (1633–1695)
Most Men make little other use of their
Speech than to give evidence against their
own Understanding.
['Of Folly and Fools' (1750)]

HOLMES, Oliver Wendell (1809–1894)
And, when you stick on conversation's burrs,
Don't strew your pathway with those dreadful
urs.
['A Rhymed Lesson' (1848)]

O'BRIAN, Patrick (1828–1909)
Question and answer is not a civilized form of
conversation.
[*Clarissa Oakes* (1992)]

SENECA (c.4 BC–AD 65)
Conversation has a kind of charm about it, an
insinuating and insidious something that
elicits secrets from us just like love or liquor.
[*Epistles*]

SHAKESPEARE, William (1564–1616)
He draweth out the thread of his verbosity
finer than the staple of his argument.
[*Love's Labour Lost*, V.i]

**TALLEYRAND, Charles-Maurice de
(1754–1838)**
Speech was given to man to disguise his
thoughts.
[Attr.]

TANNEN, Deborah (1945–)
Each person's life is lived as a series of
conversations.
[*The Observer*, 1992]

WEST, Dame Rebecca (1892–1983)
There is no such thing as conversation. It is
an illusion. There are intersecting
monologues, that is all.
[*There is No Conversation* (1935)]

See **SILENCE**

COOKERY

BRILLAT-SAVARIN, Anthelme (1755–1826)
The discovery of a new dish does more for the
happiness of mankind than the discovery of a
star.
[*Physiologie du Goût* (1825)]

CLEESE, John (1939–)
The English contribution to world cuisine –
the chip.
[*A Fish Called Wanda*, film, 1988]

FERN, Fanny (1811–1872)
The way to a man's heart is through his
stomach.
[*Willis Parton*]

GALSWORTHY, John (1867–1933)
The French cook; we open tins.
[*Treasury of Humorous Quotations*]

LEITH, Prue (1940–)
Cuisine is when things taste like what they are.
[Lecture, 'The Fine Art of Food', 1987]

MEREDITH, George (1828–1909)
Kissing don't last: cookery do!
[*The Ordeal of Richard Feverel* (1859)]

MEREDITH, Owen (1831–1891)
We may live without poetry, music and art;
We may live without conscience, and live
without heart;
We may live without friends; we may live
without books;
But civilized man cannot live without cooks.
['Lucile' (1860)]

POST, Emily (1873–1960)
To the old saying that man built the house
but woman made of it a 'home' might be
added the modern supplement that woman
accepted cooking as a chore but man has
made of it a recreation.
[*Etiquette* (1922)]

SAKI (1870–1916)
The cook was a good cook, as cooks go; and
as cooks go she went.
[*Reginald* (1904)]

SLATER, Nigel (1958–)
Cooking is about not cheating yourself of
pleasure.
[*Slice of Life*, BBC TV programme]

ULLMAN, Tracey (1959–)
The most remarkable thing about my mother
is that for 30 years she served nothing but
leftovers. The original meal was never found.
[*The Observer*, 1999]

See **DINING, FOOD**

THE COUNTRY

CONGREVE, William (1670–1729)
I nauseate walking; 'tis a country diversion, I
loathe the country.
[*The Way of the World* (1700)]

COWPER, William (1731–1800)
God made the country, and man made the
town.
[*The Task* (1785)]

DOYLE, Sir Arthur Conan (1859–1930)
It is my belief, Watson, founded upon my experience, that the lowest and vilest alleys of London do not present a more dreadful record of sin than does the smiling and beautiful countryside.
['Copper Beeches' (1892)]

HAZLITT, William (1778–1830)
There is nothing good to be had in the country, or, if there is, they will not let you have it.
[*The Round Table* (1817)]

KILVERT, Francis (1840–1879)
It is a fine thing to be out on the hills alone. A man could hardly be a beast or a fool alone on a great mountain.
[*Diary*, 1871]

SACKVILLE-WEST, Vita (1892–1962)
The country habit has me by the heart,
For he's bewitched for ever who has seen,
Not with his eyes but with his vision, Spring
Flow down the woods and stipple leaves with sun.
['Winter' (1926)]

SMITH, Sydney (1771–1845)
I have no relish for the country; it is a kind of healthy grave.
[Letter to Miss G. Harcourt, 1838]

WILDE, Oscar (1854–1900)
Anybody can be good in the country.
[*The Picture of Dorian Gray* (1891)]

See **CITIES**

COURAGE

ARISTOTLE (384–322 BC)
I count him braver who overcomes his desires than him who overcomes his enemies.
[In Stobaeus, *Florilegium*]

BARRIE, Sir J.M. (1860–1937)
Courage is the thing. All goes if courage goes.
[Address, St Andrews University, 1922]

EARHART, Amelia (1898–1937)
Courage is the price that Life exacts for granting peace.
['Courage' (1927)]

HEMINGWAY, Ernest (1898–1961)
(Definition of 'guts')
Grace under pressure.
[Attr.]

HOWARD, Sir Michael (1922–)
The important thing when you are going to do something brave is to have someone on hand to witness it.
[*The Observer*, 1980]

IBÁRRURI, Dolores ('La Pasionaria') (1895–1989)
It is better to die on your feet than to live on your knees.
[Speech, Paris, 1936]

LEACOCK, Stephen (1869–1944)
It takes a good deal of physical courage to ride a horse. This, however, I have. I get it at about forty cents a flask, and take it as required.
[*Literary Lapses* (1910)]

NAPOLEON I (1769–1821)
As for moral courage, he said he had very rarely encountered two o'clock in the morning courage; that is, the courage of the unprepared.
[*Mémorial de Sainte Hélène*]

USTINOV, Sir Peter (1921–2004)
Courage is often lack of insight, whereas cowardice in many cases is based on good information.
[Attr.]

See **PATRIOTISM**

COWARDICE

ELIZABETH I (1533–1603)
If thy heart fails thee, climb not at all.
[In Fuller, *The History of the Worthies of England* (1662)]

HOUSMAN, A.E. (1859–1936)
The man that runs away
Lives to die another day.
[*A Shropshire Lad* (1896)]

JOHNSTON, Brian (1912–1994)
(When asked by his commanding officer what steps he would take if he came across a German battalion)
Long ones, backwards.
[Quoted in his obituary, *The Sunday Times*]

ROCHESTER (Earl of) (1647–1680)
For all men would be cowards if they durst.
['A Satire Against Reason and Mankind' (1679)]

SHAW, George Bernard (1856–1950)
As an old soldier I admit the cowardice: it's as universal as sea sickness, and matters just as little.
[*Man and Superman* (1903)]

VOLTAIRE (1694–1778)
Marriage is the only adventure open to the cowardly.
[Attr.]

Crime

ADLER, Freda (1934–)
(On rape)
Perhaps it is the only crime in which the victim becomes the accused and, in reality, it is she who must prove her good reputation, her mental soundness, and her impeccable propriety.
[*Sisters in Crime* (1975)]

ALLEN, Fred (1894–1956)
He's a good boy; everything he steals he brings right home to his mother.
[Attr.]

BACON, Francis (1561–1626)
Opportunity makes a thief.
[Letter to Essex, 1598]

**THE BIBLE
(King James Version)**
Whoso sheddeth man's blood, by man shall his blood be shed.
[*Genesis*, 9:6]

BRECHT, Bertolt (1898–1956)
What is robbing a bank compared with founding a bank?
[*The Threepenny Opera* (1928)]

BULWER-LYTTON, Edward (1803–1873)
In other countries poverty is a misfortune – with us it is a crime.
[*England and the English* (1833)]

CAPONE, Al (1899–1947)
I've been accused of every death except the casualty list of the World War.
[In Allsop, *The Bootleggers* (1961)]

CHESTERTON, G.K. (1874–1936)
Thieves respect property; they merely wish the property to become their property that they may more perfectly respect it.
[Attr.]

CONGREVE, William (1670–1729)
He that first cries out stop thief, is often he that has stolen the treasure.
[*Love for Love* (1695)]

FARBER, Barry (1859–1930)
Crime expands according to our willingness to put up with it.
[Attr.]

FARQUHAR, George (1678–1707)
Crimes, like virtues, are their own rewards.
[*The Inconstant* (1702)]

FRY, Elizabeth (1780–1845)
Punishment is not for revenge, but to lessen crime and reform the criminal.
[Journal entry]

GOLDMAN, Emma (1869–1940)
Crime is naught but misdirected energy.
[*Anarchism* (1910)]

LA BRUYÈRE, Jean de (1645–1696)
If poverty is the mother of crime, lack of intelligence is its father.
[*Les caractères ou les moeurs de ce siècle* (1688)]

LEWES, G.H. (1817–1878)
Murder, like talent, seems occasionally to run in families.
[*The Physiology of Common Life* (1859)]

LIGHTNER, Candy (1946–)
Death by drunken driving is a socially acceptable form of homicide.
[*San José Mercury*, April 1981]

RACINE, Jean (1639–1699)
Crime has its degrees, as virtue does.
[*Phèdre* (1677)]

RAINS, Claude (1889–1967)
Major Strasser has been shot. Round up the usual suspects.
[*Casablanca*, film, 1942]

ROSTAND, Jean (1894–1977)
Kill one man, and you are a murderer. Kill millions of men, and you are a conqueror. Kill them all, and you are a god.
[*Thoughts of a Biologist* (1939)]

SHAKESPEARE, William (1564–1616)
The robb'd that smiles steals something from the thief.
[*Othello*, I.iii]

SPENCER, Herbert (1820–1903)
A clever theft was praiseworthy amongst the Spartans; and it is equally so amongst Christians, provided it be on a sufficiently large scale.
[*Social Statics* (1850)]

WAUGH, Evelyn (1903–1966)
I came to the conclusion many years ago that almost all crime is due to the repressed desire for aesthetic expression.
[*Decline and Fall* (1928)]

See **MURDER, PUNISHMENT**

CRITICISM

ARNOLD, Matthew (1822–1888)
I am bound by my own definition of criticism:
a disinterested endeavour to learn and
propagate the best that is known and thought
in the world.
[*Essays in Criticism* (1865)]

AUDEN, W.H. (1907–1973)
One cannot review a bad book without
showing off.
[*The Dyer's Hand and Other Essays* (1963)]

BULLET, Gerald (1893–1958)
So, when a new book comes his way,
By someone still alive to-day,
Our Honest John, with right good will,
Sharpens his pencil for the kill.
['A Reviewer']

BURGESS, Anthony (1917–1993)
I know how foolish critics can be, being one
myself.
[*The Observer*, 1980]

BYRON, Lord (1788–1824)
A man must serve his time to every trade
Save censure – critics all are ready made.
Take hackney'd jokes from Miller, got by rote,
With just enough of learning to misquote.
[*English Bords and Scotch Reviewers* (1809)]

CHURCHILL, Charles (1731–1764)
Though by whim, envy, or resentment led,
They damn those authors whom they never
read.
[*The Candidate* (1764)]

CHURCHILL, Sir Winston (1874–1965)
I do not resent criticism, even when, for the
sake of emphasis, it parts for the time with
reality.
[Speech, 1941]

COLLINS, Jackie (1937–)
The biggest critics of my books are people
who never read them.

CONRAN, Shirley (1932–)
(On Julie Burchill)
I cannot take seriously the criticism of
someone who doesn't know how to use a
semicolon.
[Attr.]

DISRAELI, Benjamin (1804–1881)
You know who the critics are? The men who
have failed in literature and art.
[*Lothair* (1870)]

FRANCE, Anatole (1844–1924)
A good critic is one who tells of his own soul's
adventures among masterpieces.
[*La Vie Littéraire* (1888)]

FRY, Christopher (1907–2005)
I sometimes think
His critical judgement is so exquisite
It leaves us nothing to admire except his
opinion.
[*The Dark is Light Enough* (1954)]

HAMPTON, Christopher (1946–)
Asking a working writer what he thinks about
critics is like asking a lamp-post how it feels
about dogs.
[*The Sunday Times Magazine*, 1977]

HUXLEY, Aldous (1894–1963)
Parodies and caricatures are the most
penetrating of criticisms.
[*Point Counter Point* (1928)]

JOHNSON, Samuel (1709–1784)
(Of literary criticism)
You may abuse a tragedy, though you cannot
write one, You may scold a carpenter who has
made you a bad table, though you cannot
make a table. It is not your trade to make
tables.
[In Boswell, *The Life of Samuel Johnson*
(1791)]
The man who is asked by an author what he
thinks of his work, is put to the torture, and is
not obliged to speak the truth.
[In Boswell, *The Life of Samuel Johnson* (1791)]

LA BRUYÈRE, Jean de (1645–1696)
The pleasure of criticizing takes away from us
the pleasure of being moved by some very
fine things.
[*Les caractères ou les moeurs de ce siècle* (1688)]

MARX, Groucho (1895–1977)
I was so long writing my review that I never
got around to reading the book.
[Attr.]

MAUGHAM, William Somerset (1874–1965)
People ask you for criticism, but they only
want praise.
[*Of Human Bondage* (1915)]

MOORE, George (1852–1933)
The lot of critics is to be remembered by what
they failed to understand.
[*Impressions and Opinions* (1891)]

PARKER, Dorothy (1893–1967)
This is not a novel to be tossed aside lightly.
It should be thrown with great force.
[In Gaines, *Wit's End*]

POPE, Alexander (1688–1744)
Nor in the Critic let the Man be lost.
Good-nature and good-sense must ever join;
To err is human, to forgive, divine.
[*An Essay on Criticism* (1711)]

PORSON, Richard (1759–1808)
(On Southey's poems)
Your works will be read after Shakespeare and
Milton are forgotten – and not till then.
[In Meissen, *Quotable Anecdotes*]

**QUILLER-COUCH, Sir Arthur ('Q')
(1863–1944)**
The best is the best, though a hundred judges
have declared it so.
[*Oxford Book of English Verse* (1900)]

SHAW, George Bernard (1856–1950)
A dramatic critic ... leaves no turn unstoned.
[*New York Times*, 1950]

SIBELIUS, Jean (1865–1957)
Pay no attention to what the critics say.
No statue has ever been put up to a critic.
[Attr.]

SONTAG, Susan (1933–2004)
Interpretation is the revenge of the intellect
upon art.
[*Evergreen Review*, 1964]

STEINBECK, John (1902–1968)
(On critics)
Unless the bastards have the courage to give
you unqualified praise, I say ignore them.
[In J.K. Galbraith, *A Life in Our Times* (1981)]

STOPPARD, Tom (1937–)
I doubt that art needed Ruskin any more than
a moving train needs one of its passengers to
shove it.
[*The Times Literary Supplement*, 1977]

SWIFT, Jonathan (1667–1745)
So, naturalists observe, a flea
Hath smaller fleas that on him prey;
And these have smaller fleas to bite 'em,
And so proceed ad infinitum.
Thus every poet, in his kind,
Is bit by him that comes behind.
['On Poetry' (1733)]

TYNAN, Kenneth (1927–1980)
A critic is a man who knows the way but can't
drive the car.
[*New York Times Magazine*, 1966]

VOLTAIRE (1694–1778)
(Reviewing Rousseau's poem 'Ode to
Posterity')
I do not think this poem will reach its
destination.
[Attr.]

WILDE, Oscar (1854–1900)
The man who sees both sides of a question is
a man who sees absolutely nothing at all.
['The Critic as Artist' (1891)]

See **ACTORS, INSULTS, POETS, WRITERS**

CRUELTY

BLAKE, William (1757–1827)
Cruelty has a Human Heart
And Jealousy a Human Face,
Terror the Human Form Divine,
And Secrecy the Human Dress.
['A Divine Image' (c. 1832)]

COWPER, William (1731–1800)
I would not enter on my list of friends
(Tho' grac'd with polish'd manners and fine
sense,
Yet wanting sensibility) the man
Who needlessly sets foot upon a worm.
[*The Task* (1785)]

DANIELS, Dr Anthony (1949–)
Cruelty is like hope: it springs eternal.
[*The Observer*, 1998]

FROUDE, James Anthony (1818–1894)
Fear is the parent of cruelty.
[*Short Sudies on Great Subjects* (1877)]

GIDE, André (1869–1951)
Cruelty is the first of God's attributes.
[*The counterfeiters*]

TROTSKY, Leon (1879–1940)
In a serious struggle there is no worse cruelty
than to be magnanimous at an inappropriate
time.
[*The History of the Russian Revolution* (1933)]

See **VIOLENCE**

CRYING

BYRON, Lord (1788–1824)
Oh! too convincing – dangerously dear –
In woman's eye the unanswerable tear!
[*The Corsair* (1814)]

CRISP, Quentin (1908–1999)
Tears were to me what glass beads are to
African traders.
[*The Naked Civil Servant* (1968)]

CROMPTON, Richmal (1890–1969)
Violet Elizabeth dried her tears. She saw that
they were useless and she did not believe in
wasting her effects. 'All right,' she said calmly,
'I'll thcream then. I'll thcream, an' thcream,
an' thcream till I'm thick.'
[*Still William* (1925)]

DICKENS, Charles (1812–1870)
We need never be ashamed of our tears.
[*Great Expectations* (1861)]
'It opens the lungs, washes the countenance,
exercises the eyes, and softens down the
temper', said Mr Bumble. 'So cry away.'
[*Oliver Twist* (1838)]

LIBERACE, Wladziu Valentino (1919–1987)
(Remark made after hostile criticism)
I cried all the way to the bank.
[*Autobiography* (1973)]

SAINT-EXUPÉRY, Antoine de (1900–1944)
It is such a mysterious place, the land of
tears.
[*The Little Prince* (1943)]

CULTURE

ARNOLD, Matthew (1822–1888)
Culture, the acquainting ourselves with the
best that has been known and said in the
world, and thus the history of the human spirit.
[*Literature and Dogma*]

BANDA, Dr Hastings (1905–1997)
I wish I could bring Stonehenge to Nyasaland
to show there was a time when Britain had a
savage culture.
[*The Observer*, 1963]

BELLOW, Saul (1915–2005)
If culture means anything, it means knowing
what value to set upon human life; it's not
somebody with a mortarboard reading Greek.
I know a lot of facts, history. That's not
culture. Culture is the openness of the
individual psyche ... to the news of being.
[*The Glasgow Herald*, 1985]

CARLYLE, Thomas (1795–1881)
The great law of culture is: let each become
all that he was created capable of being.
['Jean Paul Friedrich Richter' (1839)]

DARWIN, Charles (1809–1882)
The highest possible stage in moral culture is
when we recognize that we ought to control
our thoughts.
[*The Descent of Man* (1871)]

FRYE, Northrop (1912–1991)
Creative culture is infinitely porous – it
absorbs influences from all over the world.
[*Maclean's*, 1991]

GOERING, Hermann (1893–1946)
When I hear anyone talk of Culture, I reach for
my revolver.
[Attr.]

KENNY, Mary (1944–)
Decadent cultures usually fall in the end, and
robust cultures rise to replace them. Our own
cultural supermarket may eventually be
subject to a takeover bid: the most likely
challenger being, surely, Islam.
[*Sunday Telegraph*, 1993]

KOESTLER, Arthur (1905–1983)
Two half-truths do not make a truth, and two
half-cultures do not make a culture.
[*The Ghost in the Machine* (1961)]

MCLUHAN, Marshall (1911–1980)
In a culture like ours, long accustomed to
splitting and dividing all things as a means of
control, it is sometimes a bit of a shock to be
reminded that, in operational and practical
fact, the medium is the message.
[*Understanding Media* (1964)]

MANTEL, Hilary (1952–)
(On travel)
I saw the world as some sort of exchange
scheme for my ideals, but the world deserves
better than this. When you come across an
alien culture you must not automatically
respect it. You must sometimes pay it the
compliment of hating it.
['Last Months in Al Hamra' (1987)]

MUSSOLINI, Benito (1883–1945)
In a statesman so-called 'culture' is, after all,
a useless luxury.
[*Il Populo d'Italia*, 1919]

WALLACE, Edgar (1875–1932)
What is a highbrow? He is a man who has
found something more interesting than
women.
[*New York Times*, 1932]

WHARTON, Edith (1862–1937)
Mrs Ballinger is one of the ladies who pursue
Culture in bands, as though it were dangerous
to meet it alone.
[*Xingu and Other Stories* (1916)]

See **CIVILIZATION, SCIENCE**

CURIOSITY

BACON, Francis (1561–1626)
They are ill discoverers that think there is no
land, when they can see nothing but sea.
[*The Advancement of Learning* (1605)]

BAX, Sir Arnold (1883–1953)
One should try everything once, except incest
and folk-dancing.
[*Farewell my Youth* (1943)]

THE BIBLE
(King James Version)
Be not curious in unnecessary matters: for
more things are shewed unto thee than men
understand.
[*Apocrypha, Ecclesiasticus*, 3:23]

CARROLL, Lewis (1832–1898)
'If everybody minded their own business,' said
the Duchess in a hoarse growl, 'the world
would go round a deal faster than it does.'
[*Alice's Adventures in Wonderland* (1865)]

JOHNSON, Samuel (1709–1784)
A generous and elevated mind is
distinguished by nothing more certainly than
an eminent degree of curiosity.
[In Boswell, *The Life of Samuel Johnson* (1791)]

LAMB, Charles (1775–1834)
Not many sounds in life, and I include all
urban and all rural sounds, exceed in interest
a knock at the door.
['Valentine's Day' (1823)]

MORITA, Akio (1920–1999)
Curiosity is the key to creativity.
[*Made in Japan* (1986)]

CUSTOM

BAILLIE, Joanna (1762–1851)
What custom hath endear'd
We part with sadly, though we prize it not.
[*Basil* (1798)]

BECKETT, Samuel (1906–1989)
The air is full of our cries. But habit is a great
deadener.
[*Waiting for Godot* (1955)]

CRABBE, George (1754–1832)
Habit with him was all the test of truth,
'It must be right: I've done it from my youth.'
[*The Borough* (1810)]

HUME, David (1711–1776)
Custom, then, is the great guide of human life.
[*Philosophical Essays Concerning Human
Understanding* (1748)]

PÉGUY, Charles (1873–1914)
Memory and habit are the harbingers of
death.
[*Note conjointe sur M. Descartes*]

SHAKESPEARE, William (1564–1616)
Age cannot wither her, nor custom stale
Her infinite variety. Other women cloy
The appetites they feed, but she makes
hungry
Where most she satisfies.
[*Antony and Cleopatra*, II.ii]

It is a custom
More honour'd in the breach than the
observance.
[*Hamlet*, I.iv]

CYNICISM

ALLEN, Woody (1935–)
The lion and the calf shall lie down together
but the calf won't get much sleep.
[*Without Feathers* (1976)]

BIERCE, Ambrose (1842–c.1914)
Cynic: A blackguard whose faulty vision sees
things as they are, not as they ought to be.
[*The Enlarged Devil's Dictionary* (1961)]

CHEKHOV, Anton (1860–1904)
After all, the cynicism of real life can't be
outdone by any literature: one glass won't get
someone drunk when he's already had a
whole barrel.
[Letter to M.V. Kiseleva, 1887]

COZZENS, James Gould (1903–1978)
A cynic is just a man who found out when he
was about ten that there wasn't any Santa
Claus, and he's still upset.
[Attr.]

HARRIS, Sydney J. (1917–1986)
A cynic is not merely one who reads bitter
lessons from the past, he is one who is
prematurely disappointed in the future.
[*On the Contrary* (1962)]

HELLMAN, Lillian (1905–1984)
Cynicism is an unpleasant way of saying the
truth.
[*The Little Foxes* (1939)]

HURST, Fannie (1889–1968)
It takes a clever man to turn cynic, and a wise man to be clever enough not to.
[Attr.]

MEREDITH, George (1828–1909)
Cynicism is intellectual dandyism.
[*The Egoist* (1879)]

WILDE, Oscar (1854–1900)
(In a lecture on Dickens)
One would have to have a heart of stone to read the death of Little Nell without laughing.
[In H. Pearson, *Lives of the Wits*]
Cecil Graham: What is a cynic?
Lord Darlington: A man who knows the price of everything and the value of nothing.
[*Lady Windermere's Fan* (1892)]

DANCING

AUSTEN, Jane (1775–1817)
Fine dancing, I believe, like virtue, must be its own reward.
[*Emma* (1816)]

BANKHEAD, Tallulah (1903–1968)
(Said on dropping fifty dollars into a tambourine held out by a Salvation Army collector)
Don't bother to thank me. I know what a perfectly ghastly season it's been for you Spanish dancers.
[Attr.]

BURNEY, Fanny (1752–1840)
Dancing? Oh, dreadful! How it was ever adopted in a civilized country I cannot find out; 'tis certainly a Barbarian exercise, and of savage origin.
[*Cecilia* (1782)]

CHESTERFIELD, Lord (1694–1773)
Custom has made dancing sometimes necessary for a young man; therefore mind it while you learn it, that you may learn to do it well, and not be ridiculous, though in a ridiculous act.
[Letter to his son, 1746]

DUNCAN, Isadora (1878–1927)
I have discovered the dance. I have discovered the art which has been lost for two thousand years.
[*My Life* (1927)]

SHAKESPEARE, William (1564–1616)
You and I are past our dancing days.
[*Romeo and Juliet*, I.v]

When you do dance, I wish you
A wave o' th' sea, that you might ever do
Nothing but that; move still, still so,
And own no other function.
[*The Winter's Tale*, IV.iv]

SURTEES, R.S. (1805–1864)
These sort of boobies think that people come to balls to do nothing but dance; whereas everyone knows that the real business of a ball is either to look out for a wife, to look after a wife, or to look after somebody else's wife.
[*Mr Facey Romford's Hounds* (1865)]

YEATS, W.B. (1865–1939)
All men are dancers and their tread
Goes to the barbarous clangour of a gong.
['Nineteen Hundred and Nineteen' (1921)]

DANGER

BURKE, Edmund (1729–1797)
Dangers by being despised grow great.
[Speech on the Petition of the Unitarians, 1792]

CHAPMAN, George (c.1559–c.1634)
Danger (the spurre of all great mindes) is ever
The curbe to your tame spirits.
[*Revenge of Bussy D'Ambois* (1613)]

CORNEILLE, Pierre (1606–1684)
When we conquer without danger our triumph is without glory.
[*Le Cid* (1637)]

EMERSON, Ralph Waldo (1803–1882)
In skating over thin ice, our safety is in our speed.
['Prudence' (1841)]
As soon as there is life there is danger.
[*Society and Solitude* (1870)]

GAY, John (1685–1732)
How, like a moth, the simple maid,
Still plays about the flame!
[*The Beggar's Opera* (1728)]

MCCARTHY, Cormac (1933–)
There are dragons in the wings of the world.
[*The Guardian*, 1995]

SHAKESPEARE, William (1564–1616)
Out of this nettle, danger, we pluck this flower, safety.
[*Henry IV. Part 1*, II.iii]

STEVENSON, Robert Louis (1850–1894)
The bright face of danger.
['The Lantern-Bearers' (1892)]

AUBER, Daniel François Esprit (1782–1871)
(Remark made at a funeral)
This is the last time I will take part as an amateur.
[Attr.]

BACON, Francis (1561–1626)
Men fear death as children fear to go in the dark; and as that natural fear in children is increased with tales, so is the other.
[*Essays* (1625)]

BHAGAVADGITA
I am become death, the destroyer of worlds.
[Quoted by J. Robert Oppenheimer after testing the first atomic bomb]

BOWRA, Sir Maurice (1898–1971)
Any amusing deaths lately?
[Attr.]

BUTLER, Samuel (1835–1902)
When you have told anyone you have left him a legacy the only decent thing to do is to die at once.
[In Festing Jones, *Samuel Butler: A Memoir*]

DIBDIN, Charles (1745–1814)
What argufies pride and ambition?
Soon or late death will take us in tow:
Each bullet has got its commission,
And when our time's come we must go.
['Each Bullet has its Commission']

DICKINSON, Emily (1830–1886)
Because I could not stop for Death –
He kindly stopped for me–
The Carriage held but just Ourselves –
And Immortality.
['Because I could not stop for Death' (c.1863)]

FONTAINE, Jean de la (1621–1695)
Death does not take the wise man by surprise, he is always prepared to leave.
['La Mort et le mourant']

FORSTER, E.M. (1879–1970)
Death destroys a man; the idea of Death saves him.
[*Howard's End* (1910)]

HENDRIX, Jimi (1942–1970)
Once you're dead, you're made for life.
[Attr.]

HENLEY, William Ernest (1849–1903)
Madam Life's a piece in bloom
Death goes dogging everywhere:
She's the tenant of the room,
He's the ruffian on the stair.
[*Echoes* (1877)]

HUXLEY, Aldous (1894–1963)
Death ... It's the only thing we haven't succeeded in completely vulgarizing.
[*Eyeless in Gaza* (1936)]

HUXLEY, Henrietta (1825–1915)
And if there be no meeting past the grave,
If all is darkness, silence, yet 'tis rest.
Be not afraid ye waiting hearts that weep;
For still He giveth His beloved sleep,
And if an endless sleep He wills, so best.
[Lines on the grave of her husband, 1895]

KIPLING, Rudyard (1865–1936)
(To a magazine which incorrectly reported his death)
I've just read that I am dead. Don't forget to delete me from your list of subscribers.
[Attr.]

KOESTLER, Arthur (1905–1983)
(Of the atomic bomb)
Hitherto man had to live with the idea of death as an individual; from now onward mankind will have to live with the idea of its death as a species.
[Attr.]

LARKIN, Philip (1922–1985)
The anaesthetic from which none come round.
['Aubade' (1988)]

MAETERLINCK, Maurice (1862–1949)
The living are just the dead on holiday.
[Attr.]

MILLAY, Edna St Vincent (1892–1950)
Down, down, down into the darkness of the grave
Gently they go, the beautiful, the tender, the kind;
Quietly they go, the intelligent, the witty, the brave.
I know. But I do not approve. And I am not resigned.
['Dirge without Music' (1928)]

MOLIÈRE (1622–1673)
One dies only once, and then for such a long time!
[*Le Dépit Amoureux* (1656)]

OWEN, Wilfred (1893–1918)
What passing-bells for these who die as cattle?
Only the monstrous anger of the guns.
Only the stuttering rifles' rapid rattle
Can patter out their hasty orisons.
['Anthem for Doomed Youth' (1917)]

POWER, Marguerite (Countess of Blessington) (1789–1849)
It is better to die young than to outlive all one loved, and all that rendered one lovable.
[*The Confessions of an Elderly Gentleman* (1836)]

SAKI (1870–1916)
Waldo is one of those people who would be enormously improved by death.
[*Beasts and Super-Beasts* (1914)]

SASSOON, Siegfried (1886–1967)
Stumbling along the trench in the dusk, dead men and living lying against the sides of the trenches – one never knew which were dead and which living. Dead and living were nearly one, for death was in all our hearts.
[*Diary*, April 1917]

SCHOPENHAUER, Arthur (1788–1860)
After your death you will be what you were before your birth.
[*Parerga and Paralipomena* (1851)]

SÉVIGNÉ, Marquise de (1626–1696)
I find death so terrible that I hate life more for leading me towards it than for the thorns encountered on the way.
[Letter to Mme de Grignan, 1672]

SHAKESPEARE, William (1564–1616)
Fear no more the heat o' th' sun
Nor the furious winter's rages;
Thou thy worldly task hast done,
Home art gone, and ta'en thy wages.
Golden lads and girls all must,
As chimney-sweepers, come to dust.
[*Cymbeline*, IV.ii]
This fell sergeant Death Is strict in his arrest.
[*Hamlet*, V.ii]
Cowards die many times before their deaths:
The valiant never taste of death but once.
[*Julius Caesar*, II.ii]
Men must endure
Their going hence, even as their coming hither:
Ripeness is all.
[*King Lear*, V.ii]

SHAW, George Bernard (1856–1950)
Life levels all men: death reveals the eminent.
[*Man and Superman* (1903)]

SHELLEY, Percy Bysshe (1792–1822)
Death is the veil which those who live call life:
They sleep, and it is lifted.
[*Prometheus Unbound* (1820)]

SMITH, Stevie (1902–1971)
If there wasn't death, I think you couldn't go on.
[*The Observer*, 1969]

SOUTHEY, Robert (1774–1843)
My name is Death: the last best friend am I.
[*Carmen Nuptiale* (1816)]

THOMAS, Dylan (1914–1953)
Though they go mad they shall be sane,
Though they sink through the sea they shall rise again;
Though lovers be lost love shall not;
And death shall have no dominion.
['And death shall have no dominion' (1936)]

TWAIN, Mark (1835–1910)
The report of my death was an exaggeration.
[Cable, 1897]

WRIGHT, Judith (1915–2000)
Death marshals up his armies round us now.
Their footsteps crowd too near.
Lock your warm hand above the chilling heart
and for a time I live without my fear.
Grope in the night to find me and embrace,
for the dark preludes of the drums begin,
and round us, round the company of lovers,
death draws his cordons in.
['The Company of Lovers' (1946)]

YEATS, W.B. (1865–1939)
Nor dread nor hope attend
A dying animal;
A man awaits his end
Dreading and hoping all.
['Death' (1933)]

YOUNG, Edward (1683–1765)
Life is the desert, life the solitude; Death joins us to the great majority.
[*The Revenge* (1721)]

See **EPITAPHS, GRIEF, LAST WORDS, MORTALITY, MURDER, SLEEP, SUICIDE**

DEATH: DYING

ALEXANDER THE GREAT (356–323 BC)
I am dying with the help of too many physicians.
[Attr.]

ALLEN, Woody (1935–)
It's not that I'm afraid to die. I just don't want to be there when it happens.
[*Without Feathers* (1976)]

BACON, Francis (1561–1626)
I do not believe that any man fears to be dead, but only the stroke of death.
[*The Remaines of ... Lord Verulam* (1648)]

BARRIE, Sir J.M. (1860–1937)
To die will be an awfully big adventure.
[*Peter Pan* (1904)]

BETJEMAN, Sir John (1906–1984)
There was sun enough for lazing upon beaches,
There was fun enough for far into the night.
But I'm dying now and done for,
What on earth was all the fun for?
For I'm old and ill and terrified and tight.
['Sun and Fun' (1954)]

BUTLER, Samuel (1835–1902)
It costs a lot of money to die comfortably.
[*The Note-Books of Samuel Butler* (1912)]

CHARLES II (1630–1685)
He had been, he said, a most unconscionable time dying; but he hoped that they would excuse it.
[In Macaulay, *The History of England* (1849)]

CHILDERS, Erskine (1870–1922)
(Writing about his imminent execution)
It seems perfectly simple and inevitable, like lying down after a long day's work.
[Prison letter to his wife]

CRASHAW, Richard (c.1612–1649)
And when life's sweet fable ends,
Soul and body part like friends;
No quarrels, murmurs, no delay;
A kiss, a sigh, and so away.
['Temperance' (1652)]

DICKINSON, Emily (1830–1886)
I heard a Fly buzz – when I died ...
With Blue – uncertain stumbling Buzz–
Between the light – and me –
And then the Windows failed –
and then I could not see to see.
['I heard a Fly buzz – when I died' (c. 1862)]

JOHNSON, Samuel (1709–1784)
It matters not how a man dies, but how he lives. The act of dying is not of importance, it lasts so short a time.
[In Boswell, *The Life of Samuel Johnson* (1791)]

MAUGHAM, William Somerset (1874–1965)
Dying is a very dull, dreary affair. And my advice to you is to have nothing whatever to do with it.
[In R. Maugham, *Escape from the Shadows* (1972)]

PLATH, Sylvia (1932–1963)
Dying Is an art, like everything else. I do it exceptionally well.
['Lady Lazarus' (1963)]

POPE, Alexander (1688–1744)
I mount! I fly!
O Grave! where is thy victory?
O Death! where is thy sting?
['The Dying Christian to his Soul' (1730)]

SHAKESPEARE, William (1564–1616)
Nothing in his life
Became him like the leaving it: he died
As one that had been studied in his death
To throw away the dearest thing he ow'd
As 'twere a careless trifle.
[*Macbeth*, I.iv]

SMITH, Logan Pearsall (1865–1946)
I cannot forgive my friends for dying; I do not find these vanishing acts of theirs at all amusing.
[*Afterthoughts* (1931)]

THOMAS, Dylan (1914–1953)
Do not go gentle into that good night,
Old age should burn and rave at close of day;
Rage, rage against the dying of the light.
['Do Not Go Gentle into that Good Night' (1952)]

TWAIN, Mark (1835–1910)
All say, 'How hard it is to die' – a strange complaint to come from the mouths of people who have had to live.
[*Pudd'nhead Wilson's Calendar* (1894)]

See **EPITAPHS, GRIEF, LAST WORDS, MORTALITY, MURDER, SLEEP, SUICIDE**

DEBT

FOX, Henry Stephen (1791–1846)
(Remark after an illness)
I am so changed that my oldest creditors would hardly know me.
[Quoted by Byron in a letter to John Murray, 1817]

FRANKLIN, Benjamin (1706–1790)
Creditors have better memories than debtors.
[*Poor Richard's Almanac* (1758)]

IBSEN, Henrik (1828–1906)
Home life ceases to be free and beautiful as soon as it is founded on borrowing and debt.
[*A Doll's House* (1879)]

MUMFORD, Ethel (1878–1940)
In the midst of life we are in debt.
[*Altogether New Cynic's Calendar* (1907)]

SHERIDAN, Richard Brinsley (1751–1816)
(Handing one of his creditors an IOU)
Thank God, that's settled.
[In Shriner, *Wit, Wisdom, and Foibles of the Great* (1918)]
(After being refused a loan of £25 from a friend who asked him to repay the £500 he had already borrowed)
My dear fellow, be reasonable; the sum you ask me for is a very considerable one, whereas I only ask you for twenty-five pounds.
[Attr.]

WARD, Artemus (1834–1867)
Let us all be happy, and live within our means, even if we have to borrer the money to do it with.
['Science and Natural History']

WILDE, Oscar (1854–1900)
It is only by not paying one's bills that one can hope to live in the memory of the commercial classes.
[*The Chameleon*, 1894]

WODEHOUSE, P.G. (1881–1975)
I don't owe a penny to a single soul – not counting tradesmen, of course.
['Jeeves and the Hard-Boiled Egg' (1919)]

DECEPTION

ALLEN, Woody (1935–)
I was thrown out of NYU my freshman year for cheating in my metaphysics final. I looked into the soul of the boy sitting next to me.
[*Annie Hall*, film, 1977]

BERKELEY, Bishop George (1685–1753)
It is impossible that a man who is false to his friends and neighbours should be true to the public.
[*Maxims Concerning Patriotism* (1750)]

CARSWELL, Catherine (1879–1946)
It wasn't a woman who betrayed Jesus with a kiss.
[*The Savage Pilgrimage* (1932)]

CHAUCER, Geoffrey (c.1340–1400)
The smylere with the knyf under the cloke.
[*The Canterbury Tales* (1387)]

FADIMAN, Clifton (1904–1999)
Experience teaches you that the man who looks you straight in the eye, particularly if he adds a firm handshake, is hiding something.
[*Enter, Conversing*]

FONTAINE, Jean de la (1621–1695)
It is a double pleasure to trick the trickster.
['Le coq et le renard']

GAY, John (1685–1732)
To cheat a man is nothing; but the woman must have fine parts indeed who cheats a woman!
[*The Beggar's Opera* (1728)]

HENRY, O. (1862–1910)
It was beautiful and simple as all truly great swindles are.
['The Octopus Marooned' (1908)]

HILL, Joe (1879–1914)
You will eat (You will eat)
Bye and bye (Bye and bye)
In that glorious land above the sky (Way up high)
Work and pray (Work and pray)
Live on hay (Live on hay)
You'll get pie in the sky when you die (That's a lie.).
['The Preacher and the Slave,' song, 1911]

SCOTT, Sir Walter (1771–1832)
O what a tangled web we weave, When first we practise to deceive!
[*Marmion* (1808)]

SHAKESPEARE, William (1564–1616)
O villain, villain, smiling, damned villain!
My tables – meet it is I set it down
That one may smile, and smile, and be a villain.
[*Hamlet*, I.v]

THURBER, James (1894–1961)
You can fool too many of the people too much of the time.
[*The New Yorker*, 1939]

VIRGIL (70–19 BC)
Who may deceive a lover?
[*Aeneid*]

See **APPEARANCE, HYPOCRISY, LIES**

DEMOCRACY

ATTLEE, Clement (1883–1967)
Democracy means government by discussion but it is only effective if you can stop people talking.
[Speech, 1957]

BEVERIDGE, William Henry (1879–1963)
The trouble in modern democracy is that men do not approach to leadership until they have lost the desire to lead anyone.
[*The Observer*, 1934]

CHURCHILL, Sir Winston (1874–1965)
Many forms of government have been tried,
and will be tried in this world of sin and woe.
No one pretends that democracy is perfect or
all-wise. Indeed, it has been said that
democracy is the worst form of Government
except all those other forms that have been
tried from time to time.
[Speech, 1947]

DEMOSTHENES (c.384–322 BC)
There is one safeguard, which is an advantage
and security for all, but especially to
democracies against despots. What is it?
Distrust.
[*Philippics*]

**FLERS, Marquis de (1872–1927) and
CAILLAVET, Arman de (1869–1915)**
Democracy is the name we give the people
whenever we need them.
[*L'habit vert*]

FO, Dario (1926–)
Correct! You said it! Scandal is the manure of
democracy.
[*Accidental Death of an Anarchist* (1974)]

FORSTER, E.M. (1879–1970)
So Two cheers for Democracy: one because it
admits variety and two because it permits
criticism. Two cheers are quite enough: there
is no occasion to give three. Only Love the
Beloved Republic deserves that.
[*Two Cheers for Democracy* (1951)]

IBSEN, Henrik (1828–1906)
The most dangerous foe to truth and freedom
in our midst is the compact majority. Yes, the
damned, compact liberal majority.
[*An Enemy of the People* (1882)]

LINCOLN, Abraham (1809–1865)
No man is good enough to govern another
man without that other's consent.
[Speech, 1854]
The ballot is stronger than the bullet.
[Speech, 1856]

NIEBUHR, Reinhold (1892–1971)
Man's capacity for justice makes democracy
possible, but man's inclination to injustice
makes democracy necessary.
[*The Children of Light and the Children of
Darkness* (1944)]

SHAW, George Bernard (1856–1950)
Democracy substitutes election by the
incompetent many for appointment by the
corrupt few.
[*Man and Superman* (1903)]

TOCQUEVILLE, Alexis de (1805–1859)
I sought the image of democracy, in order to
learn what we have to fear and to hope from
its progress.
[*De la Démocratie en Amérique* (1840)]

WEBSTER, Daniel (1782–1852)
The people's government, made for the
people, made by the people, and answerable
to the people.
[Speech, 1830]

WILLIAMS, Tennessee (1911–1983)
Knowledge – Zzzzzp! Money – Zzzzzp! –
Power! That's the cycle democracy is built on!
[*The Glass Menagerie* (1945)]

WILSON, Woodrow (1856–1924)
The world must be made safe for democracy.
[Speech, 1917]

See **CLASS, GOVERNMENT**

DESPAIR

CAMUS, Albert (1913–1960)
He who despairs over an event is a coward,
but he who holds hopes for the human
condition is a fool.
[*The Rebel* (1951)]

FITZGERALD, F. Scott (1896–1940)
In the real dark night of the soul it is always
three o'clock in the morning.
[*The Crack-Up* (1945)]

GREENE, Graham (1904–1991)
Despair is the price one pays for setting
oneself an impossible aim.
[*Heart of the Matter* (1948)]

HOPKINS, Gerard Manley (1844–1889)
Not, I'll not, carrion comfort, Despair, not
feast on thee;
Not untwist – slack they may be – these last
strands of man
In me or, most weary, cry I can no more. I can;
Can something, hope, wish day come, not
choose not to be.
['Carrion Comfort' (1885)]

KAFKA, Franz (1883–1924)
Do not despair, not even about the fact that
you do not despair.
[*Diary*, 1913]

ST JOHN OF THE CROSS (1542–1591)
The dark night of the soul.
[Title of poem]

SHAKESPEARE, William (1564-1616)
I shall despair. There is no creature loves me;
And if I die no soul will pity me:
And wherefore should they, since that I myself
Find in myself no pity to myself?
[*Richard III*, V.iii]

SHAW, George Bernard (1856-1950)
He who has never hoped can never despair.
[*Caesar and Cleopatra* (1901)]

THOREAU, Henry David (1817-1862)
The mass of men lead lives of quiet desperation.
[*Walden* (1854)]

See **SUFFERING**

DESTINY

AESCHYLUS (525-456 BC)
Things are where things are, and, as fate has willed,
So shall they be fulfilled.
[*Agamemnon*, trans. Browning]

ARNOLD, Matthew (1822-1888)
Yet they, believe me, who await
No gifts from chance, have conquered fate.
['Resignation' (1849)]

AURELIUS, Marcus (121-180)
Nothing happens to any thing which that thing is not made by nature to bear.
[*Meditations*]

BACON, Francis (1561-1626)
If a man look sharply, and attentively, he shall see Fortune: for though she be blind, yet she is not invisible.
[*Essays* (1625)]

BOWEN, Elizabeth (1899-1973)
Fate is not an eagle, it creeps like a rat.
[*The House in Paris* (1935)]

BÜCHNER, Georg (1813-1837)
We are puppets on strings worked by unknown forces; we ourselves are nothing, nothing!
[*Danton's Death* (1835)]

CHURCHILL, Sir Winston (1874-1965)
I felt as if I were walking with destiny, and that all my past life had been but a preparation for this hour and this trial.
[*The Gathering Storm*]

CLAUDIUS CAECUS, Appius (4th-3rd century BC)
Each man is the architect of his own destiny.
[In Sallust, *Ad Caesarem*]

CRISP, Quentin (1908-1999)
Believe in fate, but lean forward where fate can see you.
[Attr.]

DELILLE, Abbé Jacques (1738-1813)
Relations are made by fate, friends by choice.
[*Malheur et pitié* (1803)]

EMERSON, Ralph Waldo (1803-1882)
The bitterest tragic element in life to be derived from an intellectual source is the belief in a brute Fate or Destiny.
[*Natural History of Intellect* (1893)]

FITZGERALD, Edward (1809-1883)
'Tis all a Chequer-board of Nights and Days
Where Destiny with Men for Pieces plays:
Hither and thither moves, and mates, and slays,
And one by one back in the Closet lays.
[*The Rubáiyát of Omar Khayyám* (1859)]
The Moving Finger writes; and, having writ,
Moves on: nor all thy Piety nor Wit
Shall lure it back to cancel half a Line,
Nor all thy Tears wash out a Word of it.
[*The Rubáiyát of Omar Khayyám* (1859)]

FORD, John (c.1586-1639)
Tempt not the stars, young man, thou canst not play
With the severity of fate.
[*The Broken Heart* (1633)]

GAY, John (1685-1732)
'Tis a gross error, held in schools,
That Fortune always favours fools.
[*Fables* (1738)]

HARE, Maurice Evan (1886-1967)
There once was a man who said, 'Damn!
It is borne in upon me I am
An engine that moves
In predestinate grooves,
I'm not even a bus, I'm a tram.'
['Limerick,' 1905]

HITLER, Adolf (1889-1945)
I go the way that Providence bids me go with the certainty of a sleepwalker.
[Speech, Munich, 1936]

HORACE (65-8 BC)
Do not ask – it is forbidden to know – what end the gods have in store for me or for you.
[*Odes*]

JONSON, Ben (1572-1637)
Blind Fortune still
Bestows her gifts on such as cannot use them.
[*Every Man out of His Humour* (1599)]

LOOS, Anita (1893–1981)
Fate keeps on happening.
[*Gentlemen Prefer Blondes* (1925)]

MACHIAVELLI (1469–1527)
Fortune, like a woman, is friendly to the young, because they show her less respect, they are more daring and command her with audacity.
[*The Prince* (1532)]

MALLARMÉ, Stéphane (1842–1898)
A throw of the dice will never eliminate chance.
[Title of work, 1897]

READE, Charles (1814–1884)
Sow an act, and you reap a habit. Sow a habit, and you reap a character. Sow a character, and you reap a destiny.
[Attr.]

SCHOPENHAUER, Arthur (1788–1860)
Fate shuffles the cards and we play.
['Aphorisms for Wisdom' (1851)]

SHAKESPEARE, William (1564–1616)
Men at some time are masters of their fates:
The fault, dear Brutus, is not in our stars,
But in ourselves, that we are underlings.
[*Julius Caesar*, I.ii]
There is a tide in the affairs of men
Which, taken at the flood, leads on to fortune;
Omitted, all the voyage of their life
Is bound in shallows and in miseries.
[*Julius Caesar*, IV.iii.]

SINGER, Isaac Bashevis (1904–1991)
We have to believe in free will. We've got no choice.
[*The Times*, 1982]

TERENCE (c.190–159 BC)
Fortune favours the brave.
[*Phormia*]

See **PURPOSE**

THE DEVIL

BAUDELAIRE, Charles (1821–1867)
My dear brothers, never forget when you hear the progress of the Enlightenment praised, that the Devil's cleverest ploy is to persuade you that he doesn't exist.
[Attr.]

THE BIBLE
(King James Version)
Resist the devil, and he will flee from you.
[*James*, 4:7]

BROWNING, Elizabeth Barrett (1806–1861)
The devil's most devilish when respectable.
[*Aurora Leigh* (1857)]

BUTLER, Samuel (1835–1902)
An apology for the devil: it must be remembered that we have heard only one side of the case; God has written all the books.
[*The Note-Books of Samuel Butler* (1912)]

DOSTOEVSKY, Fyodor (1821–1881)
I think if the devil doesn't exist, and man has created him, he has created him in his own image and likeness.
[*The Brothers Karamazov* (1880)]

HILL, Rowland (1744–1833)
(Referring to his writing of hymns)
He did not see any reason why the devil should have all the good tunes.
[In Broome, *The Rev. Rowland Hill* (1881)]

LAWRENCE, D.H. (1885–1930)
It is no good casting out devils. They belong to us, we must accept them and be at peace with them.
['The Reality of Peace' (1936)]

MILTON, John (1608–1674)
Abasht the Devil stood,
And felt how awful goodness is.
[*Paradise Lost* (1667)]

SHAKESPEARE, William (1564–1616)
The devil can cite Scripture for his purpose.
[*The Merchant of Venice*, I.iii]

WILDE, Oscar (1854–1900)
We are each our own devil, and we make
This world our hell.
[*The Duchess of Padua* (1883)]

See **HELL**

DIARIES

BANKHEAD, Tallulah (1903–1968)
Only good girls keep diaries. Bad girls don't have the time.
[Attr.]

MINNELLI, Liza (1946–)
In Hollywood now when people die they don't say, 'Did he leave a will?' but 'Did he leave a diary?'.
[*The Observer*, 1989]

DINING

TERRY, Dame Ellen (1847–1928)
What is a diary as a rule? A document useful to the person who keeps it, dull to the contemporary who reads it, invaluable to the student, centuries afterwards, who treasures it!
[*The Story of My Life* (1933)]

TOLSTOY, Sophie (1844–1919)
(Of Tolstoy)
He would like to destroy his old diaries and to appear before his children and the public only in his patriarchal robes. His vanity is enormous!
[*A Diary of Tolstoy's Wife*, 1860–1891]

DINING

BOWRA, Sir Maurice (1898–1971)
I'm a man
More dined against than dining.
[In Betjeman, *Summoned by Bells* (1960)]

EVARTS, William Maxwell (1818–1901)
(Of a dinner given by US President and temperance advocate Rutherford B. Hayes)
It was a brilliant affair; water flowed like champagne.
[Attr.]

GULBENKIAN, Nubar (1896–1972)
The best number for a dinner party is two: myself and a damn good head waiter.
[*The Observer*, 1965]

JOHNSON, Samuel (1709–1784)
This was a good dinner enough, to be sure; but it was not a dinner to ask a man to.
[In Boswell, *The Life of Samuel Johnson* (1791)]
A man seldom thinks with more earnestness of anything than he does of his dinner.
[In Piozzi, *Anecdotes of the Late Samuel Johnson* (1786)]
A man is in general better pleased when he has a good dinner upon his table, than when his wife talks Greek.
[In Hawkins, *Life of Samuel Johnson* (1787)]

MAUGHAM, William Somerset (1874–1965)
At a dinner party one should eat wisely but not too well, and talk well but not too wisely.
[*A Writer's Notebook* (1949)]

PEPYS, Samuel (1633–1703)
Strange to see how a good dinner and feasting reconciles everybody.
[*Diary*, 1665]

SWIFT, Jonathan (1667–1745)
He showed me his bill of fare to tempt me to dine with him; Poh, said I, I value not your bill of fare; give me your bill of company.
[*Journal to Stella*, 1711]

WILDE, Oscar (1854–1900)
(Said to Frank Harris who was listing the houses he had dined at)
Dear Frank, we believe you; you have dined in every house in London – once.
[Attr.]

See **FOOD**

DIPLOMACY

CROMWELL, Oliver (1599–1658)
A man-of-war is the best ambassador.
[Attr.]

FROST, Robert (1874–1963)
A diplomat is a man who always remembers a woman's birthday but never remembers her age.
[Attr.]

PEARSON, Lester B. (1897–1972)
Diplomacy is letting someone else have your way.
[*The Observer*, 1965]

USTINOV, Sir Peter (1921–2004)
A diplomat these days is nothing but a head-waiter who's allowed to sit down* occasionally.
[*Romanoff and Juliet* (1956)]

WOTTON, Sir Henry (1568–1639)
An ambassador is an honest man sent to lie abroad for the good of his country.
[Written in an album, 1606]

DIVORCE

ATWOOD, Margaret (1939–)
A divorce is like an amputation; you survive, but there's less of you.
[*Time*, 1973]

KERR, Jean (1923–2003)
A lawyer is never entirely comfortable with a friendly divorce, anymore than a good mortician wants to finish his job and then have the patient sit up on the table.
[*Time*, 1961]

PARKER, Dorothy (1893–1967)
(Said of her husband on the day their divorce became final)
Oh, don't worry about Alan ... Alan will always land on somebody's feet.
[In J. Keats, *You Might As Well Live* (1970)]

THORNDIKE, Dame Sybil (1882-1976)
(Replying to a query as to whether she had ever considered divorce during her long marriage to Sir Lewis Casson)
Divorce? Never. But murder often!

[Attr.]

WEST, Dame Rebecca (1892-1983)
If our divorce laws were improved, we could at least say that if marriage does nobody much good it does nobody any harm.

[*The Clarion*]

Dogs

BEERBOHM, Sir Max (1872-1956)
You will find that the woman who is really kind to dogs is always one who has failed to inspire sympathy in men.

[*Zuleika Dobson* (1911)]

BENNETT, Alan (1934-)
It's the one species I wouldn't mind seeing vanish from the face of the earth. I wish they were like the white rhino – six of them left in the Serengeti National Park, and all males.

[Attr.]

ELIOT, George (1819-1880)
Though, as we know, she was not fond of pets that must be held in the hands or trodden on, she was always attentive to the feelings of dogs, and very polite if she had to decline their advances.

[*Middlemarch* (1872)]

HUXLEY, Aldous (1894-1963)
To his dog, every man is Napoleon; hence the constant popularity of dogs.

[Attr.]

MUIR, Frank (1920-1998)
Dogs, like horses, are quadrupeds. That is to say, they have four rupeds, one at each corner, on which they walk.

[*You Can't Have Your Kayak and Heat It*, with Dennis Norden]

NASH, Ogden (1902-1971)
A door is what a dog is perpetually on the wrong side of.

['A Dog's Best Friend Is His Illiteracy' (1952)]

SPARROW, John (1906-1992)
That indefatigable and unsavoury engine of pollution, the dog.

[Letter to *The Times*, 1975]

STREATFIELD, Sir Geoffrey Hugh Benbow (1897-1978)
I loathe people who keep dogs. They are cowards who haven't got the guts to bite people themselves.

[*A Madman's Diary*]

See **ANIMALS, CHILDREN**

Doubt

AUSTEN, Jane (1775-1817)
Where so many hours have been spent in convincing myself that I am right, is there not some reason to fear I may be wrong?

[*Sense and Sensibility* (1811)]

BACON, Francis (1561-1626)
If a man will begin with certainties, he shall end in doubts; but if he will be content to begin with doubts, he shall end in certainties.

[*The Advancement of Learning* (1605)]

BORGES, Jorge Luis (1899-1986)
I have known what the Greeks knew not: uncertainty.

[*The Garden of Paths which Diverge* (1941)]

BOYD, William (1952-)
What now? What next? All these questions. All these doubts. So few certainties. But then I have taken new comfort and refuge in the doctrine that advises one not to seek tranquillity in certainty, but in permanently suspended judgement.

[*Brazzaville Beach* (1990)]

BROWNING, Robert (1812-1889)
All we have gained then by our unbelief
Is a life of doubt diversified by faith,
For one of faith diversified by doubt:
We called the chess-board white, – we call it black.

['Bishop Blougram's Apology' (1855)]

BUTLER, Samuel (1835-1902)
My Lord, I do not believe. Help thou mine unbelief.

[*Samuel Butler's Notebooks* (1951)]

DARROW, Clarence (1857-1938)
(Remark during the trial of John Scopes, 1925, for teaching evolution in school)
I do not consider it an insult but rather a compliment to be called an agnostic. I do not pretend to know where many ignorant men are sure – that is all that agnosticism means.

[Attr.]

DENT, Alan (1905–1978)
This is the tragedy of a man who could not make up his mind.
[Introduction to film *Hamlet*, 1948]

HUXLEY, T.H. (1825–1895)
I am too much of a sceptic to deny the possibility of anything.
[Letter to Herbert Spencer, 1886]

KORAN
There is no doubt in this book.
[Chapter 1]

NEWMAN, John Henry (Cardinal) (1801–1890)
Ten thousand difficulties do not make one doubt.
[*Apologia pro Vita Sua* (1864)]

TENNYSON, Alfred (Lord) (1809–1892)
There lives more faith in honest doubt,
Believe me, than in half the creeds.
[*In Memoriam A. H. H.* (1850)]

See **UNCERTAINTY**

DREAMS

BACON, Francis (1561–1626)
Dreams and predictions of astrology ... ought to serve but for winter talk by the fireside.
[*Essays* (1625)]

BUNN, Alfred (1796–1860)
I dreamt that I dwelt in marble halls,
With vassals and serfs at my side.
[*The Bohemian Girl* (1843)]

CALDERÓN DE LA BARCA, Pedro (1600–1681)
For I see, since I am asleep, that I dream while I am awake.
[*Life is a Dream* (1636)]

CHUANG TSE (c.369–286 BC)
I do not know whether I was then a man dreaming I was a butterfly, or whether I am now a butterfly dreaming I am a man.
[*Chuang Tse* (1889)]

CLARKE, Sir Arthur C. (1917–2008)
(Voice of computer HAL 9000)
Dr Chandra, will I dream?
[Film *2001, A Space Odyssey*, (1969)]

FREUD, Sigmund (1856–1939)
The interpretation of dreams is the royal road to a knowledge of the unconscious activities of the mind.
[*The Interpretation of Dreams*, (1909)]

LAWRENCE, T.E. (1888–1935)
All men dream: but not equally. Those who dream by night in the dusty recesses of their minds wake in the day to find that it was vanity; but the dreamers of the day are dangerous men, for they may act their dream with open eyes, to make it possible.
[*The Seven Pillars of Wisdom* (1926)]

MONTAIGNE, Michel de (1533–1592)
Those who have compared our life to a dream were, by chance, more right than they thought ... We are awake while sleeping, and sleeping while awake.
[*Essais* (1580)]

POE, Edgar Allan (1809–1849)
All that we see or seem
Is but a dream within a dream.
['A Dream within a Dream' (1849)]

SHAKESPEARE, William (1564–1616)
O God, I could be bounded in a nutshell and count myself a king of infinite space, were it not that I have bad dreams.
[*Hamlet*, II.ii]

We are such stuff
As dreams are made on; and our little life
Is rounded with a sleep.
[*The Tempest*, IV.i]

TENNYSON, Alfred (Lord) (1809–1892)
Dreams are true while they last, and do we not live in dreams?
['The Higher Pantheism' (1867)]

YEATS, W.B. (1865–1939)
In dreams begins responsibility.
[*Responsibilities* (1914)]

See **BED, SLEEP**

DRESS

AESOP (6th century BC)
It is not only fine feathers that make fine birds.
['The Jay and the Peacock']

ASHFORD, Daisy (1881–1972)
You look rather rash, my dear, your colours don't quite match your face.
[*The Young Visiters* (1919)]

BONGAY, Amy
(Commenting on the fact that the fashion industry had begun to find supermodels too demanding)
It's a terrible sign. It will be the death of this profession if designers start using real people on the catwalks and in their advertising.
[*Daily Mail*, 1995]

CHANEL, Coco (1883–1971)
(On Dior's New Look)
These are clothes by a man who doesn't know women, never had one and dreams of being one.
[*Scotland on Sunday*, 1995]

CURIE, Marie (1867–1934)
(Referring to a wedding dress)
I have no dress except the one I wear every day. If you are going to be kind enough to give me one, please let it be practical and dark so that I can put it on afterwards to go to the laboratory.
[Letter to a friend, 1894]

DARROW, Clarence (1857–1938)
I go to a better tailor than any of you and pay more for my clothes. The only difference is that you probably don't sleep in yours.
[In E. Fuller, *2500 Anecdotes*]
It is only when the mind and character slumber that the dress can be seen.
[*Letters and Social Aims* (1875)]

FARQUHAR, George (1678–1707)
A lady, if undrest at Church, looks silly,
One cannot be devout in dishabilly.
[*The Stage Coach* (1704)]

FORBES, Miss C.F. (1817–1911)
The sense of being well-dressed gives a feeling of inward tranquillity which religion is powerless to bestow.
[In Emerson, *Social Aims* (1876)]

GASKELL, Elizabeth (1810–1865)
[The Cranford ladies'] dress is very independent of fashion; as they observe, 'What does it signify how we dress here at Cranford, where everybody knows us?' And if they go from home, their reason is equally cogent, 'What does it signify how we dress here, where nobody knows us?'.
[*Cranford* (1853)]

HEWETT, Dorothy (1923–2002)
Gentlemen may remove any garment consistent with decency. Ladies may remove any garment consistent with charm.
['Beneath the Arches']

LOOS, Anita (1893–1981)
You have got to be a Queen to get away with a hat like that.
[*Gentlemen Prefer Blondes* (1925)]

NASH, Ogden (1902–1971)
Sure, deck your lower limbs in pants;
Yours are the limbs, my sweeting.
You look divine as you advance –
Have you seen yourself retreating?
['What's the Use?' (1940)]

O'ROURKE, P.J. (1947–)
The only really firm rule of taste about cross dressing is that neither sex should ever wear anything they haven't yet figured out how to go to the bathroom in.
[*Modern Manners* (1984)]

PARKER, Dorothy (1893–1967)
Where's the man could ease a heart,
Like a satin gown?
['The Satin Dress' (1937)]
Brevity is the soul of lingerie.
[In Woollcott, *While Rome Burns* (1934)]

PARTON, Dolly (1946–)
You'd be surprised how much it costs to look this cheap.
[In Carole McKenzie, *Quotable Women* (1992)]

SWIFT, Jonathan (1667–1745)
She wears her clothes, as if they were thrown on with a pitchfork.
[*Polite Conversation* (1738)]

WEST, Mae (1892–1980)
You can say what you like about long dresses, but they cover a multitude of shins.
[*Peel Me a Grape*]

WHITEHORN, Katherine (1926–)
Hats divide generally into three classes: offensive hats, defensive hats, and shrapnel.
[*Shouts and Murmurs* (1963)]

WILDE, Oscar (1854–1900)
A well-tied tie is the first serious step in life.
[*A Woman of No Importance* (1893)]

WODEHOUSE, P.G. (1881–1975)
The Right Hon was a tubby little chap who looked as if he had been poured into his clothes and had forgotten to say 'When!'.
[*Very Good, Jeeves* (1930)]

DUTY

ANONYMOUS
Straight is the line of Duty
Curved is the line of Beauty
Follow the first and thou shallt see
The second ever following thee.

BIERCE, Ambrose (1842–c.1914)
Duty: That which sternly impels us in the direction of profit, along the line of desire.
[*The Enlarged Devil's Dictionary* (1967)]

GILBERT, W.S. (1836–1911)
The question is, had he not been a thing of beauty,
Would she be swayed by quite as keen a sense of duty?
[*The Pirates of Penzance* (1880)]

GRANT, Ulysses S. (1822–1885)
No personal consideration should stand in the way of performing a public duty.
[Note on letter, 1875]

HOOPER, Ellen Sturgis (1816–1841)
I slept, and dreamed that life was Beauty;
I woke, and found that life was Duty.
['Beauty and Duty' (1840)]

IBSEN, Henrik (1828–1906)
What's a man's first duty? The answer's brief:
To be himself.
[*Peer Gynt* (1867)]

LEE, Robert E. (1807–1870)
Duty then is the sublimest word in our language. Do your duty in all things. You cannot do more. You should never wish to do less.
[Inscription in the Hall of Fame]

MILNER, Alfred (1854–1925)
If we believe a thing to be bad, and if we have a right to prevent it, it is our duty to try to prevent it and to damn the consequences.
[Speech, 1909]

NELSON, Lord (1758–1805)
(Nelson's last signal at the Battle of Trafalgar, 1805)
England expects every man to do his duty.
[In Southey, *The Life of Nelson* (1860)]

PEACOCK, Thomas Love (1785–1866)
Sir, I have quarrelled with my wife; and a man who has quarrelled with his wife is absolved from all duty to his country.
[*Nightmare Abbey* (1818)]

SHAKESPEARE, William (1564–1616)
Every subject's duty is the King's; but every subject's soul is his own.
[*Henry V*, IV.i]

SHAW, George Bernard (1856–1950)
When a stupid man is doing something he is ashamed of, he always declares that it is his duty.
[*Caesar and Cleopatra* (1901)]

STEVENSON, Robert Louis (1850–1894)
There is no duty we so much underrate as the duty of being happy.
[*Virginibus Puerisque* (1881)]

TENNYSON, Alfred (Lord) (1809–1892)
O hard, when love and duty clash!
[*The Princess* (1847)]

WASHINGTON, George (1732–1799)
To persevere in one's duty and be silent is the best answer to calumny.
[*Moral Maxims*]

WILDE, Oscar (1854–1900)
Duty is what one expects of others, it is not what one does oneself.
[*A Woman of No Importance* (1893)]

ECONOMICS

BAGEHOT, Walter (1826–1877)
No real English gentleman, in his secret soul, was ever sorry for the death of a political economist.
['The First Edinburgh Reviewers' (1858)]

BLAIR, Tony (1953–)
I want Britain to be a stake-holder economy where everyone has a chance to get on and succeed, where there is a clear sense of national purpose and where we leave behind some of the battles between Left and Right which really are not relevant in the new global economy of today.
[Speech in Singapore, 1996]

CARLYLE, Thomas (1795–1881)
(Of Political Economics)
And the Social Science, – not a 'gay science', ... no, a dreary, desolate, and indeed quite abject and distressing one; what we might call ... the dismal science.
[*Latter-Day Pamphlets* (1850)]

DOUGLAS-HOME, Sir Alec (1903–1995)
When I have to read economic documents I have to have a box of matches and start moving them into position to illustrate and simplify the points to myself.
[Interview in *The Observer*, 1962]

EDEN, Anthony (1897–1977)
Everybody is always in favour of general economy and particular expenditure.
[*The Observer*, 1956]

EISENHOWER, Dwight D. (1890–1969)
Every gun that is made, every warship launched, every rocket fired signifies, in the final sense, a theft from those who hunger and are not fed, those who are cold and are not clothed. This world in arms is not spending money alone. It is spending the sweat of its labourers, the genius of its scientists, the hopes of its children.
[Speech, 1953]

FRIEDMAN, Milton (1912–2006)
There's no such thing as a free lunch.
[Title of book]

GALBRAITH, J.K. (1908–2006)
Economics is extremely useful as a form of employment for economists.
[Attr.]
If all else fails, immortality can always be assured by spectacular error.
[Attr.]

GEORGE, Eddie (1938–2009)
There are three kinds of economist. Those who can count and those who can't.
[The Observer Review, 1996]

HELLER, Walter (1915–1987)
(Definition of an economist)
Someone who can't see something working in practice without asking whether it would work in theory.
[Attr.]

HENDERSON, Leon (1895–1986)
Having a little inflation is like being a little pregnant.
[Attr.]

JONES, Barry Owen (1932–)
Academic economists have about the status and reliability of astrologers or the readers of Tarot cards. If the medical profession was as lacking in resources we would not have advanced very far beyond the provision of splints for broken arms.
[In John Wilkes (ed.), The Future of Work]

KEYNES, John Maynard (1883–1946)
It is better that a man should tyrannize over his bank balance than over his fellow-citizens.
[The General Theory of Employment, Interest and Money (1936)]

KING, Sir Mervyn (1948–)
(The task of a central bank)
Taking away the punchbowl just as the party in the financial system is getting going.

LEVIN, Bernard (1928–2004)
Inflation in the Sixties was a nuisance to be endured, like varicose veins or French foreign policy.
[The Pendulum Years (1970)]

MALTHUS, Thomas Robert (1766–1834)
Population, when unchecked, increases in a geometrical ratio. Subsistence only increases in an arithmetical ratio.
[Essay on the Principle of Population (1798)]

MELLON, Andrew William (1855–1937)
A nation is not in danger of financial disaster merely because it owes itself money.
[Attr.]

ROOSEVELT, Franklin Delano (1882–1945)
We have always known that heedless self-interest was bad morals; we know now that it is bad economics.
[First Inaugural Address, 1933]

RUTSKOI, Alexander (1947–)
The dollar is Russia's national currency now, the rouble is just a sweetie paper. We've handed our sword to America.
[Newsweek, 1994]

SCHUMACHER, E.F. (1911–1977)
Small is Beautiful. A study of economics as if people mattered.
[Title of book, 1973]

SELLAR, Walter (1898–1951) and YEATMAN, Robert Julian (1897–1968)
The National Debt is a very Good Thing and it would be dangerous to pay it off, for fear of Political Economy.
[1066 And All That (1930)]

SHAW, George Bernard (1856–1950)
If all economists were laid end to end, they would not reach a conclusion.
[Attr.]

TRUMAN, Harry S. (1884–1972)
It's a recession when your neighbour loses his job; it's a depression when you lose your own.
[The Observer, 1958]

YELTSIN, Boris (1931–2007)
I am for the market, not for the bazaar.
[The Times, 1992]

EDITING

ALLEN, Fred (1894-1956)
(Remark to writers who had heavily edited one of his scripts)
Where were you fellows when the paper was blank?
[Attr.]

AUBREY, John (1626-1697)
He [Shakespeare] was wont to say that he 'never blotted out a line of his life'; said Ben Jonson, 'I wish he had blotted out a thousand.'
[*Brief Lives* (c. 1693)]

CHEEVER, John (1912-1982)
Trust your editor, and you'll sleep on straw.
[In Susan Cheever, *Home Before Dark* (1984)]

HUBBARD, Elbert (1856-1915)
Editor: a person employed by a newspaper whose business it is to separate the wheat from the chaff and to see that the chaff is printed.
[*A Thousand and One Epigrams* (1911)]

JOHNSON, Samuel (1709-1784)
Read over your compositions, and where ever you meet with a passage which you think is particularly fine, strike it out.
[In Boswell, *The Life of Samuel Johnson* (1791)]

MAYER, Louis B. (1885-1957)
(Comment to writers who had objected to changes in their work)
The number one book of the ages was written by a committee, and it was called The Bible.
[In Halliwell, *The Filmgoer's Book of Quotes* (1973)]

TWAIN, Mark (1835-1910)
As to the Adjective: when in doubt, strike it out.
[*Pudd'nhead Wilson's Calendar* (1894)]
See **BOOKS, NEWSPAPERS, PUBLISHING**

EDUCATION

ARISTOTLE (384-322 BC)
The roots of education are bitter, but the fruit is sweet.
[In Diogenes Laertius, *Lives of Philosophers*]

ARNOLD, Thomas (1795-1842)
My object will be, if possible, to form Christian men, for Christian boys I can scarcely hope to make.
[Letter, 1828]

ASCHAM, Roger (1515-1568)
I said ... how, and why, young children were sooner allured by love, than driven by beating, to attain good learning.
[*The Scholemoster* (1570)]

BACON, Francis (1561-1626)
Reading maketh a full man; conference a ready man; and writing an exact man.
[*Essays* (1625)]

BANKHEAD, Tallulah (1903-1968)
I read Shakespeare and the Bible and I can shoot dice. That's what I call a liberal education.
[Attr.]

BIERCE, Ambrose (1842-c.1914)
Education: That which discloses to the wise and disguises from the foolish their lack of understanding.
[*The Cynic's Word Book* (1906)]

BLAIR, Tony (1953-)
Ask me my three main priorities for government, and I tell you: education, education, education.
[Speech to Labour Party conference, 1996]

BROUGHAM, Lord Henry (1778-1868)
Education makes a people easy to lead, but difficult to drive; easy to govern, but impossible to enslave.
[Attr.]

BUCHAN, John (1875-1940)
To live for a time close to great minds is the best kind of education.
[*Memory Hold the Door*]

BUSH, George W. (1946-)
(On returning to Yale to accept an honorary degree)
To those of you who received honors, awards and distinctions, I say well done. And to the C students, I say you, too, can be president of the United States.
[*The Sunday Times*, May 2001]

Rarely is the question asked: is our children learning?
[Campaign speech, 2000]

CHESTERTON, G.K. (1874-1936)
Education is simply the soul of a society as it passes from one generation to another.
[*The Observer*, 1924]

CODY, Henry John (1868-1951)
Education is casting false pearls before real swine.
[Attr.]

COOPER, Roger (1936–)
(After five years in an Iranian prison)
I can say that anyone who, like me, has been
educated in English public schools and served
in the ranks of the British Army is quite at
home in a Third World prison.
[*Newsweek*, 1991]

COWARD, Sir Noël (1899–1973)
I've over-educated myself in all the things I
shouldn't have known at all.
[*Mild Oats* (1931)]

D'SOUZA, Dinesh (1961–)
If education cannot help separate truth from
falsehood, beauty from vulgarity, right from
wrong, then what can it teach us?
[*Atlantic Monthly*, 1991]

DICKENS, Charles (1812–1870)
Now, what I want is, Facts. Teach these boys
and girls nothing but Facts. Facts alone are
wanted in life. Plant nothing else, and root
out everything else ... Stick to Facts, sir!
[*Hard Times* (1854)]

DIOGENES (THE CYNIC) (c.400–325 BC)
Education is something that tempers the
young and consoles the old, gives wealth to
the poor and adorns the rich.
[In Diogenes Laertius, *Lives of Eminent
Philosophers*]

EMERSON, Ralph Waldo (1803–1882)
I pay the schoolmaster, but 'tis the
schoolboys that educate my son.
[*Journals*]

HUXLEY, Aldous (1894–1963)
The solemn foolery of scholarship for
scholarship's sake.
[*The Perennial Philosophy* (1945)]

JOHNSON, Samuel (1709–1784)
All intellectual improvement arises from
leisure.
[In Boswell, *The Life of Samuel Johnson* (1791)]

KANT, Immanuel (1724–1804)
Man is the only creature which must be
educated.
[*On Pedagogy* (1803)]

KRAUS, Karl (1874–1936)
Education is what most people receive, many
pass on and few actually have.
[*Pro domo et mundo* (1912)]

MCIVER, Charles D. (1860–1906)
When you educate a man you educate an
individual; when you educate a woman you
educate a whole family.
[Address at women's college]

MORAVIA, Alberto (1907–1990)
The ratio of literacy to illiteracy is constant,
but nowadays the illiterates can read and
write.
[*The Observer*, 1979]

ROUSSEAU, Jean-Jacques (1712–1778)
One is only curious in proportion to one's
level of education.
[*Émile ou De l'éducation* (1762)]

SKINNER, B.F. (1904–1990)
Education is what survives when what has
been learned has been forgotten.
[*New Scientist*, 1964]

SPARK, Muriel (1918–2006)
To me education is a leading out of what is
already there in the pupil's soul. To Miss
Mackay it is a putting in of something that is
not there, and that is not what I call
education, I call it intrusion.
[*The Prime of Miss Jean Brodie* (1961)]

STOCKS, Mary (Baroness) (1891–1975)
Today we enjoy a social structure which offers
equal opportunity in education. It is indeed
regrettably true that there is no equal
opportunity to take advantage of the equal
opportunity.
[*Still More Commonplace* (1973)]

TREVELYAN, G.M. (1876–1962)
Education ... has produced a vast population
able to read but unable to distinguish what is
worth reading.
[*English Social History* (1942)]

USTINOV, Sir Peter (1921–2004)
People at the top of the tree are those
without qualifications to detain them at the
bottom.
[Attr.]

WILDE, Oscar (1854–1900)
Education is an admirable thing, but it is well
to remember from time to time that nothing
that is worth knowing can be taught.
['The Critic as Artist' (1891)]

See **KNOWLEDGE, LEARNING, SCHOOL,
TEACHERS, UNIVERSITY**

Egoism

ADLER, Alfred (1870–1937)
(On hearing that an egocentric had fallen in love)
Against whom?

[Attr.]

ALI, Muhammad (1942–)
I am the greatest.

[Catchphrase]

BACON, Francis (1561–1626)
It was prettily devised of Aesop, 'The fly sat upon the axletree of the chariot-wheel and said, what a dust do I raise.'

['Of Vain-Glory' (1625)]

BARNES, Peter (1931–2004)
I know I am God because when I pray to him I find I'm talking to myself.

[The Ruling Class (1968)]

BIERCE, Ambrose (1842–c.1914)
Egotist: A person of low taste, more interested in himself than in me.

[The Cynic's Word Book (1906)]

BULMER-THOMAS, Ivor (b.1905–1993)
(Of Harold Wilson)
If ever he went to school without any boots it was because he was too big for them.

[Remark, 1949]

BUTLER, Samuel (1835–1902)
The advantage of doing one's praising for oneself is that one can lay it on so thick and exactly in the right places.

[The Way of All Flesh (1903)]

CHAMFORT, Nicolas (1741–1794)
Someone said of a great egotist: 'He would burn your house down to cook himself a couple of eggs.'

[Caractères et anecdotes]

CHURCHILL, Charles (1731–1764)
(Of Thomas Franklin, Professor of Greek, Cambridge)
He sicken'd at all triumphs but his own.

[The Rosciad (1761)]

DULLES, John Foster (1888–1959)
(Reply when asked if he had ever been wrong)
Yes, once – many, many years ago. I thought I had made a wrong decision. Of course, it turned out that I had been right all along. But I was wrong to have thought that I was wrong.

[Attr.]

ELIOT, George (1819–1880)
He was like a cock, who thought the sun had risen to hear him crow.

[Adam Bede (1859)]

GORTON, John Grey (1911–2002)
I am always prepared to recognize that there can be two points of view – mine, and one that is probably wrong.

[In Trengove, John Grey Gorton]

HARTLEY, L.P. (1895–1972)
'Should I call myself an egoist?' Miss Johnstone mused.'Others have called me so. They merely meant I did not care for them.'

[Simonetta Perkins (1925)]

JEROME, Jerome K. (1859–1927)
Conceit is the finest armour a man can wear.

[Idle Thoughts of an Idle Fellow (1886)]

KEITH, Penelope (1940–)
Shyness is just egotism out of its depth.

[The Observer, 1988]

KOURNIKOVA, Anna (1981–)
Frankly, I am beautiful, famous and gorgeous.

[Scotland an Sunday, 1998]

MEREDITH, George (1828–1909)
In ... the book of Egoism, it is written, Possession without obligation to the object possessed approaches felicity.

[The Egoist (1879)]

ROUX, Joseph (1834–1886)
The egoist does not tolerate egoism.

[Meditations of a Parish Priest (1886)]

SITWELL, Dame Edith (1887–1964)
I have often wished I had time to cultivate modesty ... But I am too busy thinking about myself.

[The Observer, 1950]

STRACHEY, Lytton (1880–1932)
(Of Hurrell Froude)
The time was out of joint, and he was only too delighted to have been born to set it right.

[Eminent Victorians (1918)]

SUZUKI, D.T. (1870–1966)
The individual ego asserts itself strongly in the West. In the East, there is no ego. The ego is non-existent and, therefore, there is no ego to be crucified.

[Mysticism: Christian and Buddhist (1957)]

TROLLOPE, Anthony (1815–1882)
As for conceit, what man will do any good who is not conceited? Nobody holds a good opinion of a man who has a low opinion of himself.
[*Orley Farm* (1862)]

WILDE, Oscar (1854–1900)
I am the only person in the world I should like to know thoroughly.
[*Lady Windermere's Fan* (1892)]

See **PRIDE, SELF**

Enemies

THE BIBLE
(King James Version)
Love your enemies, bless them that curse you, do good to them that hate you, and pray for them which despitefully use you, and persecute you.
[*Matthew*, 5:44]

BRETON, Nicholas (c.1545–c.1626)
I wish my deadly foe, no worse Than want of friends, and empty purse.
['A Farewell to Town' (1577)]

BURKE, Edmund (1729–1797)
He that wrestles with us strengthens our nerves, and sharpens our skill. Our antagonist is our helper.
[*Reflections on the Revolution in France* (1790)]

CALLAS, Maria (1923–1977)
When my enemies stop hissing, I shall know I'm slipping.
[Arianna Stassinopoulos *Maria Callas* (1981)]

CONRAD, Joseph (1857–1924)
You shall judge of a man by his foes as well as by his friends.
[*Lord Jim* (1900)]

KISSINGER, Henry (1923–)
Even a paranoid can have enemies.
[*Time*, 1977]

LESAGE, Alain-René (1668–1747)
They made peace between us; we embraced, and since that time we have been mortal enemies.
[*Le Diable boiteux*]

LINKLATER, Eric (1899–1974)
With a heavy step Sir Matthew left the room and spent the morning designing mausoleums for his enemies.
[*Juan in America* (1931)]

NARVÁEZ, Ramón María (1800–1868)
(On his deathbed, when asked by a priest if he forgave his enemies)
I do not have to forgive my enemies, I have had them all shot.
[Attr.]

PUZO, Mario (1920–1999)
Keep your friends close, but your enemies closer.
[*The Godfather, Part II*, film, 1974]

ROOSEVELT, Franklin Delano (1882–1945)
I ask you to judge me by the enemies I have made.
[*The Observer*, 1932]

WILDE, Oscar (1854–1900)
A man cannot be too careful in the choice of his enemies.
[*The Picture of Dorian Gray* (1891)]

England

AGATE, James (1877–1947)
The English instinctively admire any man who has no talent and is modest about it.
[Attr.]

BAGEHOT, Walter (1826–1877)
Of all nations in the world the English are perhaps the least a nation of pure philosophers.
[*The English Constitution* (1867)]

BEHAN, Brendan (1923–1964)
He was born an Englishman and remained one for years.
[*The Hostage* (1958)]

BRADBURY, Malcolm (1932–2001)
I like the English. They have the most rigid code of immorality in the world.
[*Eating People is Wrong* (1954)]

BRIGHT, John (1811–1889)
England is the mother of Parliaments.
[Speech, 1865]

BROOKE, Rupert (1887–1915)
If I should die, think only this of me:
That there's some corner of a foreign field
That is for ever England.
['The Soldier' (1914)]

BROWNE, Sir Thomas (1605–1682)
All places, all airs make unto me one country; I am in England, everywhere, and under any meridian.
[*Religio Medici* (1643)]

BROWNING, Robert (1812-1889)
Oh, to be in England
Now that April's there,
And whoever wakes in England
Sees, some morning, unaware,
That the lowest boughs and the brushwood
sheaf
Round the elm-tree bole are in tiny leaf,
While the chaffinch sings on the orchard bough
In England – now!
['Home Thoughts, from Abroad' (1845)]

BUTLER, Samuel (1835-1902)
The wish to spread those opinions that we
hold conducive to our own welfare is so
deeply rooted in the English character that
few of us can escape its influence.
[*Erewhon* (1872)]

BYRON, Lord (1788-1824)
The English winter – ending in July,
To recommence in August.
[*Don Juan* (1824)]

CARLYLE, Thomas (1795-1881)
(When asked what the population of England
was)
Thirty millions, mostly fools.
[Attr.]

COMPTON-BURNETT, Dame Ivy (1884-1969)
Well, the English have no family feelings. That
is, none of the kind you mean. They have
them, and one of them is that relations must
cause no expense.
[*Parents and Children* (1941)]

COWPER, William (1731-1800)
England, with all thy faults, I love thee still –
My country!
[*The Task* (1785)]

DEFOE, Daniel (c.1661-1731)
Your Roman-Saxon-Danish-Norman English.
[*The True-Born Englishman* (1701)]

FORSTER, E.M. (1879-1970)
It is not that the Englishman can't feel – it is
that he is afraid to feel. He has been taught at
his public school that feeling is bad form. He
must not express great joy or sorrow, or even
open his mouth too wide when he talks – his
pipe might fall out if he did.
[*Abinger Harvest* (1936)]

GOLDING, William (1911-1993)
We've got to have rules and obey them. After
all, we're not savages. We're English; and the
English are best at everything. So we've got to
do the right things.
[*Lord of the Flies* (1954)]

HAZLITT, William (1778-1830)
The English (it must be owned) are rather a
foul-mouthed nation.
[*Table-Talk* (1822)]

HERBERT, Sir A.P. (1890-1971)
The Englishman never enjoys himself except
for a noble purpose.
[*Uncommon Law* (1935)]

HUGO, Victor (1802-1885)
England has two books: the Bible and
Shakespeare. England made Shakespeare but
the Bible made England.
[Attr.]

JOAD, C.E.M. (1891-1953)
It will be said of this generation that it found
England a land of beauty and left it a land of
beauty spots.
[*The Observer*, 1953]

JOYCE, James (1882-1941)
We feel in England that we have treated you
Irish rather unfairly. It seems history is to blame.
[*Ulysses* (1922)]

KINGSLEY, Charles (1819-1875)
'Tis the hard grey weather
Breeds hard English men.
['Ode to the North-East Wind' (1854)]

KIPLING, Rudyard (1865-1936)
For Allah created the English mad – the
maddest of all mankind!
[*The Five Nations* (1903)]

MACAULAY, Lord (1800-1859)
The history of England is emphatically the
history of progress.
['Sir James Mackintosh' (1843)]

MACINNES, Colin (1914-1976)
England is … a country infested with people
who love to tell us what to do, but who very
rarely seem to know what's going on.
[*England, Half English*]

MARY (Queen of Scots) (1542-1587)
England is not all the world.
[Said at her trial, 1586]

MIKES, George (1912-1987)
An Englishman, even if he is alone, forms an
orderly queue of one.
[*How to be an Alien* (1946)]

O'CONNELL, Daniel (1775-1847)
The Englishman has all the qualities of a
poker except its occasional warmth.
[Attr.]

PEPYS, Samuel (1633–1703)
But Lord! to see the absurd nature of
Englishmen, that cannot forbear laughing and
jeering at everything that looks strange.
[*Diary*, 1662]

RHODES, Cecil (1853–1902)
Remember that you are an Englishman, and
have consequently won first prize in the
lottery of life.
[In Ustinov, *Dear Me* (1977)]

SANTAYANA, George (1863–1952)
England is the paradise of individuality,
eccentricity, heresy, anomalies, hobbies, and
humours.
[*Soliloquies in England* (1922)]

SEELEY, Sir John Robert (1834–1895)
We [the English] seem as it were to have
conquered and peopled half the world in a fit
of absence of mind.
[*The Expansion of England* (1883)]

SHAKESPEARE, William (1564–1616)
This royal throne of kings, this scept'red isle,
This earth of majesty, this seat of Mars,
This other Eden, demi-paradise,
This fortress built by Nature for herself
Against infection and the hand of war,
This happy breed of men, this little world,
This precious stone set in the silver sea,
Which serves it in the office of a wall,
Or as a moat defensive to a house,
Against the envy of less happier lands;
This blessed plot, this earth, this realm, this
England.
[*Richard II*, II.i]

STEINER, George (1929–)
This land is blessed with a powerful
mediocrity of mind. It has saved you from
communism and from fascism.
[*The Observer*, 1998]

SULLY, Duc de (1559–1641)
The English enjoy themselves sadly, according
to the custom of their country.
[*Memoirs* (1638)]

WELLS, H.G. (1866–1946)
In England we have come to rely upon a
comfortable time-lag of fifty years or a
century intervening between the perception
that something ought to be done and a
serious attempt to do it.
[*The Work, Wealth and Happiness of Mankind*
(1931)]

WELSH, Irvine (1957–)
It's nae good blamin' it oan the English fir
colonising us. Ah don't hate the English.
They're just wankers. We can't even pick a
decent vibrant, healthy culture to be
colonised by.
[*Trainspotting* (1994)]

WILDE, Oscar (1854–1900)
The English have a miraculous power of
turning wine into water.
[Attr.]

WINTERS, Shelley (1922–2006)
I did a picture in England one winter and it
was so cold I almost got married.
[*New York Times*, April 1956]

See **CITIES, PATRIOTISM**

ENVIRONMENT

BOTTOMLEY, Gordon (1874–1948)
When you destroy a blade of grass
You poison England at her roots:
Remember no man's foot can pass
Where evermore no green life shoots.
['To Ironfounders and Others' (1912)]

CARSON, Rachel Louise (1907–1964)
As man proceeds towards his announced goal
of the conquest of nature, he has written a
depressing record of destruction directed not
only against the earth he inhabits but against
the life that shares it with him.
[*The Silent Spring* (1962)]

MCLEAN, Joyce (1860–1904)
There's an old saying which goes: Once the
last tree is cut and the last river poisoned, you
will find you cannot eat your money.
[*The Globe and Mail*, 1989]

MEAD, Margaret (1901–1978)
We are living beyond our means. As a people
we have developed a life-style that is draining
the earth of its priceless and irreplaceable
resources without regard for the future of our
children and people all around the world.
[*Redbook*]

See **COUNTRY**

ENVY

BEERBOHM, Sir Max (1872–1956)
The dullard's envy of brilliant men is always
assuaged by the suspicion that they will come
to a bad end.
[*Zuleika Dobson* (1911)]

THE BIBLE
(King James Version)
Through envy of the devil came death into the world.

[Apocrypha, *Wisdom of Solomon*, 2:24]

FIELDING, Henry (1707-1754)
Some folks rail against other folks because other folks have what some folks would be glad of.

[*Joseph Andrews* (1742)]

GAY, John (1685-1732)
Fools may our scorn, not envy raise,
For envy is a kind of praise.

[*Fables* (1727)]

MOORE, Brian (1921-1999)
How many works of the imagination have been goaded into life by envy of an untalented contemporary's success.

[*An Answer from Limba* (1994)]

SHAKESPEARE, William (1564-1616)
(Of Cassius)
Such men as he be never at heart's ease
Whiles they behold a greater than themselves,
And therefore are they very dangerous.

[*Julius Caesar*, I.ii]

See **JEALOUSY**

ANONYMOUS
All who come my grave to see
Avoid damp beds and think of me.

[Epitaph of Lydia Eason, St Michael's, Stoke]

(On a child dead of snake-bite)
From a subtle serpents Bite he cride
our RoseBud cut he drup'd his head and died,
He was his Fathers glorey
And Mothers pride.

[Memorial to John Howorth, died 8 October 1804 at 11 years, St John's Churchyard, Wilberforce, New South Wales]

God took our flour,
Our little Nell;
He thought He too
Would like a smell.

[In Thomas Wood, *Cobbers*]

Here lie I and my four daughters,
Killed by drinking Cheltenham waters.
Had we but stuck to Epsom salts,
We wouldn't have been in these here vaults.

['Cheltenham Waters']

Here lie I by the chancel door;
They put me here because I was poor.
The further in, the more you pay,
But here lie I as snug as they.

[Epitaph, Devon churchyard]

Here lies a child that took one peep of Life
And viewed its endless troubles with dismay,
Gazed with an anguish'd glance upon the strife
And sickening at the sight flew fast away.
What though for many the gate of Heaven is shut,
It stands wide open for this little Butt.

[Epitaph on Allena Butt, who had died when only 6 weeks old]

Here lies a man who was killed by lightning;
He died when his prospects seemed to be brightening.
He might have cut a flash in this world of trouble,
But the flash cut him, and he lies in the stubble.

[Epitaph, Torrington, Devon]

Here lies a poor woman who always was tired,
For she lived in a place where help wasn't hired.
Her last words on earth were,
Dear friends I am going
Where washing ain't done nor sweeping nor sewing,
And everything there is exact to my wishes,
For there they don't eat and there's no washing of dishes ...
Don't mourn for me now, don't mourn for me never,
For I'm going to do nothing for ever and ever.

[Epitaph in Bushey churchyard]

Here lies Fred,
Who was alive and is dead;
Had it been his father,
I had much rather;
Had it been his brother,
Still better than another;
Had it been his sister,
No one would have missed her;
Had it been the whole generation,
Still better for the nation:
But since 'tis only Fred,
Who was alive and is dead,-
There's no more to be said.

[In Horace Walpole, *Memoirs of George II* (1847)]

Here lies my wife,
Here lies she;
Hallelujah!
Hallelujee!

[Epitaph, Leeds churchyard]

Here lies the body of Mary Ann Lowder,
She burst while drinking a seidlitz powder.
Called from the world to her heavenly rest.
She should have waited till it effervesced.
[Epitaph]

Here lies the body of Richard Hind,
Who was neither ingenious, sober, nor kind.
[Epitaph]

Here lies Will Smith – and, what's something rarish,
He was born, bred, and hanged, all in the same parish.
[Epitaph]

Mary Ann has gone to rest,
Safe at last on Abraham's breast,
Which may be nuts for Mary Ann,
But is certainly rough on Abraham.
[Epitaph]

My sledge and anvil lie declined
My bellows too have lost their wind
My fire's extinct, my forge decayed,
And in the Dust my Vice is laid
My coals are spent, my iron's gone
My Nails are Drove, My Work is done.
[Epitaph in Nettlebed churchyard]

Reader, one moment stop and think,
That I am in eternity, and you are on the brink.
[Tombstone inscription at Perth, Scotland]

Remember man, as thou goes by,
As thou art now so once was I,
As I am now so must thou be,
Remember man that thou must die.
[Headstone in Straiton, Ayrshire]

Rest in peace – until we meet again.
[Widow's epitaph for husband; in Mitford,
The American Way of Death]

Sacred to the memory of Captain Anthony Wedgwood
Accidentally shot by his gamekeeper
Whilst out shooting
'Well done thou good and faithful servant'.
[Epitaph]

Stranger! Approach this spot with gravity!
John Brown is filling his last cavity.
[Epitaph of a dentist]

That we spent, we had:
That we gave, we have:
That we left, we lost.
[Epitaph of the Earl of Devonshire]

This is the grave of Mike O'Day
Who died maintaining his right of way.
His right was clear, his will was strong.
But he's just as dead as if he'd been wrong.
[Epitaph]

Warm summer sun shine kindly here:
Warm summer wind blow softly here:
Green sod above lie light, lie light:
Good-night, Dear Heart: good-night, good-night.
[Memorial to Clorinda Haywood,
St Bartholomew's, Edgbaston]

ARBUTHNOT, John (1667-1735)
Here continueth to rot the body of Francis Chartres.
[First line of epitaph]

ATKINSON, Surgeon-Captain E.L. (1882-1929)
Hereabouts died a very gallant gentleman,
Captain L.E.G. Oates of the Inniskilling
Dragoons. In March 1912, returning from the
Pole, he walked willingly to his death in a
blizzard, to try and save his comrades, beset
by hardships.
[Epitaph on a cairn and cross erected in the
Antarctic, November 1912]

BENCHLEY, Robert (1889-1945)
(Suggesting an epitaph for an actress)
She sleeps alone at last.
[Attr.]

BRAY, John Jefferson (1912-1995)
A hundred canvasses and seven sons
He left, and never got a likeness once.
['Epitaph on a Portrait Painter']

BURNS, Robert (1759-1796)
Here lie Willie Michie's banes:
O Satan, when ye tak him,
Gie him the schulin' o' your weans,
For clever Deils he'll mak them!
['Epitaph for William Michie, Schoolmaster of
Cleish Parish, Fifeshire' (1787)]

BYRON, Lord (1788-1824)
With death doomed to grapple,
Beneath this cold slab, he
Who lied in the chapel
Now lies in the Abbey.
['Epitaph for William Pitt' (1820)]

DOUGLAS, James (Earl of Morton) (c.1516-1581)
(Said during the burial of John Knox, 1572)
Here lies he who neither feared nor flattered any flesh.
[Attr.]

DRYDEN, John (1631-1700)
Here lies my wife: here let her lie!
Now she's at rest, and so am I.
['Epitaph intended for his wife']

FIELDS, W.C. (1880–1946)
On the whole, I'd rather be in Philadelphia.
[His own epitaph]

FRANKLIN, Benjamin (1706–1790)
The body of Benjamin Franklin, printer,
(Like the cover of an old book,
Its contents worn out,
And stript of its lettering and gilding)
Lies here, food for worms!
Yet the work itself shall not be lost,
For it will, as he believed, appear once more
In a new
And more beautiful edition,
Corrected and amended
By its Author!
[Epitaph for himself, 1728]

FROST, Robert (1874–1963)
I would have written of me on my stone:
I had a lover's quarrel with the world.
['The Lesson for Today' (1942)]

HUME, David (1711–1776)
Within this circular idea
Call'd vulgarly a tomb,
The ideas and impressions lie
That constituted Hume.
[Epitaph on his monument on Calton Hill, Edinburgh]

KAUFMAN, George S. (1889–1961)
(Suggestion for his own epitaph)
Over my dead body!
[Attr.]

KEATS, John (1795–1821)
Here lies one whose name was writ in water.
[Epitaph for himself]

KIPLING, Rudyard (1865–1936)
A Soldier of the Great War Known unto God.
[Inscription on the graves of unidentified soldiers, 1919]

MENCKEN, H.L. (1880–1956)
If, after I depart this vale, you ever remember me and have thought to please my ghost, forgive some sinner and wink your eye at some homely girl.
[Smart Set, 1921, Epitaph]

MILL, John Stuart (1806–1873)
Were there but a few hearts and intellects like hers this earth would already become the hoped-for heaven.
[Epitaph for his wife, Harriet, 1859]

PARKER, Dorothy (1893–1967)
(Her own epitaph)
Excuse my dust.
[In Alexander Woollcott, *While Rome Burns* (1934)]

ROCHESTER (Earl of) (1647–1680)
Here lies our sovereign lord the King
Whose word no man relies on,
Who never said a foolish thing,
Nor ever did a wise one.
[Epitaph written for Charles II (1706)]

ROSSETTI, Christina (1830–1894)
O Earth, lie heavily upon her eyes;
Seal her sweet eyes weary of watching.
['Rest' (1862)]

SCOTT, Sir Walter (1771–1832)
Here lies one who might be trusted with untold gold, but not with unmeasured whisky.
[Epitaph for his favourite servant, Tom Purdie]

SHAKESPEARE, William (1564–1616)
(Epitaph on his tomb)
Good friend, for Jesu's sake forbear,
To dig the dust enclosed here.
Blest be the man that spares these stones,
And curst be he that moves my bones.
[Attr.]

SMITH, Joseph (1805–1844)
No man knows my history.
[Funeral sermon, written by himself]

STURGES, Preston (1898–1959)
(Suggested epitaph for himself)
Now I've laid me down to die
I pray my neighbours not to pry
Too deeply into sins that I
Not only cannot here deny
But much enjoyed as time flew by.
[In Halliwell, *The Filmgoer's Book of Quotes* (1973)]

WILDE, Oscar (1854–1900)
All her bright golden hair
Tarnished with rust,
She that was young and fair
Fallen to dust.
['Requiescat' (1881)]

WREN, Sir Christopher (1632–1723)
(Si monumentum requiris, circumspice.)
If you are looking for his memorial, look around you.
[Inscription written by his son, in St Paul's Cathedral, London]

EQUALITY

ANTHONY, Susan B. (1820–1906)
There never will be complete equality until women themselves help to make laws and elect lawmakers.
[*The Arena*, 1897]

BALZAC, Honoré de (1799–1850)
Equality may perhaps be a right, but no power on earth can ever turn it into a fact.
[*La Duchesse de Langeais* (1834)]

BARRIE, Sir J.M. (1860–1937)
His Lordship may compel us to be equal upstairs, but there will never be equality in the servants' hall.
[*The Admirable Crichton* (1902)]

BURNS, Robert (1759–1796)
The rank is but the guinea's stamp,
The man's the gowd for a' that ...
For a' that, an' a' that,
It's comin yet for a' that,
That man to man the world o'er
Shall brithers be for a' that.
['A Man's a Man for a' that' (1795)]

HUXLEY, Aldous (1894–1963)
That all men are equal is a proposition to which, at ordinary times, no sane human being has ever given his assent.
[*Proper Studies* (1927)]

JOHNSON, Samuel (1709–1784)
Your levellers wish to level down as far as themselves; but they cannot bear levelling up to themselves.
[In Boswell, *The Life of Samuel Johnson* (1791)]
It is better that some should be unhappy than that none should be happy, which would be the case in a general state of equality.
[In Boswell, *The Life of Samuel Johnson* (1791)]

KING, Martin Luther (1929–1968)
I have a dream that one day this nation will rise up and live out the true meaning of its creed: – 'We hold these truths to be self-evident, that all men are created equal'.
[Speech at Civil Rights March on Washington, August 28, 1963]

MANDELA, Nelson (1918–)
I have fought against white domination, and I have fought against black domination. I have cherished the ideal of a democratic and free society in which all persons will live together in harmony and with equal opportunities. It is an ideal which I hope to live for and achieve. But, if needs be, it is an ideal for which I am prepared to die.
[Statement in the dock, 1964]

MURDOCH, Iris (1919–1999)
The cry of equality pulls everyone down.
[*The Observer*, 1987]

ORWELL, George (1903–1950)
All animals are equal, but some animals are more equal than others.
[*Animal Farm* (1945)]

RAINBOROWE, THOMAS (d. 1648–)
The poorest he that is in England hath a life to live as the greatest he.
[Speech in Army debates, 1647]

WEDGWOOD, Josiah (1730–1795)
Am I not a man and a brother?
[Motto adopted by Anti-Slavery Society]

See **CLASS FEMINISM**

ERROR

AESCHYLUS (525–456 BC)
Even he who is wiser than the wise may err.
[*Fragments*]

BANVILLE, Théodore Faullain de (1823–1891)
Those who do nothing are never wrong.
[*Odes funambulesques*]

BOLINGBROKE, Henry (1678–1751)
Truth lies within a little and certain compass, but error is Immense.
[*Reflections upon Exile* (1716)]

DESTOUCHES, Philippe Néricault (1680–1754)
The absent are always in the wrong.
[*L'Obstacle Imprévu* (1717)]

DRYDEN, John (1631–1700)
Errors, like straws, upon the surface flow; He who would search for pearls must dive below.
[*All for Love* (1678)]

ELIOT, George (1819–1880)
Errors look so very ugly in persons of small means – one feels they are taking quite a liberty in going astray; whereas people of fortune may naturally indulge in a few delinquencies.
[*Scenes of Clerical Life* (1858)]

JOHNSON, Samuel (1709–1784)
(Asked the reason for a mistake in his Dictionary)
Ignorance, madam, sheer ignorance.
[In Boswell, *The Life of Samuel Johnson* (1791)]

LOCKE, John (1632–1704)
It is one thing to show a man that he is in error, and another to put him in possession of truth.
[*Essay concerning Human Understanding* (1690)]

PHELPS, E.J. (1822–1900)
The man who makes no mistakes does not usually make anything.
[Speech, 1899]

POPE, Alexander (1688–1744)
A man should never be ashamed to own he has been in the wrong, which is but saying, in other words, that he is wiser today than he was yesterday.
[*Miscellanies* (1727)]

REAGAN, Ronald (1911–2004)
You know, by the time you reach my age, you've made plenty of mistakes if you've lived your life properly.
[*The Observer*, 1987]

SCHOPENHAUER, Arthur (1788–1860)
There is only one innate error, and that is that we are here in order to be happy.
[*The World as Will and Idea* (1859)]

STRAW, Jack (1946–)
The only people who never make mistakes are those who have never taken a decision.
[*The Observer*, May 1999]

TELLER, Edward (1908–2003)
An expert is a man who has made all the mistakes which can be made in a very narrow field.
[Remark, 1972]

WEST, Mae (1892–1980)
To err is human, but it feels divine.
[In Simon Rose, *Classic Film Guide* (1995)]

See **TRUTH**

EUROPE

ASCHERSON, Neal (1932–)
Europe and the United States together invented representative democracy and human rights. But Europe invented fascism and communism all by itself.
[Article, *The Observer*, June 1998]

BALDWIN, James (1924–1987)
Europe has what we [Americans] do not have yet, a sense of the mysterious and inexorable limits of life, a sense, in a word, of tragedy. And we have what they sorely need: a sense of life's possibilities.
[Attr.]

DELORS, Jacques (1925–)
Europe is not just about material results, it is about spirit. Europe is a state of mind.
[*The Independent*, May 1994]

FANON, Frantz (1925–1961)
When I search for man in the technique and style of Europe, I see only a succession of negations of man, and an avalanche of murders.
[*The Wretched of the Earth* (1961)]

FISHER, H.A.L. (1856–1940)
Purity of race does not exist. Europe is a continent of energetic mongrels.
[*History of Europe* (1935)]

GOLDSMITH, Oliver (c.1728–1774)
On whatever side we regard the history of Europe, we shall perceive it to be a tissue of crimes, follies, and misfortunes.
[*The Citizen of the World* (1762)]

MCCARTHY, Mary (1912–1989)
The immense popularity of American movies abroad demonstrates that Europe is the unfinished negative of which America is the proof.
[*On the Contrary* (1961)]

SHERMAN, Sir Alfred (1919–2006)
Britain does not wish to be ruled by a conglomerate in Europe which includes Third World nations such as the Greeks and Irish, nor for that matter the Italians and French, whose standards of political morality are not ours, and never will be.
[*The Independent*, August 1990]

THATCHER, Margaret (1925–2013)
Historians will one day look back and think it a curious folly that just as the Soviet Union was forced to recognize reality by dispersing power to its separate states and by limiting the powers of its central government, some people in Europe were trying to create a new artificial state by taking powers from national states and concentrating them at the centre.
[Speech, 1994]

VICTORIA, Queen (1819–1901)
I am sick of all this horrid business of politics, and Europe in general, and I think you will hear of me going with the children to live in Australia, and to think of Europe as the Moon!
[Letter to her daughter, the Princess Royal, 1859]

See **BRITAIN, ENGLAND, FRANCE, IRELAND, SCOTLAND**

EVIL

ANONYMOUS
Honi soit qui mal y pense. Evil be to him who evil thinks.
[Motto of the Order of the Garter]

ARENDT, Hannah (1906–1975)
(Of Eichmann)
It was as though in those last minutes he was summing up the lessons that this long course in human wickedness had taught us – the lesson of the fearsome, word-and-thought-defying banality of evil.
[Eichmann in Jerusalem (1963)]

BOILEAU-DESPRÉAUX, Nicolas (1636–1711)
The fear of one evil often leads us into a greater one.
[L'Art Poétique (1674)]

BURKE, Edmund (1729–1797)
The only thing necessary for the triumph of evil is for good men to do nothing.
[Attr.]

CONRAD, Joseph (1857–1924)
The belief in a supernatural source of evil is not necessary; men alone are quite capable of every wickedness.
[Under Western Eyes (1911)]

DELBANCO, Andrew (1952–)
The idea of evil is something on which the health of society depends. We have an obligation to name evil and oppose it in ourselves as well as in others.
[The Guardian, 1995]

GOLDSMITH, Oliver (c. 1728–1774)
Don't let us make imaginary evils, when you know we have so many real ones to encounter.
[The Good Natur'd Man (1768)]

HATTERSLEY, Roy (1932–)
Familiarity with evil breeds not contempt but acceptance.
[The Guardian, 1993]

HAZLITT, William (1778–1830)
To great evils we submit, we resent little provocations.
[Table-Talk (1822)]

KEMPIS, Thomas á (c.1380–1471)
Of two evils the lesser is always to be chosen.
[De Imitatione Christi (1892)]

LA ROCHEFOUCAULD (1613–1680)
There is scarcely a single man clever enough to know all the evil he does.
[Maximes (1678)]

MCCARTHY, Mary (1912–1989)
If someone tells you he is going to make 'a realistic decision' you immediately understand that he has resolved to do something bad.
[On the Contrary (1961)]

NEWMAN, John Henry (Cardinal) (1801–1890)
Whatever is the first time persons hear evil, it is quite certain that good has been beforehand with them, and they have a something within them which tells them it is evil.
[Parochial and Plain Sermons]

NIETZSCHE, Friedrich Wilhelm (1844–1900)
Whoever struggles with monsters might watch that he does not thereby become a monster. When you stare into an abyss for a long time, the abyss also stares into you.
[Beyond Good and Evil (1886)]

POPE, Alexander (1688–1744)
Vice is a monster of so frightful mien,
As, to be hated, needs but to be seen;
Yet soon too oft, familiar with her face,
We first endure, then pity, then embrace.
[An Essay on Man (1733)]

SHAKESPEARE, William (1564–1616)
How oft the sight of means to do ill deeds
Make deeds ill done!
[King John, IV.ii]
Through tatter'd clothes small vices do appear;
Robed and furr'd gowns hide all.
[King Lear, IV.vi]

WEST, Mae (1892–1980)
Whenever I'm caught between two evils, I take the one I've never tried.
[Klondike Annie, film, 1936]

WILDE, Oscar (1854–1900)
Wickedness is a myth invented by good people to account for the curious attractiveness of others.
[The Chameleon, 1894]

See **GOOD AND EVIL, SIN**

EVOLUTION

BLACKWELL, Antoinette Brown (1825-1921)
Mr Darwin ... has failed to hold definitely before his mind the principle that the difference of sex, whatever it may consist in, must itself be subject to natural selection and to evolution.
[*The Sexes Throughout Nature* (1875)]

CONGREVE, William (1670-1729)
I confess freely to you, I could never look long upon a monkey, without very mortifying reflections.
[Letter to Mr Dennis, 1695]

DARWIN, Charles (1809-1882)
I have called this principle, by which each slight variation, if useful, is preserved, by the term of Natural Selection.
[*The Origin of Species* (1859)]
We must, however, acknowledge, as it seems to me, that man with all his noble qualities ... still bears in his bodily frame the indelible stamp of his lowly origin.
[*The Descent of Man* (1871)]

DARWIN, Charles Galton (1887-1962)
The evolution of the human race will not be accomplished in the ten thousand years of tame animals, but in the million years of wild animals, because man is and will always be a wild animal.
[*The Next Ten Million Years*]

DISRAELI, Benjamin (1804-1881)
Is man an ape or an angel? Now I am on the side of the angels.
[Speech, 1864]

SPENCER, Herbert (1820-1903)
It cannot but happen ... that those will survive whose functions happen to be most nearly in equilibrium with the modified aggregate of external forces ... This survival of the fittest implies multiplication of the fittest.
[*The Principles of Biology* (1864)]

VONNEGUT, Kurt (1922-2007)
I was taught that the human brain was the crowning glory of evolution so far, but I think it's a very poor scheme for survival.
[*The Observer*, December 1987]

EXCESS

BEST, George (1946-2005)
I spent a lot of money on booze, birds and fast cars. The rest I just squandered.
[Attr.]

BLAKE, William (1757-1827)
The road of excess leads to the palace of Wisdom.
['Proverbs of Hell' (1793)]

LETTERMAN, David (1947-)
Sometimes something worth doing is worth overdoing.
[CBS Late Show, 1994]

WILDE, Oscar (1854-1900)
Moderation is a fatal thing, Lady Hunstanton. Nothing succeeds like excess.
[*A Woman of No Importance* (1893)]

EXERCISE

DRYDEN, John (1631-1700)
Better to hunt in fields, for health unbought,
Than fee the doctor for a nauseous draught.
The wise, for cure, on exercise depend;
God never made his work, for man to mend.
[*Epistles* (1700)]

FORD, Henry (1863-1947)
Exercise is bunk. If you are healthy, you don't need it: if you are sick you shouldn't take it.
[Attr.]

HUTCHINS, Robert M. (1899-1977)
Whenever I feel like exercise, I lie down until the feeling passes.
[In Jarman, *The Guinness Dictionary of Sports Quotations* (1990)]

O'TOOLE, Peter (1932-)
The only exercise I get these days is from walking behind the coffins of friends who took too much exercise.
[*The Observer*, 1998]

See **HEALTH**

EXILE

AYTOUN, W.E. (1813-1865)
They bore within their breasts the grief
That fame can never heal –
The deep, unutterable woe
Which none save exiles feel.
['The Island of the Scots' (1849)]

THE BIBLE
(King James Version)
I have been a stranger in a strange land.
[*Exodus*, 2:22]

GREGORY VII (c.1020–1085)
(Last words)
I have loved righteousness and hated iniquity: therefore I die in exile.
[In Bowden, *The Life and Pontificate of Gregory VII* (1840)]

SANTAYANA, George (1863–1952)
People who feel themselves to be exiles in this world are mightily inclined to believe themselves citizens of another.
[Attr.]

SPARK, Muriel (1918–2006)
It was Edinburgh that bred within me the conditions of exiledom; and what have I been doing since then but moving from exile to exile? It has ceased to be a fate, it has become a calling.
['What Images Return']

EXPERIENCE

ALI, Muhammad (1942–)
The man who views the world at fifty the same as he did at twenty has wasted thirty years of his life.
[*Playboy Magazine*, November 1975]

ANONYMOUS
Experience is the comb that nature gives us when we are bald.

ANTRIM, Minna (1861–1950)
Experience is a good teacher, but she sends in terrific bills.
[*Naked Truth and Veiled Allusions* (1902)]

BAX, Sir Arnold (1883–1953)
You should make a point of trying every experience once, excepting incest and folk-dancing.
[*Farewell My Youth* (1943)]

BOWEN, Elizabeth (1899–1973)
Experience isn't interesting till it begins to repeat itself – in fact, till it does that, it hardly is experience.
[*The Death of the Heart* (1938)]

EMERSON, Ralph Waldo (1803–1882)
The years teach much which the days never know.
['Experience' (1844)]

HEGEL, Georg Wilhelm (1770–1831)
What experience and history teach us, however, is this, that peoples and governments have never learned anything from history.
[*Lectures on the Philosophy of History* (1837)]

HOLMES, Oliver Wendell (1809–1894)
A moment's insight is sometimes worth a life's experience.
[*The Professor at the Breakfast-Table* (1860)]

HUXLEY, Aldous (1894–1963)
Experience is not what happens to a man. It is what a man does with what happens to him.
[Attr.]

MACCAIG, Norman (1910–1996)
Experience teaches that it doesn't.
[*A World of Difference* (1983)]

WILDE, Oscar (1854–1900)
Experience is the name every one gives to their mistakes.
[*Lady Windermere's Fan* (1892)]

See **HISTORY, PAST**

FACTS

BARRIE, Sir J.M. (1860–1937)
Facts were never pleasing to him. He acquired them with reluctance and got rid of them with relief. He was never on terms with them until he had stood them on their heads.
[*The Greenwood Hot* (1937)]

BURNS, Robert (1759–1796)
But facts are chiels that winna ding,
And downa be disputed.
['A Dream' (1786)]

DOYLE, Sir Arthur Conan (1859–1930)
'I should have more faith,' he said; 'I ought to know by this time that when a fact appears opposed to a long train of deductions it invariably proves to be capable of bearing some other interpretation.'
[*A Study in Scarlet* (1887)]

HUXLEY, Aldous (1894–1963)
Facts do not cease to exist because they are ignored.
[*Proper Studies* (1927)]

JAMES, Henry (1843–1916)
The fatal futility of Fact.
[*Prefaces* (1897)]

RYLE, Gilbert (1900-1976)
A myth is, of course, not a fairy story. It is the presentation of facts belonging to one category in the idioms appropriate to another. To explode a myth is accordingly not to deny the facts but to re-allocate them.
[*The Concept of Mind* (1949)]

See **TRUTH**

FAILURE

CIANO, Count Galeazzo (1903-1944)
As always, victory finds a hundred fathers, but defeat is an orphan.
[*Diary*, 1942]

COWARD, Sir Noël (1899-1973)
(On Randolph Churchill)
Dear Randolph, utterly unspoiled by failure.
[Attr.]

HARE, Augustus (1792-1834)
Half the failures in life arise from pulling in one's horse as he is leaping.
[*Guesses at Truth* (1827)]

HELLER, Joseph (1923-1999)
He was a self-made man who owed his lack of success to nobody.
[*Catch-22* (1961)]

HEMINGWAY, Ernest (1898-1961)
But man is not made for defeat ... A man can be destroyed but not defeated.
[*The Old Man and the Sea* (1952)]

KEATS, John (1795-1821)
I would sooner fail than not be among the greatest.
[Letter to James Hessey, 1818]

NEWMAN, Paul (1925-2008)
Show me a good loser and I'll show you a loser.
[*The Observer*, 1982]

SHAKESPEARE, William (1564-1616)
Macbeth: If we should fail? Lady Macbeth: We fail!
But screw your courage to the sticking place, And we'll not fail.
[*Macbeth*, I.vii]

WILDE, Oscar (1854-1900)
We women adore failures. They lean on us.
[*A Woman of No Importance* (1893)]

See **SUCCESS**

FAME

ALLEN, Fred (1894-1956)
A celebrity is a person who works hard all his life to become known, then wears dark glasses to avoid being recognized.
[Attr.]

BERNERS, Lord (1883-1950)
(Of T.E. Lawrence)
He's always backing into the limelight.
[Attr.]

BOORSTIN, Daniel J (1914-2004)
The celebrity is a person who is known for his well-knownness.
[*The Image* (1962)]

BYRON, Lord (1788-1824)
(Remark on the instantaneous success of Childe Harold)
I awoke one morning and found myself famous.
[In Moore, *Letters and Journals of Lord Byron* (1830)]

CAINE, Sir Michael (1933-)
Rich and famous people can't be friends with unknowns. I had to dump all mine. You go to dinner with them and you never know when they are going to ask you for something.
[*The Sunday Times*, July 2001]

CALDERÓN DE LA BARCA, Pedro (1600-1681)
Fame, like water, bears up the lighter things, and lets the weighty sink.
[Attr.]

CATO THE ELDER (234-149 BC)
I would much rather have men ask why I have no statue than why I have one.
[In Plutarch, *Lives*]

CURTIS, Tony (1925-2010)
It is like having a kind of Alzheimer's disease where everyone knows you and you don't know anyone.
[*The Sunday Times*, April 2001]

GRAINGER, James (c.1721-1766)
What is fame? an empty bubble;
Gold? a transient, shining trouble.
['Solitude' (1755)]

GREENE, Graham (1904-1991)
Fame is a powerful aphrodisiac.
[*Radio Times*, 1964]

HUGO, Victor (1802-1885)
Fame? It's glory in small change.
[*Ruy Blas* (1838)]

HUXLEY, Aldous (1894-1963)
I'm afraid of losing my obscurity.
Genuineness only thrives in the dark. Like
celery.

[*Those Barren Leaves* (1925)]

LEBOWITZ, Fran (1946-)
The best fame is a writer's fame: it's enough
to get a table at a good restaurant, but not
enough that you get interrupted when you
eat.

[*The Observer*, May 1993]

MELBA, Dame Nellie (1861-1931)
(To the editor of the Argus)
I don't care what you say, for me or against
me, but for heaven's sake say something
about me.

[In Thompson, *On Lips of Living Men*]

MONTAIGNE, Michel de (1533-1592)
Fame and tranquillity cannot dwell under the
same roof.

[*Essais* (1580)]

PECK, Gregory (1916-2003)
(On the fact that no-one in a crowded
restaurant recognized him)
If you have to tell them who you are, you
aren't anybody.

[In S. Harris, *Pieces of Eight*]

ROBERTS, Julia (1967-)
Define superstar. It has nothing to do with
the person. I still walk around the
supermarket and buy toilet paper.

[*The Sunday Times*, March 2001]

TACITUS (AD c.56-c.120)
The desire for fame is the last thing to be put
aside, even by the wise.

[*Histories*]

TEMPLE, Shirley (1928-)
I stopped believing in Santa Claus when I was
six. Mother took me to see him in a
department store and he asked for my
autograph.

WARHOL, Andy (c.1926-1987)
In the future everyone will be world famous
for fifteen minutes.

[Catalogue for an exhibition, 1968]

WILDE, Oscar (1854-1900)
There is only one thing in the world worse
than being talked about, and that is not being
talked about.

[*The Picture of Dorian Gray* (1891)]

See **CELEBRITY, REPUTATION**

FAMILIES

BEERBOHM, Sir Max (1872-1956)
They were a tense and peculiar family, the
Oedipuses, weren't they?

[Attr.]

BELLOC, Hilaire (1870-1953)
Mothers of large families (who claim to
common sense)
Will find a Tiger well repays the trouble and
expense.

[*The Bad Child's Book of Beasts* (1896)]

DICKENS, Charles (1812-1870)
Accidents will occur in the best-regulated
families.

[*David Copperfield* (1850)]

ELIZABETH II (1926-)
Like all the best families, we have our share of
eccentricities, of impetuous and wayward
youngsters and of family disagreements.

[*Daily Mail*, October 1989]

HAZLITT, William (1778-1830)
A person may be indebted for a nose or an
eye, for a graceful carriage or a voluble
discourse, to a great-aunt or uncle, whose
existence he has scarcely heard of.

[*London Magazine*, 1821]

HOPE, Anthony (1863-1933)
Good families are generally worse than any
others.

[*The Prisoner of Zenda* (1894)]

JACKSON, Shirley (1919-1965)
It has long been my belief that in times of
great stress, such as a 4-day vacation, the
thin veneer of family wears off almost at
once, and we are revealed in our true
personalities.

[*Raising Demons* (1956)]

JOHN PAUL II (1920-2005)
Treasure your families – the future of
humanity passes by way of the family.

[Speech, 1982]

LEACH, Sir Edmund (1910-1989)
Far from being the basis of the good society,
the family, with its narrow privacy and tawdry
secrets, is the source of all our discontents.

[BBC Reith Lecture, 1967]

LINCOLN, Abraham (1809-1865)
I don't know who my grandfather was; I am
much more concerned to know what his
grandson will be.

[In Gross, *Lincoln's Own Stories*]

FASCISM

MARX, Groucho (1895–1977)
You're a disgrace to our family name of
Wagstaff, if such a thing is possible.
[*Horse Feathers*, film, 1932]

MITCHELL, Julian (1935–)
The sink is the great symbol of the bloodiness
of family life. All life is bad, but family life is
worse.
[*As For as You Can Go* (1963)]

MONTAIGNE, Michel de (1533–1592)
There is scarcely any less trouble in running a
family than in governing an entire state ... and
domestic matters are no less importunate for
being less important.
[*Essais* (1580)]

NASH, Ogden (1902–1971)
One would be in less danger
From the wiles of a stranger
If one's own kin and kith
Were more fun to be with.
['Family Court' (1931)]

POUND, Ezra (1885–1972)
Oh how hideous it is
To see three generations of one house
gathered together!
It is like an old tree with shoots,
And with some branches rotted and falling.
['Commission' (1916)]

**THACKERAY, William Makepeace
(1811–1863)**
If a man's character is to be abused, say what
you will, there's nobody like a relation to do
the business.
[*Vanity Fair* (1848)]

TOLSTOY, Leo (1828–1910)
All happy families resemble one another, but
every unhappy family is unhappy in its own
way.
[*Anna Karenina* (1877)]

WODEHOUSE, P.G. (1881–1975)
It is no use telling me that there are bad
aunts and good aunts. At the core they are all
alike. Sooner or later, out pops the cloven
hoof.
[*The Code of the Woosters* (1938)]

See **ANCESTORS, BIRTH, CHILDREN,
FATHERS, MARRIAGE, MOTHERS,
PREGNANCY**

FASCISM

BERLUSCONI, Silvio (1936–)
Mussolini never killed anyone, he just sent
dissenters abroad for a vacation.
[*La voce de Rimini*, 2003]

BEVAN, Aneurin (1897–1960)
Fascism is not in itself a new order of society.
It is the future refusing to be born.
[Attr.]

**IBÁRRURI, Dolores ('La Pasionaria')
(1895–1989)**
Wherever they pass, they [the fascists] sow
death and desolation.
[*Speeches and Articles* (1938)]

MCKENNEY, Ruth (1911–1972)
If modern civilisation had any meaning it was
displayed in the fight against Fascism.
[In Seldes, *The Great Quotations* (1960)]

MOSLEY, Sir Oswald (1896–1980)
Before the organization of the Blackshirt
movement free speech did not exist in this
country.
[In *New Statesman*, *This England*]

MUSSOLINI, Benito (1883–1945)
(On Hitler's seizing power)
Fascism is a religion; the twentieth century
will be known in history as the century of
Fascism.
[In Seldes, *Sawdust Caesar*]

PLATH, Sylvia (1932–1963)
Every woman adores a Fascist,
The boot in the face, the brute
Brute heart of a brute like you.
['Daddy' (1963)]

FASHION

AUSTEN, Jane (1775–1817)
A person and face, of strong, natural, sterling
insignificance, though adorned in the first
style of fashion.
[*Sense and Sensibility* (1811)]

BAILEY, David (1938–)
I never cared for fashion much, amusing little
seams and witty little pleats: it was the girls I
liked.
[*The Independent*, November 1990]

BEATON, Cecil (1904–1980)
(On the miniskirt)
Never in the history of fashion has so little
material been raised so high to reveal so
much that needs to be covered so badly.

CASSINI, Oleg (1913–2006)
Fashion anticipates, and elegance is a state of mind.

[*In My Own Fashion* (1987)]

CHANEL, Coco (1883–1971)
(Remark at a press conference, 1967)
Fashion is reduced to a question of hem lengths. Haute couture is finished because it's in the hands of men who don't like women.

[In Madsen, *Coco Chanel* (1990)]

CIBBER, Colley (1671–1757)
One had as good be out of the world, as out of the fashion.

[*Love's Last Shift* (1696)]

RADNER, Gilda (1946–1989)
I base most of my fashion taste on what doesn't itch.

[*It's Always Something* (1989)]

See **APPEARANCE, STYLE**

FATHERS

THE BIBLE
(King James Version)
The fathers have eaten sour grapes, and the children's teeth are set on edge.

[*Ezekiel*, 18:2]

BURTON, Robert (1577–1640)
Diogenes struck the father when the son swore.

[*Anatomy of Melancholy* (1621)]

CHESTERFIELD, Lord (1694–1773)
As fathers commonly go, it is seldom a misfortune to be fatherless; and considering the general run of sons, as seldom a misfortune to be childless.

[Attr.]

CODE NAPOLÉON
Investigations into paternity are forbidden.

[Article 340]

RUSSELL, Bertrand (1872–1970)
The fundamental defect of fathers is that they want their children to be a credit to them.

[Attr.]

SHAKESPEARE, William (1564–1616)
It is a wise father that knows his own child.

[*The Merchant of Venice*, II.ii]

TENNYSON, Alfred (Lord) (1809–1892)
How many a father have I seen,
A sober man, among his boys,
Whose youth was full of foolish noise.

[*In Memoriam A. H. H.* (1850)]

TURNBULL, Margaret (1872–1942)
No man is responsible for his father. That is entirely his mother's affair.

[*Alabaster Lamps* (1925)]

TWAIN, Mark (1835–1910)
When I was a boy of 14 my father was so ignorant I could hardly stand to have the old man around. But when I got to be 21, I was astonished at how much he had learned in seven years.

[In Mackay, *The Harvest of a Quiet Eye* (1977)]

See **CHILDREN, FAMILIES, MOTHERS**

FEAR

ALLEN, Woody (1935–)
I'm really a timid person – I was beaten up by Quakers.

[*Sleeper*, film, 1973]

BOWEN, Elizabeth (1899–1973)
Proust has pointed out that the predisposition to love creates its own objects: is this not true of fear?

[*Collected Impressions* (1950)]

CERVANTES, Miguel de (1547–1616)
Fear has many eyes and can see things which are underground.

[*Don Quixote* I (1605)]

CHURCHILL, Sir Winston (1874–1965)
When I look back on all these worries I remember the story of the old man who said on his deathbed that he had had a lot of trouble in his life, most of which had never happened.

[*Their Finest Hour*]

CURIE, Marie (1867–1934)
Nothing in life is to be feared, it is only to be understood. Now is the time to understand more, so that we may fear less.

[Attr.]

DELANEY, Shelagh (1939–2011)
I'm not frightened of the darkness outside. It's the darkness inside houses I don't like.

[*A Taste of Honey* (1959)]

FOCH, Ferdinand (1851–1929)
None but a coward dares to boast that he has never known fear.

[Attr.]

PARRIS, Matthew (1949–)
Terror of discovery and fear of reproval slip into our unconscious minds during infancy and remain there forever, always potent, usually unacknowledged.

[*The Spectator*, 1996]

PLATO (c.429–347 BC)
Nothing in the affairs of men is worthy of great anxiety.
[*Republic*]

ROOSEVELT, Franklin Delano (1882–1945)
The only thing we have to fear is fear itself.
[First Inaugural Address, 1933]

SHAW, George Bernard (1856–1950)
There is only one universal passion: fear.
[*The Man of Destiny* (1898)]

STEPHENS, James (1882–1950)
Curiosity will conquer fear even more than bravery will.
[*The Crock of Gold* (1912)]

THOMAS, Lewis (1913–1993)
Worrying is the most natural and spontaneous of all human functions. It is time to acknowledge this, perhaps even to learn to do it better.
[*More Notes of a Biology Watcher*]

VOLTAIRE (1694–1778)
Fear follows crime, and is its punishment.
[*Sémiramis* (1748)]

See **DEATH**

FEMINISM

ANTHONY, Susan B. (1820–1906)
Men their rights and nothing more; women their rights and nothing less.
[*Motto of The Revolution*, 1868]

ATKINSON, Ti-Grace (c.1938–)
Feminism is the theory: lesbianism is the practice.
[Attr. in *Amazons, Bluestockings and Crones: A Feminist Dictionary*]

BROWN, Arnold (1936–)
Uncle Harry was an early feminist ... Our family would often recount how, at a race-meeting in Ayr, he threw himself under a suffragette.
[*Are You Looking at Me, Jimmy?*]

BURCHILL, Julie (1960–)
The freedom that women were supposed to have found in the Sixties largely boiled down to easy contraception and abortion; things to make life easier for men, in fact.
[*Born again Cows* (1986)]
A good part – and definitely the most fun part – of being a feminist is about frightening men.
[*Time Out*, November 1989]

FAUST, Beatrice Eileen (1939–)
If the women's movement can be summed up in a single phrase, it is 'the right to choose'.
[*Women, Sex and Pornography* (1980)]

FOURIER, François Charles Marie (1772–1837)
The extension of women's privileges is the basic principle of all social progress.
[*Théorie des Quatre Mouvements* (1808)]

GREER, Germaine (1939–)
If women understand by emancipation the adoption of the masculine role then we are lost indeed.
[*The Female Eunuch* (1970)]

JOHNSTON, Jill (1929–2010)
Feminists who still sleep with men are delivering their most vital energies to the oppressor.
[*Lesbian Nation: The Feminist Solution* (1973)]
No one should have to dance backwards all their life.
[In Miles, *The Women's History of the World* (1988)]

KEY, Ellen (1849–1926)
The emancipation of women is practically the greatest egoistic movement of the nineteenth century, and the most intense affirmation of the right of the self that history has yet seen.
[*The Century of the Child* (1909)]

LOOS, Anita (1893–1981)
I'm furious about the Women's Liberationists. They keep getting up on soapboxes and proclaiming that women are brighter than men. That's true, but it should be kept very quiet or it ruins the whole racket.
[*The Observer*, 1973]

MARTINEAU, Harriet (1802–1876)
Is it to be understood that the principles of the Declaration of Independence bear no relation to half of the human race?
[*Society in America* (1837)]

O'BRIEN, Edna (1930–)
The vote, I thought, means nothing to women. We should be armed.
[In Erica Jong, *Fear of Flying* (1973)]

ORBACH, Susie (1946–)
Fat is a Feminist Issue.
[Title of book, 1978]

PAGLIA, Camille (1947–)
Women and children first is an unscientific sentimentality which must be opposed.
[*The Observer*, 1998]

PANKHURST, Dame Christabel (1880–1958)
We are here to claim our right as women, not only to be free, but to fight for freedom. It is our privilege, as well as our pride and our joy, to take some part in this militant movement, which, as we believe, means the regeneration of all humanity.
[Speech, 1911]

SHAW, George Bernard (1856–1950)
Give women the vote, and in five years there will be a crushing tax on bachelors.
[*Man and Superman* (1903)]

SOLANAS, Valerie (1940–1998)
(SCUM (Society for Cutting Up Men), manifesto, 1968)
Every man, deep down, knows he's a worthless piece of shit.
[In Bassnett, *Feminist Experiences: The Women's Movement in Four Cultures* (1986)]

STEINEM, Gloria (1934–)
Some of us have become the men we wanted to marry.
[*The Observer*, 1982]

TWEEDIE, Jill (1936–1993)
I blame the women's movement for ten years in a boiler suit.
[Attr.]

WELDON, Fay (1931–)
There has to be a halt in the gender war and feminism must extend its remit to include the rights of men.
[*The Observer*, 1998]

WHITTLESEY, Faith (1939–)
Remember, Ginger Rogers did everything Fred Astaire did, but she did it backwards and in high heels.

WOLLSTONECRAFT, Mary (1759–1797)
(Of women)
I do not wish them to have power over men; but over themselves.
[*A Vindication of the Rights of Woman* (1792)]

See **EQUALITY, MEN AND WOMEN, WOMEN**

FICTION

ALDISS, Brian (1925–)
Science fiction is no more written for scientists than ghost stories are written for ghosts.
[*Penguin Science Fiction* (1961)]

CECIL, Lord David (1902–1986)
It does not matter that Dickens' world is not lifelike: it is alive.
[*Early Victorian Novelists* (1934)]

CHANDLER, Raymond (1888–1959)
When I started out to write fiction I had the great disadvantage of having absolutely no talent for it … If more than two people were on scene I couldn't keep one of them alive.
[Letter to Paul Brooks, 1949]

CHESTERTON, G.K. (1874–1936)
A good novel tells us the truth about its hero; but a bad novel tells us the truth about its author.
[*Heretics* (1905)]

DAVISON, Frank Dalby (1893–1970)
You need a skin as thin as a cigarette paper to write a novel and the hide of an elephant to publish it.
[*Meanjin*, 1982]

DISRAELI, Benjamin (1804–1881)
When I want to read a novel I write one.
[Attr.]

GIBBON, Edward (1737–1794)
The romance of Tom Jones, that exquisite picture of human manners, will outlive the palace of the Escurial and the imperial eagle of the house of Austria.
[*Memoirs of My Life and Writings* (1796)]

LARKIN, Philip (1922–1985)
(Referring to modern novels)
Far too many relied on the classic formula of a beginning, a muddle, and an end.
[*New Fiction*, 1978]

LAWRENCE, D.H. (1885–1930)
The novel is the one bright book of life.
[*Phoenix* (1936)]

NABOKOV, Vladimir (1899–1977)
A novelist is, like all mortals, more fully at home on the surface of the present than in the ooze of the past.
[*Strong Opinions* (1973)]

SHAW, George Bernard (1856–1950)
It is clear that a novel cannot be too bad to be worth publishing … It certainly is possible for a novel to be too good to be worth publishing.
[*Plays Pleasant and Unpleasant* (1898)]

STENDHAL (1783–1842)
A novel is a mirror walking along a wide road.
[*Le Rouge et le Noir* (1830)]

THEROUX, Paul (1941–)
Fiction gives us a second chance that life
denies us.
[*New York Times*, July 1976]

WILDE, Oscar (1854–1900)
The good ended happily, and the bad
unhappily. That is what Fiction means.
[*The Importance of Being Earnest* (1895)]

WOOLF, Virginia (1882–1941)
A woman must have money and a room of
her own if she is to write fiction.
[*A Room of One's Own* (1929)]

See **BOOKS, LITERATURE, WRITERS,
WRITING**

FLATTERY

AUSTEN, Jane (1775–1817)
It is happy for you that you possess the talent
of flattering with delicacy. May I ask whether
these pleasing attentions proceed from the
impulse of the moment, or are the result of
previous study?
[*Pride and Prejudice* (1813)]

BIERCE, Ambrose (1842–c.1914)
Flatter: To impress another with a sense of
one's own merit.
[*The Enlarged Devil's Dictionary* (1961)]

DISRAELI, Benjamin (1804–1881)
(To Queen Victoria)
We authors, Ma'am.
[Attr.]

FONTAINE, Jean de la (1621–1695)
My dear Monsieur, know that every flatterer
lives at the expense of the one who listens to
him.
['Le corbeau et le renard']

HALIFAX, Lord (1633–1695)
It is flattering some Men to endure them.
['Of Company' (1750)]

SHAW, George Bernard (1856–1950)
What really flatters a man is that you think
him worth flattering.
[*John Bull's Other Island* (1907)]

See **PRAISE**

FLYING

EARHART, Amelia (1898–1937)
Flying might not be all plain sailing, but the
fun of it is worth the price.
[*The Fun of It* (1932)]

**ELIZABETH (the Queen Mother)
(1900–2002)**
(On her love of helicopters)
The chopper has changed my life as
conclusively as that of Anne Boleyn.
[*The Guardian*, August 2000]

WELLES, Orson (1915–1985)
There are only two emotions in a plane:
boredom and terror.
[*The Times*, May 1985]

FOOD

ATWOOD, Margaret (1939–)
Eating is our earliest metaphor, preceding our
consciousness of gender difference, race,
nationality, and language. We eat before we
talk.
[*The CanLit Foodbook: From Pen to Palate –
A Collection of Tasty Literary Fare* (1987)]

BAREHAM, Lindsey (1948–)
Good mashed potato is one of the great
luxuries of life and I don't blame Elvis for
eating it every night for the last year of his life.
[*In Praise of the Potato* (1989)]

BRILLAT-SAVARIN, Anthelme (1755–1826)
Tell me what you eat and I will tell you what
you are.
[*Physiologie du Goût* (1825)]

CERVANTES, Miguel de (1547–1616)
Hunger is the best sauce in the world.
[*Don Quixote* (1615)]

DAHL, Roald (1916–1990)
Do you know what breakfast cereal is made
of? It's made of all those little curly wooden
shavings you find in pencil sharpeners!
[*Charlie and the Chocolate Factory* (1964)]

DAVID, Elizabeth (1913–1992)
To eat figs off the tree in the very early
morning, when they have been barely
touched by the sun, is one of the exquisite
pleasures of the Mediterranean.
[*Italian Food* (1954)]

DAVIES, David (1742–1819)
Though the potato is an excellent root,
deserving to be brought into general use, yet
it seems not likely that the use of it should
ever be normal in the country.
[*The Case of the Labourers in Husbandry* (1795)]

DE VRIES, Peter (1910–1993)
Gluttony is an emotional escape, a sign
something is eating us.
[*Comfort me with Apples* (1956)]

FADIMAN, Clifton (1904–1999)
Cheese – milk's leap toward immortality.
[*Any Number Can Play* (1957)]

FRANKLIN, Benjamin (1706–1790)
To lengthen thy life, lessen thy meals.
[*Poor Richard's Almanac* (1733)]

FULLER, Thomas (1608–1661)
He was a very valiant man who first ventured
on eating of oysters.
[*The History of the Worthies of England* (1662)]

GARFIELD, James A. (1831–1881)
Man cannot live by bread alone; he must have
peanut butter.
[Inaugural address, 4 March 1881]

GROENING, Matt (1954–)
Groundskeeper Willie: Get yer haggis right
here! Chopped heart and lungs, boiled in a
wee sheep's stomach! Tastes as good as it
sounds!
[*The Simpsons*, TV cartoon series]

HERBERT, George (1593–1633)
A cheerful look makes a dish a feast.
[*Jacula Prudentum* (1640)]

JOHNSON, Samuel (1709–1784)
I look upon it, that he who does not mind his
belly will hardly mind anything else.
[In Boswell, *The Life of Samuel Johnson* (1791)]

LAWSON, Nigella (1960–)
Diets are like boyfriends – it never really works
to go back to them.
[*Sunday Times*, 2006]

LEBOWITZ, Fran (1946–)
Food is an important part of a balanced diet.
[*Metropolitan Life* (1978)]

LUTYENS, Sir Edwin Landseer (1869–1944)
(Comment made in a restaurant)
This piece of cod passes all understanding.
[In Robert Lutyens, *Sir Edwin Lutyens* (1942)]

MCCARTNEY, Linda (1941–1998)
I don't eat anything with a face.
[BBC News Online, obituary, 1998]

MOLIÈRE (1622–1673)
One should eat to live, not live to eat.
[*L'Avare* (1669)]

MONROE, Marilyn (1926–1962)
(On having matzo balls for supper at Arthur
Miller's parents)
Isn't there another part of the matzo you can
eat?
[Attr.]

PETER, Laurence J. (1919–1990)
The noblest of all dogs is the hot-dog; it feeds
the hand that bites it.
[*Quotations for Our Time* (1977)]

PIGGY, Miss
Never eat anything at one sitting that you
can't lift.
[*Woman's Hour*, 1992]

POPE, Alexander (1688–1744)
Fame is at best an unperforming cheat;
But 'tis substantial happiness, to eat.
['Prologue for Mr D'Urfey's Last Play' (1727)]

ROUSSEAU, Émile (1929–)
Great eaters of meat are in general more cruel
and ferocious than other men. The English
are known for their cruelty.
[Attr.]

SECOMBE, Sir Harry (1921–2001)
My advice if you insist on slimming: Eat as
much as you like – just don't swallow it.
[*Daily Herald*, 1962]

SHAKESPEARE, William (1564–1616)
Methinks sometimes I have no more wit than
a Christian or an ordinary man has; but I am a
great eater of beef, and I believe that does
harm to my wit.
[*Twelfth Night*, I.iii]

SHAW, George Bernard (1856–1950)
There is no love sincerer than the love of food.
[*Man and Superman* (1903)]

VOLTAIRE (1694–1778)
(On learning that coffee was considered a
slow poison)
I think it must be so, for I have been drinking
it for sixty-five years and I am not dead yet.
[Attr.]

WEBSTER, John (c.1580–c.1625)
I saw him even now going the way of all flesh,
that is to say towards the kitchen.
[*Westward Hoe* (1607)]

WODEHOUSE, P.G. (1881–1975)
The lunches of fifty-seven years had caused
his chest to slip down to the mezzanine floor.
[*The Heart of a Goof* (1926)]

See **COOKERY, DINING, VEGETARIANISM**

FOOLISHNESS

BARNUM, Phineas T. (1810–1891)
There's a sucker born every minute.
[Attr.]

BEECHER, Henry Ward (1813–1887)
(On receiving a note containing only one word: 'Fool')
I have known many an instance of a man writing a letter and forgetting to sign his name, but this is the only instance I have ever known of a man signing his name and forgetting to write the letter.
[Attr.]

BLAKE, William (1757–1827)
If the fool would persist in his folly he would become wise.
['Proverbs of Hell' (1793)]

COWPER, William (1731–1800)
A fool must now and then be right, by chance.
['Conversation' (1782)]

FIELDING, Henry (1707–1754)
One fool at least in every married couple.
[Amelia (1751)]

FRANKLIN, Benjamin (1706–1790)
Experience keeps a dear school, but fools will learn in no other.
[Poor Richard's Almanac (1743)]

HORACE (65–8 BC)
Mix a little folly with your plans: it is sweet to be silly at the right moment.
[Odes]

IBSEN, Henrik (1828–1906)
Fools are in a terrible, overwhelming majority, all the wide world over.
[An Enemy of the People (1882)]

MOLIÈRE (1622–1673)
The greatest folly of all is wanting to busy oneself in setting the world to rights.
[Le Misanthrope (1666)]

POPE, Alexander (1688–1744)
For Fools rush in where Angels fear to tread.
[An Essay on Criticism (1711)]

ROWLAND, Helen (1875–1950)
The follies which a man regrets most in his life are those which he didn't commit when he had the opportunity.
[A Guide to Men (1922)]

SCHILLER, Johann Christoph Friedrich (1759–1805)
Gods themselves struggle in vain with stupidity.
[The Maid of Orleans (1801)]

SHAKESPEARE, William (1564–1616)
He uses his folly like a stalking-horse, and under the presentation of that he shoots his wit.
[As You Like It, V.iv]

STEVENSON, Robert Louis (1850–1894)
For God's sake give me the young man who has brains enough to make a fool of himself!
[Virginibus Puerisque (1881)]

SWIFT, Jonathan (1667–1745)
Hated by fools, and fools to hate,
Be that my motto and my fate.
['To Mr Delany' (1718)]

THOREAU, Henry David (1817–1862)
Any fool can make a rule and every fool will mind it.
[Attr.]

TUSSER, Thomas (c.1524–1580)
A fool and his money be soon at debate.
[Five Hundred Points of Good Husbandry (1557)]

YOUNG, Edward (1683–1765)
Be wise with speed;
A fool at forty is a fool indeed.
[Love of Fame, the Universal Passion (1728)]

See **IGNORANCE, STUPIDITY**

FORCE

ASIMOV, Isaac (1920–1992)
Violence is the last refuge of the incompetent.
[Foundation (1951)]

BRIEN, Alan (1925–2008)
Violence is the repartee of the illiterate.
[Punch, 1973]

BRIGHT, John (1811–1889)
Force is not a remedy.
[Speech, 1880]

BRONOWSKI, Jacob (1908–1974)
The wish to hurt, the momentary intoxication with pain, is the loophole through which the pervert climbs into the minds of ordinary men.
[The Face of Violence (1954)]

BURKE, Edmund (1729–1797)
The use of force alone is but temporary. It may subdue for a moment; but it does not remove the necessity of subduing again: and a nation is not governed, which is perpetually to be conquered.
[Speech on Conciliation with America (1775)]

FONTAINE, Jean de la (1621–1695)
The reason of the strongest is always the best.
['Le loup et l'agneau']

HORACE (65–8 BC)
Brute force without judgement collapses under its own weight.
[Odes]

INGE, William Ralph (1860–1954)
A man may build himself a throne of bayonets, but he cannot sit upon it.
[*Philosophy of Plotinus* (1923)]

KING, Martin Luther (1929–1968)
A riot is at bottom the language of the unheard.
[*Chaos or Community* (1967)]

ROOSEVELT, Theodore (1858–1919)
There is a homely old adage which runs, 'Speak softly and carry a big stick; you will go far.'
[Speech, 1903]

See **POWER, VIOLENCE**

FOREIGNERS

CRISP, Quentin (1908–1999)
I don't hold with abroad and think that foreigners speak English when our backs are turned.
[*The Naked Civil Servant* (1968)]

ERASMUS (c.1466–1536)
Is not the Turk a man and a brother?
[*Querela Pacis*]

MEYNELL, Hugo (1727–1780)
For anything I see, foreigners are fools.
[In Boswell, *The Life of Samuel Johnson* (1791)]

MITFORD, Nancy (1904–1973)
Abroad is unutterably bloody and foreigners are fiends.
[*The Pursuit of Love* (1945)]

TROLLOPE, Anthony (1815–1882)
We cannot bring ourselves to believe it possible that a foreigner should in any respect be wiser than ourselves. If any such point out to us our follies, we at once claim those follies as the special evidences of our wisdom.
[*Orley Farm* (1862)]

TWAIN, Mark (1835–1910)
They spell it Vinci and pronounce it Vinchy; foreigners always spell better than they pronounce.
[*The Innocents Abroad* (1869)]

See **TRAVEL**

FORGETTING

BROWNE, Sir Thomas (1605–1682)
Oblivion is a kind of Annihilation.
[*Christian Morals* (1716)]

CALVERLEY, C.S. (1831–1884)
I cannot sing the old songs now!
It is not that I deem them low;
'Tis that I can't remember how
They go.
['Changed' (1872)]

DISRAELI, Benjamin (1804–1881)
Nobody is forgotten when it is convenient to remember him.
[Attr.]

MARX, Groucho (1895–1977)
I never forget a face, but I'll make an exception in your case.
[*The Guardian*, 1965]

STEVENSON, Robert Louis (1850–1894)
I've a grand memory for forgetting, David.
[*Kidnapped* (1886)]

SVEVO, Italo (1861–1928)
There are three things I always forget. Names, faces and – the third I can't remember.
[Attr.]

See **MEMORY**

FORGIVENESS

AUSTEN, Jane (1775–1817)
You ought certainly to forgive them as a Christian, but never to admit them in your sight, or allow their names to be mentioned in your hearing.
[*Pride and Prejudice* (1813)]

**THE BIBLE
(King James Version)**
Father, forgive them; for they know not what they do.
[*Luke*, 23:34]

BROWNING, Robert (1812–1889)
Good, to forgive;
Best, to forget!
Living, we fret;
Dying, we live.
[*La Saisiaz* (1878)]

DIETRICH, Marlene (1901–1992)
Once a woman has forgiven her man, she must not reheat his sins for breakfast.
[*Marlene Dietrich's ABC* (1962)]

DRYDEN, John (1631–1700)
Forgiveness to the injured does belong;
But they ne'er pardon, who have done the wrong.
[*The Conquest of Granada* (1670)]

FROST, Robert (1874–1963)
Forgive, O Lord, my little jokes on Thee
And I'll forgive Thy great big one on me.
['Cluster of Faith' (1962)]

GAY, John (1685–1732)
Well, Polly; as far as one woman can forgive
another, I forgive thee.
[*The Beggar's Opera* (1728)]

HEINE, Heinrich (1797–1856)
We should forgive our enemies, but only after
they have been hanged first.

KENNEDY, Robert F. (1925–1968)
Always forgive your enemies – but never
forget their names.
[Attr.]

FRANCE

CARLYLE, Thomas (1795–1881)
France was long a despotism tempered by
epigrams.
[*History of the French Revolutian* (1837)]

COWARD, Sir Noël (1899–1973)
There's always something fishy about the
French.
[*Conversatian Piece* (1934)]

DE GAULLE, Charles (1890–1970)
One can only unite the French under the
threat of danger. One cannot simply bring
together a nation that produces 265 kinds of
cheese.
[Speech, 1951]

JOHNSON, Samuel (1709–1784)
A Frenchman must be always talking,
whether he knows anything of the matter or
not; an Englishman is content to say nothing,
when he has nothing to say.
[In Boswell, *The Life of Samuel Jahnson* (1791)]

NAPOLEON I (1769–1821)
France has more need of me than I have need
of France.
[Speech, 1813]

NOVELLO, Ivor (1893–1951)
There's something Vichy about the French.
[In Marsh, *Ambrosia and Small Beer*]

WALPOLE, Horace (1717–1797)
I do not dislike the French from the vulgar
antipathy between neighbouring nations, but
for their insolent and unfounded airs of
superiority.
[Letter, 1787]

WILDER, Billy (1906–2002)
France is a country where the money falls
apart in your hands and you can't tear the
toilet paper.
[In Halliwell, *Filmgoer's Book of Quotes* (1973)]

FREEDOM

ADDISON, Joseph (1672–1719)
A day, an hour of virtuous liberty
Is worth a whole eternity in bondage.
[*Cato* (1713)]

ANONYMOUS
As a general rule, the freedom of any people
can be judged by the volume of their laughter.
[Declaration sent to Pope John XXII by the
Scottish barons]
For so long as but a hundred of us remain
alive, we will in no way yield ourselves to the
dominion of the English. For it is not for glory,
nor riches, nor honour that we fight, but for
Freedom only, which no good man lays down
but with his life.
[Declaration of Arbroath, 1320]

BELL, Clive (1881–1964)
Only reason can convince us of those three
fundamental truths without a recognition of
which there can be no effective liberty: that
what we believe is not necessarily true; that
what we like is not necessarily good; and that
all questions are open.
[*Civilisation* (1928)]

BERLIN, Isaiah (1909–1997)
Liberty is liberty, not equality or fairness or
justice or culture, or human happiness or a
quiet conscience.
[*Four Essays on Liberty* (1969)]

BURKE, Edmund (1729–1797)
Freedom and not servitude is the cure of
anarchy; as religion, and not atheism, is the
true remedy for superstition.
[*Speech on Conciliation with America*
(1775)]
The only liberty I mean, is a liberty connected
with order; that not only exists along with
order and virtue, but which cannot exist at all
without them.
[Speech, 1774]

COLERIDGE, Hartley (1796–1849)
But what is Freedom? Rightly understood,
A universal licence to be good.
['Liberty' (1833)]

CONNOLLY, James (1868-1916)
Apostles of Freedom are ever idolised when dead, but crucified when alive.
[*Workers Republic*, 1898]

CURRAN, John Philpot (1750-1817)
The condition upon which God hath given liberty to man is eternal vigilance; which condition if he break, servitude is at once the consequence of his crime, and the punishment of his guilt.
[Speech, 1790]

DIDEROT, Denis (1713-1784)
Men will never be free until the last king is strangled with the entrails of the last priest.
[*Dithyrambe sur la Fête des Rois*]

ENGELS, Friedrich (1820-1895)
Freedom is the recognition of necessity.
[In Mackay, *The Harvest of a Quiet Eye* (1977)]

EWER, William Norman (1885-1976)
I gave my life for freedom – This I know:
For those who bade me fight had told me so.
['The Souls' (1917)]

HALIFAX, Lord (1633-1695)
Power is so apt to be insolent and Liberty to be saucy, that they are very seldom upon good Terms.
[*Political, Moral and Miscellaneous Thoughts and Reffections* (1750)]

HAZLITT, William (1778-1830)
The love of liberty is the love of others; the love of power is the love of ourselves.
[*Political Essays* (1819)]

HENRY, Patrick (1736-1799)
Give me liberty, or give me death!
[Speech, 1775]

HOFFER, Eric (1902-1983)
When people are free to do as they please, they usually imitate each other.
[*The Passionate State of Mind* (1955)]

JEFFERSON, Thomas (1743-1826)
The tree of liberty must be refreshed from time to time with the blood of patriots and tyrants. It is its natural manure.
[Letter to W.S. Smith, 1787]

KAFKA, Franz (1883-1924)
It's often better to be in chains than to be free.
[*The Trial* (1925)]

KING, Martin Luther (1929-1968)
Free at last, free at last, thank God Almighty, we are free at last!
[Speech, 1963]

KRISTOFFERSON, Kris (1936-)
Freedom's just another word for nothing left to lose.
['Me and Bobby McGee', song, 1969]

LENIN, V.I. (1870-1924)
It is true that liberty is precious – so precious that it must be rationed.
[In Sidney and Beatrice Webb, *Soviet Communism* (1936)]

LINCOLN, Abraham (1809-1865)
Those who deny freedom to others, deserve it not for themselves.
[Speech, 1856]

MACAULAY, Lord (1800-1859)
There is only one cure for the evils which newly acquired freedom produces; and that is freedom.
[*Collected Essays* (1843)]

MALCOLM X (1925-1965)
You can't separate peace from freedom because no one can be at peace unless he has his freedom.
[*Malcolm X Speaks*, 1965]

MANDELA, Nelson (1918-)
I cannot and will not give any undertaking at a time when I, and you, the people, are not free. Your freedom and mine cannot be separated.
[Message to a rally in Soweto, 1985]

MILL, John Stuart (1806-1873)
The sole end for which mankind are warranted, individually or collectively, in interfering with the liberty of action of any of their number, is self-protection.
[*On Liberty* (1859)]

MILTON, John (1608-1674)
None can love freedom heartilie, but good men; the rest love not freedom, but licence.
[*The Tenure of Kings and Magistrates* (1649)]

MONTESQUIEU, Charles (1689-1755)
Freedom is the right to do whatever the laws permit.
[*De l'esprit des lois* (1748)]

ROLAND, Madame (1754-1793)
(Remark on mounting the scaffold)
O liberty! O liberty! how many crimes are committed in your name!
[In Lamartine, *Histoire des Girondins* (1847)]

ROUSSEAU, Jean-Jacques (1712-1778)
Man was born free, and everywhere he is in chains.
[*Du Contrat Social* (1762)]

SARTRE, Jean-Paul (1905–1980)
Once freedom has exploded in the soul of a man, the gods have no more power over him.
[*The Flies* (1943)]

Man is condemned to be free.
[*Existentialism and Humanism*]

SHAW, George Bernard (1856–1950)
Liberty means responsibility. That is why most men dread it.
[*Man and Superman* (1903)]

SOLZHENITSYN, Alexander (1918–2008)
You only have power over people as long as you don't take everything away from them. But when you've robbed a man of everything he's no longer in your power – he's free again.
[*The First Circle* (1968)]

STEVENSON, Adlai (1900–1965)
My definition of a free society is a society where it is safe to be unpopular.
[Speech, Detroit, 1952]

TWAIN, Mark (1835–1910)
It is by the goodness of God that in our country we have those three unspeakably precious things: freedom of speech, freedom of conscience, and the prudence never to practise either of them.
[*Following the Equator* (1897)]

VOLTAIRE (1694–1778)
Liberty was born in England from the quarrels of tyrants.
[*Lettres philosophiques* (1734)]

WASHINGTON, George (1732–1799)
Liberty, when it begins to take root, is a plant of rapid growth.
[Letter, 1788]

WILSON, Woodrow (1856–1924)
The history of liberty is a history of resistance.
[Speech, 1912]

FRIENDSHIP

ADAMS, Henry (1838–1918)
One friend in a lifetime is much; two are many; three are hardly possible. Friendship needs a certain parallelism of life, a community of thought, a rivalry of aim.
[*The Education of Henry Adams* (1918)]

ARISTOTLE (384–322 BC)
On being asked what is a friend, he said 'A single soul dwelling in two bodies.'
[In Diogenes Laertius, *Lives of Philosophers*]

BACON, Francis (1561–1626)
It is the worst solitude, to have no true friendships.
[*The Advancement of Learning* (1605)]

BELLOC, Hilaire (1870–1953)
From quiet homes and first beginning,
Out to the undiscovered ends,
There's nothing worth the wear of winning,
But laughter and the love of friends.
[*Verses* (1910)]

THE BIBLE
(King James Version)
A faithful friend is a sturdy shelter: he that has found one has found a treasure. There is nothing so precious as a faithful friend, and no scales can measure his excellence.
[*Apocrypha, Ecclesiasticus*]

BIERCE, Ambrose (1842–c.1914)
Antipathy: The sentiment inspired by one's friend's friend.
[*The Enlarged Devil's Dictionary* (1961)]

BRADBURY, Malcolm (1932–2001)
I've noticed your hostility towards him ... I ought to have guessed you were friends.
[*The History Man* (1975)]

BYRON, Lord (1788–1824)
Friendship is Love without his wings.
['L'amitié est l'amour sans ailes' (1806)]

CANNING, George (1770–1827)
Give me the avowed, erect and manly foe;
Firm I can meet, perhaps return the blow;
But of all plagues, good Heaven, thy wrath can send,
Save me, oh, save me, from the candid friend.
['New Morality' (1821)]

COLETTE (1873–1954)
My true friends have always given me that supreme proof of devotion, a spontaneous aversion for the man I loved.
[*Break of Day* (1928)]

COLTON, Charles Caleb (c.1780–1832)
Friendship often ends in love; but love in friendship – never.
[*Lacon* (1820)]

DES HOTEL, Rob and BATALI, Dean
Willow: Well, I like you. You're nice, and you're funny and you don't smoke, and okay, werewolf, but that's not all the time. I mean, three days out of the month I'm not much fun to be around, either.
[*Buffy the Vampire Slayer*, TV series, 1998]

EMERSON, Ralph Waldo (1803–1882)
Let the soul be assured that somewhere in the universe it should rejoin its friend, and it would be content and cheerful alone for a thousand years.
['Friendship' 1841]
The only reward of virtue is virtue; the only way to have a friend is to be one.
['Friendship' (1841)]

JOHNSON, Samuel (1709–1784)
If a man does not make new acquaintance as he advances through life, he will soon find himself left alone. A man, Sir, should keep his friendship in constant repair.
[In Boswell, *The Life of Samuel Johnson* (1791)]
How few of his friends' houses would a man choose to be at when he is sick.
[In Boswell, *The Life of Samuel Johnson* (1791)]

KINGSMILL, Hugh (1889–1949)
Friends are God's apology for relations.
[In Ingrams, *God's Apology* (1977)]

LA ROCHEFOUCAULD (1613–1680)
In the misfortunes of our closest friends, we always find something which is not displeasing to us.
[*Maximes* (1665)]

LEWIS, C.S. (1898–1963)
Friendship is unnecessary, like philosophy, like art. ... It has no survival value; rather it is one of those things that give value to survival.
[*The Four Loves* (c. 1936)]

MEDICI, Cosima de' (1389–1464)
We read that we ought to forgive our enemies; but we do not read that we ought to forgive our friends.
[In Bacon, *Apophthegms* (1625)]

POPE, Alexander (1688–1744)
True friendship's laws are by this rule express'd,
Welcome the coming, speed the parting guest.
[*The Odyssey* (1726)]
How often are we to die before we go quite off this stage? In every friend we lose a part of ourselves, and the best part.
[Letter to Swift, 1732]

SHAKESPEARE, William (1564–1616)
Friendship is constant in all other things
Save in the office and affairs of love.
[*Much Ado About Nothing*, II.i]

TWAIN, Mark (1835–1910)
The holy passion of Friendship is of so sweet and steady and loyal and enduring a nature that it will last through a whole lifetime, if not asked to lend money.
[*Pudd'nhead Wilson's Calendar* (1894)]

VIDAL, Gore (1925–2012)
Whenever a friend succeeds, a little something in me dies.
[*The Sunday Times Magazine*, 1973]

WAUGH, Evelyn (1903–1966)
We cherish our friends not for their ability to amuse us, but for our ability to amuse them.
[Attr.]

WHITMAN, Walt (1819–1892)
I no doubt deserved my enemies, but I don't believe I deserved my friends.
[In Bradford, *Biography and the Human Heart*]

YEATS, W.B. (1865–1939)
Think where man's glory most begins and ends,
And say my glory was I had such friends.
['The Municipal Gallery Revisited' (1937)]

See **ENEMIES**

THE FUTURE

ACHESON, Dean (1893–1971)
Always remember that the future comes one day at a time.
[*Sketches From Life*]

BALDWIN, James (1924–1987)
The future is ... black.
[*The Observer*, 1963]

BENJAMIN, Walter (1892–1940)
He who asks fortune-tellers the future unwittingly forfeits an inner intimation of coming events that is a thousand times more exact than anything they may say.
[*One-Way Street* (1928)]

BERRA, Yogi (1925–)
The future ain't what it used to be.
[Attr.]

BIERCE, Ambrose (1842–c.1914)
Future: That period of time in which our affairs prosper, our friends are true and our happiness is assured.
[*The Cynic's Word Book* (1906)]

CAMUS, Albert (1913–1960)
The future is the only kind of property that the masters willingly concede to slaves.
[*The Rebel* (1951)]

CHURCHILL, Sir Winston (1874-1965)
The empires of the future are empires of the mind.
[Speech, 1943]

CLARK, Lord Kenneth (1903-1983)
One may be optimistic, but one can't exactly be joyful at the prospect before us.
[End of TV series, *Civilization*]

COLERIDGE, Samuel Taylor (1772-1834)
Often do the spirits
Of great events stride on before the events,
And in to-day already walks tomorrow.
['Death of Wallenstein' (1800)]

CONFUCIUS (c.550-c.478 BC)
Study the past, if you would divine the future.
[*Analects*]

COWARD, Sir Noël (1899-1973)
I don't give a hoot about posterity. Why should I worry about what people think of me when I'm dead as a doornail anyway?
[*Present Laughter* (1943)]

CRISP, Quentin (1908-1999)
I still lived in the future – a habit which is the death of happiness.
[*The Naked Civil Servant* (1968)]

DIX, Dorothy (1870-1951)
I have learned to live each day as it comes, and not to borrow trouble by dreading tomorrow. It is the dark menace of the future that makes cowards of us.
[*Dorothy Dix, Her Book* (1926)]

EINSTEIN, Albert (1879-1955)
I never think of the future. It comes soon enough.
[Interview, 1930]

HUGO, Victor (1802-1885)
In the twentieth century, war will be dead, the scaffold will be dead, hatred will be dead, frontier boundaries will be dead, dogmas will be dead; man will live. He will possess something higher than all these – a great country, the whole earth, and a great hope, the whole heaven.
[*The Future of Man*]

JOHNSON, Samuel (1709-1784)
The future is purchased by the present.
[Attr.]

KAY, Alan (1940-)
The best way of predicting the future is to invent it.
[Attr.]

LEWIS, C.S. (1898-1963)
The Future is something which everyone reaches at the rate of sixty minutes an hour, whatever he does, whoever he is.
[*The Screwtape Letters* (1942)]

MAUGHAM, William Somerset (1874-1965)
It is bad enough to know the past; it would be intolerable to know the future.
[In R. Hughes *Foreign Devil* (1972)]

MITCHELL, Margaret (1900-1949)
After all, tomorrow is another day.
[*Gone with the Wind* (1936)]

ORWELL, George (1903-1950)
If you want a picture of the future, imagine a boot stamping on a human face – for ever.
[*Nineteen Eighty-Four* (1949)]

PROUST, Marcel (1871-1922)
What we call our future is the shadow which our past throws in front of us.
[*A l'ombre des jeunes filles en fleurs* (1918)]

QUAYLE, Dan (1947-)
The future will be better tomorrow.
[Attr.]

STEFFENS, Lincoln (1866-1936)
(Remark after visiting Russia in 1919)
I have seen the future; and it works.
[Letter to Marie Howe, 1919]

WELL, Simone (1909-1943)
The future is made of the same stuff as the present.
[*On Science, Necessity, and the Love of God*]

WELLS, H.G. (1866-1946)
One thousand years more. That's all Homo sapiens has before him.
[In H. Nicolson, *Diary*]

See **PAST, PRESENT, TIME**

GARDENS

ADDISON, Joseph (1672-1719)
I value my garden more for being full of blackbirds than of cherries, and very frankly give them fruit for their songs.
[*The Spectator*, 1712]

ATWOOD, Margaret (1939-)
Gardening is not a rational act.
[*Bluebeard's Egg* (1986)]

BROWN, Thomas Edward (1830-1897)
A garden is a lovesome thing, God wot!
['My Garden' (1893)]

COWLEY, Abraham (1618-1667)
God the first garden made, and the first city
Cain.
['The Garden' (1668)]

EMERSON, Ralph Waldo (1803-1882)
What is a weed? A plant whose virtues have
not yet been discovered.
[*Fortune of the Republic* (1878)]

GURNEY, Dorothy (1858-1932)
The kiss of the sun for pardon,
The song of the birds for mirth,
One is nearer God's Heart in a garden
Than anywhere else on earth.
['God's Garden' (1913)]

RUSSELL, Bertrand (1872-1970)
Every time I talk to a savant I feel quite sure
that happiness is no longer a possibility. Yet
when I talk to my gardener, I'm convinced of
the opposite.
[Attr.]

SHAKESPEARE, William (1564-1616)
'Tis in ourselves that we are thus or thus. Our
bodies are our gardens to the which our wills
are gardeners.
[*Othello*, I.iii]

SIMMONS, John (1937-)
A weed is simply a plant that you don't want.
[*The Observer*, 1983]

TENNYSON, Alfred (Lord) (1809-1892)
Come into the garden, Maud,
For the black bat, night, has flown,
Come into the garden, Maud,
I am here at the gate alone;
And the woodbine spices are wafted abroad,
And the musk of the rose is blown.
[*Maud* (1855)]

VOLTAIRE (1694-1778)
'That is well said,' replied Candide, 'but we
must cultivate our garden.'
[*Candide* (1759)]

Generosity

BARRIE, Sir J.M. (1860-1937)
Never ascribe to an opponent motives
meaner than your own.
[Address, St Andrews University, 1922]

**THE BIBLE
(King James Version)**
It is more blessed to give than to receive.
[*Acts of the Apostles*, 20:35]
God loveth a cheerful giver.
[*II Corinthians*, 9:7]

CORNEILLE, Pierre (1606-1684)
The manner of giving is worth more than the
gift.
[*Le Menteur* (1643)]

GIBBS, Sir Philip (1877-1962)
It is better to give than to lend, and it costs
about the same.
[Attr.]

**TALLEYRAND, Charles-Maurice de
(1754-1838)**
Don't trust first impulses; they are always
generous.
[Attr.]

See **BENEFACTORS, CHARITY**

Genius

ANONYMOUS
The difference between genius and stupidity
is that genius has its limits.

BEERBOHM, Sir Max (1872-1956)
I have known no man of genius who had not
to pay, in some affliction or defect either
physical or spiritual, for what the gods had
given him.
[*And Even Now* (1920)]

DALI, Salvador (1904-1989)
I'm going to live forever. Geniuses don't die.
[*The Observer*, 1986]

DOYLE, Sir Arthur Conan (1859-1930)
Mediocrity knows nothing higher than itself,
but talent instantly recognizes genius.
[*The Valley of Fear* (1914)]

EDISON, Thomas Alva (1847-1931)
Genius is one per cent inspiration and
ninety-nine per cent perspiration.
[*Life*, 1932]

HAZLITT, William (1778-1830)
Rules and models destroy genius and art.
['Thoughts on Taste' (1818)]

HOPE, Anthony (1863-1933)
Unless one is a genius, it is best to aim at
being intelligible.
[*The Dolly Dialogues* (1894)]

HOPKINS, Jane Ellice (1836-1904)
Gift, like genius, I often think, only means an
infinite capacity for taking pains.
[*Work amongst Working Men*, 1870]

HUBBARD, Elbert (1856–1915)
One machine can do the work of fifty ordinary men. No machine can do the work of one extraordinary man.
[*A Thousand and One Epigrams* (1911)]

KENNEDY, John F. (1917–1963)
(At a dinner held at the White House for Nobel prizewinners)
... probably the greatest concentration of talent and genius in this house, except for perhaps those times when Thomas Jefferson ate alone.
[*New York Times*, 1962]

MEREDITH, Owen (1831–1891)
Genius does what it must, and Talent does what it can.
['Last Words of a Sensitive Second-Rate Poet' (1868)]

SWIFT, Jonathan (1667–1745)
When a true genius appears in the world, you may know him by this sign, that the dunces are all in confederacy against him.
[*Thoughts on Various Subjects* (1711)]

VIDAL, Gore (1925–2012)
(Of Andy Warhol)
A genius with the IQ of a moron.
[*The Observer*, June 1989]

WELLES, Orson (1915–1985)
Everybody denies I am a genius – but nobody ever called me one!
[In *Halliwell's Filmgoers' Companion* (1984)]

WHISTLER, James McNeill (1834–1903)
(Replying to a lady inquiring whether he thought genius hereditary)
I cannot tell you that, madam. Heaven has granted me no offspring.
[In Seitz, *Whistler Stories* (1913)]

WILDE, Oscar (1854–1900)
(Spoken to André Gide)
Do you want to know the great tragedy of my life? I have put all of my genius into my life; all I've put into my works is my talent.
[In Gide, *Oscar Wilde* (1910)]
(At the New York Customs)
I have nothing to declare except my genius.
[In Harris, *Oscar Wilde* (1918)]

See **TALENT**

ALLEN, Fred (1894–1956)
A gentleman is any man who wouldn't hit a woman with his hat on.
[Attr.]

ANONYMOUS
When Adam delved, and Eve span,
Who was then a gentleman?
[Attr. John Ball, 1381]

BURKE, Edmund (1729–1797)
Somebody has said, that a king may make a nobleman but he cannot make a Gentleman.
[Letter to William Smith, 1795]

CHIFLEY, Joseph Benedict (1885–1951)
My experience of gentlemen's agreements is that, when it comes to the pinch, there are rarely enough bloody gentlemen about.
[In Crisp, *Ben Chifley* (1960)]

CURZON, Lord (1859–1925)
Gentlemen do not take soup at luncheon.
[In Woodward, *Short Journey* (1942)]

FURPHY, Joseph (1843–1912)
For there is no such thing as a democratic gentleman; the adjective and the noun are hyphenated by a drawn sword.
[*Such is Life* (1903)]

LINTON, W.J. (1812–1897)
For he is one of Nature's Gentlemen, the best of every time.
[*Nature's Gentleman*]

MATTHEWS, Brander (1852–1929)
A gentleman need not know Latin, but he should at least have forgotten it.
[Attr.]

NELSON, Lord (1758–1805)
(To his midshipmen)
Recollect that you must be a seaman to be an officer; and also, that you cannot be a good officer without being a gentleman.
[In Southey, *The Life of Nelson* (1860)]

NEWMAN, John Henry (Cardinal) (1801–1890)
It is almost a definition of a gentleman to say that he is one who never inflicts pain.
['Knowledge and Religious Duty' (1852)]

SHAW, George Bernard (1856–1950)
I am a gentleman: I live by robbing the poor.
[*Man and Superman* (1903)]

STEVENSON, Robert Louis (1850–1894)
Between the possibility of being hanged in all innocence, and the certainty of a public and merited disgrace, no gentleman of spirit could long hesitate.
[*The Wrong Box* (1889)]

SURTEES, R.S. (1805–1864)
The only infallible rule we know is, that the man who is always talking about being a gentleman never is one.
[*Ask Mamma* (1858)]

GLORY

ANONYMOUS
Sic transit gloria mundi. Thus passes the glory of the world.
[Spoken during the coronation of a new Pope]

BLAKE, William (1757–1827)
The pride of the peacock is the glory of God.
['Proverbs of Hell' (c. 1793)]

BYRON, Lord (1788–1824)
Glory, like the phoenix 'midst her fires,
Exhales her odours, blazes, and expires.
[*English Bards and Scotch Reviewers* (1809)]

CAMPBELL, Thomas (1777–1844)
The combat deepens. On, ye brave,
Who rush to glory, or the grave!
['Hohenlinden']

FONTAINE, Jean de la (1621–1695)
No flowery path leads to glory.
['Les deux aventuriers et le talisman']

GRAY, Thomas (1716–1771)
The boast of heraldry, the pomp of pow'r,
And all that beauty, all that wealth e'er gave,
Awaits alike th' inevitable hour,
The paths of glory lead but to the grave ....
['Elegy Written in a Country Churchyard' (1751)]

SHAKESPEARE, William (1564–1616)
Like madness is the glory of this life.
[*Timon of Athens*, I.ii]

WEBSTER, John (c.1580–c.1625)
Glories, like glow-worms, afar off shine bright,
But, looked too near, have neither heat nor light.
[*The Duchess of Malfi* (1623)]

WORDSWORTH, William (1770–1850)
Not in entire forgetfulness,
And not in utter nakedness,
But trailing clouds of glory do we come
From God, who is our home:
Heaven lies about us in our infancy!
['Ode: Intimations of Immortality' (1807)]

GOALS

BERLIN, Isaiah (1909–1997)
Injustice, poverty, slavery, ignorance – these may be cured by reform or revolution. But men do not live only by fighting evils. They live by positive goals, individual and collective, a vast variety of them, seldom predictable, at times incompatible.
['Political Ideas in the Twentieth Century' (1969)]

KAFKA, Franz (1883–1924)
There is a goal but no way of reaching it; what we call the way is hesitation.
[*Reflections on Sin, Sorrow, Hope and the True Way*]

LONGFELLOW, Henry Wadsworth (1807–1882)
If you would hit the mark, you must aim a little above it;
Every arrow that flies feels the attraction of earth.
['Elegiac Verse' (1880)]

SANTAYANA, George (1863–1952)
Fanaticism consists in redoubling your effort when you have forgotten your aim.
[*The Life of Reason* (1906)]

SIDNEY, Sir Philip (1554–1586)
Who shoots at the midday sun, though he be sure he shall never hit the mark, yet as sure he is he shall shoot higher than who aims but at a bush.
[*New Arcadia* (1590)]

SMITH, Logan Pearsall (1865–1946)
When people come and talk to you of their aspirations, before they leave you had better count your spoons.
[*Afterthoughts* (1931)]

STEVENSON, Robert Louis (1850–1894)
An aspiration is a joy forever.
[*Virginibus Puerisque* (1881)]

See **AMBITION**

GOD

AGATHON (c.445–400 BC)
Even God is deprived of this one thing only:
the power to undo what has been done.
[In Aristotle, *Nicomachean Ethics*]

ALLEN, Woody (1935–)
Not only is there no God, but try getting a
plumber on weekends.
[*Getting Even* (1971)]
The worst that can be said is that he's an
under-achiever.
[*Love and Death*, film, 1976]
If only God would give me some clear sign!
Like making a large deposit in my name at a
Swiss bank.
[*Without Feathers* (1976)]

BALDWIN, James (1924–1987)
If the concept of God has any validity or any
use, it can only be to make us larger, freer,
and more loving. If God cannot do this, then it
is time we got rid of Him.
[*The Fire Next Time* (1963)]

THE BIBLE
(King James Version)
In the beginning God created the heaven and
the earth.
And the earth was without form, and void;
and darkness was upon the face of the deep.
And the Spirit of God moved upon the face of
the waters.
And God said, Let there be light: and there
was light.
[*Genesis*, 1:1–3]
For the Lord seeth not as man seeth: for man
looketh on the outward appearance, but the
Lord looketh on the heart.
[*I Samuel*, 16:7]
God is a Spirit: and they that worship him
must worship him in spirit and in truth.
[*John*, 4:24]

BONHOEFFER, Dietrich (1906–1945)
In all important questions, man has learned
to cope without recourse to God as a working
hypothesis.
[Letter to a friend, 1944]

BROOKE, Rupert (1887–1915)
Because God put His adamantine fate
Between my sullen heart and its desire,
I swore that I would burst the Iron Gate,
Rise up, and curse Him on His throne of fire.
['Failure' (1905–1908)]

BROWNING, Elizabeth Barrett (1806–1861)
God answers sharp and sudden on some
prayers,
And thrusts the thing we have prayed for in
our face,
A gauntlet with a gift in't.
[*Aurora Leigh* (1857)]

COWPER, William (1731–1800)
God moves in a mysterious way
His wonders to perform;
He plants his footsteps in the sea,
And rides upon the storm.
[*Olney Hymns* (1779)]

DE VRIES, Peter (1910–1993)
It is the final proof of God's omnipotence that
he need not exist in order to save us.
[*The Mackerel Plaza* (1958)]

DUHAMEL, Georges (1884–1966)
I have too much respect for the idea of God to
make it responsible for such an absurd world.
[*Chronique des Pasquier* (1948)]

EINSTEIN, Albert (1879–1955)
God does not play dice.
[Attr.]

EMPEDOCLES (c.490–c.430 BC)
God is a circle whose centre is everywhere
and whose circumference is nowhere.
[Attr.]

GALILEO GALILEI (1564–1642)
I do not feel obliged to believe that the same
God who has endowed us with sense, reason,
and intellect has intended us to forgo their use.
[Attr.]

GREENE, Graham (1904–1991)
Those who marry God ... can become
domesticated too – it's just as hum-drum a
marriage as all the others.
[*A Burnt-Out Case* (1961)]

HALDANE, J.B.S. (1892–1964)
(Reply when asked what inferences could be
drawn about the nature of God from a study
of his works)
The Creator ... has a special preference for
beetles.
[Lecture, 1951]

HUGHES, Sean (1966–)
I'd like to thank God for fucking up my life and at
the same time not existing, quite a special skill.
[*The Independent*, 1993]

HUGHES, Ted (1930–1998)
God is a good fellow, but His mother's against
him.
[*Wodwo* (1967)]

KEMPIS, Thomas á (c.1380–1471)
For man proposes, but God disposes.
[*De Imitatione Christi* (1892)]

KOESTLER, Arthur (1905–1983)
God seems to have left the receiver off the
hook, and time is running out.
[*The Ghost in the Machine* (1961)]

MENCKEN, H.L. (1880–1956)
God is the immemorial refuge of the
incompetent, the helpless, the miserable. They
find not only sanctuary in His arms, but also a
kind of superiority, soothing to their macerated
egos; He will set them above their betters.
[*Notebooks* (1956)]
It takes a long while for a naturally trustful
person to reconcile himself to the idea that
after all God will not help him.
[*Notebooks* (1956)]

NIETZSCHE, Friedrich Wilhelm (1844–1900)
God is dead: but men's natures are such that
for thousands of years yet there will perhaps
be caves in which his shadow will be seen.
[*The Gay Science* (1887)]

OWEN, John (c.1560–1622)
God and the doctor we alike adore
But only when in danger, not before;
The danger o'er, both are alike requited,
God is forgotten, and the Doctor slighted.
[*Epigrams*]

PASCAL, Blaise (1623–1662)
I cannot forgive Descartes; in all his
philosophy he did his best to dispense with
God. But he could not avoid making Him set
the world in motion with a flick of His finger;
after that he had no more use for God.
[*Pensées* (1670)]

SARTRE, Jean-Paul (1905–1980)
God is absence. God is the solitude of man.
[*Le Diable et le Bon Dieu* (1951)]

SHAKESPEARE, William (1564–1616)
There's a divinity that shapes our ends,
Rough-hew them how we will.
[*Hamlet*, V.ii]
As flies to wanton boys are we to th' gods –
They kill us for their sport.
[*King Lear*, IV.i]

SQUIRE, Sir J.C. (1884–1958)
God heard the embattled nations sing and
shout
'Gott strafe England!' and 'God save the King!'
God this, God that, and God the other thing –
'Good God!' said God, 'I've got my work cut
out.'
[*The Survival of the Fittest* (1916)]

VOLTAIRE (1694–1778)
God is not on the side of the big batallions,
but of the best marksmen.
['The Piccini Notebooks' (c. 1735–1750)]
If God did not exist, it would be necessary to
invent him.
[*Epîtres*, 'A l'auteur du livre des trois
imposteurs']

WALKER, Alice (1944–)
I think it pisses God off if you walk by the
color purple in a field somewhere and don't
notice it.
[*The Color Purple*, film, 1985]

See **ATHEISM, BELIEF**

GOOD AND EVIL

THE BIBLE
(King James Version)
Ye shall be as gods, knowing good and evil.
[*Genesis*, 3:5]

BURNS, Robert (1759–1796)
Whatever mitigates the woes or increases the
happiness of others, this is my criterion of
goodness; and whatever injures society at
large, or any individual in it, this is my
measure of iniquity.
[Attr.]

GOLDSMITH, Oliver (c.1728–1774)
We must touch his weaknesses with a
delicate hand. There are some faults so nearly
allied to excellence, that we can scarce weed
out the vice without eradicating the virtue.
[*The Good Natur'd Man* (1768)]

LERMONTOV, Mikhail (1814–1841)
What is the greatest good and evil? – two
ends of an invisible chain which come closer
together the further they move apart.
[*Vadim* (1834)]

SHAKESPEARE, William (1564–1616)
The evil that men do lives after them;
The good is oft interred with their bones.
[*Julius Caesar*, III.ii]
Some rise by sin, and some by virtue fall.
[*Measure for Measure*, II.i]

SURTEES, R.S. (1805–1864)
More people are flattered into virtue than
bullied out of vice.
[*The Analysis of the Hunting Field* (1846)]

VANBRUGH, Sir John (1664-1726)
Belinda: Ay, but you know we must return good for evil.
Lady Brute: That may be a mistake in the translation.

[*The Provok'd Wife* (1697)]

See **GOODNESS**

GOODNESS

ARISTOTLE (384-322 BC)
In all things the middle state is to be praised. But it is sometimes necessary to incline towards overshooting and sometimes to shooting short of the mark, since this is the easiest way of hitting the mean and the right course.

[*Nicomachean Ethics*]

BARTH, Karl (1886-1968)
Men have never been good, they are not good, they never will be good.

[*Time*, 1954]

BLAKE, William (1757-1827)
He who would do good to another must do it in Minute Particulars. General Good is the plea of the Scoundrel, hypocrite & flatterer.

[*Jerusalem* (1804-1820)]

BUDDHA (c.563-483 BC)
This Ayrian Eightfold Path, that is to say: Right view, right aim, right speech, right action, right living, right effort, right mindfulness, right contemplation.

[In Woodward, *Some Sayings of the Buddha*]

BURKE, Edmund (1729-1797)
When bad men combine, the good must associate; else they will fall, one by one, an unpitied sacrifice in a contemptible struggle.

[*Thoughts on the Cause of the Present Discontents* (1770)]

CONFUCIUS (c.550-c.478 BC)
True goodness springs from a man's own heart. All men are born good.

[*Analects*]

HUTCHESON, Francis (1694-1746)
That action is best, which procures the greatest happiness for the greatest numbers.

[*An Inquiry into the Original of our Ideas of Beauty and Virtue* (1725)]

LANDOR, Walter Savage (1775-1864)
Goodness does not more certainly make men happy than happiness makes them good.

[*Imaginary Conversations* (1853)]

MACHIAVELLI (1469-1527)
Men never do anything good except out of necessity.

[*Discourse*]

PLATO (c.429-347 BC)
The good is the beautiful.

[*Lysis*]

SHAKESPEARE, William (1564-1616)
How far that little candle throws his beams! So shines a good deed in a naughty world.

[*The Merchant of Venice*, V.i]

VOLTAIRE (1694-1778)
The best is the enemy of the good.

['Art dramatique' (1770)]

WEST, Mae (1892-1980)
When I'm good I'm very good, but when I'm bad I'm better.

[*I'm No Angel*, film, 1933]

WILDE, Oscar (1854-1900)
It is better to be beautiful than to be good. But ... it is better to be good than to be ugly.

[*The Picture of Dorion Gray* (1891)]

See **BEAUTY, BENEFACTORS, GOOD AND EVIL, MORALITY, VIRTUE**

GOSSIP

BIERCE, Ambrose (1842-C. 1914)
Backbite: To speak of a man as you find him when he can't find you.

[*The Enlarged Devil's Dictionary* (1961)]

CHESTERFIELD, Lord (1694-1773)
In the case of scandal, as in that of robbery, the receiver is always thought as bad as the thief.

[Letter to his son, 1748]

CONGREVE, William (1670-1729)
Retired to their tea and scandal, according to their ancient custom.

[*The Double Dealer* (1694)]

They come together like the Coroner's Inquest, to sit upon the murdered reputations of the week.

[*The Way of the World* (1700)]

LONGWORTH, Alice Roosevelt (1884-1980)
(Embroidered on a cushion at her home in Washington)
If you haven't anything nice to say about anyone, come and sit by me.

[*New York Times*, 1980]

OUIDA (1839-1908)
A cruel story runs on wheels, and every hand oils the wheels as they run.

[*Wisdom, Wit and Pathos*, 'Moths']

POPE, Alexander (1688–1744)
At ev'ry word a reputation dies.
[*The Rape of the Lock* (1714)]

RUSSELL, Bertrand (1872–1970)
No one gossips about other people's secret virtues.
[*On Education* (1926)]

See **SECRETS**

GOVERNMENT

ACTON, Lord (1834–1902)
The danger is not that a particular class is unfit to govern. Every class is unfit to govern.
[Letter to Mary Gladstone, 1881]

ANONYMOUS
Anarchy may not be the best form of government, but it's better than no government at all.

BAGEHOT, Walter (1826–1877)
A severe though not unfriendly critic of our institutions said that 'the cure for admiring the House of Lords was to go and look at it.'
[*The English Constitution* (1867)]

BEVERIDGE, William Henry (1879–1963)
The object of government in peace and in war is not the glory of rulers or of races, but the happiness of the common man.
[Report on Social Insurance and Allied Services (1942)]

BURKE, Edmund (1729–1797)
All government, indeed every human benefit and enjoyment, every virtue, and every prudent act, is founded on compromise and barter.
[*Speech on Conciliation with America* (1775)]
In all forms of Government the people is the true legislator.
[*Tracts on the Popery Laws* (1812)]

CAMPBELL-BANNERMAN, Sir Henry (1836–1908)
Good government could never be a substitute for government by the people themselves.
[Speech, 1905]

FRIEDMAN, Milton (1912–2006)
Governments never learn. Only people learn.
[*The Observer*, 1996]

HOBBES, Thomas (1588–1679)
They that are discontented under monarchy, call it tyranny; and they that are displeased with aristocracy, call it oligarchy: so also, they which find themselves grieved under a democracy, call it anarchy, which signifies want of government; and yet I think no man believes, that want of government, is any new kind of government.
[*Leviathan* (1651)]

JOHNSON, Samuel (1709–1784)
I would not give half a guinea to live under one form of government rather than another. It is of no moment to the happiness of an individual.
[In Boswell, *The Life of Samuel Johnson* (1791)]

KEYNES, John Maynard (1883–1946)
The important thing for government is not to do things which individuals are doing already, and to do them a little better or a little worse; but to do those things which at present are not done at all.
['The End of Laissez-Faire' (1926)]

MAISTRE, Joseph de (1753–1821)
Each country has the government it deserves.
[Letter, 1811]

MENCKEN, H.L. (1880–1956)
The worst government is the most moral. One composed of cynics is often very tolerant and human. But when fanatics are on top there is no limit to oppression.
[*Notebooks* (1956)]

PAINE, Thomas (1737–1809)
Man is not the enemy of Man, but through the medium of a false system of government.
[*The Rights of Man* (1791)]

RIPPON, Geoffrey (1924–1997)
Governments don't retreat, they simply advance in another direction.
[*The Observer*, 1981]

ROGERS, Will (1879–1935)
I don't make jokes – I just watch the government and report the facts.
[Attr.]

RUSKIN, John (1819–1900)
Government and cooperation are in all things the laws of life; anarchy and competition, the laws of death.
[*Unto this Last* (1862)]

VOLTAIRE (1694–1778)
In governments there must be both shepherds and butchers.
['The Piccini Notebooks']

See **CAPITALISM, DEMOCRACY, MONARCHY AND ROYALTY, POLITICIANS, POLITICS**

GREATNESS

AMIEL, Henri-Frédéric (1821–1881)
The age of great men is going; the epoch of the ant-hill, of life in multiplicity, is beginning.
[*Journal*, 1851]

ASQUITH, Margot (1864–1945)
Mrs Asquith remarked indiscreetly that if Kitchener was not a great man, he was, at least, a great poster.
[In Sir Philip Magnus, *Kitchener: Portrait of an Imperialist* (1958)]

BEERBOHM, Sir Max (1872–1956)
Great men are but life-sized. Most of them, indeed, are rather short.
[Attr.]

CAMPBELL, Thomas (1777–1844)
What millions died – that Caesar might be great!
[*Pleasures of Hope* (1799)]

CARLYLE, Thomas (1795–1881)
No great man lives in vain. The History of the world is but the Biography of great men.
['The Hero as Divinity' (1841)]

CHAPMAN, George (c.1559–c.1634)
They're only truly great who are truly good.
[*Revenge for Honour* (1654)]

EMERSON, Ralph Waldo (1803–1882)
Is it so bad, then, to be misunderstood? Pythagoras was misunderstood, and Socrates, and Jesus, and Luther, and Copernicus, and Galileo, and Newton, and every pure and wise spirit that ever took flesh. To be great is to be misunderstood.
[*Essays, First Series* (1841)]

FIELDING, Henry (1707–1754)
Greatness consists in bringing all manner of mischief on mankind, and goodness in removing it from them.
[*Jonathan Wild* (1743)]

FRAZER, Sir James (1854–1941)
The world cannot live at the level of its great men.
[*The Golden Bough* (1900)]

LA ROCHEFOUCAULD (1613–1680)
The glory of great men must always be measured by the means they have used to obtain it.
[*Maximes* (1678)]

SHAKESPEARE, William (1564–1616)
Be not afraid of greatness. Some are born great, some achieve greatness, and some have greatness thrust upon 'em.
[*Twelfth Night*, II.v]

WALPOLE, Horace (1717–1797)
They who cannot perform great things themselves may yet have a satisfaction in doing justice to those who can.
[Attr.]

GUILT

ARENDT, Hannah (1906–1975)
It is quite gratifying to feel guilty if you haven't done anything wrong: how noble! Whereas it is rather hard and certainly depressing to admit guilt and to repent.
[*Eichmann in Jerusalem: A Report on the Banality of Evil* (1963)]

GOETHE (1749–1832)
For all guilt is avenged on earth.
[*Wilhelm Meister's Apprentice Years* (1796)]

GOLDSMITH, Oliver (c.1728–1774)
When lovely woman stoops to folly And finds too late that men betray, What charm can soothe her melancholy, What art can wash her guilt away? The only art her guilt to cover, To hide her shame from every eye, To give repentance to her lover And wring his bosom – is to die.
[*The Vicar of Wakefield* (1766)]

HORACE (65–8 BC)
This be your wall of brass, to have nothing on your conscience, no reason to grow pale with guilt.
[*Epistles*]

KENNEDY, A.L. (1965–)
Guilt is of course not an emotion in the Celtic countries, it is simply a way of life – a kind of gleefully painful social anaesthetic.
[*So I am Glad* (1995)]

MCGOUGH, Roger (1937–)
You will put on a dress of guilt and shoes with broken high ideals.
['Comeclose and Sleepnow' (1967)]

RUSKIN, John (1819–1900)
Life without industry is guilt.
['The Relation of Art to Morals' (1870)]

SHAKESPEARE, William (1564–1616)
Will all great Neptune's ocean wash this
blood Clean from my hand? No; this my hand
will rather
The multitudinous seas incarnadine, Making
the green one red.
[*Macbeth*, II.ii]
Out, damned spot! out, I say! One, two; why
then 'tis time to do't. Hell is murky. Fie, my lord,
fie! a soldier, and afeard? What need we fear
who knows it, when none can call our pow'r
to account? Yet who would have thought the
old man to have had so much blood in him?
[*Macbeth*, V.i]
Here's the smell of the blood still. All the
perfumes of Arabia will not sweeten this little
hand. Oh, oh, oh!
[*Macbeth*, V.i]

STEVENSON, Robert Louis (1850–1894)
What hangs people ... is the unfortunate
circumstance of guilt.
[*The Wrong Box* (1889)]

See **CONSCIENCE, REGRET**

GRIEF

AUSTEN, Jane (1775–1817)
We met ... Dr Hall in such very deep
mourning that either his mother, his wife, or
himself must be dead.
[Letter to Cassandra Austen, 1799]

BYRON, Lord (1788–1824)
(A cypress)
Dark tree, still sad when others' grief is fled,
The only constant mourner o'er the dead!
['The Giaour' (1813)]

COWPER, William (1731–1800)
Grief is itself a med'cine.
['Charity' (1782)]

DICKINSON, Emily (1830–1886)
The Bustle in a House
The Morning after Death
Is solemnest of industries
Enacted upon Earth –
The Sweeping up the Heart
And putting Love away
We shall not want to use again
Until Eternity.
['The Bustle in a House' (c. 1866)]

ELLIOT, Jean (1727–1805)
I've heard them lilting, at our yowe-milking,
Lasses a'lilting before the dawn o' day;
But now they are moaning on ilka green
loaning –
The Flowers of the Forest are a' wede away.
['The Flowers of the Forest' (1756)]

FORD, John (c.1586–1639)
They are the silent griefs which cut the
heart-strings.
[*The Broken Heart* (1633)]

GRAVES, Robert (1895–1985)
His eyes are quickened so with grief,
He can watch a grass or leaf
Every instant grow ...
Across two counties he can hear
And catch your words before you speak.
The woodlouse or the maggot's weak
Clamour rings in his sad ear,
And noise so slight it would surpass Credence.
['Lost Love' (1921)]

JOHNSON, Samuel (1709–1784)
Grief is a species of idleness.
[Letter to Mrs. Thrale, 1773]

LOWELL, James Russell (1819–1891)
Sorrow, the great idealizer.
[Attr.]

PROUST, Marcel (1871–1922)
Happiness alone is beneficial for the body, but
it is grief that develops the powers of the mind.
[*Le Temps retrouvé* (1926)]

SHAKESPEARE, William (1564–1616)
Grief fills the room up of my absent child,
Lies in his bed, walks up and down with me,
Puts on his pretty looks, repeats his words,
Remembers me of all his gracious parts,
Stuffs out his vacant garments with his form;
Then have I reason to be fond of grief.
[*King John*, III.iv]
What, man! Ne'er pull your hat upon your
brows;
Give sorrow words. The grief that does not speak
Whispers the o'erfraught heart and bids it break.
[*Macbeth*, IV.iii]

SHELLEY, Percy Bysshe (1792–1822)
Ah, woe is me! Winter is come and gone,
But grief returns with the revolving year.
[*Adonais* (1821)]

STOWE, Harriet Beecher (1811–1896)
The bitterest tears shed over graves are for
words left unsaid and deeds left undone.
[*Little Foxes* (1866)]

TENNYSON, Alfred (Lord) (1809–1892)
Death has made
His darkness beautiful with thee.
[*In Memoriam A.H.H.* (1850)]

WORDSWORTH, William (1770–1850)
Surprised by joy – impatient as the Wind
I turned to share the transport – Oh! with whom
But thee, deep buried in the silent tomb.
['Surprised by joy' (1815)]

GUILT

ARENDT, Hannah (1906–1975)
It is quite gratifying to feel guilty if you
haven't done anything wrong: how noble!
Whereas it is rather hard and certainly
depressing to admit guilt and to repent.
[*Eichmann in Jerusalem: A Report on the
Banality of Evil* (1963)]

GOETHE (1749–1832)
For all guilt is avenged on earth.
[*Wilhelm Meister's Apprentice Years* (1796)]

GOLDSMITH, Oliver (c.1728–1774)
When lovely woman stoops to folly
And finds too late that men betray,
What charm can soothe her melancholy,
What art can wash her guilt away?
The only art her guilt to cover,
To hide her shame from every eye,
To give repentance to her lover
And wring his bosom – is to die.
[*The Vicar of Wakefield* (1766)]

HORACE (65–8 BC)
This be your wall of brass, to have nothing on
your conscience, no reason to grow pale with
guilt.
[*Epistles*]

KENNEDY, A.L. (1965–)
Guilt is of course not an emotion in the Celtic
countries, it is simply a way of life – a kind of
gleefully painful social anaesthetic.
[*So I am Glad* (1995)]

MCGOUGH, Roger (1937–)
You will put on a dress of guilt and shoes with
broken high ideals.
['Comeclose and Sleepnow' (1967)]

RUSKIN, John (1819–1900)
Life without industry is guilt.
['The Relation of Art to Morals' (1870)]

SHAKESPEARE, William (1564–1616)
Will all great Neptune's ocean wash this blood
Clean from my hand? No this my hand will
rather
The multitudinous seas incarnadine,
Making the green one red.
[*Macbeth*, II.ii]
Out, damned spot! out, I say! One, two; why
then 'tis time to do't. Hell is murky. Fie, my
lord, fie! a soldier, and afeard? What need we
fear who knows it, when none can call our
pow'r to account? Yet who would have thought
the old man to have had so much blood in him?
[*Macbeth*, V.i]

Here's the smell of the blood still. All the
perfumes of Arabia will not sweeten this little
hand. Oh, oh, oh!
[*Macbeth*, V.i]

STEVENSON, Robert Louis (1850–1894)
What hangs people ... is the unfortunate
circumstance of guilt.
[*The Wrong Box* (1889)]

See **CONSCIENCE, REGRET**

HAPPINESS

ADAMS, Scott (1957–)
Smile, it confuses people.
[*The Dilbert Principle*]

ARISTOTLE (384–322 BC)
One swallow does not make a summer,
neither does one fine day; similarly one day or
brief time of happiness does not make a
person entirely happy.
[*Nicomachean Ethics*]

BERGMAN, Ingrid (1915–1982)
Happiness is good health – and a bad
memory.
[In Simon Rose, *Classic Film Guide* (1995)]

BOETHIUS (c.475–524)
Nothing is miserable unless you think it so;
conversely, every lot is happy to one who is
content with it.
[*De Consolatione Philosophiae*]

CAMPBELL, Thomas (1777–1844)
One moment may with bliss repay
Unnumber'd hours of pain.
['The Ritter Bann']

COLERIDGE, Samuel Taylor (1772–1834)
We ne'er can be
Made happy by compulsion.
['The Three Graves' (1809)]

DRYDEN, John (1631–1700)
Happy the man, and happy he alone,
He, who can call to-day his own:
He who, secure within, can say,
Tomorrow do thy worst, for I have lived
to-day.
[*Sylvae* (1685)]

ELIOT, George (1819–1880)
The happiest women, like the happiest
nations, have no history.
[*The Mill on the Floss* (1860)]

EMERSON, Ralph Waldo (1803–1882)
To fill the hour, – that is happiness.
[*Essays, Second Series* (1844)]

FRANKLIN, Benjamin (1706–1790)
Be in general virtuous, and you will be happy.
['On Early Marriages']

JOHNSON, Samuel (1709–1784)
There is nothing which has yet been contrived by man, by which so much happiness is produced as by a good tavern or inn.
[In Boswell, *The Life of Samuel Johnson* (1791)]

MARMION, Shackerley (1603–1639)
Great joys, like griefs, are silent.
[*Holland's Leaguer* (1632)]

MILL, John Stuart (1806–1873)
Ask yourself whether you are happy, and you cease to be so.
[*Autobiography* (1873)]

ROONEY, Mickey (1920–)
Had I been brighter, the ladies been gentler, the Scotch been weaker, had the gods been kinder, had the dice been hotter, this could have been a one-sentence story: Once upon a time I lived happily ever after.
[Attr.]

ROUSSEAU, Jean-Jacques (1712–1778)
Happiness: a good bank account, a good cook, and a good digestion.
[*Treasury of Humorous Quotations*]

SAGAN, Françoise (1935–2004)
What is that wall that always rises up between human beings and their most intimate desire, their frightening will to be happy? ... Is it a nostalgia nurtured from childhood?
[*Le Garde du coeur* (1968)]

SAINT-EXUPÉRY, Antoine de (1900–1944)
If you want to understand the meaning of happiness, you must see it as a reward and not as a goal.
[*Carnets*]

SHAKESPEARE, William (1564–1616)
O, how bitter a thing it is to look into happiness through another man's eyes!
[*As You Like It*, V.ii]

SHAW, George Bernard (1856–1950)
We have no more right to consume happiness without producing it than to consume wealth without producing it.
[*Candida* (1898)]
A lifetime of happiness! No man alive could bear it: it would be hell on earth.
[*Man and Superman* (1903)]

SMITH, Sydney (1771–1845)
Mankind are always happy for having been happy, so that if you make them happy now, you make them happy twenty years hence by the memory of it.
[*Sketches of Moral Philosophy* (1849)]

SOLON (c.638–c.559 BC)
Until [a man] dies, be careful to call him not happy but lucky.
[In Herodotus, *Histories*]

SZASZ, Thomas (1920–2012)
Happiness is an imaginary condition, formerly often attributed by the living to the dead, now usually attributed by adults to children, and by children to adults.
[*The Second Sin* (1973)]

TOLSTOY, Leo (1828–1910)
If you want to be happy, be.
[Attr.]

WAUGH, Evelyn (1903–1966)
I can't quite explain it, but I don't believe one can ever be unhappy for long provided one does just exactly what one wants to and when one wants to.
[*Decline and Fall* (1928)]

WELDON, Fay (1931–)
I don't believe in happiness: why should we expect to be happy? In such a world as this, depression is rational, rage reasonable.
[*The Observer*, 1995]

WHATELY, Richard (1787–1863)
Happiness is no laughing matter.
[*Apophthegms* (1854)]

See **LAUGHTER, PLEASURE**

HATRED

BYRON, Lord (1788–1824)
Now hatred is by far the longest pleasure;
Men love in haste, but they detest at leisure.
[*Don Juan* (1824)]

DE VRIES, Peter (1910–1993)
Everybody hates me because I'm so universally liked.
[*The Vale of Laughter* (1967)]

FIELDS, W.C. (1880–1946)
I am free of all prejudice. I hate everyone equally.
[Attr.]

GABOR, Zsa-Zsa (1919–)
I never hated a man enough to give him his diamonds back.

[*The Observer*, 1957]

HAZLITT, William (1778–1830)
Violent antipathies are always suspicious, and betray a secret affinity.

[*Table-Talk* (1822)]

HOFFER, Eric (1902–1983)
Passionate hatred can give meaning and purpose to an empty life.

[Attr.]

JUNG CHANG (1952–)
He [Mao Zedong] was, it seemed to me, really a restless fight promoter by nature and good at it. He understood ugly human instincts such as envy and resentment, and knew how to mobilize them for his ends. He ruled by getting people to hate each other.

[*Wild Swans* (1991)]

NASH, Ogden (1902–1971)
Any kiddie in school can love like a fool,
But hating, my boy, is an art.

[*Happy Days* (1933)]

ROSTEN, Leo (1908–1997)
(Of W.C. Fields; often attributed to him)
Any man who hates dogs and babies can't be all bad.

[Speech, 1939]

RUSSELL, Bertrand (1872–1970)
Few people can be happy unless they hate some other person, nation or creed.

[Attr.]

TACITUS (AD c.56–c.120)
It is part of human nature to hate those whom you have injured.

[*Agricola*]

See **LOVE**

HEALTH

BUTLER, Samuel (1835–1902)
The healthy stomach is nothing if not conservative. Few radicals have good digestions.

[*The Note-Books of Samuel Butler* (1912)]

DAVIS, Adelle (1904–1974)
Thousands upon thousands of persons have studied disease. Almost no one has studied health.

[*Let's Eat Right to Keep Fit* (1954)]

JAY, Douglas (1907–1996)
For in the case of nutrition and health, just as in the case of education, the gentleman in Whitehall really does know better what is good for people than the people know themselves.

[*The Socialist Case* (1947)]

JUVENAL (c.60–130)
Your prayers should be for a healthy mind in a healthy body.

[*Satires*]

MARTIAL (c.AD 40–c.104)
It is not to live but to be healthy that makes a life.

[*Epigrammata*]

SMITH, Sydney (1771–1845)
I am convinced digestion is the great secret of life.

[Letter to Arthur Kinglake, 1837]

SWIFT, Jonathan (1667–1745)
I row after health like a waterman, and ride after it like a postboy, and find little success.

[Attr.]

TUSSER, Thomas (c.1524–1580)
Make hunger thy sauce, as a medicine for health.

[*Five Hundred Points of Good Husbandry* (1557)]

WALTON, Izaak (1593–1683)
Look to your health; and if you have it, praise God, and value it next to a good conscience; for health is the second blessing that we mortals are capable of; a blessing money cannot buy.

[*The Compleat Angler* (1653)]

See **EXERCISE, ILLNESS, MEDICINE**

HEAVEN

BORGES, Jorge Luis (1899–1986)
Let heaven exist, even if my place be hell.

['*The Library of Babel*' (1941)]

BROWN, Helen Gurley (1922–2012)
(Promotional line for Cosmopolitan magazine)
Good girls go to heaven, bad girls go everywhere.

[Attr.]

BROWNING, Robert (1812–1889)
On the earth the broken arcs; in the heaven, a perfect round.

['Abt Vogler' (1864)]

DE QUINCEY, Thomas (1785–1859)
Thou hast the keys of Paradise, oh just, subtle, and mighty opium!
[*Confessions of an English Opium Eater* (1822)]

FITZGERALD, Edward (1809–1883)
Here with a Loaf of Bread beneath the Bough,
A Flask of Wine, a Book of Verse – and Thou
Beside me singing in the Wilderness –
And Wilderness is Paradise enow.
[*The Rubáiyát of Omar Khayyám* (1859)]

LICHTENBERG, Georg (1742–1799)
Probably no invention came more easily to man than Heaven.
[*Aphorisms*]

PROUST, Marcel (1871–1922)
The true paradises are the paradises we have lost.
[*Le Temps retrouvé* (1926)]

SHAKESPEARE, William (1564–1616)
Heaven is above all yet: there sits a Judge
That no king can corrupt.
[*Henry VIII*, III.i]

SHAW, George Bernard (1856–1950)
Heaven, as conventionally conceived, is a place so inane, so dull, so useless, so miserable, that nobody has ever ventured to describe a whole day in heaven, though plenty of people have described a day at the seaside.
[*Misalliance* (1914)]

SMITH, Sydney (1771–1845)
My idea of heaven is, eating pâté de foie gras to the sound of trumpets.
[In H. Pearson, *The Smith of Smiths* (1934)]

See **AFTERLIFE**

Hell

BERNANOS, Georges (1888–1948)
Hell, madam, is to love no longer.
[*The Diary of a Country Priest*, (1936)]

BUNYAN, John (1628–1688)
Then I saw there was a way to Hell, even from the gates of heaven.
[*The Pilgrim's Progress* (1678)]

BURTON, Robert (1577–1640)
If there is a hell upon earth, it is to be found in a melancholy man's heart.
[*Anatomy of Melancholy* (1621)]

CLARE, Dr Anthony (1942–2007)
Hell is when you get what you think you want.
[*The Observer*, 1983]

ELIOT, T.S. (1888–1965)
Hell is oneself;
Hell is alone, the other figures in it
Merely projections. There is nothing to escape from
And nothing to escape to.
One is always alone.
[*The Cocktail Party* (1950)]

LEWIS, C.S. (1898–1963)
There is wishful thinking in Hell as well as on earth.
[*The Screwtape Letters* (1942)]

MILTON, John (1608–1674)
Here we may reign secure, and in my choice
To reign is worth ambition though in Hell:
Better to reign in Hell, then serve in Heav'n.
[*Paradise Lost* (1667)]

Long is the way
And hard, that out of Hell leads
up to Light.
[*Paradise Lost* (1667)]

SADE, Marquis de (1740–1814)
There is no other hell for man than the stupidity and wickedness of his own kind.
[*Histoire de Juliette* (1797)]

SARTRE, Jean-Paul (1905–1980)
Hell is other people.
[*In Camera* (1944)]

SHAW, George Bernard (1856–1950)
A perpetual holiday is a good working definition of hell.
[Attr.]

TEILHARD DE CHARDIN, Pierre (1881–1955)
You have told me, O God, to believe in hell. But you have forbidden me to think, with absolute certainty, of any man as damned.
[*Le Milieu divin*]

VIRGIL (70–19 BC)
The gates of Hell are open night and day;
Smooth the descent and easy is the way:
But to return, and view the cheerful skies,
In this the task and mighty labour lies.
[*Aeneid*]

See **DEVIL**

Heroes

BRECHT, Bertolt (1898–1956)
Andrea: Unhappy the country that has no heroes!
Galileo: Unhappy the country that needs heroes.
[*Life of Galileo* (1938–1939)]

CORNUEL, Madame Anne-Marie Bigot de (1605–1694)
No man is a hero to his valet.
[In *Lettres de Mlle Aïssé á Madame C* (1787)]

GAMBETTA, Léon (1838–1882)
Heroic times have passed away.
[Saying]

HARRIS, Max (1921–1995)
The Australian world is peopled with good blokes and bastards, but not heroes.
[In Coleman (ed.), *Australian Civilization*]

HENDERSON, Hamish (1919–2002)
There were our own, there were the others. Their deaths were like their lives, human and animal.
There were no gods and precious few heroes.
[*Elegies for the Dead in Cyrenaica* (1948)]

LANDOR, Walter Savage (1775–1864)
Hail, ye indomitable heroes, hail!
Despite of all your generals ye prevail.
['The Crimean Heroes']

MACKENZIE, Sir Compton (1883–1972)
Ever since the first World War there has been an inclination to denigrate the heroic aspect of man.
[*On Moral Courage* (1962)]

MORELL, Thomas (1703–1784)
See, the conquering hero comes! Sound the trumpets, beat the drums!
[*Joshua* (1748)]

ORWELL, George (1903–1950)
The high sentiments always win in the end, leaders who offer blood, toil, tears and sweat always get more out of their followers than those who offer safety and a good time. When it comes to the pinch, human beings are heroic.
[*Horizon*, 1941]

ROGERS, Will (1879–1935)
Heroing is one of the shortest-lived professions there is.
[In Grove, *The Will Rogers Book* (1961)]

See **COURAGE, PATRIOTISM, WAR**

HISTORY

ANGELOU, Maya (1928–)
History, faced with courage, need not be lived again.
[Speech at the Inauguration of President Clinton, 1993]

ANONYMOUS
Every time history repeats itself the price goes up.

AUSTEN, Jane (1775–1817)
Real solemn history, I cannot be interested in … The quarrels of popes and kings, with wars or pestilences, in every page; the men all so good for nothing, and hardly any women at all, it is very tiresome.
[*Northanger Abbey* (1818)]

BALFOUR, A.J. (1848–1930)
History does not repeat itself. Historians repeat each other.
[Attr.]

BEECHAM, Sir Thomas (1879–1961)
When the history of the first half of this century comes to be written – properly written – it will be acknowledged the most stupid and brutal in the history of civilisation.
[Attr.]

CARLYLE, Thomas (1795–1881)
History a distillation of rumour.
[*History of the French Revolution* (1837)]
Happy the people whose annals are blank in history-books!
[*History of Frederick the Great* (1865)]

CATHER, Willa (1873–1947)
The history of every country begins in the heart of a man or a woman.
[*O Pioneers!* (1913)]

COLERIDGE, Samuel Taylor (1772–1834)
If men could learn from history, what lessons it might teach us! But passion and party blind our eyes, and the light which experience gives is a lantern on the stern, which shines only on the waves behind us!
[*Table Talk* (1835)]

EBAN, Abba (1915–2002)
History teaches us that men and nations behave wisely once they have exhausted all other alternatives.
[Speech, 1970]

FORD, Henry (1863–1947)
(Popularly remembered as 'History is bunk')
History is more or less bunk. It's tradition. We don't want tradition. We want to live in the present and the only history that is worth a tinker's damn is the history we make today.
[*Chicago Tribune*, 1916]

FUKUYAMA, Francis (1952–)
What we may be witnessing is not just the end of the Cold War but the end of history as such: that is, the end point of man's ideological evolution and the universalism of Western liberal democracy.
[*The Independent*, 1989]

GIBBON, Edward (1737–1794)
History ... is, indeed, little more than the register of the crimes, follies, and misfortunes of mankind.
[*Decline and Fall of the Roman Empire* (1776–88)]

JOYCE, James (1882–1941)
History is a nightmare from which I am trying to awake.
[*Ulysses* (1922)]

KOESTLER, Arthur (1905–1983)
The most persistent sound which reverberates through men's history is the beating of war drums.
[*Janus: A Summing Up* (1978)]

LANG, Ian (1940–)
History is littered with dead opinion polls.
[*The Independent*, 1994]

MACLEOD, Iain (1913–1970)
History is too serious to be left to historians.
[*The Observer*, 1961]

MCLUHAN, Marshall (1911–1980)
The hydrogen bomb is history's exclamation point. It ends an agelong sentence of manifest violence.
[Attr.]

MARX, Karl (1818–1883)
Hegel says somewhere that all great events and personalities in world history reappear in one way or another. He forgot to add: the first time as tragedy, the second as farce.
[*The Eighteenth Brumaire of Louis Napoleon* (1852)]

PÉGUY, Charles (1873–1914)
It is impossible to write ancient history because we do not have enough sources, and impossible to write modern history because we have far too many.
[*Clio*]

POPPER, Sir Karl (1902–1994)
There is no history of mankind, there are only many histories of all kinds of aspects of human life. And one of these is the history of political power. This is elevated into the history of the world.
[*The Open Society and its Enemies* (1945)]

SAKI (1870–1916)
The people of Crete unfortunately make more history than they can consume locally.
[*The Chronicles of Clovis* (1911)]

SAMUEL, Lord (1870–1963)
Hansard is history's ear, already listening.
[*The Observer*, 1949]

SELLAR, Walter (1898–1951) and YEATMAN, Robert Julian (1897–1968)
A Bad Thing: America was thus clearly top nation, and History came to a.
[*1066 And All That* (1930)]

TAYLOR, A.J.P. (1906–1990)
(Of Napoleon III)
He was what I often think is a dangerous thing for a statesman to be – a student of history; and like most of those who study history, he learned from the mistakes of the past how to make new ones.
[*The Listener*, 1963]

TOLSTOY, Leo (1828–1910)
Historians are like deaf people who go on answering questions that no one has asked them.
[Attr.]

WELLS, H.G. (1866–1946)
Human history becomes more and more a race between education and catastrophe.
[*The Outline of History* (1920)]

See **EXPERIENCE, PAST**

HOLLYWOOD

BURCHILL, Julie (1960–)
Fame is no sanctuary from the passing of youth ... suicide is much easier and more acceptable in Hollywood than growing old gracefully.
[*Girls on Film* (1986)]

GRANT, Cary (1904–1986)
We have our factory, which is called a stage. We make a product, we color it, we title it and we ship it out in cans.
[*Newsweek*, June 1969]

HAWN, Goldie (1945–)
There are only three ages for women in Hollywood – Babe, District Attorney, and Driving Miss Daisy.

HOPPER, Hedda (1890–1966)
In Hollywood gratitude is Public Enemy Number One.
[*From Under My Hat* (1952)]

JONG, Erica (1942-)
Where is Hollywood located? Chiefly between the ears. In that part of the American brain lately vacated by God.
[*How To Save Your Own Life* (1977)]

LEVANT, Oscar (1906-1972)
Strip the phoney tinsel off Hollywood and you'll find the real tinsel underneath.
[Attr.]

MATURE, Victor (1915-1999)
Hollywood: Where the stars twinkle until they wrinkle.

MIZNER, Wilson (1876-1933)
A trip through a sewer in a glass-bottomed boat.

MONROE, Marilyn (1926-1962)
Hollywood is a place where they'll pay you $50,000 for a kiss and 50 cents for your soul.
[Attr.]

REED, Rex (1938-)
In Hollywood, if you don't have happiness, you send out for it.
[In J.R. Colombo, *Colombo's Hollywood*]

STALLINGS, Laurence (1894-1968)
Hollywood - a place where the inmates are in charge of the asylum.
[Attr.]

WILDER, Billy (1906-2002)
People copy, people steal. Most of the pictures they make nowadays are loaded down with special effects. I couldn't do that. I quit smoking because I couldn't reload my Zippo.
[*The New York Times*]

See **CINEMA, SHOWBUSINESS**

HOME

ACE, Jane (1905-1974)
Home wasn't built in a day.
[In G. Ace, *The Fine Art of Hypochondria* (1966)]

ANONYMOUS
Be it ever so humble there's no place like home for sending one slowly crackers.

BEAUVOIR, Simone de (1908-1986)
The ideal of happiness has always taken material form in the house, whether cottage or castle; it stands for permanence and separation from the world.
[*The Second Sex* (1949)]

DE WOLFE, Elsie (1865-1950)
It is the personality of the mistress that the home expresses. Men are forever guests in our homes, no matter how much happiness they may find there.
[*The House in Good Taste* (1920)]

DOUGLAS, Norman (1868-1952)
Many a man who thinks to found a home discovers that he has merely opened a tavern for his friends.
[*South Wind* (1917)]

FLETCHER, John (1579-1625)
Charity and beating begins at home.
[*Wit Without Money* (c. 1614)]

FROST, Robert (1874-1963)
'Home is the place where, when you have to go there,
They have to take you in.'
'I should have called it
Something you somehow haven't to deserve.'
['The Death of the Hired Man' (1914)]

LUCE, Clare Boothe (1903-1987)
A man's home may seem to be his castle on the outside; inside, it is more often his nursery.
[Attr.]

MEYER, Agnes (1887-c.1970)
What the nation must realise is that the home, when both parents work, is non-existent. Once we have honestly faced the fact, we must act accordingly.
[*Washington Post*, 1943]

MORE, Hannah (1745-1833)
The sober comfort, all the peace which springs
From the large aggregate of little things;
On these small cares of daughter, wife, or friend,
The almost sacred joys of home depend.
['Sensibility' (1782)]

MORRIS, William (1834-1896)
If you want a golden rule that will fit everybody, this is it: Have nothing in your houses that you do not know to be useful, or believe to be beautiful.
[*Hopes and Fears for Art* (1882)]

ROWLAND, Helen (1875-1950)
'Home' is any four walls that enclose the right person.
[*Reflections of a Bachelor Girl* (1909)]

SHAW, George Bernard (1856-1950)
The great advantage of a hotel is that it's a refuge from home life.
[*You Never Can Tell* (1898)]

STOWE, Harriet Beecher (1811–1896)
Home is a place not only of strong affections, but of entire unreserve; it is life's undress rehearsal, its backroom, its dressing room, from which we go forth to more careful and guarded intercourse, leaving behind us much debris of cast-off and everyday clothing.
[*Little Foxes* (1866)]

THATCHER, Margaret (1925–2013)
Home is where you come to when you have nothing better to do.
[*Vanity Fair* May 1991]

See **TRAVEL**

Honesty

AUDEN, W.H. (1907–1973)
Only God can tell the saintly from the suburban,
Counterfeit values always resemble the true;
Neither in Life nor Art is honesty bohemian,
The free behave much as the respectable do.
['New Year Letter' (1941)]

BLAKE, William (1757–1827)
Always be ready to speak your mind, and a base man will avoid you.
[Attr.]

BROWNE, Sir Thomas (1605–1682)
I have tried if I could reach that great resolution ... to be honest without a thought of Heaven or Hell.
[*Religio Medici* (1643)]

CARLYLE, Thomas (1795–1881)
Make yourself an honest man and then you may be sure there is one rascal less in the world.
[Attr.]

CROMWELL, Oliver (1599–1658)
A few honest men are better than numbers.
[Letter to Sir William Spring, 1643]

DEFOE, Daniel (c.1661–1731)
Necessity makes an honest man a knave.
[*Serious Reflections of Robinson Crusoe* (1720)]

FITZGERALD, F. Scott (1896–1940)
I am one of the few honest people that I have ever known.
[*The Great Gatsby* (1926)]

RICHELIEU (Cardinal) (1585–1642)
If you give me six lines written by the most honest man, I will find something in them to hang him.
[Attr.]

WHATELY, Richard (1787–1863)
Honesty is the best policy, but he who is governed by that maxim is not an honest man.
[*Apophthegms* (1854)]

See **TRUTH**

Honour

EMERSON, Ralph Waldo (1803–1882)
The louder he talked of his honor, the faster we counted our spoons.
[*Conduct of Life* (1860)]

HARE, Augustus (1792–1834)
Purity is the feminine, Truth the masculine, of Honour.
[*Guesses at Truth* (1827)]

MARX, Groucho (1895–1977)
Remember, men, we're fighting for this woman's honour; which is probably more than she ever did.
[*Duck Soup*, film, 1933]

RACINE, Jean (1639–1699)
Without money, honour is no more than a disease.
[*Les Plaideurs* (1668)]

Hope

BACON, Francis (1561–1626)
Hope is a good breakfast, but it is a bad supper.
['Apophthegms']

CHESTERTON, G.K. (1874–1936)
Hope is the power of being cheerful in circumstances which we know to be desperate.
[*Heretics* (1905)]

FRANKLIN, Benjamin (1706–1790)
He that lives upon hope will die fasting.
[*Poor Richard's Almanac* (1758)]

HERBERT, George (1593–1633)
He that lives in hope danceth without music.
[*Jacula Prudentum* (1640)]

ILLICH, Ivan (1926–2002)
We must rediscover the distinction between hope and expectation.
[*Deschooling Society* (1971)]

KERR, Jean (1923–2003)
Hope is the feeling you have that the feeling you have isn't permanent.
[*Finishing Touches* (1973)]

OSBORNE, John (1929–1994)
(A notice in his bathroom)
Since I gave up hope I feel so much better.
[*The Independent*, 1994]

POPE, Alexander (1688–1744)
Hope springs eternal in the human breast;
Man never Is, but always To be blest.
[*An Essay on Man* (1733)]

TERENCE (c.190–159 BC)
Where there's life, there's hope.
[*Heauton Timoroumenos*]

See **AMBITION, DESIRE, OPTIMISM**

HOUSEWORK

ALCOTT, Louisa May (1832–1888)
Housekeeping ain't no joke.
[*Litle Women* (1868)]

BEAUVOIR, Simone de (1908–1986)
Few tasks are more like the torture of
Sisyphus than housework, with its endless
repetition ... The housewife wears herself out
marking time: she makes nothing, simply
perpetuates the present.
[*The Second Sex* (1949)]

BINCHY, Maeve (1940–2012)
I don't want to hear about ironing. I don't
want to smell the iron. Why? I regard it as a
badge of servitude.
[*The Times* 1998]

CONRAN, Shirley (1932–)
I make no secret of the fact that I would rather
lie on a sofa than sweep beneath it. But you
have to be efficient if you're going to be lazy.
[*Superwoman* (1975)]

CRISP, Quentin (1908–1999)
There was no need to do any housework at
all. After the first four years the dirt doesn't
get any worse.
[*The Naked Civil Servant* (1968)]

DILLER, Phyllis (1917–1974)
Cleaning your house while your kids are
growing
Is like shoveling the walk before it stops
snowing.
[*Phyllis Diller's Housekeeping Hints*]

GIBBONS, Stella (1902–1989)
There's nothing like a thorn twig for cletterin'
dishes.
[*Cold Comfort Farm* (1932)]

**GREGORY, Lady Isabella Augusta
(1852–1932)**
I am so tired of housekeeping I dreamed I was
being served up for my guests and awoke only
when the knife was at my throat.
[In Mary-Lou Kohfeldt, *Lady Gregory* (1985)]

OAKLEY, Ann (1944–)
Housework is work directly opposed to the
possibility of human self-actualization.
[*Woman's Work: The Housewife, Past and
Present* (1974)]

WHITE, Patrick (1912–1990)
The tragedy of domesticity, that avalanche of
overcoats and boots.
[*The Aunt's Story* (1948)]

See **FEMINISM, WOMEN**

HUMANITY AND HUMAN NATURE

AUDEN, W.H. (1907–1973)
Man is a history-making creature who can
neither repeat his past nor leave it behind.
[*The Dyer's Hand* (1963)]

AUSTEN, Jane (1775–1817)
Human nature is so well disposed towards
those who are in interesting situations, that a
young person, who either marries or dies, is
sure of being kindly spoken of.
[*Emma* (1816)]

BACON, Francis (1561–1626)
There is in human nature generally more of
the fool than of the wise.
[*Essays* (1625)]

BEAUMARCHAIS (1732–1799)
Drinking when we're not thirsty and making
love all the time, madam, that is all there is to
distinguish us from other animals.
[*Le Barbier de Seville* (1775)]

BEERBOHM, Sir Max (1872–1956)
Mankind is divisible into two great classes:
hosts and guests.
[Attr.]

**THE BIBLE
(King James Version)**
Man is born unto trouble as the sparks fly
upward.
[*Job*, 5:7]
As for man, his days are as grass: as a flower
of the field, so he flourisheth.
[*Psalms*, 103:15]

BRONOWSKI, Jacob (1908–1974)
Every animal leaves traces of what it was;
man alone leaves traces of what he created.
[*The Ascent of Man* (1973)]

BÜCHNER, Georg (1813–1837)
We are puppets on strings worked by
unknown forces; we ourselves are nothing,
nothing!
[*Danton's Death* (1835)]

BURNS, Robert (1759–1796)
Man's inhumanity to man
Makes countless thousands mourn!
['Man was made to Mourn, a Dirge' (1784)]

BUTLER, Samuel (1835–1902)
'Man wants but little here below' but likes
that little good – and not too long in coming.
[*Further Extracts from the Note-Books of
Samuel Butler* (1934)]
Man is the only animal that can remain on
friendly terms with the victims he intends to
eat until he eats them.
[*Samuel Butler's Notebooks* (1951)]

CAINE, Sir Michael (1933–)
The basic rule of human nature is that
powerful people speak slowly and subservient
people quickly – because if they don't speak
fast nobody will listen to them.
[*The Times*, August 1992]

CAMPBELL, Roy (1901–1957)
I hate 'Humanity' and all such abstracts: but I
love people. Lovers of 'Humanity' generally
hate people and children, and keep parrots or
puppy dogs.
[*Light on a Dark Horse* (1951)]

CAMUS, Albert (1913–1960)
A single sentence will suffice for modern
man: he fornicated and read the papers.
[*The Fall* (1956)]

CHESTERTON, G.K. (1874–1936)
Individually, men may present a more or less
rational appearance, eating, sleeping and
scheming. But humanity as a whole is
changeful, mystical, fickle and delightful. Men
are men, but Man is a woman.
[*The Napoleon of Notting Hill* (1904)]

CONFUCIUS (c.550–c.478 BC)
Men's natures are alike; it is their habits that
carry them far apart.
[*Analects*]

DONLEAVY, J.P (1926–)
I got disappointed in human nature as well
and gave it up because I found it too much
like my own.
[*Fairy Tales of New York* (1961)]

DONNE, John (1572–1631)
No man is an Island, entire of it self; every
man is a piece of Continent, a part of the
main ... any man's death diminishes me,
because I am involved in Mankind; And
therefore never send to know for whom the
bell tolls; it tolls for thee.
[*Devotions upon Emergent Occasions* (1624)]

ELIOT, George (1819–1880)
There is a great deal of unmapped country
within us which would have to be taken into
account in an explanation of our gusts and
storms.
[*Daniel Deronda* (1876)]

FROUDE, James Anthony (1818–1894)
Wild animals never kill for sport. Man is the
only one to whom the torture and death of
his fellow creatures is amusing in itself.
[*Oceana, or England and her Colonies* (1886)]

GOLDSMITH, Oliver (c.1728–1774)
Man wants but little here below,
Nor wants that little long.
[*The Vicar of Wakefield* (1766)]

GORKY, Maxim (1868–1936)
Man and man alone is, I believe, the creator
of all things and all ideas.
[Attr.]

HAZLITT, William (1778–1830)
Man is an intellectual animal, and therefore
an everlasting contradiction to himself. His
senses centre in himself, his ideas reach to
the ends of the universe; so that he is torn in
pieces between the two, without a possibility
of its ever being otherwise.
[*Characteristics* (1823)]

JOHNSON, Samuel (1709–1784)
Sir, are you so grossly ignorant of human
nature, as not to know that a man may be
very sincere in good principles without having
good practice?
[In Boswell, *Journal of a Tour to the Hebrides*
(1785), 25 October 1773]

KEATS, John (1795–1821)
Scenery is fine – but human nature is finer.
[Letter to Benjamin Bailey, 1818]

MACHIAVELLI (1469–1527)
Men sooner forget the death of their father than the loss of their possessions.
[*The Prince*, 1532]

MILLIGAN, Spike (1918–2002)
I support all the causes that are trying to increase the sensitivity of the human race to the odious things that they do. We're a pretty horrendous crowd.
[Quoted in *The Herald*, February 2002]

MONASH, Sir John (1865–1931)
Nothing man does to the animal creation is equal to the cruelties he commits on his own kind.
[*The Seals*]

MONTAIGNE, Michel de (1533–1592)
Man is quite insane. He wouldn't know how to create a maggot, yet he creates Gods by the dozen.
[*Essais* (1580)]

NIETZSCHE, Friedrich Wilhelm (1844–1900)
What? is man only a mistake made by God, or God only a mistake made by man?
[*Twilight of the Idols* (1889)]

PASCAL, Blaise (1623–1662)
Man is only a reed, the feeblest thing in nature; but he is a thinking reed.
[*Pensées* (1670)]

PLAUTUS, Titus Maccius (c.254–184 BC)
Man is a wolf to man.
[*Asinaria*]

POPE, Alexander (1688–1744)
Know then thyself, presume not God to scan;
The proper study of Mankind is Man ...
Created half to rise, and half to fall;
Great lord of all things, yet a prey to all;
Sole judge of truth, in endless error hurl'd:
The glory, jest, and riddle of the world!
[*An Essay on Man* (1733)]

PROTAGORAS (c.485–c.410 BC)
Man is the measure of all things.
[In Plato, *Theaetetus*]

ROUSSEAU, Jean-Jacques (1712–1778)
Nature made man happy and good, but ... society corrupts him and makes him miserable.
[*Rousseau juge de Jean-Jacques*]

RUSKIN, John (1819–1900)
No human being, however great, or powerful, was ever so free as a fish.
[*The Two Paths* (1859)]

SCHILLER, Johann Christoph Friedrich (1759–1805)
Man is honoured by his heart and not by his opinions.
[*Wallensteins Tod* (1801)]

SHAKESPEARE, William (1564–1616)
What a piece of work is a man! How noble in reason! how infinite in faculties! in form and moving, how express and admirable! in action, how like an angel! in apprehension, how like a god! the beauty of the world! the paragon of animals!
[*Hamlet*, II.ii]

SHAW, George Bernard (1856–1950)
Man can climb to the highest summits; but he cannot dwell there long.
[*Candida* (1898)]

TEMPLE, William (1881–1944)
It is not the ape, nor the tiger in man that I fear, it is the donkey.
[Attr.]

TERTZ, Abram (1925–1997)
Man is always both much worse and much better than is expected of him. The fields of good are just as limitless as the wastelands of evil.
[*A Voice From the Chorus* (1973)]

TWAIN, Mark (1835–1910)
Man is the Only Animal that Blushes. Or needs to.
[*Following the Equator* (1897)]

UNAMUNO, Miguel de (1864–1936)
Man, because he is man, because he is conscious, is, in relation to the ass or to a crab, already a diseased animal. Consciousness is a disease.
[*The Tragic Sense of Life* (1913)]

VALÉRY, Paul (1871–1945)
A man is infinitely more complicated than his thoughts.
[In Auden, *A Certain World*]

VOLTAIRE (1694–1778)
If God has created us in his image we have repaid him well.
[*Le Sottisier* (c. 1778)]

WAUGH, Evelyn (1903–1966)
Instead of this absurd division into sexes they ought to class people as static and dynamic.
[*Decline and Fall* (1928)]

WILDE, Oscar (1854–1900)
It is absurd to divide people into good and bad. People are either charming or tedious.
[*Lady Windermere's Fan* (1892)]

YEVTUSHENKO, Yevgeny (1933–)
In the final analysis, humanity has only two ways out – either universal destruction or universal brotherhood.
['The Spirit of Elbe' (1966)]
See **LIFE**

Humour

ADDISON, Joseph (1672–1719)
If we may believe our logicians, man is distinguished from all other creatures by the faculty of laughter.
[*The Spectator*, 1712]

ALBEE, Edward (1928–)
I have a fine sense of the ridiculous, but no sense of humour.
[*Who's Afraid of Virginia Woolf* (1962)]

AYCKBOURN, Sir Alan (1939–)
Few women care to be laughed at and men not at all, except for large sums of money.
[*The Norman Conquests* (1975)]

BARKER, Ronnie (1929–2005)
The marvellous thing about a joke with a double meaning is that it can only mean one thing.
[Attr.]

BEAUMARCHAIS (1732–1799)
I make myself laugh at everything, for fear of having to cry.
[*Le Barbier de Seville* (1775)]

BERLIN, Irving (1888–1989)
(Birthday message to Groucho Marx)
The world would not be in such a snarl, had Marx been Groucho instead of Karl.
[Attr.]

BRACKEN, Brendan (First Viscount) (1901–1958)
It's a good deed to forget a poor joke.
[*The Observer*, 1943]

BROWN, Thomas Edward (1830–1897)
A rich man's joke is always funny.
['The Doctor' (1887)]

BUTLER, Samuel (1835–1902)
The most perfect humour and irony is generally quite unconscious.
[*Life and Habit* (1877)]

CARLYLE, Thomas (1795–1881)
No man who has once heartily and wholly laughed can be altogether irreclaimably bad.
[*Sartor Resartus* (1834)]

CHAMFORT, Nicolas (1741–1794)
The most wasted of all days is the day one did not laugh.
[*Maximes et pensées* (1796)]

CHURCHILL, Charles (1731–1764)
A joke's a very serious thing.
[*The Ghost* (1763)]

COLBY, Frank Moore (1865–1925)
Men will confess to treason, murder, arson, false teeth, or a wig. How many of them will own up to a lack of humour?
[*Essays*]

COOK, Peter (1937–1995)
There's terrific merit in having no sense of humour, no sense of irony, practically no sense of anything at all. If you're born with these so-called defects you have a very good chance of getting to the top.
[In Ronald Bergan *Beyond the Fringe ... and Beyond* (1989)]

DODD, Ken (1931–)
(Commenting on Freud's theory that a good joke will bring relief and elation)
The trouble with Freud is that he never played the Glasgow Empire Saturday night after Rangers and Celtic had both lost.
[TV interview, 1965]

ELIOT, George (1819–1880)
A difference of taste in jokes is a great strain on the affections.
[*Daniel Deronda* (1876)]

GRIFFITHS, Trevor (1935–)
Comedy is medicine.
[*The Comedians* (1979)]

PRIESTLEY, J.B. (1894–1984)
Comedy, we may say, is society protecting itself – with a smile.
[*George Meredith* (1926)]

ROGERS, Will (1879–1935)
Everything is funny as long as it is happening to someone else.
[*The Illiterate Digest* (1924)]

SHAW, George Bernard (1856–1950)
My way of joking is to tell the truth. It's the funniest joke in the world.
[*John Bull's Other Island* (1907)]

WALTON, Izaak (1593–1683)
I love such mirth as does not make friends ashamed to look upon one another next morning.
[*The Compleat Angler* (1653)]

WILCOX, Ella Wheeler (1850-1919)
Laugh and the world laughs with you;
Weep, and you weep alone;
For the sad old earth must borrow its mirth,
But has trouble enough of its own.
['Solitude' (1917)]

WODEHOUSE, P.G. (1881-1975)
She had a penetrating sort of laugh. Rather
like a train going into a tunnel.
[The Inimitable Jeeves (1923)]

HYPOCRISY

BACON, Francis (1561-1626)
It is the wisdom of the crocodiles, that shed
tears when they would devour.
['Of Wisdom for a Man's Self' (1625)]

BYRON, Lord (1788-1824)
Be hypocritical, be cautious, be
Not what you seem but always what you see.
[Don Juan (1824)]

CHURCHILL, Charles (1731-1764)
Keep up appearances; there lies the test;
The world will give thee credit for the rest.
Outward be fair, however foul within;
Sin if thou wilt, but then in secret sin.
['Night' (1761)]

DICKENS, Charles (1812-1870)
With affection beaming in one eye, and
calculation shining out of the other.
[Martin Chuzzlewit (1844)]

EMERSON, Ralph Waldo (1803-1882)
The book written against fame and learning
has the author's name on the title-page.
[Journals]

GAY, John (1685-1732)
An open foe may prove a curse, But a
pretended friend is worse.
[Fables (1727)]

LA ROCHEFOUCAULD (1613-1680)
Hypocrisy is a homage that vice pays to
virtue.
[Maximes (1678)]

MAUGHAM, William Somerset (1874-1965)
Hypocrisy is the most difficult and nerve-
racking vice that any man can pursue; it
needs an unceasing vigilance and a rare
detachment of spirit. It cannot, like adultery
or gluttony, be practised at spare moments;
it is a whole-time job.
[Cakes and Ale (1930)]

MILTON, John (1608-1674)
For neither Man nor Angel can discern
Hypocrisie, the onely evil that walks
Invisible, except to God alone.
[Paradise Lost (1667)]

WILDE, Oscar (1854-1900)
I hope that you have not been leading a
double life, pretending to be wicked and
being really good all the time. That would be
hypocrisy.
[The Importance of Being Earnest (1895)]

YOUNG, Edward (1683-1765)
A man I knew who lived upon a smile,
And well it fed him; he look'd plump and fair,
While rankest venom foam'd through every
vein.
[Night-Thoughts on Life, Death and Immortality
(1742-1746)]

See **DECEPTION**

IDEALISM

DALAI LAMA (1935-)
History shows that most of the positive or
beneficial developments in human society
have occurred as the result of care and
compassion. Consider, for example, the
abolition of the slave trade - Ideals are the
engine of progress.
[The Times, June 1999]

KING, Martin Luther (1929-1968)
I submit to you that if a man hasn't
discovered something he will die for, he isn't
fit to live.
[Speech in Detroit, June 23, 1963]

LAWRENCE, D.H. (1885-1930)
Away with all ideals. Let each individual act
spontaneously from the for ever incalculable
prompting of the creative wellhead within
him. There is no universal law.
[Phoenix (1936)]

MCCARTNEY, Paul (1942-)
The issues are the same. We wanted peace
on earth, love, and understanding between
everyone around the world. We have learned
that change comes slowly.
[The Observer, 1987]

TARKINGTON, Booth (1869-1946)
An ideal wife is any woman who has an ideal
husband.
[Attr.]

THATCHER, Margaret (1925-2013)
If a woman like Eva Peron with no ideals can get that far, think how far I can go with all the ideals that I have.
[*The Sunday Times*, 1980]

IDEAS

ALAIN, Emile-Auguste Chartier (1868-1951)
Nothing is more dangerous than an idea when you only have one idea.
[*Remarks on Religion* (1938)]

BOWEN, Elizabeth (1899-1973)
One can live in the shadow of an idea without grasping it.
[*The Heat of the Day* (1949)]

GEDDES, Patrick (1854-1932)
When an idea is dead it is embalmed in a textbook.
[In Boardman, *The Worlds of Patrick Geddes* (1978)]

HOLMES, Oliver Wendell (Jr) (1841-1935)
Many ideas grow better when transplanted into another mind than in the one where they sprang up.
[In Bowen, *Yankee from Olympus* (1945)]

HUGO, Victor (1802-1885)
One can resist the invasion of an army; but one cannot resist the invasion of ideas.
[*Histoire d'un Crime* (1852)]

LEWIS, Wyndham (1882-1957)
'Dying for an idea,' again, sounds well enough, but why not let the idea die instead of you?
[*The Art of Being Ruled* (1926)]

MACDONALD, Ramsay (1866-1937)
Society goes on and on and on. It is the same with ideas.
[Speech, 1935]

MARQUIS, Don (1878-1937)
An idea isn't responsible for the people who believe in it.
[*New York Sun*]

MEDAWAR, Sir Peter Brian (1915-1987)
The human mind treats a new idea the way the body treats a strange protein – it rejects it.
[Attr.]

PAXMAN, Jeremy (1950-)
The English way with ideas is not to kill them but to let them die of neglect.
[*The Observer*, 1998]

SHAW, George Bernard (1856-1950)
This creature Man, who in his own selfish affairs is a coward to the backbone, will fight for an idea like a hero.
[*Man and Superman* (1903)]

SWIFT, Jonathan (1667-1745)
A nice man is a man of nasty ideas.
[*Thoughts on Various Subjects* (1711)]

See **MIND, OPINIONS, THOUGHT**

IDLENESS AND UNEMPLOYMENT

ADAMS, Scott (1957-)
Of course I don't look busy, I did it right the first time.
[The *Dilbert Principle*]

ANONYMOUS
Doing nothing gets pretty tiresome because you can't stop and rest.

BOILEAU-DESPRÉAUX, Nicolas (1636-1711)
What a terrible burden it is to have nothing to do!
[*Epitres* (c.1690)]

BRUMMEL, Beau (1778-1840)
I always like to have the morning well-aired before I get up.
[In Macfarlane, *Reminiscences of a Literary Life* (1917)]

CHESTERFIELD, Lord (1694-1773)
Idleness is only the refuge of weak minds, and the holiday of fools.
[Letter to his son, 1749]

CHRISTIE, Dame Agatha (1890-1976)
We owe most of our great inventions and most of the achievements of genius to idleness – either enforced or voluntary.
[*The Moving Finger* (1942)]

EWART, Gavin (1916-1995)
After Cambridge – unemployment. No one wanted much to know.
Good degrees are good for nothing in the business world below.
['The Sentimental Education']

FITZGERALD, F. Scott (1896-1940)
'What'll we do with ourselves this afternoon?' cried Daisy,' and the day after that, and the next thirty years?'.
[*The Great Gatsby* (1925)]

FURPHY, Joseph (1843-1912)
Unemployed at last!
[*Such is Life* (1903)]

HEWETT, Dorothy (1923–2002)
For dole bread is bitter bread
Bitter bread and sour
There's grief in the taste of it
There's weevils in the flour.
['Weevils in the Flour']

HOOVER, Herbert (1874–1964)
When a great many people are unable to find
work, unemployment results.
[In Boller, *Presidential Anecdotes* (1981)]

JEROME, Jerome K. (1859–1927)
It is impossible to enjoy idling thoroughly
unless one has plenty of work to do.
[*Idle Thoughts of an Idle Fellow* (1886)]

JOSEPH, Jenny (1932–)
I was raised to feel that doing nothing was a
sin. I had to learn to do nothing.
[*The Observer*, 1998]

JOWETT, Benjamin (1817–1893)
Research! A mere excuse for idleness; it has
never achieved, and will never achieve any
results of the slightest value.
[In Logan Pearsall Smith, *Unforgotten Years*]

MARX, Karl (1818–1883)
Without doubt machinery has greatly
increased the number of well-to-do idlers.
[*Das Kapital* (1867)]

MAUGHAM, William Somerset (1874–1965)
It was such a lovely day I thought it was a pity
to get up.
[*Our Betters* (1923)]

NASH, Ogden (1902–1971)
I would live my life in nonchalance and
insouciance
Were it not for making a living, which is rather
a nouciance.
['Introspective Reflection' (1940)]

THURBER, James (1894–1961)
It is better to have loafed and lost than never
to have loafed at all.
[*Fables for Our Time* (1940)]

WARD, Artemus (1834–1867)
I am happiest when I am idle. I could live for
months without performing any kind of
labour, and at the expiration of that time I
should feel fresh and vigorous enough to go
right on in the same way for numerous more
months.
[*Artemus Ward in London* (1867)]

See **BED**

AUBREY, John (1626–1697)
Sciatica: he cured it, by boiling his buttock.
[*Brief Lives* (c.1693)]

AUSTIN, Alfred (1835–1913)
(On the illness of the Prince of Wales)
Across the wires the electric message came:
'He is no better, he is much the same.'
[Attr.]

BACON, Francis (1561–1626)
The remedy is worse than the disease.
['Of Seditions and Troubles' (1625)]

CHEKHOV, Anton (1860–1904)
If many remedies are suggested for a disease,
that means the disease is incurable.
[*The Cherry Orchard* (1904)]

DAVIES, Robertson (1913–1995)
Not to be healthy … is one of the few sins
that modern society is willing to recognise
and condemn.
[*The Cunning Man* (1994)]

EMERSON, Ralph Waldo (1803–1882)
A person seldom falls sick, but the bystanders
are animated with a faint hope that he will die.
[*Conduct of Life* (1860)]

GALBRAITH, J.K. (1908–2006)
Much of the world's work, it has been said, is
done by men who do not feel quite well. Marx
is a case in point.
[*The Age of Uncertainty*]

HELLER, Joseph (1923–1999)
Hungry Joe collected lists of fatal diseases and
arranged them in alphabetical order so that
he could put his finger without delay on any
one he wanted to worry about.
[*Catch-22* (1961)]

HIPPOCRATES (c.460–357 BC)
For extreme illnesses extreme remedies are
most fitting.
[*Aphorisms*]

MCAULEY, James Philip (1917–1976)
(After his first cancer operation; to a friend)
Well, better a semi-colon than a full stop!
[In Coleman, *The Heart of James McAuley*
(1980)]

PERELMAN, S.J. (1904–1979)
I've got Bright's disease and he's got mine.
[Attr.]

See **HEALTH, MEDICINE**

IMAGINATION

AUSTEN, Jane (1775–1817)
A lady's imagination is very rapid; it jumps
from admiration to love, from love to
matrimony, in a moment.
[*Pride and Prejudice* (1813)]

BACALL, Lauren (1924–)
Imagination is the highest kite that one can fly.
[*Lauren Bacall, By Myself*]

BLAKE, William (1757–1827)
What is now proved was once only imagin'd.
['Proverbs of Hell', (c.1793)]

EINSTEIN, Albert (1879–1955)
Imagination is more important than
knowledge.
[*On Science*]

ELIOT, George (1819–1880)
He said he should prefer not to know the
sources of the Nile, and that there should be
some unknown regions preserved as
hunting-grounds for the poetic imagination.
[*Middlemarch* (1872)]

JOUBERT, Joseph (1754–1824)
Imagination is the eye of the soul.
[Attr.]

ROBINSON, Roland Edward (1912–1992)
Where does imagination start but from
primeval images in man's barbaric heart?
['Mopoke']

STEAD, Christina (1902–1983)
I don't know what imagination is, if not an
unpruned, tangled kind of memory.
[*Letty Fox: Her Luck* (1946)]

VIDAL, Gore (1925–2012)
It is the spirit of the age to believe that any
fact, no matter how suspect, is superior to
any imaginative exercise, no matter how true.
[*French Letters: Theories of the New Novel*]

IMMORTALITY

ALLEN, Woody (1935–)
I don't want to achieve immortality through
my work ... I want to achieve it by not dying.
[Attr.]

BECKETT, Samuel (1906–1989)
Clov: Do you believe in the life to come?
Hamm: Mine was always that.
[*Endgame* (1958)]

EMERSON, Ralph Waldo (1803–1882)
Other world! There is no other world! Here or
nowhere is the whole fact.
['Natural Religion']

ERTZ, Susan (1894–1985)
Someone has somewhere commented on the
fact that millions long for immortality who
don't know what to do with themselves on a
rainy Sunday afternoon.
[*Anger in the Sky* (1943)]

HAZLITT, William (1778–1830)
No young man believes he shall ever die.
['On the Feeling of Immortality in Youth'
(1827)]

HELLER, Joseph (1923–1999)
He had decided to live forever or die in the
attempt.
[*Catch-22* (1961)]

PLATO (c.429–347 BC)
Let us be persuaded ... to consider that the
soul is immortal and capable of enduring all
evil and all good and so we shall always hold
to the upward way and pursue justice with
wisdom.
[*Republic*]

STASSINOPOULOS, Arianna (1950–)
Our current obsession with creativity is the
result of our continued striving for
immortality in an era when most people no
longer believe in an afterlife.
[*The Female Woman* (1973)]

THOREAU, Henry David (1817–1862)
(On being asked his opinion of the hereafter)
One world at a time.
[Attr.]

See **ETERNITY, MORTALITY**

INCOME

AUSTEN, Jane (1775–1817)
A large income is the best recipe for
happiness I ever heard of. It certainly may
secure all the myrtle and turkey part of it.
[*Mansfield Park* (1814)]

BUTLER, Samuel (1835–1902)
All progress is based upon a universal innate
desire on the part of every organism to live
beyond its income.
[*The Note-Books of Samuel Butler* (1912)]

DICKENS, Charles (1812–1870)
Annual income twenty pounds, annual expenditure nineteen nineteen six, result happiness. Annual income twenty pounds, annual expenditure twenty pounds ought and six, result misery.
[*David Copperfield* (1850)]

PARKINSON, C. Northcote (1909–1993)
Expenditure rises to meet income.
[Attr.]

SAKI (1870–1916)
I'm living so far beyond my income that we might almost be said to be living apart.
[Attr.]

All decent people live beyond their incomes nowadays and those who aren't respectable live beyond other people's. A few gifted individuals manage to do both.
[*The Chronicles of Clovis* (1911)]

SAUNDERS, Ernest (1935–)
I was on a basic £100,000 a year. You don't make many savings on that.
[*The Observer*, 1987]

SHAKESPEARE, William (1564–1616)
Remuneration! O, that's the Latin word for three farthings.
[*Love's Labour Lost*, III.i]

SMITH, Logan Pearsall (1865–1946)
There are few sorrows, however poignant, in which a good income is of no avail.
[*Afterthoughts* (1931)]

See **MONEY AND WEALTH**

INDECISION

ASQUITH, Margot (1864–1945)
(Of Sir Stafford Cripps)
He has a brilliant mind until he makes it up.
[In *The Wit of the Asquiths*]

BEVAN, Aneurin (1897–1960)
We know what happens to people who stay in the middle of the road. They get run over.
[*The Observer*, 1953]

THE BIBLE
(King James Version)
How long halt ye between two opinions?
[*I Kings* 18:21]

BROOKS, Mel (1926–)
He who hesitates is poor.
[*The Producers*, film, 1968]

JAMES, William (1842–1910)
There is no more miserable human being than one in whom nothing is habitual but indecision.
[*Principles of Psychology* (1890)]

NASH, Ogden (1902–1971)
If I could but spot a conclusion, I should race to it.
['All, All Are Gone, The Old Familiar Quotations' (1952)]

SMITH, Sir Cyril (1928–2010)
If the fence is strong enough I'll sit on it.
[*The Observer*, 1974]

TWAIN, Mark (1835–1910)
I must have a prodigious quantity of mind; it takes me as much as a week, sometimes, to make it up.
[*The Innocents Abroad* (1869)]

See **UNCERTAINTY**

INDEPENDENCE

AESOP (6th century BC)
The gods help those who help themselves.
['Hercules and the Waggoner']

BRANCUSI, Constantin (1876–1957)
(Refusing Rodin's invitation to work in his studio)
Nothing grows well in the shade of a big tree.
[Attr.]

GIBBON, Edward (1737–1794)
The first of earthly blessings, independence.
[*Memoirs of My Life and Writings* (1796)]

IBSEN, Henrik (1828–1906)
The strongest man in the world is the man who stands alone.
[*An Enemy of the People* (1882)]

MARRYAT, Frederick (1792–1848)
I think it much better that ... every man paddle his own canoe.
[*Settlers in Canada* (1844)]

THOREAU, Henry David (1817–1862)
I would rather sit on a pumpkin and have it all to myself than be crowded on a velvet cushion.
[*Walden* (1854)]

INGRATITUDE

CHILLINGWORTH, William (1602–1644)
I once knew a man out of courtesy help a lame dog over a stile, and he for requital bit his fingers.
[*The Religion of Protestants* (1637)]

GARCÍA MÁRQUEZ, Gabriel (1928–)
There are no limits to human ingratitude.
[*No-one Writes to the Colonel* (1961)]

HUXLEY, Aldous (1894–1963)
Most human beings have an almost infinite
capacity for taking things for granted.
[*Themes and Variations* (1950)]

LA ROCHEFOUCAULD (1613–1680)
Over-great haste to repay an obligation is a
form of ingratitude.
[*Maximes* (1678)]

LOUIS XIV (1638–1715)
Every time I make an appointment I make a
hundred men discontented and one
ungrateful.
[In Voltaire, *Siècle de Louis XIV*]

SHAKESPEARE, William (1564–1616)
Blow, blow, thou winter wind,
Thou art not so unkind
As man's ingratitude ...
Thy tooth is not so keen,
Freeze, freeze, thou bitter sky,
That dost not bite so nigh
As benefits forgot.
[*As You Like It*, II.vii]

INSULTS

ALLEN, Dave (1936–2005)
If I had a head like yours, I'd have it circumcised.
[In Gus Smith, *God's Own Comedian*]

AUSTEN, Jane (1775–1817)
You have delighted us long enough.
[*Pride and Prejudice* (1813)]

BAKER, Josephine (1906–1975)
I like Frenchmen very much, because even
when they insult you they do it so nicely.
[Attr.]

CHESTERFIELD, Lord (1694–1773)
An injury is much sooner forgotten than an
insult.
[Letter to his son, 1746]

CORNEILLE, Pierre (1606–1684)
He who allows himself to be insulted,
deserves to be.
[*Héraclius* (1646)]

GILBERT, W.S. (1836–1911)
I shouldn't be sufficiently degraded in my
own estimation unless I was insulted with a
very considerable bribe.
[*The Mikado* (1885)]

JOHNSON, Samuel (1709–1784)
(To an abusive Thames waterman)
Sir, your wife, under pretence of keeping a
bawdy-house, is a receiver of stolen goods.
[In Boswell, *The Life of Samuel Johnson* (1791)]

KELLY, Ned (1855–1880)
A parcel of big, ugly, fat-necked wombat
headed magpie legged narrow hipped splew
footed sons of Irish Bailiffs or English
landlords which is better known as Officers of
Justice or Victorian Police.
[In *The Jerilderie Letter*]

LLOYD GEORGE, David (1863–1945)
(Of Sir Douglas Haig)
He was brilliant to the top of his army boots.
[Attr.]

PARKER, Dorothy (1893–1967)
(Reply to the comment, 'Anyway, she's always
very nice to her inferiors')
Where does she find them?
[In Lyttelton Hart-Davis, *Letters*]

SHERIDAN, Richard Brinsley (1751–1816)
If it is abuse, – why one is always sure to hear
of it from one damned good-natured friend or
another!
[*The Critic* (1779)]

THURBER, James (1894–1961)
A man should not insult his wife publicly, at
parties. He should insult her in the privacy of
the home.
[*Thurber Country* (1953)]

WILDER, Billy (1906–2002)
(Said to singer Cliff Osmond)
You have Van Gogh's ear for music.
[Attr.]

See **ACTORS, CRITICISM, POLITICIANS**

INTELLECTUALS

AGNEW, Spiro T. (1918–1996)
A spirit of national masochism prevails,
encouraged by an effete corps of impudent
snobs who characterize themselves as
intellectuals.
[*New York Times*, October 1969]

AUDEN, W.H. (1907–1973)
To the man-in-the-street, who, I'm sorry to
say,
Is a keen observer of life,
The word intellectual suggests straight away
A man who's untrue to his wife.
[*Collected Poems*, 1939–1947]

BANKHEAD, Tallulah (1903–1968)
I've been called many things, but never an intellectual.
[Tallulah (1952)]

BARZUN, Jacques (1907–2012)
The intellectuals' chief cause of anguish are one another's works.
[The House of Intellect (1959)]

BLAKE, William (1757–1827)
I care not whether a Man is Good or Evil; all that I care Is whether he is a Wise Man or a Fool. Go! put off Holiness And put on Intellect.
[Jerusalem (1804–1820)]

BRENAN, Gerald (1894–1987)
Intellectuals are people who believe that ideas are of more importance than values. That is to say, their own ideas and other people's values.
[Thoughts in a Dry Season (1978)]

SCHWEITZER, Albert (1875–1965)
'Hello, friend,' I shout,' Won't you help us?' 'I am an intellectual and don't carry wood around,' came the answer. 'You're lucky,' I replied. 'I too wanted to become an intellectual, but I didn't manage it.'
[Mitteilungen aus Lambarene (1928)]

STEVENSON, Adlai (1900–1965)
Eggheads of the world unite; you have nothing to lose but your yolks.
[Attr.]

See **INTELLIGENCE, MIND, THOUGHT**

INTELLIGENCE

ALLEN, Woody (1935–)
My brain: it's my second favourite organ.
[Sleeper, film, 1973]

BALDWIN, Stanley (1867–1947)
The intelligent are to the intelligentsia what a gentleman is to a gent.
[Attr.]

BOGARDE, Dirk (1921–1999)
I'm not very clever, but I'm quite intelligent.
[Attr.]

DOYLE, Sir Arthur Conan (1859–1930)
I am a brain, Watson. The rest of me is a mere appendix.
[The Case Book of Sherlock Holmes (1927)]

FREUD, Sigmund (1856–1939)
The voice of the intellect is a soft one, but it does not rest till it has gained a hearing.
[The Future of an Illusion]

LA ROCHEFOUCAULD (1613–1680)
The height of cleverness is to be able to conceal it.
[Maximes (1678)]

MACAULAY, Lord (1800–1859)
The highest intellects, like the tops of mountains, are the first to catch and to reflect the dawn.
['Sir James Mackintosh' (1843)]

MANN, Thomas (1875–1955)
Every intellectual attitude is latently political.
[The Observer, 1974]

NIETZSCHE, Friedrich Wilhelm (1844–1900)
Wit is the epigram for the death of an emotion.
[Human, All too Human (1886)]

PASCAL, Blaise (1623–1662)
The more intelligence one has the more people one finds original. Commonplace people see no difference between men.
[Pensées (1670)]

SCHOPENHAUER, Arthur (1788–1860)
Intellect is invisible to the man who has none.
[Aphorismen zur Lebensweisheit]

SHAKESPEARE, William (1564–1616)
Brevity is the soul of wit.
[Hamlet, II.ii]
Look, he's winding up the watch of his wit; by and by it will strike.
[The Tempest, II.i]
This fellow is wise enough to play the fool; And to do that well craves a kind of wit.
[Twelfth Night, III.i]

WHITEHEAD, A.N. (1861–1947)
Intelligence is quickness to apprehend as distinct from ability, which is capacity to act wisely on the thing apprehended.
[Dialogues (1954)]

See **INTELLECTUALS, KNOWLEDGE, MIND, PERCEPTION, THOUGHT, WISDOM**

THE INTERNET

CHOMSKY, Noam (1928–)
The Internet is an élite organisation; most of the population of the world has never even made a phone call.
[The Observer Review, 1996]

FASULO, Tom
Surfing on the Internet is like sex; everyone boasts about doing more than they actually do. But in the case of the Internet, it's a lot more.

GERSTNER, Lou (1942–)
The killer app[lication] will not be a shrink-wrapped program that sells in millions. The killer app will be a Web site that touches millions of people and helps them to do what they want to do.

GIBSON, William (1948–)
Cyberspace: A consensual hallucination experienced daily by billions of legitimate operators, in every nation.
[*Neuromancer* (1984)]

SIRIAM, M.G.
Looking at the proliferation of personal web pages on the net, it looks like very soon everyone on earth will have 15 Megabytes of fame.

WILENSKY, Robert (1951–)
We've all heard that a million monkeys banging on a million typewriters will eventually reproduce the entire works of Shakespeare. Now, thanks to the Internet, we know this is not true.
[*Mail on Sunday*, February 1997]

See **COMPUTERS, MEDIA, TECHNOLOGY**

INVENTION

ANONYMOUS
Every revolutionary idea – in science, politics, art, or whatever – evokes three stages of reaction in a hearer:
• It is completely impossible – don't waste my time.
• It is possible, but it is not worth doing.
• I said it was a good idea all along.

BACON, Francis (1561–1626)
He that will not apply new remedies must expect new evils; for time is the greatest innovator.
[*Essays* (1625)]

BIERCE, Ambrose (1842–c.1914)
An inventor is a person who makes an ingenious arrangement of wheels, levers and springs, and believes it civilization.
[*The Devil's Dictionary*, 1958]

EDISON, Thomas Alva (1847–1931)
To invent, you need a good imagination and a pile of junk.
[Attr.]

EMERSON, Ralph Waldo (1803–1882)
Invention breeds invention.
[*Society and Solitude* (1870)]

FRANKLIN, Benjamin (1706–1790)
(On being asked the use of a new invention)
What is the use of a new-born child?
[In Parton, *Life and Times of Benjamin Franklin* (1864)]

See **SCIENCE**

IRELAND

ALLINGHAM, William (1824–1889)
Not men and women in an Irish street
But Catholics and Protestants you meet.
[Attr.]

ANONYMOUS
Anyone who isn't confused here doesn't really understand what's going on.
[Belfast citizen, 1970]

ASCHERSON, Neal (1932–)
Peace in Northern Ireland has to built on its divisions, not on a fiction of unity which does not yet exist.
[*The Observer*, 1998]

BATES, Daisy May (1863–1951)
There are a few fortunate races that have been endowed with cheerfulness as their main characteristic, the Australian Aborigine and the Irish being among these.
[*The Passing of the Aborigines* ... (1938)]

BEHAN, Brendan (1923–1964)
Pat: He was an Anglo-Irishman.
Meg: In the blessed name of God, what's that?
Pat: A Protestant with a horse.
[*The Hostage* (1958)]
Other people have a nationality. The Irish and the Jews have a psychosis.
[*Richard's Cork Leg* (1972)]

DE VALERA, Eamon (1882–1975)
Whenever I wanted to know what the Irish people wanted, I had only to examine my own heart and it told me straight off what the Irish people wanted.
[*Dáil Éireann*, 1922]

DISRAELI, Benjamin (1804–1881)
A starving population, an absentee aristocracy, and an alien Church, and in addition the weakest executive in the world. That is the Irish question.
[Speech, 1844]

DOYLE, Roddy (1958-)
The Irish are the niggers of Europe ... An'
Dubliners are the niggers of Ireland ... An' the
northside Dubliners are the niggers o' Dublin
– Say it loud. I'm black an' I'm proud.
[*The Commitments* (1987)]

GOGARTY, Oliver St John (1878-1957)
Politics is the chloroform of the Irish people,
or rather the hashish.
[*As I Was Going Down Sackville Street* (1937)]

JOYCE, James (1882-1941)
Ireland is the old sow that eats her farrow.
[*A Portrait of the Artist as a Young Man* (1916)]

O'FAOLAIN, Sean (1900-1991)
An Irish Quaker is a fellow who prefers
women to drink.
[Attr. on Nigel Rees BBC programme,
Quote Unquote, 1999]

SHAW, George Bernard (1856-1950)
An Irishman's heart is nothing but his
imagination.
[*John Bull's Other Island* (1907)]

SMITH, Sydney (1771-1845)
The moment the very name of Ireland is
mentioned, the English seem to bid adieu to
common feeling, common prudence, and to
common sense, and to act with the barbarity
of tyrants, and the fatuity of idiots.
[*Letters of Peter Plymley* (1807)]

YEATS, W.B. (1865-1939)
Behind Ireland fierce and militant, is Ireland
poetic, passionate, remembering, idyllic,
fanciful, and always patriotic.
['Popular Ballad Poetry of Ireland', 1889]

JEALOUSY

JONG, Erica (1942-)
Jealousy is all the fun you think they had.
[*Fear of Flying* (1973)]

MILTON, John (1608-1674)
Nor jealousie
Was understood, the injur'd
Lover's Hell.
[*Paradise Lost* (1667)]

SAGAN, Françoise (1935-2004)
To jealousy nothing is more frightful than
laughter.
[Attr.]

SHAKESPEARE, William (1564-1616)
O, beware, my lord, of jealousy;
It is the green-ey'd monster which doth mock
The meat it feeds on.
[*Othello*, III.iii]

Trifles light as air
Are to the jealous confirmations strong
As proofs of holy writ.
[*Othello*, III.iii]

Jealous souls will not be answer'd so;
They are not ever jealous for the cause,
But jealous for they are jealous.
[*Othello*, III.iv]

WELLS, H.G. (1866-1946)
Moral indignation is jealousy with a halo.
[*The Wife of Sir Isaac Harman* (1914)]

See **ENVY**

JEWELLERY

DICKENS, Charles (1812-1870)
It was not a bosom to repose upon, but it was
a capital bosom to hang jewels upon.
[*Little Dorrit* (1857)]

LENNON, John (1940-1980)
Those in the cheaper seats clap your hands.
And the rest of you, if you'll just rattle your
jewellery.
[Remark, Royal Variety Performance, 1963]

LOOS, Anita (1893-1981)
Any girl who was a lady would not even think
of having such a good time that she did not
remember to hang on to her jewelry.
[*Gentlemen Prefer Blondes* (1925)]

ROBIN, Leo (1900-1984)
Diamonds Are A Girl's Best Friend.
[Song title, 1949]

WEST, Mae (1892-1980)
'Goodness, what beautiful diamonds!'
'Goodness had nothing to do with it!'.
[*Night After Night*, film, 1932]

JUDAISM

BALFOUR, A.J. (1848-1930)
His Majesty's Government views with favour
the establishment in Palestine of a national
home for the Jewish people.
['The Balfour Declaration', 1917]

BLUE, Rabbi Lionel (1930–)
There is always a danger in Judaism of seeing history as a sort of poker game played between Jews and God, in which the presence of others is noted but not given much importance.
[*The Observer*, 1982]

HEINE, Heinrich (1797–1856)
It is extremely difficult for a Jew to be converted, for how can he bring himself to believe in the divinity of – another Jew?
[Attr.]

JOHNSON, Paul (1928–)
For me this is a vital litmus test: no intellectual society can flourish where a Jew feels even slightly uneasy.
[*The Sunday Times Magazine*, 1977]

LAWRENCE, D.H. (1885–1930)
The very best that is in the Jewish blood: a faculty for pure disinterestedness, and warm, physically warm love, that seems to make the corpuscles of the blood glow.
[*Kangaroo* (1923)]

MARX, Groucho (1895–1977)
(When excluded, on racial grounds, from a beach club)
Since my daughter is only half-Jewish, could she go into the water up to her knees?
[*The Observer*, 1977]

MILLER, Jonathan (1934–)
I'm not really a Jew; just Jew-ish, not the whole hog.
[*Beyond the Fringe* (1961)]

MILLIGAN, Spike (1918–2002)
Q. Are you Jewish?
A. No, a tree fell on me.
[*Private Eye*, 1973]

ROTH, Philip (1933–)
A Jewish man with parents alive is a fifteen-year-old boy, and will remain a fifteen-year-old boy until they die.
[*Portnoy's Complaint* (1969)]

STEIN, Gertrude (1874–1946)
The Jews have produced only three originative geniuses: Christ, Spinoza, and myself.
[In Mellow, *Charmed Circle* (1974)]

ZANGWILL, Israel (1864–1926)
No Jew was ever fool enough to turn Christian unless he was a clever man.
[*Children of the Ghetto* (1892)]

See **PREJUDICE, RACE, RELIGION**

JUDGEMENT

AUGUSTINE, Saint (354–430)
The judgement of the world is sure.
[*Contra Epistolam Parmeniani*]

**THE BIBLE
(King James Version)**
Judge not, that ye be not judged.
[*Matthew*, 7:1]
By their fruits ye shall know them.
[*Matthew*, 7:20]
He that is without sin among you, let him first cast a stone at her.
[*Luke*, 8:7]

BRUNO, Giordano (1548–1600)
(Said to the cardinals who excommunicated him)
Perhaps your fear in passing judgement is greater than mine in receiving it.
[Attr.]

CAMUS, Albert (1913–1960)
Don't wait for the Last Judgement. It is taking place every day.
[*The Fall* (1956)]

COMPTON-BURNETT, Dame Ivy (1884–1969)
Appearances are not held to be a clue to the truth. But we seem to have no other.
[*Manservant and Maidservant* (1947)]

COWPER, William (1731–1800)
Judgment drunk, and brib'd to lose his way, Winks hard, and talks of darkness at noon-day.
['The Progress of Error' (1782)]

MONTAIGNE, Michel de (1533–1592)
It is a dangerous and serious presumption, and argues an absurd temerity, to condemn what we do not understand.
[*Essais* (1580)]

PLINY THE ELDER (AD 23–79)
The cobbler should not judge beyond his last.
[*Historia Naturalis*]

SHAKESPEARE, William (1564–1616)
What judgment shall I dread, doing no wrong?
[*The Merchant of Venice*, IV.i]

JUSTICE AND INJUSTICE

BENNETT, Arnold (1867–1931)
The price of justice is eternal publicity.
[*Things That Have Interested Me*]

KINDNESS

BINGHAM, Sir Thomas (1933-)
(Discussing the rising costs of going to law)
We cannot for ever be content to
acknowledge that in England justice is open
to all - like the Ritz Hotel.
[*Independent on Sunday*, 1994]

BLACKSTONE, Sir William (1723-1780)
It is better that ten guilty persons escape than
one innocent suffer.
[*Commentaries on the Laws of England* (1765-1769)]

BURROUGHS, William S. (1914-1999)
If you can't be just, be arbitrary.
[*Naked Lunch* (1959)]

CARLYLE, Jane Welsh (1801-1866)
When one has been threatened with a great
injustice, one accepts a smaller as a favour.
[Journal, 1855]

FIELDING, Henry (1707-1754)
Thwackum was for doing justice, and leaving
mercy to Heaven.
[*Tom Jones* (1749)]

FRANCE, Anatole (1844-1924)
To disarm the strong and arm the weak would
be to change a social order which I have been
commissioned to preserve. Justice is the
means whereby established injustices are
sanctioned.
[*Crainquebille* (1904)]

JUNIUS (1769-1772)
The injustice done to an individual is
sometimes of service to the public.
[Letters (1769-1771)]

KELLY, Ned (1855-1880)
There never was such a thing as justice in the
English laws but any amount of injustice to
be had.
[In *Overland*, 1981]

KING, Martin Luther (1929-1968)
Injustice anywhere is a threat to justice
everywhere.
[Letter from Birmingham Jail, 1963]

LA ROCHEFOUCAULD (1613-1680)
The love of justice in most men is no more
than the fear of suffering injustice.
[*Maximes* (1678)]

LINCOLN, Abraham (1809-1865)
The probability that we may fail in the
struggle ought not to deter us from the
support of a cause we believe to be just.
[Speech, 1859]

MAGNA CARTA (1215-)
To no one will we sell, to no one will we deny,
or delay, right or justice.
[Clause 40]

MENCKEN, H.L. (1880-1956)
Injustice is relatively easy to bear: what stings
is justice.
[Attr.]

MILTON, John (1608-1674)
Yet I shall temper so
Justice with Mercie.
[*Paradise Lost* (1667)]

ROUX, Joseph (1834-1886)
We love justice greatly, and just men but little.
[*Meditations of a Parish Priest* (1886)]

SHAKESPEARE, William (1564-1616)
What stronger breastplate than a heart
untainted?
Thrice is he arm'd that hath his quarrel just;
And he but naked, though lock'd up in steel,
Whose conscience with injustice is corrupted.
[*Henry VI, Part 2*, III.ii]

SHIRLEY, James (1596-1666)
Only the actions of the just
Smell sweet, and blossom in their dust.
[*The Contention of Ajax and Ulysses* (1659)]

STOPPARD, Tom (1937-)
This is a British murder inquiry and some
degree of justice must be seen to be more or
less done.
[*Jumpers* (1972)]

WILDE, Oscar (1854-1900)
For Man's grim Justice goes its way,
And will not swerve aside:
It slays the weak, it slays the strong,
It has a deadly stride.
[*The Ballad of Reading Gaol* (1898)]

See **JUDGEMENT, LAW**

KINDNESS

ANONYMOUS
Be kind to unkind people - they need it the
most.

CONFUCIUS (c.550-c.478 BC)
Recompense injury with justice and
recompense kindness with kindness.
[*Analects*]

DAVIES, William Henry (1871-1940)
I love thee for a heart that's kind -
Not for the knowledge in thy mind.
['Sweet Stay-at-Home' (1913)]

GIDE, André (1869–1951)
True kindness presupposes the faculty of imagining as one's own the suffering and joy of others.

[Attr.]

JOHNSON, Samuel (1709–1784)
Always, Sir, set a high value on spontaneous kindness. He whose inclination prompts him to cultivate your friendship of his own accord, will love you more than one whom you have been at pains to attach to you.

[In Boswell, *The Life of Samuel Johnson* (1791)]

SHAKESPEARE, William (1564–1616)
I must be cruel, only to be kind.

[*Hamlet*, III.iv]

WILCOX, Ella Wheeler (1850–1919)
So many gods, so many creeds,
So many paths that wind and wind,
While just the art of being kind
Is all the sad world needs.

['The World's Need' (1917)]

WILLIAMS, Tennessee (1911–1983)
I have always depended on the kindness of strangers.

[*A Streetcar Named Desire* (1947)]

See **CHARITY**

KNOWLEDGE

ADAMS, Henry (1838–1918)
They know enough who know how to learn.

[*The Education of Henry Adams* (1918)]

BACON, Francis (1561–1626)
Knowledge itself is power.

['Of Heresies' (1597)]

**THE BIBLE
(King James Version)**
He that increaseth knowledge increaseth sorrow.

[*Ecclesiastes* 1:18]

HOLMES, Oliver Wendell (1809–1894)
It is the province of knowledge to speak and it is the privilege of wisdom to listen.

[*The Poet at the Breakfast-Table* (1872)]

JOAD, C.E.M. (1891–1953)
There was never an age in which useless knowledge was more important than in ours.

[*The Observer*, 1951]

JOHNSON, Samuel (1709–1784)
Integrity without knowledge is weak and useless, and knowledge without integrity is dangerous and dreadful.

[Rasselas (1759)]

MACAULAY, Lord (1800–1859)
Knowledge advances by steps, and not by leaps.

['History' (1828)]

MILTON, John (1608–1674)
The first and wisest of them all professd
To know this onely, that he nothing knew.

[*Paradise Regained* (1671)]

MUMFORD, Ethel (1878–1940)
Knowledge is power if you know it about the right person.

[In Cowan, *The Wit of Women*]

POPPER, Sir Karl (1902–1994)
Our knowledge can only be finite, while our ignorance must necessarily be infinite.

[*Conjectures and Refutations* (1963)]

SHARPE, Tom (1928–2013)
His had been an intellectual decision founded on his conviction that if a little knowledge was a dangerous thing, a lot was lethal.

[*Porterhouse Blue* (1974)]

SHERIDAN, Richard Brinsley (1751–1816)
Madam, a circulating library in a town is an ever-green tree of diabolical knowledge! – It blossoms through the year! – And depend on it, Mrs Malaprop, that they who are so fond of handling the leaves, will long for the fruit at last.

[*The Rivals* (1775)]

See **EDUCATION, LEARNING, WISDOM**

LANGUAGE

CHURCHILL, Sir Winston (1874–1965)
(Marginal comment on a document)
This is the sort of English up with which I will not put.

[In Gowers, *Plain Words* (1948)]

DAY, Clarence Shepard (1874–1935)
Imagine the Lord talking French! Aside from a few odd words in Hebrew, I took it completely for granted that God had never spoken anything but the most dignified English.

[*Life with Father* (1935)]

DICKENS, Charles (1812–1870)
There was no light nonsense about Miss Blimber ... She was dry and sandy with working in the graves of deceased languages. None of your live languages for Miss Blimber. They must be dead – stone dead – and then Miss Blimber dug them up like a Ghoul.

[*Dombey and Son* (1848)]

EMERSON, Ralph Waldo (1803–1882)
Language is fossil poetry.

['The Poet' (1844)]

FRANKLIN, Benjamin (1706-1790)
Write with the learned, pronounce with the vulgar.
[*Poor Richard's Almanac* (1738)]

GOETHE (1749-1832)
Whoever is not acquainted with foreign languages knows nothing of his own.
[On *Art and Antiquity* (1827)]

GOLDWYN, Samuel (1882-1974)
Let's have some new clichés.
[*The Observer*, 1948]

JESPERSEN, Otto (1860-1943)
In his whole life man achieves nothing so great and so wonderful as what he achieved when he learned to talk.
[*Language* (1904)]

JOHNSON, Samuel (1709-1784)
Language is the dress of thought.
[*The Lives of the Most Eminent English Poets* (1781)]

LANGLAND, William (c.1330-c.1400)
Grammere, that grounde is of alle.
[*The Vision of William Concerning Piers the Plowman*]

LÉVI-STRAUSS, Claude (1908-2009)
Language is a kind of human reason, which has its own internal logic of which man knows nothing.
[*The Savage Mind* (1962)]

LIVELY, Penelope (1933-2000)
Language tethers us to the world; without it we spin like atoms.
[*Moon Tiger* (1987)]

MACAULAY, Lord (1800-1859)
The English Bible, a book which, if everything else in our language should perish, would alone suffice to show the whole extent of its beauty and power.
['John Dryden' (1843)]

MILLIGAN, Spike (1918-2002)
The cliche is the handrail of the crippled mind.
[Quoted in *The Herald*, February 2002]

NARAYAN, R.K. (1906-2001)
English is a very adaptable language. And it's so transparent it can take on the tint of any country.
[Radio conversation, 1968]

PARKER, Dorothy (1893-1967)
(Of an acquaintance)
You know, she speaks eighteen languages. And she can't say 'No' in any of them.
[In J. Keats, *You Might As Well Live* (1970)]

SHAW, George Bernard (1856-1950)
England and America are two countries separated by the same language.
[*Reader's Digest*, 1942]

SIGISMUND (1368-1437)
(Responding to criticism of his Latin)
I am the Roman Emperor and am above grammar.
[Attr.]

SPENSER, Edmund (c.1522-1599)
So now they have made our English tongue, a gallimaufray or hodgepodge of al other speches.
[*The Shepheardes Calender* (1579)]

SULLIVAN, Annie (1866-1936)
Language grows out of life, out of its needs and experiences ... Language and knowledge are indissolubly connected; they are interdependent. Good work in language presupposes and depends on a real knowledge of things.
[Speech, 1894]

TOMLIN, Lily (1939-)
Man invented language in order to satisfy his deep need to complain.
[In Pinker, *The Language Instinct* (1994)]

TUCHOLSKY, Kurt (1890-1935)
English is a simple, yet hard language. It consists entirely of foreign words pronounced wrongly.
[*Scraps* (1973)]

See **CLASS, STYLE, WORDS, WRITING**

LAST WORDS

ADDISON, Joseph (1672-1719)
See in what peace a Christian can die.

APPEL, George (d.1928-)
(Executed in the electric chair)
Well, gentlemen, you are about to see a baked Appel.

BANKHEAD, Tallulah (1903-1968)
Codeine ... bourbon.
[Attr.]

BARNUM, Phineas T. (1810-1891)
How were the receipts today at Madison Square Garden?
[Attr.]

BARRIE, Sir J.M. (1860-1937)
I can't sleep.
[Attr.]

BARRYMORE, Ethel (1879-1959)
Is everybody happy? I want everybody to be happy. I know I'm happy.
[Attr.]

BEETHOVEN, Ludwig van (1770-1827)
Friends applaud, the comedy is finished.
[Attr.]

BELL, Alexander Graham (1847-1922)
So little done. So much to do.

BOGART, Humphrey (1899-1957)
I should never have changed from scotch to martinis.
[In Simon Rose, *Classic Film Guide* (1995)]

CHUBBUCK, Chris (d.1974)
(US newsreader before shooting herself during a broadcast.)
And now, in keeping with Channel 40's policy of always bringing you the latest in blood and guts, in living color, you're about to see another first – an attempted suicide.

GEORGE V (1865-1936)
(To Lord Wigram, his secretary; sometimes quoted as his last words)
How is the Empire?
[Attr.]

GILMORE, Gary (d.1977)
(Executed by firing squad)
Let's do it!
[Attr.]

GOETHE (1749-1832)
More light!
[Attr.]

HEGEL, Georg Wilhelm (1770-1831)
Only one man ever understood me ... And he didn't understand me.
[In B. Conrad, *Famous Last Words* (1962)]

HOBBES, Thomas (1588-1679)
I am about to take my last voyage, a great leap in the dark.
[In Watkins, *Anecdotes of Men of Learning* (1808)]

HOLLAND, First Lord (Henry Fox) (1705-1774)
(Said during his last illness)
If Mr Selwyn calls, let him in: if I am alive I shall be very glad to see him, and if I am dead he will be very glad to see me.
[Attr.]

HUME, David (1711-1776)
I am dying as fast as my enemies, if I have any, could wish, and as cheerfully as my best friends could desire.

IBSEN, Henrik (1828-1906)
(Ibsen's last words; his nurse had just remarked that he was feeling a little better)
On the contrary!
[Attr.]

LATIMER, Bishop Hugh (c.1485-1555)
(Said shortly before being put to death)
Be of good comfort, Master Ridley, and play the man. We shall this day light such a candle by God's grace in England, as (I trust) shall never be put out.
[In Foxe, *Actes and Monuments* (1562-1563)]

LE MESURIER, John (1912-1983)
It's all been rather lovely.
[Quoted in *The Times*, 1983]

MARCO POLO (c.1254-1324)
I have not told half of what I saw.
[In W. Durant, *The Story of Civilization*]

MORE, Sir Thomas (1478-1535)
After his head was upon the block, [he] lift it up again, and gently drew his beard aside, and said, This hath not offended the king.
[In Francis Bacon, *Apophthegms New and Old* (1625)]

MORRIS, William (1834-1896)
I want to get Mumbo-Jumbo out of the world.
[Attr.]

NELSON, Lord (1758-1805)
(At the Battle of Trafalgar, 1805)
Thank God, I have done my duty.
[In Robert Southey, *The Life of Nelson* (1860)]

NERO (37-68)
What a great artist dies with me!
[In Suetonius, *Lives of the Caesars*]

O'NEILL, Eugene (1888-1953)
I knew it. I knew it. Born in a hotel room – and God damn it – died in a hotel room.
[Attr.]

OATES, Captain Lawrence (1880-1912)
I am just going outside, and may be some time.
[Captain Scott's diary]

PALMERSTON, Lord (1784-1865)
Die, my dear Doctor, that's the last thing I shall do!
[Attr.]

PAVLOVA, Anna (1881–1931)
Get my swan costume ready.
[Attr.]

PERELMAN, S.J. (1904–1979)
(Giving his reasons for refusing to see a priest as he lay dying)
I am curious to see what happens in the next world to one who dies unshriven.
[Attr.]

PICASSO, Pablo (1881–1973)
Drink to me.
[Attr.]

PITT, William (1759–1806)
I think I could eat one of Bellamy's veal pies.
[Attr.]

POPE, Alexander (1688–1744)
Here am I, dying of a hundred good symptoms.
[In Spence, *Anecdotes*]

RABELAIS, François (c.1494–c.1553)
I am going to seek a great perhaps ... Bring down the curtain, the farce is played out.
[Attr.]

RALEIGH, Sir Walter (c.1552–1618)
(On feeling the edge of the axe before his execution)
'Tis a sharp remedy, but a sure one for all ills.
[Attr.]

REYNOLDS, Sir Joshua (1723–1792)
I should desire that the last words which I should pronounce in this Academy, and from this place, might be the name of – Michael Angelo.
[*Discourses on Art*, XV (1790)]

RHODES, Cecil (1853–1902)
So little done, so much to do!
[In Lewis Mitchell, *Life of Rhodes* (1910)]

SANDERS, George (1906–1972)
Dear World, I am leaving you because I am bored. I feel I have lived long enough. I am leaving you with your worries in this sweet cesspool – good luck.
[Suicide note]

SARO-WIWA, Ken (1941–1995)
Lord take my soul, but the struggle continues.
[*The Observer*, 1995]

SAROYAN, William (1908–1981)
Everybody has got to die, but I have always believed an exception would be made in my case. Now what?
[*Time*, 1984]

SCOTT, Captain Robert (1868–1912)
For God's sake look after our people.
[*Journal*, 25 March 1912]
Had we lived, I should have had a tale to tell of the hardihood, endurance, and courage of my companions which would have stirred the heart of every Englishman. These rough notes and our dead bodies must tell the tale.
[Message to the Public, 1912]

SEDGWICK, John (1813–1864)
(His last words, in response to a suggestion that he should not show himself over the parapet during the Battle of the Wilderness)
Nonsense, they couldn't hit an elephant at this dist –.
[Attr.]

SMITH, Adam (1723–1790)
I believe we must adjourn this meeting to some other place.

SOCRATES (469–399 BC)
Crito, we owe a cock to Asclepius. Pay it and do not neglect it.
[Attr. in Plato, *Phoedo*]

SPENCER, Sir Stanley (1891–1959)
(Thanking the nurse who had given him his nightly injection, just before he died)
Beautifully done.
[In Collis, *Stanley Spencer* (1962)]

SPENKELINK, John (d.1979)
(Executed in the electric chair)
Capital punishment: them without the capital get the punishment.
[Attr.]

STEIN, Gertrude (1874–1946)
Just before she [Stein] died she asked, 'What is the answer?' No answer came. She laughed and said, 'In that case, what is the question?' Then she died.
[In Sutherland, *Gertrude Stein* (1951)]

STRACHEY, Lytton (1880–1932)
If this is dying, then I don't think much of it.
[In Michael Holroyd, *Lytton Strachey: A Critical Biography* (1968)]

THURBER, James (1894–1961)
God bless ... God damn.
[Attr.]

TOLSTOY, Leo (1828–1910)
(Refusing to reconcile himself with the Russian Orthodox Church as he lay dying)
Even in the valley of the shadow of death, two and two do not make six.
[Attr.]

VEGA CARPIO, Félix Lope de (1562–1635)
(On learning that he was about to die)
All right, then, I'll say it: Dante makes me sick.
[Attr.]

VESPASIAN (AD 9–79)
Woe is me, I think I am becoming a god.
[In Suetonius, *Lives of the Caesars*]

WILDE, Oscar (1854–1900)
(As he lay dying in a drab Paris bedroom)
Either that wallpaper goes, or I do.

LAW

ADAMS, Richard (1846–1908)
You have been acquitted by a Limerick jury and you may now leave the dock without any other stain on your character.
[In Healy, *The Old Munster Circuit*]

BACON, Francis (1561–1626)
One of the Seven was wont to say: 'That laws were like cobwebs; where the small flies were caught, and the great brake through.'
[*Apophthegms New and Old* (1624)]

BENTHAM, Jeremy (1748–1832)
Lawyers are the only persons in whom ignorance of the law is not punished.
[Attr.]

BIERCE, Ambrose (1842–c.1914)
Lawsuit: A machine which you go into as a pig and come out as a sausage.
[*The Cynic's Word Book* (1906)]

BRAXFIELD, Lord (1722–1799)
Let them bring me prisoners, and I'll find them law.
[Attr. by Cockburn]

CARROLL, Lewis (1832–1898)
'I'll be judge, I'll be jury,' said cunning old Fury: 'I'll try the whole cause, and condemn you to death.'
[*Alice's Adventures in Wonderland* (1865)]

CHAPMAN, George (c.1559–c.1634)
I'm asham'd the law is such an Ass.
[*Revenge for Honour* (1654)]

COETZEE, J.M. (1940–)
All we can do is to uphold the laws, all of us, without allowing the memory of justice to fade.
[*Waiting for the Barbarians* (1980)]

EMERSON, Ralph Waldo (1803–1882)
Good men must not obey the laws too well.
['Politics' (1844)]

FRANCE, Anatole (1844–1924)
The law, in its majestic equality, forbids the rich as well as the poor to sleep under bridges, to beg in the streets, and to steal bread.
[*Le Lys Rouge* (1894)]

GIRAUDOUX, Jean (1882–1944)
All of us here know that there is no better way of exercising the imagination than the study of law. No poet has ever interpreted nature as freely as a lawyer interprets reality.
[*La Guerre de Troie n'aura pas lieu* (1935)]

HOLMES, Hugh (Lord Justice Holmes) (1840–1916)
An elderly pensioner on being sentenced to fifteen years' penal servitude cried 'Ah! my Lord, I'm a very old man, and I'll never do that sentence.' The judge replied 'Well try to do as much of it as you can'.
[In Healy, *The Old Munster Circuit* (1939)]

INGRAMS, Richard (1937–)
I have come to regard the law courts not as a cathedral but rather as a casino.
[*The Guardian*, 1977]

LOCKE, John (1632–1704)
Wherever Law ends, Tyranny begins.
[*Second Treatise of Civil Government* (1690)]

MACHIAVELLI (1469–1527)
Good examples are borne out of good education, which is the outcome of good legislation; and good legislation is borne out of those uprisings which are unduly damned by so many people.
[*Discourse*]

MORTIMER, Sir John (1923–2009)
No brilliance is needed in the law. Nothing but common sense, and relatively clean finger nails.
[*A Voyage Round My Father* (1971)]

PUZO, Mario (1920–1999)
A lawyer with his briefcase can steal more than a thousand men with guns.
[*The Godfather* (1969)]

RICHELIEU (Cardinal) (1585–1642)
To pass a law and not have it enforced is to authorize the very thing you wish to prohibit.
[*Mémoires*]

ROBESPIERRE, Maximilien (1758–1794)
Any law which violates the indefeasible rights of man is in essence unjust and tyrannical; it is no law.
[*Déclaration des Droits de l'homme* (1793)]

ROUSSEAU, Jean-Jacques (1712–1778)

Laws are always useful to those who have possessions, and harmful to those who have nothing.

[*Du Contrat Social* (1762)]

SELDEN, John (1584–1654)

Ignorance of the law excuses no man; not that all men know the law, but because 'tis an excuse every man will plead, and no man can tell how to confute him.

[*Table Talk* (1689)]

SWIFT, Jonathan (1667–1745)

Laws are like cobwebs, which may catch small flies, but let wasps and hornets break through.

[*A Critical Essay upon the Faculties of the Mind* (1709)]

See **CRIME, JUSTICE**

LEARNING

ADDISON, Joseph (1672–1719)

The truth of it is, learning ... makes a silly man ten thousand times more insufferable, by supplying variety of matter to his impertinence, and giving him an opportunity of abounding in absurdities.

[*The Man of the Town*]

ARISTOTLE (384–322 BC)

What we have to learn to do, we learn by doing.

[*Nicomachean Ethics*]

ASCHAM, Roger (1515–1568)

There is no such whetstone, to sharpen a good wit and encourage a will to learning, as is praise.

[*The Scholemaster* (1570)]

BACON, Francis (1561–1626)

Studies serve for delight, for ornament, and for ability.

['Of Studies' (1625)]

Crafty men condemn studies; simple men admire them; and wise men use them.

['Of Studies' (1625)]

CHESTERFIELD, Lord (1694–1773)

Wear your learning, like your watch, in a private pocket; and do not merely pull it out and strike it merely to show you have one.

[Letter to his son, 1748]

CONFUCIUS (c.550–c.478 BC)

Learning without thought is labour lost; thought without learning is perilous.

[*Analects*]

FOOTE, Samuel (1720–1777)

For as the old saying is,
When house and land are gone and spent
Then learning is most excellent.

[*Taste* (1752)]

HUXLEY, T.H. (1825–1895)

Try to learn something about everything and everything about something.

[Memorial stone]

MILTON, John (1608–1674)

Where there is much desire to learn, there of necessity will be much arguing, much writing, many opinions; for opinion in good men is but knowledge in the making.

[*Areopagitica* (1644)]

OVID (43 BC–AD 18)

Add the fact that to have diligently studied the liberal arts refines behaviour and does not allow it to be savage.

[*Epistulae Ex Ponto*]

POPE, Alexander (1688–1744)

A little learning is a dangerous thing;
Drink deep, or taste not the Pierian spring:
There shallow draughts intoxicate the brain,
And drinking largely sobers us again.

[*An Essay on Criticism* (1711)]

WHITE, Patrick (1912–1990)

'I dunno,' Arthur said. 'I forget what I was taught. I only remember what I've learnt.'

[*The Solid Mandala* (1966)]

See **EDUCATION, KNOWLEDGE, SCHOOL, UNIVERSITY**

LIES

ANONYMOUS

An abomination unto the Lord, but a very present help in time of trouble.

[Definition of a lie]

ARMSTRONG, Sir Robert (1927–)

(Replying to an allegation in court that a letter he had written on behalf of the British Government had contained a lie)
It contains a misleading impression, not a lie. It was being economical with the truth.

[*The Observer*, 1986]

BACON, Francis (1561–1626)

But it is not the lie that passeth through the mind, but the lie that sinketh in, and settleth in it, that doth the hurt.

['Of Truth' (1625)]

BELLOC, Hilaire (1870-1953)
Matilda told such Dreadful Lies,
It made one Gasp and Stretch one's Eyes;
Her Aunt, who, from her Earliest Youth,
Had kept a Strict Regard for Truth,
Attempted to Believe Matilda:
The effort very nearly killed her.
['Matilda' (1907)]

BERLUSCONI, Silvio (1936-)
By definition, as a Prime Minister I cannot be
a liar.
[Italian Radio, 2006]

BUTLER, Samuel (1835-1902)
Any fool can tell the truth, but it requires a
man of some sense to know how to lie well.
[*The Note-Books of Samuel Butler* (1912)]

BYRON, Lord (1788-1824)
And, after all, what is a lie? 'Tis but The truth
in masquerade.
[*Don Juan* (1824)]

CALLAGHAN, James (1912-2005)
A lie can be half-way round the world before
the truth has got its boots on.
[Speech, 1976]

CORNEILLE, Pierre (1606-1684)
One needs a good memory after telling lies.
[*Le Menteur* (1643)]

DAVIES, Robertson (1913-1995)
Better a noble lie than a miserable truth.
[In Twigg, *Conversations with Twenty-four
Canadian Writers* (1981)]

EVANS, Harold (1928-)
The camera cannot lie. But it can be an
accessory to untruth.
[Attr.]

HAMPTON, Christopher (1946-)
You see, I always divide people into two
groups. Those who live by what they know to
be a lie, and those who live by what they
believe, falsely, to be the truth.
[*The Philanthropist* (1970)]

HERVEY, Lord (1696-1743)
Whoever would lie usefully should lie seldom.
[In Croker, *Memoirs of the Reign of George II*
(1848)]

HITLER, Adolf (1889-1945)
The broad mass of a nation ... will more easily
fall victim to a big lie than to a small one.
[*Mein Kampf* (1925)]

IBSEN, Henrik (1828-1906)
Take the saving lie from the average man and
you take his happiness away, too.
[*The Wild Duck* (1884)]

MADOFF, Bernard (1938-)
(On his investment scheme following its
collapse)
It's all just one big lie.
[*Washington Post*, 2008]

MAUGHAM, William Somerset (1874-1965)
She's too crafty a woman to invent a new lie
when an old one will serve.
[*The Constant Wife* (1927)]

NIETZSCHE, Friedrich Wilhelm (1844-1900)
We need lies ... in order to live.
[*Fragments* (1880-1889)]

PROUST, Marcel (1871-1922)
One of those telegrams of which M. de
Guermantes had wittily fixed the formula:
'Cannot come, lie follows'.
[*Le Temps retrouvé* (1926)]

SAKI (1870-1916)
A little inaccuracy sometimes saves tons of
explanation.
[*The Square Egg* (1924)]

TENNYSON, Alfred (Lord) (1809-1892)
A lie which is all a lie may be met and fought
with outright,
But a lie which is part a truth is a harder
matter to fight.
['The Grandmother' (1859)]

WILDE, Oscar (1854-1900)
The final revelation is that Lying, the telling of
beautiful untrue things, is the proper aim of Art.
['The Decay of Lying' (1889)]

See **ART, DECEPTION, HONESTY, TRUTH**

LIFE

ACKERMAN, Diane (1948-)
It began in mystery, and it will end in mystery,
but what a savage and beautiful country lies
in between.
[*A Natural History of the Senses* (1990)]

ADAMS, Douglas (1952-2001)
The Answer to the Great Question Of ... Life,
the Universe and Everything ... Is ... Forty-two.
[*The Hitch Hiker's Guide to the Galaxy* (1979)]

ADAMS, Henry (1838-1918)
Chaos often breeds life, when order breeds
habit.
[*The Education of Henry Adams* (1918)]

ADAMS, Scott (1957–)
Accept that some days you're the pigeon, and
some days you're the statue.
[*The Dilbert Principle*]

ADLER, Polly (1900–1953)
I am one of those people who just can't help
getting a kick out of life – even when it's a
kick in the teeth.
[*A House Is Not a Home* (1953)]

ARISTOTLE (384–322 BC)
Just as at the Olympic games it is not the
handsomest or strongest men who are
crowned with victory but the successful
competitors, so in life it is those who act
rightly who carry off all the prizes and rewards.
[*Nicomachean Ethics*]

ARNOLD, Matthew (1822–1888)
Is it so small a thing
To have enjoy'd the sun,
To have liv'd light in the spring,
To have lov'd, to have thought, to have done?
['Empedocles on Etna' (1852)]

AURELIUS, Marcus (121–180)
Remember that no one loses any other life
than this which he now lives, nor lives any
other than this which he now loses.
[*Meditations*]

BALFOUR, A.J. (1848–1930)
Nothing matters very much, and very few
things matter at all.
[Attr.]

BENNETT, Alan (1934–)
You know life … it's rather like opening a tin
of sardines. We are all of us looking for the key.
[*Beyond the Fringe* (1962)]

BENTLEY, Nicolas (1907–1978)
One should not exaggerate the importance of
trifles. Life, for instance, is much too short to
be taken seriously.
[Attr.]

BERRYMAN, John (1914–1972)
Life, friends, is boring. We must not say so.
[*Dream Songs* (1964)]

BLAKE, William (1757–1827)
For every thing that lives is holy, life delights
in life.
[*America: a Prophecy* (1793)]

BRENAN, Gerald (1894–1987)
We should live as if we were going to live
forever, yet at the back of our minds
remember that our time is short.
[*Thoughts in a Dry Season* (1978)]

BRONTË, Charlotte (1816–1855)
Life, believe, is not a dream,
So dark as sages say;
Oft a little morning rain
Foretells a pleasant day!
['Life' (1846)]

BROWNE, Sir Thomas (1605–1682)
Life itself is but the shadow of death, and souls
but the shadows of the living. All things fall
under this name. The sun itself is but the dark
simulacrum, and light but the shadow of God.
[The *Garden of Cyrus* (1658)]
The long habit of living indisposeth us for
dying.
[*Hydriotaphia: Urn Burial* (1658)]

BUCHAN, John (1875–1940)
It's a great life if you don't weaken.
[*Mr Standfast* (1919)]

BUTLER, Samuel (1835–1902)
Life is one long process of getting tired.
[*The Note-Books of Samuel Butler* (1912)]
To live is like love, all reason is against it, and
all healthy instinct for it.
[*The Note-Books of Samuel Butler* (1912)]

CHAMFORT, Nicolas (1741–1794)
Living is an illness to which sleep provides
relief every sixteen hours. It's a palliative.
Death is the remedy.
[*Maximes et pensées* (1796)]

CHAPLIN, Charlie (1889–1977)
Life is a tragedy when seen in close-up, but a
comedy in long-shot.
[*The Guardian*, 1977]

CLARE, John (1793–1864)
And what is Life? – an hour glass on the run
A mist retreating from the morning sun
A busy bustling still repeated dream
Its length? – A moment's pause, a moment's
thought
And happiness? A Bubble on the stream
That in the act of seizing shrinks to nought.
['What is Life?' (1820)]
If life had a second edition, how I would
correct the proofs.
[Letter to a friend]

COCTEAU, Jean (1889–1963)
Life is falling sideways.
[*Opium* (1930)]

CONRAN, Shirley (1932–)
Life is too short to stuff a mushroom.
[*Superwoman* (1975)]

COOK, Peter (1937-1995)
Life is a matter of passing the time enjoyably. There may be other things in life, but I've been too busy passing my time enjoyably to think very deeply about them.
[*The Guardian*, January 1994]

COUBERTIN, Pierre de (1863-1937)
The most important thing in life is not the winning but the taking part; the essential thing is not conquering but fighting well.
[Speech, 1908]

CROWFOOT (1821-1890)
What is life? It is the flash of a firefly in the night. It is the breath of a buffalo in the wintertime. It is the little shadow which runs across the grass and loses itself in the sunset.
[Last words]

DAVIES, William Henry (1871-1940)
What is this life if, full of care, We have no time to stand and stare?
[*Songs of Joy* (1911)]

DAWKINS, Richard (1941-)
The essence of life is statistical improbability on a colossal scale.
[*The Blind Watchmaker* (1986)]

DISRAELI, Benjamin (1804-1881)
Next to knowing when to seize an opportunity, the most important thing in life is to know when to forego an advantage.
[Attr.]

EINSTEIN, Albert (1879-1955)
Only a life lived for others is a life worthwhile.
['Defining Success']

FRANKLIN, Benjamin (1706-1790)
Dost thou love life? Then do not squander time, for that's the stuff life is made of.
[*Poor Richard's Almanac* (1746)]

GAY, John (1685-1732)
Life is a jest; and all things show it. I thought so once; but now I know it.
['My Own Epitaph' (1720)]

GORDON, Adam Lindsay (1833-1870)
Life is mostly froth and bubble, Two things stand like stone, Kindness in another's trouble, Courage in your own.
[Ye Wearie Wayfarer (1866)]

HUBBARD, Elbert (1856-1915)
Life is just one damned thing after another.
[*Philistine*, 1909]

JAMES, Henry (1843-1916)
Live all you can; it's a mistake not to. It doesn't so much matter what you do in particular, so long as you have your life. If you haven't had that then what have you had?
[*The Ambassadors* (1903)]

JEANS, Sir James Hopwood (1877-1946)
Life exists in the universe only because the carbon atom possesses certain exceptional properties.
[*The Mysterious Universe* (1930)]

JOHNSON, Samuel (1709-1784)
Human life is everywhere a state in which much is to be endured, and little to be enjoyed.
[*Rasselas* (1759)]

JUNG, Carl Gustav (1875-1961)
As far as we are able to understand, the only aim of human existence is to kindle a light in the darkness of mere being.
[*Memories, Dreams, Thoughts* (1962)]

KIERKEGAARD, Søren (1813-1855)
Life can only be understood backwards; but it must be lived forwards.
[*Life*]

LEARY, Timothy (1920-1996)
If you take the game of life seriously, if you take your nervous system seriously, if you take your sense organs seriously, if you take the energy process seriously, you must turn on, tune in, and drop out.
[*Politics of Ecstasy* (1968)]

LENNON, John (1940-1980)
Life is what happens to you while you're busy making other plans.
['Beautiful Boy', song, 1980]

LEWIS, C.S. (1898-1963)
Term, holidays, term, holidays, till we leave school, and then work, work, work till we die.
[*Surprised by Joy* (1955)]

LEWIS, Sir George Cornewall (1806-1863)
Life would be tolerable but for its amusements.
[In *Dictionary of National Biography*]

LONGFELLOW, Henry Wadsworth (1807-1882)
Lives of great men all remind us We can make our lives sublime, And, departing, leave behind us Footprints on the sands of time
['A Psalm of Life' (1838)]

MALAMUD, Bernard (1914-1986)
Life is a tragedy full of joy.
[*New York Times*, January 1979]

MARTIAL (c.AD 40–c.104)
Believe me, 'I shall live' is not the saying of a wise man. Tomorrow's life is too late: live today.
[*Epigrommata*]

MAUGHAM, William Somerset (1874–1965)
Life is too short to do anything for oneself that one can pay others to do for one.
[*The Summing Up* (1938)]

MITCHELL, Joni (1943–)
I've looked at life from both sides now
From win and lose and still somehow
It's life's illusions I recall
I really don't know life at all.
['Both Sides Now', song, 1968]

NASH, Ogden (1902–1971)
When I consider how my life is spent,
I hardly ever repent.
['Reminiscent Reflection' (1931)]

NIETZSCHE, Friedrich Wilhelm (1844–1900)
Believe me! – the secret of gathering in the greatest fruitfulness and the greatest enjoyment from existence is living dangerously!
[*The Gay Science* (1887)]

PASCAL, Blaise (1623–1662)
The last act is bloody, however delightful the rest of the play may be.
[*Pensées* (1670)]

SANTAYANA, George (1863–1952)
There is no cure for birth and death save to enjoy the interval.
[*Soliloquies in England* (1922)]

SENECA (c.4 BC–AD 65)
Eternal law has arranged nothing better than this that it has given us one way in to life, but many ways out.
[*Epistulae Morales*]
Live among men as if God beheld you; speak to God as if men were listening.
[*Epistles*]

SHAKESPEARE, William (1564–1616)
All the world's a stage,
And all the men and women merely players;
They have their exits and their entrances;
And one man in his time plays many parts.
[*As You Like It*, II.vii]

SHELLEY, Percy Bysshe (1792–1822)
Lift not the painted veil which those who live Call Life.
['Sonnet' (1818)]

SMITH, Logan Pearsall (1865–1946)
There are two things to aim at in life: first, to get what you want; and, after that, to enjoy it. Only the wisest of mankind achieve the second.
[*Afterthoughts* (1931)]

SOCRATES (469–399 BC)
The unexamined life is not a life worth living for a human being.
[Attr. in Plato, *Apology*]

STOPPARD, Tom (1937–)
Life is a gamble, at terrible odds – if it was a bet, you wouldn't take it.
[*Rosencrantz and Guildenstern Are Dead* (1967)]

TERENCE (c.190–159 BC)
Where there's life, there's hope.
[*Heauton Timoroumenos*]

THOMAS, Dylan (1914–1953)
Oh, isn't life a terrible thing, thank God?
[*Under Milk Wood* (1954)]

VAUVENARGUES, Marquis de (1715–1747)
In order to achieve great things we must live as though we were never going to die.
[*Reéflexions et Maximes* (1746)]

WHITEHEAD, A.N. (1861–1947)
It is the essence of life that it exists for its own sake.
[*Nature and Life* (1934)]

WILDE, Oscar (1854–1900)
One can live for years sometimes without living at all, and then all life comes crowding into one single hour.
[*Vera, or The Nihilist* (1880)]
One's real life is so often the life that one does not lead.
['L'Envoi to Rose-Leaf and Apple-Leaf']

WODEHOUSE, P.G. (1881–1975)
I spent the afternoon musing on Life. If you come to think of it, what a queer thing Life is! So unlike anything else, don't you know, if you see what I mean.
[*My Man Jeeves* (1919)]

See **HUMANITY AND HUMAN NATURE, MORTALITY, PURPOSE, TIME**

LITERATURE

BROOKNER, Anita (1938-)
Dr Weiss, at forty, knew that her life had been ruined by literature.
[*A Start in Life* (1981)]

CONNOLLY, Cyril (1903-1974)
Literature is the art of writing something that will be read twice; journalism what will be grasped at once.
[*Enemies of Promise* (1938)]

HELLER, Joseph (1923-1999)
He knew everything about literature except how to enjoy it.
[*Catch-22* (1961)]

HORACE (65-8 BC)
In serious works and ones that promise great things, one or two purple patches are often stitched in, to glitter far and wide.
[*Ars Poetica*]

INGE, William Ralph (1860-1954)
Literature flourishes best when it is half a trade and half an art.
['The Victorian Age' (1922)]

LEWIS, Sinclair (1885-1951)
Our American professors like their literature clear, cold, pure, and very dead.
[Address to Swedish Academy, 1930]

LODGE, David (1935-)
Literature is mostly about having sex and not much about having children; life is the other way round.
[*The British Museum is Falling Down* (1965)]

LOVER, Samuel (1797-1868)
When once the itch of literature comes over a man, nothing can cure it but the scratching of a pen.
[*Handy Andy* (1842)]

NABOKOV, Vladimir (1899-1977)
Literature and butterflies are the two sweetest passions known to man.
[*Radio Times*, 1962]

TWAIN, Mark (1835-1910)
(Definition of a classic)
Something that everybody wants to have read and nobody wants to read.
['The Disappearance of Literature']

WILDE, Oscar (1854-1900)
Movement, that problem of the visible arts, can be truly realized by Literature alone. It is literature that shows us the body in its swiftness and the soul in its unrest.
['The Critic as Artist' (1891)]

WILDER, Thornton (1897-1975)
Literature is the orchestration of platitudes.
[*Time*, 1953]

See **ART, BOOKS, CRITICISM, FICTION, POETRY, POETS, READING, WRITERS, WRITING**

LONELINESS

CONRAD, Joseph (1857-1924)
Who knows what true loneliness is – not the conventional word but the naked terror? To the lonely themselves it wears a mask.
[Attr.]

HAMMARSKJÖLD, Dag (1905-1961)
Pray that your loneliness may spur you into finding something to live for, great enough to die for.
[*Diaries*, 1951]

HUBBARD, Elbert (1856-1915)
Loneliness is to endure the presence of one who does not understand.
[Attr.]

O'BRIEN, Edna (1930-)
I often get lonely for unrealistic things: for something absolute.
[*The Observer*, 1992]

SARTON, May (1912-1995)
Loneliness is the poverty of self; solitude is the richness of self.
[*Mrs Stevens Hears the Mermaids Singing* (1993)]

See **SOLITUDE**

LOTTERY

JONES, Roger
I guess I think of lotteries as a tax on the mathematically challenged.

MONKHOUSE, Bob (1928-2003)
Statistically you stand just as good a chance of winning the lottery if you don't buy a ticket.
[*The Times* 1998]

WOOD, Victoria (1953-)
Please Lord, let me prove to you that winning the lottery won't spoil me.
[*The Sunday Times*, July 2000]

ANOUILH, Jean (1910–1987)
Love is, above all else, the gift of oneself.
[*Ardéle ou la Marguerite* (1949)]

AUDEN, W.H. (1907–1973)
When it comes, will it come without warning
Just as I'm picking my nose?
Will it knock on my door in the morning,
Or tread in the bus on my toes?
Will it come like a change in the weather?
Will its greeting be courteous or rough?
Will it alter my life altogether?
O tell me the truth about love.
['Twelve Songs']

AUSTEN, Jane (1775–1817)
All the privilege I claim for my own sex ...
is that of loving longest, when existence or
when hope is gone.
[*Persuasion* (1818)]

BALZAC, Honoré de (1799–1850)
It is easier to be a lover than a husband, for
the same reason that it is more difficult to
show a ready wit all day long than to produce
an occasional bon mot.
[Attr.]

THE BIBLE
(King James Version)
Greater love hath no man than this, that a
man lay down his life for his friends.
[*John*, 15:13]

BRICE, Fanny (1891–1951)
I never liked the men I loved, and never loved
the men I liked.
[Norman Katkov *The Fabulous Fanny* (1952)]

BROWNING, Elizabeth Barrett (1806–1861)
How do I love thee? Let me count the ways.
[*Sonnets from the Portuguese* (1850)]

BURNS, Robert (1759–1796)
O, my luve's like a red, red, rose
That's newly sprung in June.
O, my luve's like the melodie,
That's sweetly play'd in tune.
['A Red Red Rose' (1794)]

BURTON, Robert (1577–1640)
No chord, nor cable can so forcibly draw, or
hold so fast, as love can do with a twined
thread.
[*Anatomy of Melancholy* (1621)]

BUTLER, Samuel (1612–1680)
For money has a power above The stars and
fate, to manage love.
[*Hudibras* (1678)]

CHAMFORT, Nicolas (1741–1794)
Love, as it exists in society, is nothing more
than the exchange of two fantasies and the
contact of two skins.
[*Maximes et pensées* (1796)]

CHER (1946–)
If grass can grow through cement, love can
find you at every time in your life.
[*The Times*, 1998]

CHEVALIER, Maurice (1888–1972)
Many a man has fallen in love with a girl in a
light so dim he would not have chosen a suit
by it.
[Attr.]

COPE, Wendy (1945–)
(2 cures for love)
1. Don't see him. Don't phone or write a
letter.
2. The easy way: get to know him better.

DIDEROT, Denis (1713–1784)
They say that love takes wit away from those
who have it, and gives it to those who have
none.
[*Paradoxe sur le Comédien*]

DOUGLAS, Lord Alfred (1870–1945)
I am the Love that dare not speak its name.
['Two Loves' (1896)]

ELLIS, Havelock (1859–1939)
Love is friendship plus sex.
[Attr.]

ETHEREGE, Sir George (c.1635–1691)
When love grows diseased, the best thing we
can do is put it to a violent death; I cannot
endure the torture of a lingering and
consumptive passion.
[*The Man of Mode* (1676)]

FARQUHAR, George (1678–1707)
Money is the sinews of love, as of war.
[*Love and a Bottle* (1698)]

FLETCHER, Phineas (1582–1650)
Love is like linen often chang'd, the sweeter.
[*Sicelides* (1614)]

FLORIAN, Jean-Pierre Claris de (1755–1794)
Love's pleasure only lasts a moment; love's
sorrow lasts one's whole life long.
['Célestine' (1784)]

GAY, John (1685–1732)
Then nature rul'd, and love, devoid of art,
Spoke the consenting language of the heart.
[*Dione* (1720)]

GREER, Germaine (1939–)
Love, love, love – all the wretched cant of it,
masking egotism, lust, masochism, fantasy
under a mythology of sentimental postures,
a welter of self-induced miseries and joys,
blinding and masking the essential
personalities in the frozen gestures of
courtship, in the kissing and the dating and
the desire, the compliments and the quarrels
which vivify its barrenness.
[*The Female Eunuch* (1970)]

HOGG, James (1770–1835)
O, love, love, love!
Love is like a dizziness;
It winna let a poor body
Gang about his biziness!
['Love is Like a Dizziness']

HUDSON, Louise (1958–)
Now I go to films alone
watch a silent telephone
send myself a valentine
whisper softly 'I am mine'.
['Men, Who Needs Them']

KAFKA, Franz (1883–1924)
Love is, that you are the knife which I plunge
into myself.
[Letter to Milena Jesenká, 1920]

KIDMAN, Nicole (1967–)
I'm past the seven-year itch. When you're
loved for your flaws, that's when you feel
really safe.
[*The Observer*, 1998]

LAMARTINE, Alphonse de (1790–1869)
Only one being is missing, and your whole
world is bereft of people.
[*Premières Méditations poétiques* (1820)]

LARKIN, Philip (1922–1985)
What will survive of us is love.
['An Arundel Tomb' (1964)]

LINDSAY, Norman (1879–1969)
The best love affairs are those we never had.
[*Bohemians of the Bulletin* (1965)]

LODGE, Thomas (1558–1625)
Love, in my bosom, like a bee,
Doth suck his sweet.
['Love, In My Bosom' (1590)]

LOWRY, Malcolm (1909–1957)
How alike are the groans of love to those of
the dying.
[*Under the Volcano* (1947)]

MOLIÈRE (1622–1673)
One is easily taken in by what one loves.
[*Tartuffe* (1664)]

NIETZSCHE, Friedrich Wilhelm (1844–1900)
There is always some madness in love. But
there is also always some reason in madness.
[*On Reading and Writing*]

O'BRIEN, Edna (1930–)
Oh, shadows of love, inebriations of love,
foretastes of love, trickles of love, but never
yet the one true love.
[*Night* (1972)]

OVID (43 BC–AD–18)
You who seek an end to love, love will yield to
business: be busy, and you will be safe.
[*Remedia Amoris*]

PARKER, Dorothy (1893–1967)
By the time you swear you're his,
Shivering and sighing,
And he vows his passion is
Infinite, undying –
Lady, make a note of this:
One of you is lying.
['Unfortunate Coincidence' (1937)]

RACINE, Jean (1639–1699)
Ah, I have loved him too much not to hate him!
[*Andromaque* (1667)]

RUSSELL, Bertrand (1872–1970)
Of all forms of caution, caution in love is
perhaps the most fatal to true happiness.
[*Marriage and Morals* (1929)]

SAINT-EXUPÉRY, Antoine de (1900–1944)
Experience shows us that love is not looking
into one another's eyes but looking together
in the same direction.
[*Wind, Sand and Stars* (1939)]

SEGAL, Erich (1937–2010)
Love means never having to say you're sorry.
[*Love Story* (1970)]

SHAKESPEARE, William (1564–1616)
Doubt thou the stars are fire;
Doubt that the sun doth move;
Doubt truth to be a liar;
But never doubt I love.
[*Hamlet*, II.ii]

SHAW, George Bernard (1856–1950)
The fickleness of the women I love is only
equalled by the infernal constancy of the
women who love me.
[*The Philanderer* (1898)]

SHELLEY, Percy Bysshe (1792–1822)
Familiar acts are beautiful through love.
[*Prometheus Unbound* (1820)]

TENNYSON, Alfred (Lord) (1809–1892)
In the Spring a young man's fancy lightly
turns to thoughts of love.
['Locksley Hall' (1838)]
I hold it true, whate'er befall;
I feel it, when I sorrow most;
'Tis better to have loved and lost
Than never to have loved at all.
[*In Memoriam A. H. H.* (1850)]

TIBULLUS (c.54–19 BC)
May I be looking at you when my last hour
has come, and as I die may I hold you with
my weakening hand.
[*Elegies*]

TOLSTOY, Leo (1828–1910)
Love is God, and when I die it means that I, a
particle of love, shall return to the general and
eternal source.
[*War and Peace* (1869)]

TROLLOPE, Anthony (1815–1882)
Love is like any other luxury. You have no
right to it unless you can afford it.
[*The Way We Live Now* (1875)]

WAX, Ruby (1953–)
This 'relationship' business is one big waste
of time. It is just Mother Nature urging you to
breed, breed, breed. Learn from nature. Learn
from our friend the spider. Just mate once
and then kill him.
[*Spectator*, 1994]

WILCOX, Ella Wheeler (1850–1919)
We flatter those we scarcely know,
We please the fleeting guest,
And deal full many a thoughtless blow
To those who love us best.
['Life's Scars' (1917)]

WILDE, Oscar (1854–1900)
Yet each man kills the thing he loves,
By each let this be heard,
Some do it with a bitter look, Some with a
flattering word,
The coward does it with a kiss,
The brave man with a sword!
[*The Ballad of Reading Gaol* (1898)]
When one is in love one begins by deceiving
oneself. And one ends by deceiving others.
[*A Woman of No Importance* (1893)]

WYCHERLEY, William (c.1640–1716)
A mistress should be like a little country
retreat near the town, not to dwell in
constantly, but only for a night and away.
[*The Country Wife* (1675)]

YEATS, W.B. (1865–1939)
A pity beyond all telling
Is hid in the heart of love.
['The Pity of Love' (1892)]

See **PASSION, SEX**

LUXURY

ASHFORD, Daisy (1881–1972)
It was a sumpshous spot all done up in gold
with plenty of looking glasses.
[*The Young Visiters* (1919)]

CHAPLIN, Charlie (1889–1977)
The saddest thing I can imagine is to get used
to luxury.
[*My Autobiography* (1964)]

GAY, John (1685–1732)
Whether we can afford it or no, we must have
superfluities.
[*Polly* (1729)]

ORTON, Joe (1933–1967)
Every luxury was lavished on you – atheism,
breast-feeding, circumcision. I had to make
my own way.
[*Loot* (1967)]

WRIGHT, Frank Lloyd (1869–1959)
Give me the luxuries of life and I will willingly
do without the necessities.
[Quoted in his obituary, April 9, 1959]

See **MONEY AND WEALTH**

MADNESS

BECKETT, Samuel (1906–1989)
We are all born mad. Some remain so.
[*Waiting for Godot* (1955)]

BEERBOHM, Sir Max (1872–1956)
Only the insane take themselves quite
seriously.
[Attr.]

CHESTERTON, G.K. (1874–1936)
The madman is not the man who has lost his
reason. The madman is the man who has lost
everything except his reason.
[*Orthodoxy* (1908)]

CLARE, John (1793–1864)
Dear Sir, – I am in a Madhouse and quite
forget your name or who you are.
[Letter, 1860]

DALI, Salvador (1904–1989)
There is only one difference between a
madman and me. I am not mad.
[*The American*, 1956]

DAVIES, Scrope Berdmore (c.1783–1852)
Babylon in all its desolation is a sight not so awful as that of the human mind in ruins.
[Letter to Thomas Raikes, 1835]

EURIPIDES (c.485–406 BC)
Whom God wishes to destroy, he first makes mad.
[Fragment]

GINSBERG, Allen (1926–1997)
I saw the best minds of my generation destroyed by madness, starving hysterical naked.
[*Howl* (1956)]

GREENE, Graham (1904–1991)
Innocence is a kind of insanity.
[The Quiet American (1955)]

HELLER, Joseph (1923–1999)
Orr was crazy and could be grounded. All he had to do was ask; and as soon as he did, he would no longer be crazy and would have to fly more missions ... Yossarian was moved very deeply by the absolute simplicity of this clause of Catch-22 and let out a respectful whistle.
[*Catch-22* (1961)]

JUNG, Carl Gustav (1875–1961)
Show me a sane man and I will cure him for you.
[*The Observer*, 1975]

KIPLING, Rudyard (1865–1936)
The mad all are in God's keeping.
[*Kim* (1901)]

LEE, Nathaniel (c.1653–1692)
(On being confined in Bedlam)
They called me mad, and I called them mad, and damn them, they outvoted me.
[In Porter, *A Social History of Madness*]

NEWTON, Sir Isaac (1642–1727)
I can calculate the motion of heavenly bodies but not the madness of people.
[Attr.]

PROUST, Marcel (1871–1922)
Everything great in the world is done by neurotics; they alone founded our religions and composed our masterpieces.
[*Le Côté de Guermantes* (1921)]

VOLTAIRE (1694–1778)
Men will always be mad and those who think they can cure them are the maddest of all.
[Letter, 1762]

See **PSYCHIATRY**

MANNERS

BRADBURY, Malcolm (1932–2001)
The English are polite by telling lies. The Americans are polite by telling the truth.
[*Stepping Westward* (1965)]

EASTMAN, Max (1883–1969)
(On chivalry)
It is but the courteous exterior of a bigot.
[*Woman Suffrage and Sentiment*]

EMERSON, Ralph Waldo (1803–1882)
Good manners are made up of petty sacrifices.
['Social Aims' (1875)]

JARRELL, Randall (1914–1965)
To Americans English manners are far more frightening than none at all.
[*Pictures from an Institution* (1954)]

LOUIS XVIII (1755–1824)
Punctuality is the politeness of kings.
[Attr.]

MANKIEWICZ, Herman J. (1897–1953)
(After being sick at the table of a fastidious host)
It's all right, Arthur. The white wine came up with the fish.
[Attr.]

STERNE, Laurence (1713–1768)
Hail ye small sweet courtesies of life.
[*A Sentimental Journey* (1768)]

THEROUX, Paul (1941–)
The Japanese have perfected good manners and made them indistinguishable from rudeness.
[*The Great Railway Bazaar* (1975)]

TWAIN, Mark (1835–1910)
Good breeding consists in concealing how much we think of ourselves and how little we think of other persons.
[*Notebooks* (1935)]

WAUGH, Evelyn (1903–1966)
Manners are especially the need of the plain. The pretty can get away with anything.
[*The Observer*, 1962]

WILLIAM OF WYKEHAM (1324–1404)
Manners maketh man.
[Motto of Winchester College and New College, Oxford]

See **GENTEEL BEHAVIOUR, RESPECT**

MARRIAGE

ALBERT (Prince Consort) (1819–1861)
Tomorrow our marriage will be 21 years old!
How many a storm has swept over it and still
it continues green and fresh and throws out
vigorous roots.

[Attr.]

ALLEN, Woody (1935–)
It was partially my fault that we got divorced
... I tended to place my wife under a pedestal.
[At a nightclub in Chicago, 1964]

ASQUITH, Margot (1864–1945)
To marry a man out of pity is folly; and, if you
think you are going to influence the kind of
fellow who has 'never had a chance, poor
devil,' you are profoundly mistaken. One can
only influence the strong characters in life,
not the weak; and it is the height of vanity to
suppose that you can make an honest man of
anyone.
[*The Autobiography of Margot Asquith* (1920)]

ASTOR, Nancy (Viscountess) (1879–1964)
I married beneath me – all women do.
[*Dictionary of National Biography*]

AUSTEN, Jane (1775–1817)
It is a truth universally acknowledged, that a
single man in possession of a good fortune,
must be in want of a wife.
[*Pride and Prejudice* (1813)]

BACON, Francis (1561–1626)
He that hath wife and children, hath given
hostages to fortune; for they are impediments
to great enterprises, either of virtue or
mischief.
['Of Marriage and Single Life' (1625)]
Wives are young men's mistresses,
companions for middle age, and old men's
nurses.
['Of Marriage and Single Life' (1625)]

BENNETT, Arnold (1867–1931)
Being a husband is a whole-time job. That is
why so many husbands fail. They cannot give
their entire attention to it.
[*The Title* (1918)]

**THE BIBLE
(King James Version)**
Therefore shall a man leave his father and his
mother, and shall cleave unto his wife: and
they shall be one flesh.
[*Genesis*, 2:24]

BLACKSTONE, Sir William (1723–1780)
Husband and wife are one, and that one is
the husband.
[In Miles, *The Women's History of the World*
(1988)]

BURTON, Robert (1577–1640)
One was never married, and that's his hell;
another is, and that's his plague.
[*Anatomy of Melancholy* (1621)]

BYRON, Lord (1788–1824)
Though women are angels, yet wed-lock's the
devil.
['To Eliza' (1806)]

COLERIDGE, Samuel Taylor (1772–1834)
The most happy marriage I can picture or
imagine to myself would be union of a deaf
man to a blind woman.
[In Allsop, *Recollections* (1836)]

DIANA, Princess of Wales (1961–1997)
(Referring to the Prince of Wales' relationship
with Camilla Parker-Bowles)
There were three of us in this marriage, so it
was a bit crowded.
[BBC television interview, 1995]

EASTWOOD, Clint (1930–)
There's only one way to have a happy
marriage and as soon as I learn what it is I'll
get married again.
[Attr.]

FARQUHAR, George (1678–1707)
It is a maxim that man and wife should never
have it in their power to hang one another.
[*The Beaux' Stratagem* (1707)]

FELTZ, Vanessa (1962–)
Marriage 2001-style, as I know to my cost, is
entirely expendable, more easily disposable
than a McDonald's wrapper.
[*The Sunday Times*, April 2001]

FRIEDMAN, Kinky (1944–)
I support gay marriage because I believe they
have a right to be just as miserable as the rest
of us.
[CBS News, 2005]

GABOR, Zsa-Zsa (1919–)
Husbands are like fires. They go out when
unattended.
[*Newsweek*, 1960]

GOLDSMITH, Oliver (c.1728–1774)
I ... chose my wife as she did her wedding
gown, not for a fine glossy surface, but such
qualities as would wear well.
[*The Vicar of Wakefield* (1766)]

JOHNSON, Samuel (1709–1784)
Marriage has many pains, but celibacy has no pleasures.
[*Rasselas* (1759)]
A gentleman who had been very unhappy in marriage married immediately after his wife died. Dr Johnson said, it was the triumph of hope over experience.
[In Boswell, *The Life of Samuel Johnson* (1791)]

KEATS, John (1795–1821)
The roaring of the wind is my wife and the Stars through the window pane are my Children.
[Letter, 1818]

KENSIT, Patsy (1968–)
I can't believe I have had three marriages. Two is one thing, but three is like someone who goes on the Jerry Springer show.
[*The Sunday Times*, February 2001]

LAMB, Charles (1775–1834)
Nothing to me is more distasteful than that entire complacency and satisfaction which beam in the countenance of a new-married couple.
[*Essays of Elia* (1823)]

MACNEICE, Louis (1907–1963)
So they were married – to be the more together –
And found they were never again so much together,
Divided by the morning tea,
By the evening paper,
By children and tradesmen's bills.
['Les Sylphides' (1941)]

MILTON, John (1608–1674)
Flesh of Flesh,
Bone of my Bone thou art, and from thy State Mine never shall be parted, weal or woe.
[*Paradise Lost* (1667)]

MITCHUM, Robert (1917–1997)
(Marriage proposal)
Stick with me kid, and you'll be farting through silk.
[In Server *Baby I Don't Care*, 2001]

MURRAY, Jenni (1950–)
Marriage is an insult and women should not touch it.
[Attr.]

NEWMAN, Andrea (1938–)
'What is the difference between marriage and prison?' 'In prison somebody else does the cooking.'
[*Love Hurts*, film, 1990]

NICHOLSON, Jack (1937–)
I've never had a strict policy on marriage. It's unwise.
[*The Sunday Times*, March 2001]

SHAKESPEARE, William (1564–1616)
Let me give light, but let me not be light,
For a light wife doth make a heavy husband.
[*The Merchant of Venice*, V.i]
Thy husband is thy lord, thy life, thy keeper,
Thy head, thy sovereign; one that cares for thee,
And for thy maintenance commits his body
To painful labour both by sea and land.
[The Taming of the Shrew, V.ii]

SHERIDAN, Richard Brinsley (1751–1816)
'Tis safest in matrimony to begin with a little aversion.
[*The Rivals* (1775)]

SMITH, Bessie (1894–1937)
No time to marry, no time to settle down;
I'm a young woman, and I ain't done runnin'around.
[Song 'Young Woman's Blues' 1927]

TAYLOR, Bishop Jeremy (1613–1667)
He that loves not his wife and children, feeds a lioness at home and broods a nest of sorrows.
[*XXV Sermons Preached at Golden Grove* (1653)]

WELDON, Fay (1931–)
... the great wonderful construct which is marriage – a construct made up of a hundred little kindnesses, a thousand little bitings back of spite, tens of thousands of minor actions of good intent – this must not, as an institution, be brought down in ruins.
[*Splitting* (1995)]

WILDE, Oscar (1854–1900)
The real drawback to marriage is that it makes one unselfish. And unselfish people are colourless.
[*The Picture of Dorian Gray* (1891)]
Twenty years of romance make a woman look like a ruin; but twenty years of marriage make her something like a public building.
[*A Woman of No Importance* (1893)]
I am not in favour of long engagements. They give people the opportunity of finding out each other's character before marriage, which I think is never advisable.
[*The Importance of Being Earnest* (1895)]

WILDER, Thornton (1897–1975)
The best part of married life is the fights.
The rest is merely so-so.
[*The Matchmaker* (1954)]

WINTERS, Shelley (1922–2006)
In Hollywood all marriages are happy. It's
trying to live together afterwards that causes
the problems.
[Attr.]

WODEHOUSE, P.G. (1881–1975)
All the unhappy marriages come from the
husbands having brains. What good are
brains to a man? They only unsettle him.
[*The Adventures of Sally* (1920)]

See **ADULTERY, FAMILY**

MARTYRDOM

BOLEYN, Anne (1507–1536)
(On hearing that she was to be executed)
The king has been very good to me. He
promoted me from a simple maid to be a
marchioness. Then he raised me to be a
queen. Now he will raise me to be a martyr.
[Attr.]

BROWNE, Sir Thomas (1605–1682)
Were the happiness of the next world as
closely apprehended as the felicities of this, it
were a martyrdom to live.
[*Hydriotaphia: Urn Burial* (1658)]

DRYDEN, John (1631–1700)
For all have not the gift of martyrdom.
[*The Hind and the Panther* (1687)]

KIERKEGAARD, Søren (1813–1855)
The tyrant dies and his rule is over; the martyr
dies and his rule begins.
[Attr.]

OSAMA BIN LADEN (1957–2011)
We have young people who are keen on death
as much as Americans are keen on life.
[Attr.]

TERTULLIAN (c.AD 160–c.225)
As often as we are mown down by you, the
more we grow in numbers; the blood of
Christians is the seed.
[*Apologeticus*]

VOLTAIRE (1694–1778)
I am very fond of truth, but not at all of
martyrdom.
[Letter to d'Alembert, 1776]

WILDE, Oscar (1854–1900)
A thing is not necessarily true because a man
dies for it.
[*Sebastian Melmoth* (1904)]

MATHEMATICS

BARRIE, Sir J.M. (1860–1937)
What is algebra exactly; is it those three-
cornered things?
[*Quality Street* (1901)]

BROWNE, Sir Thomas (1605–1682)
I have often admired the mystical way of
Pythagoras, and the secret magic of numbers.
[*Religio Medici* (1643)]

CARLYLE, Thomas (1795–1881)
It is a mathematical fact that the casting of
this pebble from my hand alters the centre of
gravity of the Universe.
[*Sartor Resartus* (1834)]

EINSTEIN, Albert (1879–1955)
As far as the laws of mathematics refer to
reality, they are not certain, and as far as they
are certain, they do not refer to reality.
[In Capra, *The Tao of Physics* (1975)]

EUCLID (fl.c.300 BC)
A line is length without breadth.
[*Elements*]

HOBBES, Thomas (1588–1679)
Geometry ... is the only science that it hath
pleased God hitherto to bestow on mankind.
[*Leviathan* (1651)]

MILLIGAN, Spike (1918–2002)
Moriarty: How are you at Mathematics?
Harry Secombe: I speak it like a native.
[*The Goon Show*]

RUSSELL, Bertrand (1872–1970)
Mathematics, rightly viewed, possesses not
only truth, but supreme beauty – a beauty
cold and austere, like that of sculpture.
[*Mysticism and Logic* (1918)]

SMITH, Sydney (1771–1845)
What would life be without arithmetic, but a
scene of horrors.
[Letters, To Miss –, 1835]

WEIL, Simone (1909–1943)
Algebra and money are essentially levellers;
the first intellectually, the second effectively.
[Attr.]

MEDIA

BAKEWELL, Joan (Baroness) (1933–)
The BBC is full of men appointing men who remind them of themselves when young, so you get the same backgrounds, the same education, and the same programmes.
[*The Observer*, 1993]

HOWARD, Philip (1933–)
The proliferation of radio and television channels has produced a wilderness of cave-dwellers instead of the promised global village.
[*The Times*, 1992]

KAVANAU, Ted (1933–)
(Statement of CNN editorial policy)
If it bleeds, it leads.
[*The Guardian*, 1999]

MCLUHAN, Marshall (1911–1980)
The medium is the message. This is merely to say that the personal and social consequences of any medium … result from the new scale that is introduced into our affairs by each extension of ourselves or by any new technology.
[*Understanding Media* (1964)]

MURDOCH, Rupert (1931–)
Monopoly is a terrible thing, till you have it.
[*The New Yorker*, 1979]

REITH, Lord (1889–1971)
It was in fact the combination of public service motive, sense of moral obligation, assured finance and the brute force of monopoly which enabled the BBC to make of broadcasting what no other country has made of it.
[Into the Wind (1949)]

STOPPARD, Tom (1937–)
The media. It sounds like a convention of spiritualists.
[*Night and Day* (1978)]

See **INTERNET, MONEY AND WEALTH, NEWS, NEWSPAPERS, TELEVISION**

MEDICINE

THE BIBLE
(King James Version)
Physician, heal thyself.
[*Luke*, 4:23]

CHEKHOV, Anton (1860–1904)
Medicine is my lawful wife but literature is my mistress. When I'm bored with one, I spend the night with the other.
[Letter to Suvorin, 1888]

FLETCHER, John (1579–1625)
I find the medicine worse than the malady.
[*The Lover's Progress* (1623)]

FRANKLIN, Benjamin (1706–1790)
He's the best physician that knows the worthlessness of the most medicines.
[*Poor Richard's Almanac* (1733)]

GOLDWYN, Samuel (1882–1974)
Any man who goes to a psychiatrist should have his head examined.
[In Zierold, *Moguls* (1969)]

HAHNEMANN, C.F.S. (1755–1843)
Like cures like.
[Motto of homeopathic medicine]

HIPPOCRATES (c.460–357 BC)
(Of medicine)
Life is short, science is so long to learn, opportunity is elusive, experience is dangerous, judgement is difficult.
[*Aphorisms* (c.415 BC)]

LOOS, Anita (1893–1981)
So then Dr Froyd said that all I needed was to cultivate a few inhibitions and get some sleep.
[*Gentlemen Prefer Blondes* (1925)]

MCLUHAN, Marshall (1911–1980)
If the nineteenth century was the age of the editorial chair, ours is the century of the psychiatrist's couch.
[*Understanding Media* (1964)]

MOLIÈRE (1622–1673)
He's an expeditious man who likes to hurry his patients along; and when you have to die, he gets it over with quicker than anyone else.
[*Monsieur de Pourceaugnac* (1670)]

QUARLES, Francis (1592–1644)
Physicians of all men are most happy; what good success soever they have, the world proclaimeth, and what faults they commit, the earth covereth.
[*Hieroglyphics of the Life of Man* (1638)]

SHAW, George Bernard (1856–1950)
Optimistic lies have such immense therapeutic value that a doctor who cannot tell them convincingly has mistaken his profession.
[*Misalliance* (1914)]

WEBSTER, John (c.1580–c.1625)
Physicians are like kings – they brook no contradiction.
[*The Duchess of Malfi* (1623)]

WILLIAMS, Tennessee (1911–1983)
(Explaining why he had stopped seeing his psychoanalyst)
He was meddling too much in my private life.
[Attr.]

See **HEALTH, ILLNESS, PSYCHIATRY**

MEMORY

APOLLINAIRE, Guillaume (1880–1918)
Memories are hunting horns whose sound dies away in the wind.
['Cors de Chasse' (1913)]

ARNOLD, Matthew (1822–1888)
And we forget because we must
And not because we will.
['Absence' (1852)]

AUSTEN, Jane (1775–1817)
There seems something more speakingly incomprehensible in the powers, the failures, the inequalities of memory, than in any other of our intelligences.
[*Mansfield Park* (1814)]

BAUDELAIRE, Charles (1821–1867)
I have more memories than if I had lived for a thousand years.
[*Les Fleurs du mal* (1857)]

BRODSKY, Joseph (1940–1996)
What memory has in common with art is the knack for selection, the taste for detail ... More than anything, memory resembles a library in alphabetical disorder, and with no collected works by anyone.
['In a Room and a Half' (1986)]

CAMPBELL, Thomas (1777–1844)
To live in hearts we leave behind
Is not to die.
['Hallowed Ground']

DISRAELI, Benjamin (1804–1881)
Nobody is forgotten when it is convenient to remember him.
[Attr.]

LA ROCHEFOUCAULD (1613–1680)
Everyone complains of his memory; nobody of his judgment.
[*Maximes* (1678)]

SCHOPENHAUER, Arthur (1788–1860)
To expect a man to retain everything that he has ever read is like expecting him to carry about in his body everything that he has ever eaten.
[*Parerga and Paralipomena* (1851)]

SHAW, George Bernard (1856–1950)
Reminiscences make one feel so deliciously aged and sad.
[*The Irrational Knot* (1905)]

See **NOSTALIGIA, PAST**

MEN AND WOMEN

ADAMS, Scott (1957–)
Needing someone is like needing a parachute. If he isn't there the first time you need him, chances are you won't be needing him again.
[*The Dilbert Principle*]

ALLRED, Gloria (1941–)
The more I know about men the more I like dogs.
[*Politically Incorrect*, 1995]

AUSTEN, Jane (1775–1817)
There certainly are not so many men of large fortune in the world as there are pretty women to deserve them.
[*Mansfield Park* (1814)]

**THE BIBLE
(King James Version)**
It is not good that the man should be alone; I will make him an help meet for him.
[*Genesis*, 2:18]

BOMBECK, Erma (1927–1996)
What's wrong with you men? Would hair stop growing on your chest if you asked directions somewhere?
[*When You Look Like Your Passport Photo,
It's Time to Go Home* (1991)]

BURCHILL, Julie (1960–)
Men have charisma; women have vital statistics.
[*Sex and Sensibility* (1992)]

BYRON, Lord (1788–1824)
Man's love is of man's life a thing apart,
'Tis woman's whole existence.
[*Don Juan* (1824)]
The more I see of men, the less I like them. If I could but say so of women too, all would be well.
[Journal, 1814]

COLERIDGE, Samuel Taylor (1772–1834)
The man's desire is for the woman; but the woman's desire is rarely other than for the desire of the man.
[*Table Talk* (1835)]

COLLINS, Joan (1933–)
I've never yet met a man who could look after me. I don't need a husband. What I need is a wife.
[*The Sunday Times*, 1987]

CONNOLLY, Cyril (1903–1974)
The true index of a man's character is the health of his wife.
[*The Unquiet Grave* (1944)]

DIETRICH, Marlene (1901–1992)
The average man is more interested in a woman who is interested in him than he is in a woman – any woman – with beautiful legs.
[News item, 1954]
Most women set out to try to change a man, and when they have changed him they do not like him.
[Attr.]

DWORKIN, Andrea (1946–2005)
Men love death. In everything they make, they hollow out a central place for death ... Men especially love murder. In art they celebrate it. In life, they commit it.
[*The Independent*, 1992]

EBNER-ESCHENBACH, Marie von (1830–1916)
A clever woman has millions of born enemies – all stupid men.
[*Aphorisms* (1880)]

ELIOT, George (1819–1880)
I'm not denyin' the women are foolish: God Almighty made 'em to match the men.
[*Adam Bede* (1859)]

EMERSON, Ralph Waldo (1803–1882)
Men are what their mothers made them.
[*The Conduct of Life* (1860)]

FORD, Anna (1943–)
It is men who face the biggest problems in the future, adjusting to their new and complicated role.
[Attr.]

FRENCH, Marilyn (1929–2009)
Whatever they may be in public life, whatever their relations with men, in their relations with women, all men are rapists, and that's all they are. They rape us with their eyes, their laws and their codes.
[*The Women's Room* (1977)]

GABOR, Zsa-Zsa (1919–)
Never despise what it says in the women's magazines: it may not be subtle but neither are men.
[*The Observer*, 1976]

GASKELL, Elizabeth (1810–1865)
A man ... is so in the way in the house!
[*Cranford* (1853)]

GREER, Germaine (1939–)
A man who is slovenly and untidy is considered normal. The woman who is either is a slut or a sloven or a slag.
[*The Times*, March 1999]

HALL, Jerry (1956–)
My mother said it was simple to keep a man, you must be a maid in the living room, a cook in the kitchen and a whore in the bedroom. I said I'd hire the other two and take care of the bedroom bit.
[*The Observer*, 1985]

HARLOW, Jean (1911–1937)
I like to wake up feeling a new man.
[In Simon Rose, *Classic Film Guide* (1995)]

HENRY, O. (1862–1910)
If men knew how women pass the time when they are alone they'd never marry.
['Memoirs of a Yellow Dog' (1906)]

HILL, Reginald (1936–2012)
He created a man who was hard of head, blunt of speech, knew which side his bread was buttered on, and above all took no notice of women. Then God sent him forth to multiply in Yorkshire.
[*Pictures of Perfection* (1994)]

HOLMES, Oliver Wendell (1809–1894)
Man has his will, – but woman has her way.
[*The Autocrat of the Breakfast-Table* (1858)]

KEILLOR, Garrison (1942–)
Years ago, manhood was an opportunity for achievement, and now it is a problem to be overcome.
[*The Book of Guys* (1994)]

KENNEDY, Florynce R. (1916–2000)
If men could get pregnant, abortion would be a sacrament.
[In Steinem, *The Verbal Karate of Florynce R. Kennedy, Esq.* (1973)]

KIPLING, Rudyard (1865–1936)
Open and obvious devotion from any sort of man is always pleasant to any sort of woman.
[*Plain Tales from the Hills* (1888)]

LAVER, James (1899–1975)
Man in every age has created woman in the image of his own desire.
[In Neustater, *Hyenas in Petticoats* (1989)]

LERNER, Alan Jay (1918–1986)
Why can't a woman be more like a man?
Men are so honest, so thoroughly square;
Eternally noble, historically fair.
[*My Fair Lady* (1956)]

MADONNA (1958–)
Give me macho, or give me death.
[*The Sunday Times*, July 2001]

MARX, Groucho (1895–1977)
A man is only as old as the woman he feels.
[Attr.]

MEAD, Margaret (1901–1978)
Women want mediocre men, and men are working to be as mediocre as possible.
[*Quote Magazine*, 1958]

MENCKEN, H.L. (1880–1956)
Men have a much better time of it than women. For one thing, they marry later. For another thing, they die earlier.
[*A Mencken Chrestomathy* (1949)]

NORRIS, Kathleen (1880–1966)
There are men I could spend eternity with. But not this life.
[*The Middle of the World* (1981)]

PALACIO VALDÉS, Armando (1853–1938)
When a man stops being a god for his wife, he can be sure that he's now less than a man.
[*Doctor Angélico's Papers* (1911)]

PARKER, Dorothy (1893–1967)
Men seldom make passes
At girls who wear glasses.
[*Not So Deep as a Well* (1937)]

POPE, Alexander (1688–1744)
Men, some to business, some to pleasure take;
But every Woman is at heart a rake:
Men, some to quiet, some to public strife;
But every lady would be queen for life.
['Epistle to a Lady' (1735)]

RAMEY, Estelle (1917–2006)
More and more it appears that, biologically, men are designed for short, brutal lives and women for long miserable ones.
[*The Observer*, 1985]

RHONDDA (Viscountess) (1883–1958)
Women must come off the pedestal. Men put us up there to get us out of the way.
[*The Observer*, 1920]

SCHREINER, Olive (1855–1920)
It is delightful to be a woman; but every man thanks the Lord devoutly that he isn't one.
[*The Story of an African Farm* (1884)]

STEINEM, Gloria (1934–)
A woman needs a man like a fish needs a bicycle.
[Attr.]

TENNYSON, Alfred (Lord) (1809–1892)
Man for the field and woman for the hearth:
Man for the sword and for the needle she:
Man with the head and woman with the heart:
Man to command and woman to obey;
All else confusion.
[*The Princess* (1847)]

WEST, Mae (1892–1980)
When women go wrong, men go right after them.
[In Weintraub, *The Wit and Wisdom of Mae West* (1967)]

WHITTON, Charlotte (1896–1975)
Whatever women do they must do twice as well as men to be thought half as good. Luckily, this is not difficult.
[*Canada Month*, 1963]

WILDE, Oscar (1854–1900)
All women become like their mothers. That is their tragedy. No man does. That's his.
[*The Importance of Being Earnest* (1895)]

See **FEMINISM, HUMANITY AND HUMAN NATURE, MARRIAGE, WOMEN**

MIND

HUBBARD, Elbert (1856–1915)
Little minds are interested in the extraordinary; great minds in the commonplace.
[*A Thousand and One Epigrams* (1911)]

JUNG, Carl Gustav (1875–1961)
The pendulum of the mind swings between sense and nonsense, and not between what is right and what is wrong.
[*Memories, Dreams, Thoughts* (1962)]

LA ROCHEFOUCAULD (1613–1680)
The mind is always fooled by the heart.
[*Maximes* (1678)]

PRIOR, Matthew (1664–1721)
Be to her virtues very kind;
Be to her faults a little blind;
Let all her ways be unconfin'd;
And clap your padlock – on her mind.
['An English Padlock' (1705)]

PUNCH
What is Matter? – Never mind.
What is Mind? – No matter.
[1855]

WELCH, Raquel (1940–)
The mind can also be an erogenous zone.
[Attr.]

See **IDEAS, INTELLIGENCE, THOUGHT**

MODESTY

BARRIE, Sir J.M. (1860–1937)
I'm a second eleven sort of chap.
[*The Admirable Crichton* (1902)]

BUCHANAN, Robert Williams (1841–1901)
She just wore
Enough for modesty – no more.
['White Rose and Red' (1873)]

CHURCHILL, Sir Winston (1874–1965)
(Of Clement Attlee)
He is a modest man who has a good deal to
be modest about.
[In *Chicago Sunday Tribune Magazine of Books*, 1954]

CONGREVE, William (1670–1729)
Ah! Madam,... you know every thing in the
world but your perfections, and you only
know not those, because 'tis the top of
perfection not to know them.
[*Incognita* (1692)]

GILBERT, W.S. (1836–1911)
Wherever valour true is found,
True modesty will there abound.
[*The Yeoman of the Guard* (1888)]

SITWELL, Dame Edith (1887–1964)
I have often wished I had time to cultivate
modesty ... But I am too busy thinking about
myself.
[*The Observer*, April 1950]

STEELE, Sir Richard (1672–1729)
These Ladies of irresistible Modesty are those
who make Virtue unamiable.
[*The Tatler*, 1710]

MONARCHY AND ROYALTY

BLAIR, Tony (1953–)
(On hearing of the death of Diana, Princess of
Wales, 31 August 1997)
She was the People's Princess, and that is
how she will stay ... in our hearts and in our
memories forever.
[*The Times*, September 1997]

BURCHILL, Julie (1960–)
(Of Princess Diana)
She is Madonna crossed with Mother Theresa
– a glorious totem of Western ideals.
[*Sex and Sensibility* (1992)]

CARNEGIE, Andrew (1835–1919)
A king is an insult to every other man in the
land.
[Letter, 1887]

ELIZABETH I (1533–1603)
(Of the approaching Armada)
I know I have the body of a weak and feeble
woman but I have the heart and stomach of a
king, and of a king of England too; and think
foul scorn that Parma or Spain, or any prince
of Europe, should dare to invade the borders
of my realm.
[Speech, 1588]

GEORGE VI (1895–1952)
We're not a family; we're a firm.
[Attr. in Lane, *Our Future King*]

HATTERSLEY, Roy (1932–)
The institution of monarchy is inherently silly.
[*The Times* 1998]

MACHIAVELLI (1469–1527)
In order to keep his people united and
faithful, a prince must not be concerned with
being reputed as a cruel man.
[*The Prince* (1532)]

**SELLAR, Walter (1898–1951) and
YEATMAN, Robert Julian (1897–1968)**
Charles II was always very merry and was
therefore not so much a king as a Monarch.
[*1066 And All That* (1930)]

SHAKESPEARE, William (1564–1616)
Uneasy lies the head that wears a crown.
[*Henry IV, Part 2*, III.i]
I think the King is but a man as I am: the
violet smells to him as it doth to me.
[*Henry V*, IV.i]

VICTORIA, Queen (1819–1901)
We are not amused.
[Attr. in Holland, *Notebooks of a Spinster Lady* (1919)]

See **GOVERNMENT**

MONEY AND WEALTH

ASTOR, John Jacob (1763–1848)
A man who has a million dollars is as well off
as if he were rich.
[Attr.]

BACON, Francis (1561–1626)
And money is like muck, not good except it be spread.
[*'Of Seditions and Troubles' (1625)*]

BALDWIN, James (1924–1987)
Money, it turned out, was exactly like sex, you thought of nothing else if you didn't have it and thought of other things if you did.
[*Nobody Knows My Name* (1961)]

BARING, Maurice (1874–1945)
If you would know what the Lord God thinks of money, you have only to look at those to whom He gives it.
[Attr.]

BEHN, Aphra (1640–1689)
Money speaks sense in a language all nations understand.
[*The Rover* (1677)]

BENCHLEY, Robert (1889–1945)
(Comment on being told his request for a loan had been granted)
I don't trust a bank that would lend money to such a poor risk.
[Attr.]

THE BIBLE
(King James Version)
The love of money is the root of all evil.
[*I Timothy*, 6:10]

BRENAN, Gerald (1894–1987)
Those who have some means think that the most important thing in the world is love. The poor know that it is money.
[*Thoughts in a Dry Season* (1978)]

BUTLER, Samuel (1835–1902)
It has been said that the love of money is the root of all evil. The want of money is so quite as truly.
[*Erewhon* (1872)]

CARNEGIE, Andrew (1835–1919)
Surplus wealth is a sacred trust which its possessor is bound to administer in his lifetime for the good of the community.
[*The Gospel of Wealth*]

DYLAN, Bob (1941–)
Money doesn't talk, it swears.
['It's Alright, Ma (I'm Only Bleeding)' (1965)]

FLYNN, Errol (1909–1959)
My difficulty is trying to reconcile my gross habits with my net income.
[Attr.]

FRANCE, Anatole (1844–1924)
In every well-governed state, wealth is a sacred thing; in democracies it is the only sacred thing.
[*Penguin Island* (1908)]

GALBRAITH, J.K. (1908–2006)
Money differs from an automobile, a mistress or cancer in being equally important to those who have it and those who do not.
[Attr.]

GETTY, J. Paul (1892–1976)
If you can actually count your money you are not really a rich man.
[In A. Barrow, *Gossip*]

HORACE (65–8 BC)
Make money: make it honestly if possible; if not make it by any means.
[*Epistles*]

HUGHES, Howard (1905–1976)
(Response when called a 'paranoid, deranged millionaire' by a newspaper)
Goddammit, I'm a billionaire.
[Attr.]

HUXLEY, Sir Julian (1887–1975)
We all know how the size of sums of money appears to vary in a remarkable way according as they are being paid in or paid out.
[*Essays of a Biologist*]

ILLICH, Ivan (1926–2002)
Man must choose whether to be rich in things or in the freedom to use them.
[*Deschooling Society* (1971)]

JOHNSON, Samuel (1709–1784)
Sir, the insolence of wealth will creep out.
[In Boswell, *The Life of Samuel Johnson* (1791)]

LAWRENCE, D.H. (1885–1930)
Money is our madness, our vast collective madness.
['Money-Madness' (1929)]

LENNON, John (1940–1980)
I don't care too much for money,
Money can't buy me love.
['Can't Buy Me Love', song, 1964, with Paul McCartney]

MILLIGAN, Spike (1918–2002)
Money can't buy friends, but you can get a better class of enemy.
[*Puckoon* (1963)]

MILNE, A.A. (1882–1956)
For one person who dreams of making fifty thousand pounds, a hundred people dream of being left fifty thousand pounds.
[*If I May*]

NICHOLSON, Jack (1937–)
I am in an age group where it is rude to discuss money, and now it is all anyone cares about.
[*The Observer*, 1999]

PARSONS, Tony (1953–)
There are few things in this world more reassuring than an unhappy Lottery winner.
[*The Observer*, 1998]

REINHARDT, Gottfried (1911–1994)
Money is good for bribing yourself through the inconveniences of life.
[In L. Ross, *Picture*]

RIVERS, Joan (1937–)
People say that money is not the key to happiness, but I always figured if you have enough money, you can have a key made.
[*Enter Talking* (1986)]

RUNYON, Damon (1884–1946)
Always try to rub up against money, for if you rub up against money long enough, some of it may rub off on you.
[*Furthermore* (1938)]

SCHOPENHAUER, Arthur (1788–1860)
Wealth is like sea-water; the more we drink, the thirstier we become; and the same is true of fame.
[*Parerga and Paralipomena* (1851)]

SICKERT, Walter (1860–1942)
Nothing knits man to man ... like the frequent passage from hand to hand of cash.
['The Language of Art']

SMITH, Logan Pearsall (1865–1946)
To suppose, as we all suppose, that we could be rich and not behave as the rich behave, is like supposing that we could drink all day and keep absolutely sober.
[*Afterthoughts* (1931)]

THATCHER, Margaret (1925–2013)
Pennies do not come from heaven. They have to be earned here on earth.
[*The Sunday Telegraph*, 1982]

TUCKER, Sophie (1884–1966)
I've been poor and I've been rich. Rich is better.
[In Cowan, *The Wit of Women*]

TWAIN, Mark (1835–1910)
A banker is a person who lends you his umbrella when the sun is shining and wants it back the minute it rains.
[Attr.]

WILLIAMS, Tennessee (1911–1983)
You can be young without money but you can't be old without it.
[*Cat on a Hot Tin Roof* (1955)]

See **CAPITALISM, EXCESS, CONSUMER SOCIETY, INCOME**

MORALITY

AYER, A.J. (1910–1989)
No morality can be founded on authority, even if the authority were divine.
[*Essay on Humanism*]

GREENE, Graham (1904–1991)
Morality comes with sad wisdom of age. When the sense of curiosity has withered.
[Attr. in *The Observer*, 1996]

HUXLEY, Aldous (1894–1963)
The quality of moral behaviour varies in inverse ratio to the number of human beings involved.
[*Grey Eminence* (1941)]

JONG, Erica (1942–)
Your morals are like roads through the Alps. They make these hairpin turns all the time.
[*Fear of Flying* (1973)]

KRAUS, Karl (1874–1936)
Morality is the tendency to throw out the bath along with the baby.
[*Pro domo et mundo* (1912)]

LAWRENCE, D.H. (1885–1930)
Morality which is based on ideas, or on an ideal, is an unmitigated evil.
[*Fantasia of the Unconscious* (1922)]

MACAULAY, Lord (1800–1859)
We know of no spectacle so ridiculous as the British public in one of its periodical fits of morality.
['Moore's Life of Byron' (1843)]

RUSSELL, Bertrand (1872–1970)
We have, in fact, two kinds of morality side by side: one which we preach but do not practise, and another which we practise but seldom preach.
[*Sceptical Essays* (1928)]

SHAW, George Bernard (1856-1950)
An Englishman thinks he is moral when he is
only uncomfortable.
[*Man and Superman* (1903)]

SPENCER, Herbert (1820-1903)
Absolute morality is the regulation of conduct
in such a way that pain shall not be inflicted.
['Prison Ethics' (1891)]

STEVENSON, Robert Louis (1850-1894)
If your morals make you dreary, depend upon
it, they are wrong.
[*Across the Plains* (1892)]

WILDE, Oscar (1854-1900)
Morality is simply the attitude we adopt
towards people whom we personally dislike.
[*An Ideal Husband* (1895)]

See **GOOD AND EVIL, GOODNESS,
PRINCIPLES, VIRTUE**

MORTALITY

ANONYMOUS
Let us be happy while we are young, for after
carefree youth and careworn age, the earth
will hold us also.
['Gaudeamus Igitur', 13th century]

AURELIUS, Marcus (121-180)
And you will give yourself peace if you
perform each act as if it were your last.
[*Meditations*]
Everything is ephemeral, both that which
remembers and that which is remembered.
[*Meditations*]

BEHN, Aphra (1640-1689)
Faith, Sir, we are here today and gone tomorrow.
[*The Lucky Chance* (1687)]

**THE BIBLE
(King James Version)**
All flesh is grass, and all the goodliness
thereof is as the flower of the field.
[*Isaiah*, 40:6]

DOWSON, Ernest (1867-1900)
They are not long, the days of wine and roses;
Out of a misty dream
Our path emerges for a while, then closes
Within a dream.
['Vitae Summa Brevis Spem Nos Vetat
Incohare Longam' (1896)]

HERRICK, Robert (1591-1674)
Gather ye Rose-buds while ye may,
Old Time is still aflying:
And this same flower that smiles today,
Tomorrow will be dying.
[*Hesperides* (1648)]

LEACOCK, Stephen (1869-1944)
I detest life-insurance agents; they always
argue that I shall someday die, which is not so.
[*Literary Lapses* (1910)]

MARTIAL (c.AD 40-c.104)
Each of us feels the good days hasten and
depart, our days that perish and are counted
against us.
[*Epigrammata*]

MARVELL, Andrew (1621-1678)
But at my back I always hear
Time's wingèd chariot hurrying near.
And yonder all before us lie Deserts of vast
eternity.
Thy beauty shall no more be found;
Nor, in thy marble vault, shall sound
My echoing song: then worms shall try
That long preserved virginity:
And your quaint honour turn to dust;
And into ashes all my lust.
The grave's a fine and private place,
But none I think do there embrace.
['To His Coy Mistress' (1681)]

MILLAY, Edna St Vincent (1892-1950)
Death devours all lovely things:
Lesbia with her sparrow
Shares the darkness, – presently
Every bed is narrow ...
After all, my erstwhile dear,
My no longer cherished, Need we say it was
not love,
Just because it perished?
['Passer Mortuus Est' (1921)]

MONTAIGNE, Michel de (1533-1592)
One should always have one's boots on and
be ready to leave.
[*Essais* (1580)]

See **DEATH, IMMORTALITY, LIFE, TIME**

MOTHERS

ALCOTT, Louisa May (1832-1888)
What do girls do who haven't any mothers to
help them through their troubles?
[*Little Women* (1868)]

BARKER, George (1913-1991)
Seismic with laughter,
Gin and chicken helpless in her Irish hand,
Irresistible as Rabelais, but most tender for
The lame dogs and hurt birds that surround her.
['Sonnet: To My Mother' (1944)]

BARZAN, Gerald
Mother always said that honesty was the best
policy, and money isn't everything. She was
wrong about other things too.
[Attr.]

CAMPBELL, David (1915-1979)
The cruel girls we loved
Are over forty,
Their subtle daughters
Have stolen their beauty;
And with a blue stare
Of cool surprise
They mock their anxious mothers
With their mothers' eyes.
['Mothers and Daughters' (c.1965)]

ELLIS, Alice Thomas (1932-2005)
Claudia ... remembered that when she'd had
her first baby she had realised with
astonishment that the perfect couple
consisted of a mother and child and not, as
she had always supposed, a man and woman.
[The Other Side of the Fire]

FISHER, Dorothy Canfield (1879-1958)
A mother is not a person to lean on but a
person to make leaning unnecessary.
[Her Son's Wife (1926)]

FRIDAY, Nancy (1937-)
Blaming mother is just a negative way of
clinging to her still.
[My Mother/My Self (1977)]

MAUGHAM, William Somerset (1874-1965)
Few misfortunes can befall a boy which bring
worse consequences than to have a really
affectionate mother.
[A Writer's Notebook (1949)]

OLSEN, Tillie (1913-2007)
More than in any other human relationship,
overwhelmingly more, motherhood means
being instantly interruptible, responsive,
responsible.
[Silences: When Writers Don't Write (1965)]

RAYNER, Claire (1931-2010)
[Motherhood] is a dead-end job. You've no
sooner learned the skills than you are
redundant.
[Weekend Guardian, 1960]

SCOTT-MAXWELL, Florida (1884-1979)
No matter how old a mother is, she watches
her middle-aged children for signs of
improvement.
[The Measure of My Days (1968)]

SHAKESPEARE, William (1564-1616)
Thou art thy mother's glass, and she in thee
Calls back the lovely April of her prime.
[Sonnet 3]

STEFANO, Joseph (1922-2006)
A boy's best friend is his mother.
[Psycho, screenplay, 1960]

WALLACE, William Ross (c.1819-1881)
The hand that rocks the cradle
Is the hand that rules the world.
['What Rules the World' (c.1865)]

See **BIRTH, CHILDREN, FAMILY, FATHERS, PREGNANCY**

MURDER

JAMES, Henry (1843-1916)
To kill a human being is, after all, the least
injury you can do him.
[Complete Tales (1867)]

MORTIMER, Sir John (1923-2009)
Murderers are really very agreeable clients. I
do think murderers get a very bad press.
[The Observer, 1999]

PORTEUS, Beilby (1731-1808)
One murder made a villain,
Millions a hero.
['Death' (1759)]

WEBSTER, John (c.1580-c.1625)
Other sins only speak; murder shrieks out.
[The Duchess of Malfi (1623)]

See **CRIME**

MUSIC

ADDISON, Joseph (1672-1719)
Music, the greatest good that mortals know,
And all of heaven we have below.
['Song for St Cecilia's Day' (1694)]

ADE, George (1866-1944)
The music teacher came twice a week to
bridge the awful gap between Dorothy and
Chopin.
[Attr.]

ALLEN, Woody (1935-)
I can't listen to that much Wagner. I start
getting the urge to conquer Poland.
[Manhattan Murder Mystery (film, 1993)]

APPLETON, Sir Edward Victor (1892–1965)
I do not mind what language an opera is sung in so long as it is a language I don't understand.
[*The Observer*, 1955]

ARMSTRONG, Louis (1900–1971)
(When asked how he felt about people copying his style)
A lotta cats copy the Mona Lisa, but people still line up to see the original.
[Attr.]

BEECHAM, Sir Thomas (1879–1961)
There are two golden rules for an orchestra: start together and finish together. The public doesn't give a damn what goes on in between.
[In Atkins and Newman, *Beecham Stories* (1978)]

BEETHOVEN, Ludwig van (1770–1827)
(Said to a violinist complaining that a passage was unplayable)
When I composed that, I was conscious of being inspired by God Almighty. Do you think I can consider your puny little fiddle when He speaks to me?
[Attr.]

BIRTWISTLE, Sir Harrison (1934–)
I get someone to write the programme notes. Then I know what the piece is about.
[*The Observer*, 1996]

BURNEY, Fanny (1752–1840)
All the delusive seduction of martial music.
[*Diary*, 1802]

CONGREVE, William (1670–1729)
Music has charms to soothe a savage breast.
[*The Mourning Bride* (1697)]

COWARD, Sir Noël (1899–1973)
Extraordinary how potent cheap music is.
[*Private Lives* (1930)]

DRYDEN, John (1631–1700)
What passion cannot Music raise and quell?
['A Song for St. Cecilia's Day' (1687)]

DURY, Ian (1942–2000)
There are few personalities in pop music. They're mostly drab, soppy little bank clerks who've had a result.
[Attr.]

FORSTER, E.M. (1879–1970)
Beethoven's Fifth Symphony is the most sublime noise that ever penetrated into the ear of man.
[*Howard's End* (1910)]

GELDOF, Bob (1954–)
I'm into pop because I want to get rich, get famous and get laid.
[Attr.]

HOLST, Gustav (1874–1934)
Never compose anything unless the not composing of it becomes a positive nuisance to you.
[Letter to W.G. Whittaker]

HUXLEY, Aldous (1894–1963)
Since Mozart's day composers have learned the art of making music throatily and palpitatingly sexual.
[*Along the Road* (1925)]

JOHN, Sir Elton (1947–)
The great thing about rock and roll is that someone like me can be a star.
[*The New York Times*, 1992]

JOHNSON, Samuel (1709–1784)
Of music Dr Johnson used to say that it was the only sensual pleasure without vice.
[In *European Magazine*, 1795]

MENCKEN, H.L. (1880–1956)
Opera in English is, in the main, just about as sensible as baseball in Italian.
[Attr.]

MORRISON, Van (1945–)
Music is spiritual. The music business is not.
[*The Times*, July 1990]

PARKER, Charlie (1920–1955)
Music is your own experience, your thoughts, your wisdom. If you don't live it, it won't come out of your horn.
[In Shapiro and Hentoff, *Hear Me Talkin'to Ya* (1955)]

PAVAROTTI, Luciano (1935–2007)
You don't need any brains to listen to music.

RANDOLPH, David (1914–)
(On Parsifal)
The kind of opera that starts at six o'clock and after it has been going three hours, you look at your watch and it says 6.20.
[In *The Frank Muir Book* (1976)]

ROSSINI, Gioacchino (1792–1868)
Give me a laundry-list and I will set it to music.
[Attr.]

SATIE, Erik (1866–1925)
(Direction on one of his piano pieces)
To be played with both hands in the pocket.
[Attr.]

SCHNABEL, Artur (1882-1951)
The notes I handle no better than many pianists. But the pauses between the notes – ah, that is where the art resides.
[*Chicago Daily News*, 1958]

SCHUBERT, Franz (1797-1828)
My compositions spring from my sorrows. Those that give the world the greatest delight were born of my deepest griefs.
[*Diary*, 1824]

SHAKESPEARE, William (1564-1616)
In sweet music is such art,
Killing care and grief of heart
Fall asleep or hearing die.
[*Henry VIII*, III.i]

SHAW, George Bernard (1856-1950)
At every one of those concerts in England you will find rows of weary people who are there, not because they really like classical music, but because they think they ought to like it.
[*Man and Superman* (1903)]

TENNYSON, Alfred (Lord) (1809-1892)
Music that gentlier on the spirit lies,
Than tir'd eyelids upon tir'd eyes.
['The Lotos-Eaters' (1832)]

THOMAS, Irene (1920-2001)
The cello is not one of my favourite instruments. It has such a lugubrious sound, like someone reading a will.
[Attr.]

TWAIN, Mark (1835-1910)
I have been told that Wagner's music is better than it sounds.
[*Autobiography* (1959 edition)]

VICIOUS, Sid (1957-1979)
You just pick a chord, go twang, and you've got music.
[Attr.]

WILLIAMSON, Malcolm (1931-2003)
Lloyd Webber's music is everywhere, but so is Aids.
[Attr.]

ZAPPA, Frank (1940-1993)
Most people wouldn't know music if it came up and bit them on the ass.
[Attr.]

See **CRITICISM**

NATIONS

INGE, William Ralph (1860-1954)
A nation is a society united by a delusion about its ancestry and by a common hatred of its neighbours.
[In Sagittarius and George, *The Perpetual Pessimist*]

KUBRICK, Stanley (1928-1999)
The great nations have always acted like gangsters, and the small nations like prostitutes.
[*The Guardian*, 1963]

PARNELL, Charles Stewart (1846-1891)
No man has a right to fix the boundary of the march of a nation: no man has a right to say to his country – thus far shalt thou go and no further.
[Speech, 1885]

WILSON, Woodrow (1856-1924)
No nation is fit to sit in judgement upon any other nation.
[Speech, 1915]

NATURE

**THE BIBLE
(King James Version)**
While the earth remaineth, seedtime and harvest, and cold and heat, and summer and winter, and day and night shall not cease.
[*Genesis*, 8:22]

BRIDGES, Robert (1844-1930)
Man masters nature not by force but by understanding.
[Attr.]

BROWNE, Sir Thomas (1605-1682)
All things are artificial, for nature is the art of God.
[*Religio Medici* (1643)]

CHESTERTON, G.K. (1874-1936)
Is ditchwater dull? Naturalists with microscopes have told me that it teems with quiet fun.
[*The Listener*, 1936]

COWPER, William (1731-1800)
Nature is but a name for an effect,
Whose cause is God.
[*The Task* (1785)]

CURIE, Marie (1867-1934)
All my life through, the new sights of Nature made me rejoice like a child.
[*Pierre Curie*]

DARWIN, Charles (1809–1882)
What a book a devil's chaplain might write on the clumsy, wasteful, blundering, low, and horribly cruel works of nature!
[Letter to J.D. Hooker, 1856]

DYLAN, Bob (1941–)
I am against nature. I don't dig nature at all. I think nature is very unnatural. I think the truly natural things are dreams, which nature can't touch with decay.
[In Robert Shelton *No Direction Home* (1986)]

FIELDING, Henry (1707–1754)
All Nature wears one universal grin.
[*Tom Thumb the Great* (1731)]

GRACIÁN, Baltasar (1601–1658)
Art is not essential where Nature is sufficient.
[*The Hero* (1637)]

GREY OWL (1888–1938)
Civilisation says, 'Nature belongs to man.' The Indian says, 'No, man belongs to nature.'
[Address at Norwich]

HAWKING, Stephen (1942–)
There are grounds for cautious optimism that we may now be near the end of the search for the ultimate laws of nature.
[*A Brief History of Time* (1988)]

HORACE (65–8 BC)
You may drive out Nature with a pitchfork, but she always comes hurrying back.
[*Epistles*]

HUGO, Victor (1802–1885)
Nature is unforgiving; she will not agree to withdraw her flowers, her music, her scents or her rays of light before the abominations of man.
[*Ninety-three* (1874)]

INGERSOLL, Robert Greene (1833–1899)
In nature there are neither rewards nor punishments – there are consequences.
[*Some Reasons Why* (1881)]

LINNAEUS, Carl (1707–1778)
Nature does not make progress by leaps and bounds.
[*Philosophia Botanica*]

RABELAIS, François (c.1494–c.1553)
Nature abhors a vacuum.
[*Gargantua* (1534)]

SHAKESPEARE, William (1564–1616)
In nature's infinite book of secrecy
A little I can read.
[*Antony and Cleopatra*, I.ii]

THOREAU, Henry David (1817–1862)
I frequently tramped eight or ten miles through the deepest snow to keep an appointment with a beech-tree, or a yellow birch, or an old acquaintance among the pines.
[*Walden* (1854)]

VOLTAIRE (1694–1778)
Know that the secret of the arts is to correct nature.
[*Epîtres*]

WHITMAN, Walt (1819–1892)
After you have exhausted what there is in business, politics, conviviality, and so on – have found that none of these finally satisfy, or permanently wear – what remains? Nature remains.
[*Specimen Days and Collect* (1882)]

WORDSWORTH, William (1770–1850)
Nature never did betray
The heart that loved her.
['Lines composed a few miles above Tintern Abbey' (1798)]

See **ANIMALS, HUMANITY AND HUMAN NATURE, SCIENCE**

NEIGHBOURS

AUSTEN, Jane (1775–1817)
For what do we live, but to make sport for our neighbours, and laugh at them in our turn?
[*Pride and Prejudice* (1813)]

**THE BIBLE
(King James Version)**
Thou shalt love thy neighbour as thyself.
[*Leviticus*, 19:18]

BRADLEY, F.H. (1846–1924)
The propriety of some persons seems to consist in having improper thoughts about their neighbours.
[*Aphorisms* (1930)]

CHESTERTON, G.K. (1874–1936)
We make our friends, we make our enemies; but God makes our next-door neighbour.
[*Heretics* (1905)]

CLEESE, John (1939–)
Loving your neighbour as much as yourself is practically bloody impossible ... You might as well have a Commandment that states, 'Thou shalt fly'.
[*The Times*, 1993]

AUSTEN, Jane (1775–1817)
Lady Middleton ... exerted herself to ask Mr Palmer if there was any news in the paper. 'No, none at all,' he replied, and read on.
[*Sense and Sensibility* (1811)]

BALDWIN, Stanley (1867–1947)
What the proprietorship of these papers is aiming at is power, and power without responsibility – the prerogative of the harlot through the ages.
[Speech at an election rally, 1931]

BENNETT, Arnold (1867–1931)
Journalists say a thing that they know isn't true, in the hope that if they keep on saying it long enough it will be true.
[*The Title* (1918)]

BENTLEY, Nicolas (1907–1978)
No news is good news; no journalists is even better.
[Attr.]

BEVAN, Aneurin (1897–1960)
I read the newspapers avidly. It is my one form of continuous fiction.
[*The Observer*, 1960]

CARLYLE, Thomas (1795–1881)
Burke said there were Three Estates in Parliament; but, in the Reporters' Gallery yonder, there sat a Fourth Estate more important far than they all.
['The Hero as Man of Letters' (1841)]

CHESTERTON, G.K. (1874–1936)
It's not the world that's got so much worse but the news coverage that's got so much better.
[Attr.]

DANA, Charles Anderson (1819–1897)
When a dog bites a man that is not news, but when a man bites a dog that is news.
[*New York Sun*, 1882]

DRAYTON, Michael (1563–1631)
Ill news hath wings, and with the wind doth go, Comfort's a cripple and comes ever slow.
[*The Borrons' Wars* (1603)]

ELDERSHAW, M. Barnard (1897–1987)
Journalists are people who take in one another's washing and then sell it.
[*Plaque with Laurel* (1937)]

HEARST, William Randolph (1863–1951)
(Instruction to artist Frederic Remington, who wished to return from peaceful Havana in spring 1898)
Please remain. You furnish the pictures and I'll furnish the war.
[Attr. in Winkler, *W.R. Hearst* (1928)]

HEPWORTH, John (1921–1995)
Most journalists of my generation died early, succumbing to one or other of the two great killers in the craft – cirrhosis or terminal alimony.
[*National Review*, 1974]

IGNATIEFF, Michael (1947–)
News is a genre as much as fiction or drama: it is a regime of visual authority, a coercive organization of images according to a stopwatch.
[*Daedalus*, 1988]

KIPLING, Rudyard (1865–1936)
(Of newspaper barons)
Power without responsibility – the prerogative of the harlot throughout the ages.
[Remark, quoted by Baldwin in 1931]

KRAUS, Karl (1874–1936)
To have no thoughts and be able to express them – that's what makes a journalist.
[*Pro domo et mundo* (1912)]

LUCE, Henry R. (1898–1967)
I became a journalist to come as close as possible to the heart of the world.
[*Esquire*, Dec 1983]

MAILER, Norman (1923–2007)
Once a newspaper touches a story, the facts are lost forever, even to the protagonists.
[*The Presidential Papers* (1976)]

MARQUIS, Don (1878–1937)
The art of newspaper paragraphing is to stroke a platitude until it purrs like an epigram.
[In Anthony, *O Rare Don Marquis* (1962)]

MILLER, Arthur (1915–2005)
A good newspaper, I suppose, is a nation talking to itself.
[*The Observer*, 1961]

MURDOCH, Rupert (1931–)
I think the important thing is that there be plenty of newspapers with plenty of people controlling them so there can be choice.
[Film interview, 1967]

MURRAY, David (1888–1962)
A reporter is a man who has renounced
everything in life but the world, the flesh, and
the devil.
[*The Observer*, 1931]

SCOTT, C.P. (1846–1932)
Comment is free, but facts are sacred.
[*Manchester Guardian*, 1921]

TOMALIN, Nicholas (1931–1973)
The only qualities essential for real success in
journalism are rat-like cunning, a plausible
manner, and a little literary ability.
[*The Sunday Times Magazine*, 1969]

WAUGH, Evelyn (1903–1966)
News is what a chap who doesn't care much
about anything wants to read. And it's only
news until he's read it. After that it's dead.
[*Scoop* (1938)]

WOLFE, Humbert (1886–1940)
You cannot hope
To bribe or twist,
thank God! the
British journalist.
But, seeing what
the man will do
unbribed, there's
no occasion to.
['Over the Fire' (1930)]

ZAPPA, Frank (1940–1993)
Rock journalism is people who can't write
interviewing people who can't talk for people
who can't read.
[In Linda Botts, *Loose Talk* (1980)]

See **MEDIA, TELEVISION**

NOSTALGIA

ADAMS, Scott (1957–)
Someday we'll look back on this and plow into
a parked car.
[*The Dilbert Principle*]

AUGIER, Emile (1820–1889)
Homesickness for the gutter.
[*Le Mariage d'Olympe* (1855)]

BYRON, Lord (1788–1824)
Ah! happy years! once more who would not
be a boy?
[*Childe Harold's Pilgrimage* (1818)]

FITZGERALD, Penelope (1916–2000)
(Her hopes for the New Year)
Conductors should be back on the buses,
packets of salt back in the crisps, clockwork
back in clocks and levers back in pens.
[*The Observer*, 1998]

HOUSMAN, A.E. (1859–1936)
Into my heart an air that kills
From yon far country blows:
What are those blue remembered hills,

What spires, what farms are those?
That is the land of lost content, I see it
shining plain,
The happy highways where I went
And cannot come again.
[*A Shropshire Lad* (1896)]

LAMB, Charles (1775–1834)
All, all are gone, the old familiar faces.
['The Old Familiar Faces']

ORWELL, George (1903–1950)
Before the war, and especially before the Boer
War, it was summer all the year round.
[*Coming Up for Air* (1939)]

THOMAS, Dylan (1914–1953)
Years and years and years ago, when I was a
boy, when there were wolves in Wales, and
birds the colour of red-flannel petticoats
whisked past the harp-shaped hills ... when
we rode the daft and happy hills bareback, it
snowed and it snowed.
[*A Child's Christmas in Wales* (1954)]

USTINOV, Sir Peter (1921–2004)
The English have an enormous nostalgia for
school. There is no other country in the world
where you see elderly gentleman dressed like
schoolboys.
[*The Observer*, 1998]

VILLON, François (b. 1431)
But where are the snows of yesteryear?
[*Le Grand Testament* (1461)]

See **MEMORY, PAST, REGRET**

NUCLEAR WEAPONS

EINSTEIN, Albert (1879–1955)
(Of his part in the development of the atom
bomb)
If only I had known, I should have become a
watchmaker.
[*New Statesman*, 1965]

KING, Martin Luther (1929–1968)
Our scientific power has outrun our spiritual power. We have guided missiles and misguided men.
[*Strength to Love*, 1963]

MCLUHAN, Marshall (1911–1980)
The hydrogen bomb is history's exclamation point. It ends an age-long sentence of manifest violence.
[Attr.]

RUSSELL, Bertrand (1872–1970)
(On the possibility of nuclear war between the USA and the USSR)
You may reasonably expect a man to walk a tightrope safely for ten minutes; it would be unreasonable to do so without accident for two hundred years.
[In Desmond Bagley, *The Tightrope Men* (1973)]

See **WAR**

OBSTINACY

ARISTOTLE (384–322 BC)
Obstinate people may be subdivided into the opinionated, the ignorant, and the boorish.
[*Nicomacheon Ethics*]

BROWNE, Sir Thomas (1605–1682)
Obstinacy in a bad cause, is but constancy in a good.
[*Religio Medici* (1643)]

MACNEICE, Louis (1907–1963)
One must not dislike people ... because they are intransigent. For that could be only playing their own game.
[*Zoo* (1938)]

MAUGHAM, William Somerset (1874–1965)
Like all weak men he laid an exaggerated stress on not changing one's mind.
[*Of Human Bondage* (1915)]

STERNE, Laurence (1713–1768)
'Tis known by the name of perseverance in a good cause, – and of obstinacy in a bad one.
[*Tristram Shandy* (1759–67)]

OPINIONS

BAEZ, Joan (1941–)
I've never had a humble opinion. If you've got an opinion, why be humble about it.
[*Scotland on Sunday*, 1992]

CONGREVE, William (1670–1729)
I am always of the opinion with the learned, if they speak first.
[*Incognita* (1692)]

EMERSON, Ralph Waldo (1803–1882)
Tomorrow a stranger will say with masterly good sense precisely what we have thought and felt all the time, and we shall be forced to take with shame our own opinion from another.
['Self-Reliance' (1841)]

HALSEY, Margaret (1910–1997)
... the English think of an opinion as something which a decent person, if he has the misfortune to have one, does all he can to hide.
[*With Malice Toward Some* (1938)]

JEFFERSON, Thomas (1743–1826)
Error of opinion may be tolerated where reason is left free to combat it.
[First inaugural address, 1801]

LOCKE, John (1632–1704)
New opinions are always suspected, and usually opposed, without any reason but because they are not already common.
[*Essay concerning Human Understanding* (1690)]

MACKINTOSH, Sir James (1765–1832)
Men are never so good or so bad as their opinions.
['Jeremy Bentham' (1830)]

MAISTRE, Joseph de (1753–1821)
Wrong opinions are like counterfeit coins, which are first minted by great wrongdoers, then spent by decent people who perpetuate the crime without knowing what they are doing.
[*Les soirées de Saint-Pétersbourg*]

MILL, John Stuart (1806–1873)
If all mankind minus one, were of one opinion, and only one person were of the contrary opinion, mankind would be no more justified in silencing that one person, than he, if he had the power, would be justified in silencing mankind.
[*On Liberty* (1859)]

SPENCER, Herbert (1820–1903)
Opinion is ultimately determined by the feelings, and not by the intellect.
[*Social Statics* (1850)]

TURGENEV, Ivan (1818–1883)
I submit to no man's opinion; I have opinions of my own.
[*Fathers and Sons* (1862)]

WENDERS, Wim (1945–)
The more opinions you have, the less you see.
[Attr.]

See **IDEAS**

OPTIMISM

CABELL, James Branch (1879–1958)
The optimist proclaims that we live in the best of all possible worlds; and the pessimist fears this is true.
[*The Silver Stallion* (1926)]

CHURCHILL, Sir Winston (1874–1965)
A pessimist sees the difficulty in every opportunity; an optimist sees the opportunity in every difficulty.

ELLIS, Havelock (1859–1939)
The place where optimism most flourishes is the lunatic asylum.
[*The Dance of Life*]

MAILER, Norman (1923–2007)
Being married six times shows a degree of optimism over wisdom, but I am incorrigibly optimistic.
[*The Observer*, 1988]

MARQUIS, Don (1878–1937)
An optimist is a guy that has never had much experience.
[*archy and mehitabel* (1927)]

O'CASEY, Sean (1880–1964)
A lament in one ear, maybe; but always a song in the other. And to me life is simply an invitation to live.
[In Eileen O'Casey, *Eileen*]

SHORTER, Clement King (1857–1926)
The latest definition of an optimist is one who fills up his crossword puzzle in ink.
[*The Observer*, 1925]

USTINOV, Sir Peter (1921–2004)
I am an optimist, unrepentant and militant. After all, in order not to be a fool an optimist must know how sad a place the world can be. It is only the pessimist who finds this out anew every day.
[*Dear Me* (1977)]

VOLTAIRE (1694–1778)
Everything is for the best in the best of all possible worlds.
[*Candide* (1759)]

See **HOPE, PESSIMISM**

PARENTS

ALLEN, Woody (1935–)
My parents were very old world. They come from Brooklyn which is the heart of the old world. Their values in life are God, and carpeting.
[In Adler and Feinman, *Woody Allen: Clown Prince of American Humor*]

BACON, Francis (1561–1626)
The joys of parents are secret, and so are their griefs and fears.
['Of Parents and Children' (1625)]

BUTLER, Samuel (1835–1902)
Parents are the last people on earth who ought to have children.
[Attr.]

COMPTON-BURNETT, Dame Ivy (1884–1969)
Don't be too hard on parents. You may find yourself in their place.
[*Elders and Betters* (1944)]

DE VRIES, Peter (1910–1993)
There are times when parenthood seems nothing but feeding the mouth that bites you.
[*The Tunnel of Love*]

EMERSON, Ralph Waldo (1803–1882)
Respect the child. Be not too much his parent. Trespass not on his solitude.
[Attr.]

FUKUYAMA, Francis (1952–)
It takes a great deal of effort to separate a mother from her infant, and a fair amount to get a father to be involved with his.
[*The Great Disruption* (1999)]

LARKIN, Philip (1922–1985)
They fuck you up, your mum and dad.
They may not mean to, but they do.
They fill you with the faults they had
And add some extra, just for you.
['This be the Verse' (1974)]

NASH, Ogden (1902–1971)
Children aren't happy with nothing to ignore,
And that's what parents were created for.
[*Happy Days* (1933)]

SPARK, Muriel (1918–2006)
Parents learn a lot from their children about coping with life.

[*The Comforters* (1957)]

WILDE, Oscar (1854–1900)
To lose one parent may be regarded as a misfortune ... to lose both seems like carelessness.

[*The Importance of Being Earnest* (1895)]

See **CHILDREN, FAMILIES, FATHERS, MOTHERS**

PASSION

CONNOLLY, Cyril (1903–1974)
The man who is master of his passions is Reason's slave.

[In V.S. Pritchett (ed.), *Turnstile One*]

DRYDEN, John (1631–1700)
A man is to be cheated into passion, but to be reasoned into truth.

[*Religio Laici* (1682)]

JUNG, Carl Gustav (1875–1961)
A man who has not gone through the hell of his passions has never overcome them either.

[*Memories, Dreams, Thoughts* (1962)]

L'ESTRANGE, Sir Roger (1616–1704)
It is with our passions as it is with fire and water, they are good servants, but bad masters.

[Translation of *Aesop's Fables*]

SHAKESPEARE, William (1564–1616)
Give me that man
That is not passion's slave, and I will wear him
In my heart's core, ay, in my heart of heart,
As I do thee.

[*Hamlet*, III.ii]

STEELE, Sir Richard (1672–1729)
Women dissemble their Passions better than Men, but ... Men subdue their Passions better than Women.

[*The Lover* (1714)]

See **LOVE**

THE PAST

BEERBOHM, Sir Max (1872–1956)
There is always something rather absurd about the past.

[Attr.]

COLETTE (1873–1954)
But the past, the beautiful past striped with sunshine, grey with mist, childish, blooming with hidden joy, bruised with sweet sorrow.... Ah! if only I could resurrect one hour of that time, one alone – but which one?

[*Paysages et portraits* (1958)]

FITZGERALD, F. Scott (1896–1940)
So we beat on, boats against the current, borne back ceaselessly into the past.

[*The Great Gatsby* (1925)]

HARTLEY, L.P. (1895–1972)
The past is a foreign country: they do things differently there.

[*The Go-Between* (1953)]

SANTAYANA, George (1863–1952)
Those who cannot remember the past are condemned to repeat it.

[*The Life of Reason* (1906)]

TERTZ, Abram (1925–1997)
In the past, people did not cling to life quite as much, and it was easier to breathe.

[*A Voice From the Chorus* (1973)]

THOMAS, Edward (1878–1917)
The past is the only dead thing that smells sweet.

['Early One Morning' (1917)]

See **EXPERIENCE, FUTURE, HISTORY, MEMORY, NOSTALGIA, PRESENT, REGRET, TIME**

PATIENCE

BIERCE, Ambrose (1842–c.1914)
Patience: A minor form of despair, disguised as a virtue.

[*The Cynic's Word Book* (1906)]

CERVANTES, Miguel de (1547–1616)
I say have patience, and shuffle the cards.

[*Don Quixote* (1615)]

FONTAINE, Jean de la (1621–1695)
Patience and time do more than force and rage.

[*Fables*]

MASSINGER, Philip (1583–1640)
Patience, the beggar's virtue.

[*A New Way to Pay Old Debts* (1633)]

SHAKESPEARE, William (1564–1616)
How poor are they that have not patience!
What wound did ever heal but by degrees?

[*Othello*, II.iii]

PATRIOTISM

TAYLOR, Elizabeth (1912-1975)
It is very strange ... that the years teach us patience; that the shorter our time, the greater our capacity for waiting.
[*A Wreath of Roses* (1950)]

See **PERSISTENCE**

PATRIOTISM

ADDISON, Joseph (1672-1719)
What pity is it
That we can die but once to serve our country!
[*Cato* (1713)]

CAVELL, Edith (1865-1915)
(Said on the eve of her execution)
Standing, as I do, in view of God and eternity I realize that patriotism is not enough. I must have no hatred or bitterness towards anyone.
[*The Times*, 1915]

CHESTERTON, G.K. (1874-1936)
They died to save their country and they only saved the world.
[*The Ballad of Saint Barbara and Other Verses* (1922)]

DECATUR, Stephen (1779-1820)
(Toast during a banquet, 1815)
Our country! In her intercourse with foreign nations, may she always be in the right; but our country, right or wrong.
[In Mackenzie, *Life of Decatur* (1846)]

DRYDEN, John (1631-1700)
Never was patriot yet, but was a fool.
[*Absalom and Achitophel* (1681)]

FORSTER, E.M. (1879-1970)
I hate the idea of causes, and if I had to choose between betraying my country and betraying my friend, I hope I should have the guts to betray my country.
[*Two Cheers for Democracy* (1951)]

GASKELL, Elizabeth (1810-1865)
That kind of patriotism which consists in hating all other nations.
[*Sylvia's Lovers* (1863)]

GOLDSMITH, Oliver (c.1728-1774)
Such is the patriot's boast, where'er we roam,
His first best country ever is at home.
['The Traveller' (1764)]

HALE, Nathan (1755-1776)
(Speech before he was executed by the British)
I only regret that I have but one life to lose for my country.
[In Johnston, *Nathan Hale* (1974)]

HORACE (65-8 BC)
Dulce et decorum est pro patria mori. It is sweet and honourable to die for one's country.
[*Odes*]

JOHNSON, Samuel (1709-1784)
Patriotism is the last refuge of a scoundrel.
[In Boswell, *The Life of Samuel Johnson* (1791)]

OWEN, Wilfred (1893-1918)
If you could hear, at every jolt, the blood
Come gargling from the froth-corrupted lungs,
Obscene as cancer, bitter as the cud
Of vile, incurable sores on innocent tongues, –
My friend, you would not tell with such high zest
To children ardent for some desperate glory,
The old Lie: Dulce et decorum est
Pro patria mori.
['Dulce et decorum est' (1917)]

PLOMER, William (1903-1973)
Patriotism is the last refuge of the sculptor.
[Attr.]

RUSSELL, Bertrand (1872-1970)
Patriots always talk of dying for their country, and never of killing for their country.
[Attr.]

SCHURZ, Carl (1829-1906)
Our country, right or wrong! When right, to be kept right; when wrong, to be put right!
[Speech, 1872]

WILDE, Oscar (1854-1900)
Patriotism is the virtue of the vicious.
[Attr.]

See **WAR**

PEACE

ANONYMOUS
Since wars begin in the minds of men, it is in the minds of men that the defences of peace must be constructed.
[Constitution of UNESCO]

BELLOC, Hilaire (1870-1953)
Pale Ebenezer thought it wrong to fight,
But Roaring Bill (who killed him) thought it right.
['The Pacifist' (1938)]

BIERCE, Ambrose (1842-c.1914)
Peace: In international affairs, a period of cheating between two periods of fighting.
[*The Cynic's Word Book* (1906)]

BRECHT, Bertolt (1898-1956)
Don't tell me that peace has broken out.
[*Mother Courage* (1939)]

EINSTEIN, Albert (1879-1955)
Peace cannot be kept by force. It can only be achieved by understanding.
[*Notes on Pacifism*]

GANDHI (1869-1948)
I wanted to avoid violence. Non-violence is the first article of my faith. It is also the last article of my creed.
[Speech, 1922]

JERROLD, Douglas William (1803-1857)
We love peace, as we abhor pusillanimity; but not peace at any price.
['Peace' (1859)]

MILTON, John (1608-1674)
Peace hath her victories
No less renowned than war.
['To the Lord General Cromwell' (1652)]

TACITUS (AD c.56-c.120)
They create a desert, and call it peace.
[*Agricola*]

WALPOLE, Horace (1717-1797)
When will the world know that peace and propagation are the two most delightful things in it?
[Letter to Sir Horace Mann, 1778]

WILSON, Woodrow (1856-1924)
There is a price which is too great to pay for peace, and that price can be put in one word. One cannot pay the price of self-respect.
[Speech, 1916]

See **WAR**

THE PEOPLE

ALCUIN (735-804)
Nor should those be heeded who are wont to say 'The voice of the people is the voice of God', since popular uproar is always akin to madness.
[Letter to Charlemagne]

BURKE, Edmund (1729-1797)
It is a general popular error to imagine the loudest complainers for the public to be the most anxious for its welfare.
[Observations on 'The Present State of the Nation' (1769)]

CARLYLE, Thomas (1795-1881)
The Public is an old woman. Let her maunder and mumble.
[Attr.]

CICERO (106-43 BC)
The good of the people is the chief law.
[*De Legibus*]

CONFUCIUS (c.550-c.478 BC)
The people may be made to follow a course of action, but they may not be made to understand it.
[*Analects*]

CROMWELL, Oliver (1599-1658)
(Referring to a cheering crowd)
The people would be just as noisy if they were going to see me hanged.
[Attr.]

DRYDEN, John (1631-1700)
Nor is the people's judgement always true:
The most may err as grossly as the few.
[*Absalom and Achitophel* (1681)]

HAZLITT, William (1778-1830)
There is not a more mean, stupid, dastardly, pitiful, selfish, spiteful, envious, ungrateful animal than the Public. It is the greatest of cowards, for it is afraid of itself.
[*Table-Talk* (1822)]

JUVENAL (c.60-130)
Two things only the people anxiously desire: bread and circuses.
[*Satires*]

KENNEDY, Robert F. (1925-1968)
One fifth of the people are against everything all the time.
[*The Observer*, 1964]

LINCOLN, Abraham (1809-1865)
You can fool some of the people all of the time, and all of the people some of the time, but you cannot fool all of the people all of the time.
[Attr.]

SCHULZ, Charles (1922-2000)
I love mankind - it's people I can't stand.
[*Go Fly a Kite, Charlie Brown*]

See **HUMANITY AND HUMAN NATURE**

PESSIMISM

BENNETT, Arnold (1867-1931)
Pessimism, when you get used to it, is just as agreeable as optimism.
[*Things That Have Interested Me*]

BEVERIDGE, William Henry (1879-1963)
Scratch a pessimist, and you find often a defender of privilege.
[*The Observer*, 1943]

COHEN, Leonard (1934-)
I don't consider myself a pessimist. I think of a pessimist as someone who is waiting for it to rain. And I feel soaked to the skin.
[*The Observer*, May 1993]

LOWELL, Robert (1917-1977)
If we see light at the end of the tunnel,
It's the light of the oncoming train.
['Since 1939' (1977)]

MALLET, Robert (1915-2002)
How many pessimists end up by desiring the
things they fear, in order to prove that they
are right.
[*Apostilles*]

MEIR, Golda (1898-1978)
Pessimism is a luxury that a Jew can never
allow himself.
[*The Observer*, 1974]

PETER, Laurence J. (1919-1990)
A pessimist is a man who looks both ways
before crossing a one-way street.
[Attr.]

See **OPTIMISM**

PHILOSOPHY

AYER, A.J. (1910-1989)
The principles of logic and metaphysics are
true simply because we never allow them to
be anything else.
[*Language, Truth and Logic* (1936)]

BOWEN, Lord (1835-1894)
On a metaphysician: A blind man in a dark room
– looking for a black hat – which isn't there.
[Attr.]

CICERO (106-43 BC)
But somehow there is nothing so absurd that
some philosopher has not said it.
[*De Divinatione*]

EDWARDS, Oliver (1711-1791)
I have tried too in my time to be a
philosopher; but, I don't know how,
cheerfulness was always breaking in.
[In Boswell, *The Life of Samuel Johnson* (1791)]

HUXLEY, T.H. (1825-1895)
I doubt if the philosopher lives, or has ever
lived, who could know himself to be heartily
despised by a street boy without some
irritation.
[*Evolution and Ethics* (1893)]

MACNEICE, Louis (1907-1963)
Good-bye now, Plato and Hegel,
The shop is closing down;
They don't want any philosopher-kings in
England,
There ain't no universals in this man's town.
[*Autumn Journal* (1939)]

NIETZSCHE, Friedrich Wilhelm (1844-1900)
What I understand philosophers to be: a
terrible explosive, in the presence of which
everything is in danger.
[*Ecce Homo* (1888)]

PASCAL, Blaise (1623-1662)
To ridicule philosophy is truly to philosophize.
[*Penseés* (1670)]

SELDEN, John (1584-1654)
Philosophy is nothing but discretion.
[*Table Talk* (1689)]

SHAKESPEARE, William (1564-1616)
There are more things in heaven and earth,
Horatio,
Than are dreamt of in your philosophy.
[*Hamlet*, I.v]

VOLTAIRE (1694-1778)
In philosophy, we must distrust the things we
understand too easily as well as the things we
don't understand.
[*Lettres philosophiques* (1734)]
Superstition sets the whole world on fire;
philosophy quenches the flames.
[*Dictionnaire philosophique* (1764)]

WHITEHEAD, A.N. (1861-1947)
Philosophy is the product of wonder.
[*Nature and Life* (1934)]

WITTGENSTEIN, Ludwig (1889-1951)
Philosophy is a struggle against the
bewitching of our minds by means of
language.
[*Philosophical Investigations* (1953)]

See **THOUGHT**

PHOTOGRAPHY

ABBOTT, Berenice (1898-1991)
Photography can never grow up if it imitates
some other medium. It has to walk alone; it
has to be itself.
[*Infinity*, 1951]

ASTOR, Nancy (Viscountess) (1879-1964)
(Refusing to pose for a close-up photograph)
Take a close-up of a woman past sixty! You
might as well use a picture of a relief map of
Ireland!
[Attr.]

BENN, Tony (1925-)
Most things in life are moments of pleasure
and a lifetime of embarrassment;
photography is a moment of embarrassment
and a lifetime of pleasure.
[*The Independent*, October 1989]

HOCKNEY, David (1937-)
(On the death of photography)
Once you can manipulate pictures on a computer you can't believe them any more. There will be no more Cartier-Bressons.
[Interview, *The Observer*, May 1999]

LAWRENCE, D.H. (1885-1930)
The modern pantheist not only sees the god in everything, he takes photographs of it.
[*St Mawr* (1925)]

VIDAL, Gore (1925-2012)
As much of an art form as interior decorating.
[Attr.]

PLAGIARISM

BIERCE, Ambrose (1842-c.1914)
Plagiarize: To take the thought or style of another writer whom one has never, never read.
[*The Enlarged Devil's Dictionary* (1961)]

MIZNER, Wilson (1876-1933)
When you steal from one author, it's plagiarism; if you steal from many, it's research.
[Attr.]

MONTAIGNE, Michel de (1533-1592)
One could say of me that in this book I have only made up a bunch of other men's flowers, providing of my own only the string to tie them together.
[*Essais* (1580)]

MORE, Hannah (1745-1833)
He lik'd those literary cooks
Who skim the cream of others' books;
And ruin half an author's graces
By plucking bon-mots from their places.

SHERIDAN, Richard Brinsley (1751-1816)
All that can be said is, that two people happened to hit on the same thought – and Shakespeare made use of it first, that's all.
[*The Critic* (1779)]

STEVENSON, Robert Louis (1850-1894)
Of all my verse, like not a single line;
But like my title, for it is not mine,
That title from a better man I stole;
Ah, how much better, had I stol'n the whole!
[*Underwoods* (1887)]

STRAVINSKY, Igor (1882-1971)
A good composer does not imitate; he steals.
[In Yates, *Twentieth Century Music* (1967)]

SULLIVAN, Sir Arthur (1842-1900)
(Accused of plagiarism)
We all have the same eight notes to work with.
[Attr.]

PLEASURE

ALCOTT, Bronson (1799-1888)
A sip is the most that mortals are permitted from any goblet of delight.
[*Table Talk* (1877)]

AUSTEN, Jane (1775-1817)
One half of the world cannot understand the pleasures of the other.
[*Emma* (1816)]

BATAILLE, Georges (1897-1962)
Pleasure only starts once the worm has got into the fruit, to become delightful happiness must be tainted with poison.
[*My Mother* (1966)]

BEHN, Aphra (1640-1689)
Variety is the soul of pleasure.
[*The Rover* (1677)]

BIERCE, Ambrose (1842-c.1914)
Debauchee: One who has so earnestly pursued pleasure that he has had the misfortune to overtake it.
[*The Cynic's Word Book* (1906)]

BURKE, Edmund (1729-1797)
I am convinced that we have a degree of delight, and that no small one, in the real misfortunes and pains of others.
[*A Philosophical Enquiry into the Origin of our Ideas of the Sublime and Beautiful* (1757)]

BURNS, Robert (1759-1796)
But pleasures are like poppies spread:
You seize the flow'r, its bloom is shed;
Or like the snow falls in the river,
A moment white – then melts for ever.
['Tam o'Shanter' (1790)]

BYRON, Lord (1788-1824)
Pleasure's a sin, and sometimes sin's a pleasure.
[*Don Juan* (1824)]

COWPER, William (1731-1800)
Remorse, the fatal egg by pleasure laid.
['The Progress of Error' (1782)]

HAZLITT, William (1778-1830)
The art of pleasing consists in being pleased.
[*The Round Table* (1817)]

JOHNSON, Samuel (1709-1784)

Pleasure is very seldom found where it is sought; our brightest blazes of gladness are commonly kindled by unexpected sparks.

[*The Idler* (1758-1760)]

No man is a hypocrite in his pleasures.

[In Boswell, *The Life of Samuel Johnson* (1791)]

KEATS, John (1795-1821)

Ever let the Fancy roam,
Pleasure never is at home.

['Fancy' (1819)]

LAMB, Charles (1775-1834)

The greatest pleasure I know, is to do a good action by stealth, and to have it found out by accident.

['Table Talk by the Late Elia']

MOLIÈRE (1622-1673)

Heaven forbids certain pleasures, it is true, but one can arrive at certain compromises.

[*Tartuffe* (1664)]

WOOLLCOTT, Alexander (1887-1943)

All the things I really like to do are either immoral, illegal, or fattening.

[In Drennan, *Wit's End* (1973)]

See **HAPPINESS**

POETRY

ASHBERY, John (1927-)

There is the view that poetry should improve your life. I think people confuse it with the Salvation Army.

[*International Herald Tribune*, October 1989]

BARROW, Isaac (1630-1677)

Poetry is a kind of ingenious nonsense.

[In Spence, *Anecdotes*]

BYRON, Lord (1788-1824)

What is poetry? – The feeling of a Former world and Future.

[*Journal*, 1821]

CAGE, John (1912-1992)

I have nothing to say, I am saying it, and that is poetry.

[*Silence* (1961)]

COLERIDGE, Samuel Taylor (1772-1834)

I wish our clever young poets would remember my homely definitions of prose and poetry; that is prose = words in their best order; poetry = the best words in the best order.

[*Table Talk* (1835)]

COPE, Wendy (1945-)

I hardly ever tire of love or rhyme –
That's why I'm poor and have a rotten time.

['Variation on Belloc's 'Fatigue'']

COWPER, William (1731-1800)

There is a pleasure in poetic pains
Which only poets know.

[*The Task* (1785)]

ELIZABETH (the Queen Mother) (1900-2002)

(On a private reading by TS Eliot of The Waste Land)

We had this rather lugubrious man in a suit, and he read a poem – I think it was called The Desert – and first the girls got the giggles, and then I did, and then even the King. Such a gloomy man. Looked as though he worked in a bank, and we didn't understand a word.

[Quoted in *The Guardian*, August 2000]

EWART, Gavin (1916-1995)

Good light verse is better than bad heavy verse any day of the week.

[*Penultimate Poems* (1989)]

FARQUHAR, George (1678-1707)

Poetry's a mere drug, Sir.

[*Love and a Bottle* (1698)]

FROST, Robert (1874-1963)

Poetry is a way of taking life by the throat.

[In Sergeant, *Robert Frost: the Trial by Existence* (1960)]

GRANVILLE-BARKER, Harley (1877-1946)

Rightly thought of there is poetry in peaches ... even when they are canned.

[*The Madras House*]

JARRELL, Randall (1914-1965)

Some poetry seems to have been written on typewriters by other typewriters.

[Attr.]

KEATS, John (1795-1821)

If Poetry comes not as naturally as Leaves to a tree it had better not come at all.

[Letter to John Taylor, 1818]

KENNEDY, John F. (1917-1963)

When power narrows the areas of man's concern, poetry reminds him of the richness and diversity of his existence.

[Speech, 1963]

KLOPSTOCK, Friedrich (1724-1803)

(Of one of his poems)
God and I both knew what it meant once; now God alone knows.

[Attr.]

LARKIN, Philip (1922-1985)

I can't understand these chaps who go round American universities explaining how they write poems: It's like going round explaining how you sleep with your wife.

[*New York Times*, August 1986]

MACAULAY, Lord (1800-1859)

As civilization advances, poetry almost necessarily declines.

[*Collected Essays* (1843)]

MOTION, Andrew (1952-)

The poetry world is very small and full of green-eyed snapping fish.

[*The Sunday Times*, January 2001]

PRESTON, Keith (1884-1927)

Of all the literary scenes
Saddest this sight to me:
The graves of little magazines
Who died to make verse free.

['The Liberators']

SHELLEY, Percy Bysshe (1792-1822)

(Poetry)
lifts the veil from the hidden beauty of the world, and makes familiar objects be as if they were not familiar.

[*A Defence of Poetry* (1821)]

THOMAS, Dylan (1914-1953)

These poems, with all their crudities, doubts, and confusions, are written for the love of Man and in praise of God, and I'd be a damn fool if they weren't.

[*Collected Poems* (1952)]

VALÉRY, Paul (1871-1945)

A poem is never finished, only abandoned.

[In Auden, *A Certain World*]

WAIN, John (1925-1994)

Poetry is to prose as dancing is to walking.

[BBC broadcast, 1976]

WILDE, Oscar (1854-1900)

There seems to be some curious connection between piety and poor rhymes.

[In Lucas, *A Critic in Pall Mall* (1919)]

ZEPHANIAH, Benjamin (1958-)

I think poetry should be alive. You should be able to dance it.

[*The Sunday Times*, August 1987]

See **CRITICISM, LITERATURE, POETS, WRITING**

POETS

AUDEN, W.H. (1907-1973)

It is a sad fact about our culture that a poet can earn much more money writing or talking about his art than he can by practising it.

[*The Dyer's Hand* (1963)]

BEER, Thomas (1889-1940)

I agree with one of your reputable critics that a taste for drawing-rooms has spoiled more poets than ever did a taste for gutters.

[*The Mauve Decade* (1926)]

COCTEAU, Jean (1889-1963)

A true poet scarcely worries about poetry, just as a gardener does not scent his roses.

[*Professional Secrets* (1922)]

COLERIDGE, Samuel Taylor (1772-1834)

No man was ever yet a great poet, without being at the same time a profound philosopher.

[*Biographia Literaria* (1817)]

CONGREVE, William (1670-1729)

It is the business of a comic poet to paint the vices and follies of human kind.

[*The Double Dealer* (1694)]

GRAVES, Robert (1895-1985)

To be a poet is a condition rather than a profession.

[Questionnaire in *Horizon*]

LARKIN, Philip (1922-1985)

Deprivation is for me what daffodils were for Wordsworth.

[*The Observer*, 1979]

PLATO (c.429-347 BC)

Poets utter great and wise things which they do not themselves understand.

[*Republic*]

POPE, Alexander (1688-1744)

Sir, I admit your gen'ral Rule
That every Poet is a Fool;
But you yourself may serve to show it,
That every Fool is not a Poet.

['Epigram from the French' (1732)]

WALLER, Edmund (1606-1687)

Poets lose half the praise they should have got,
Could it be known what they discreetly blot.

['On Roscommon's Translation of Horace']

WOOLF, Virginia (1882-1941)

I would venture to guess that Anon, who wrote so many poems without signing them, was often a woman.

[*A Room. of One's Own* (1929)]

YEATS, W.B. (1865-1939)
The poet finds and makes his mask in disappointment, the hero in defeat.
['Anima Hominis']

See **CRITICISM, POETRY, WRITERS**

POLICE

CONRAD, Joseph (1857-1924)
The terrorist and the policeman both come from the same basket.
[*The Secret Agent* (1907)]

MILLIGAN, Spike (1918-2002)
Policemen are numbered in case they get lost.
[*The Last Goon Show of All*]

O'BRIEN, Flann (1911-1966)
(Commenting on the fact that policemen always seem to look young)
A thing of duty is a boy for ever.
[Attr.]

ORWELL, George (1903-1950)
Only the Thought Police mattered.
[*Nineteen Eighty-Four* (1949)]

ROGERS, E.W. (1864-1913)
Ev'ry member of the force
Has a watch and chain, of course;
If you want to know the time,
Ask a P'liceman!
['Ask a P'liceman', song, 1889]

POLITICIANS

ADAMS, Franklin P. (1881-1960)
The trouble with this country is that there are too many politicians who believe, with a conviction based on experience, that you can fool all of the people all of the time.
[*Nods and Becks* (1944)]

ASQUITH, Margot (1864-1945)
(Of Lloyd George)
He couldn't see a belt without hitting below it.
[*As I Remember*, 1967]

BELLOC, Hilaire (1870-1953)
Judges are guided by the law; politicians by expediency.
[*El Pais*, 1994]

BRIGHT, John (1811-1889)
(Of Disraeli)
He is a self-made man, and worships his creator.
[Remark, c.1868]

BUCHWALD, Art (1925-2007)
(Of Richard Nixon)
I worship the quicksand he walks in.
[Attr.]

CAMERON, Simon (1799-1889)
An honest politician is one who, when he is bought, will stay bought.
[Remark]

CHAPLIN, Charlie (1889-1977)
I remain just one thing, and one thing only – and that is a clown. It places me on a far higher plane than any politician.
[*The Observer*, June 1960]

CRITCHLEY, Sir Julian (1930-2000)
The only safe pleasure for a parliamentarian is a bag of boiled sweets.
[*Listener*, 1982]

CUMMINGS, e. e. (1894-1962)
a politician is an arse upon which everyone has sat except a man.
[1×1 (1944), no. 10]

DE GAULLE, Charles (1890-1970)
Since a politician never believes what he says, he is quite surprised to be taken at his word.
[Attr.]

FOLEY, Rae (1900-1978)
He had the misleading air of open-hearted simplicity that people have come to demand of their politicians.
[*The Hundredth Door* (1950)]

FORD, Gerald R. (1913-2006)
(Referring to his own appointment as President)
I guess it proves that in America anyone can be President.
[In Reeves, *A Ford Not a Lincoln*]

GUINAN, Texas (1884-1933)
A politician is a fellow who will lay down your life for his country.
[Attr.]

HEALEY, Denis (1917-)
(On Geoffrey Howe's attack on his Budget proposals)
Like being savaged by a dead sheep.
[Speech, 1978]

HOWAR, Barbara (1934-)
There are no such things as good politicians and bad politicians. There are only politicians, which is to say, they all have personal axes to grind, and all too rarely are they honed for the public good.
[*Laughing All the Way* (1973)]

KHRUSHCHEV, Nikita (1894–1971)
Politicians are the same everywhere. They promise to build a bridge even when there's no river.
[Remark to journalists in the USA, 1960]

LAMONT, Norman (1942–)
The politician's prayer is: 'May my words be ever soft and low, for I may have to eat them'.
[The Sunday Times, May 2001]

LIVINGSTONE, Ken (1945–)
Being an MP is not really a job for grown-ups – you are wandering around looking for and making trouble.
[The Guardian, July 2000]

MACLENNAN, Robert (1936–)
Tony Blair has pushed moderation to extremes.
[The Observer, 1996]

MACMILLAN, Harold (1894–1986)
If people want a sense of purpose they should get it from their archbishop. They should certainly not get it from their politicians.
[In Fairlie, The Life of Politics (1968)]

MAJOR, Sir John (1943–)
People with vision usually do more harm than good.
[The Economist, 1993]

NIXON, Richard (1913–1994)
There can be no whitewash at the White House.
[The Observer, 1973]

PARKER, Dorothy (1893–1967)
(Hearing that President Coolidge had died)
How could they tell?
[In Keats, You Might As Well Live (1970)]

POMPIDOU, Georges (1911–1974)
A statesman is a politician who places himself at the service of a nation. A politician is a statesman who places the nation at his service.
[The Observer, 1973]

ROOSEVELT, Theodore (1858–1919)
The most successful politician is he who says what everybody is thinking most often and in the loudest voice.
[In Andrews, Treasury of Humorous Quotations]

SAHL, Mort (1927–)
Washington could not tell a lie; Nixon could not tell the truth; Reagan cannot tell the difference.
[The Observer, 1987]

(Of President Nixon)
Would you buy a second-hand car from this man?
[Attr.]

SHORTEN, Caroline
Most Conservatives believe that a creche is something that happens between two Range Rovers in Tunbridge Wells.
[The Independent, September 1993]

TROLLOPE, Anthony (1815–1882)
It has been the great fault of our politicians that they have all wanted to do something.
[Phineas Finn (1869)]

TRUMAN, Harry S. (1884–1972)
A statesman is a politician who's been dead ten or fifteen years.
[Attr.]

USTINOV, Sir Peter (1921–2004)
I could never be a politician. I couldn't bear to be right all the time.
[The Times, 1998]

WELCH, Joseph (1890–1960)
(Army attorney denouncing Senator Joseph McCarthy during the Army-McCarthy Congressional Hearings)
Until this moment, Senator, I think I never really gauged your cruelty or your recklessness ... Have you no sense of decency, sir, at long last? Have you left no sense of decency?
[New York Times, 1954]

WHITEHORN, Katherine (1926–)
It is a pity, as my husband says, that more politicians are not bastards by birth instead of vocation.
[The Observer, 1964]

WHITELAW, William (1918–1999)
I am not prepared to go about the country stirring up apathy.
[Attr.]

WILSON, Harold (1916–1995)
(Of Tony Benn)
He immatures with age.
[Attr., BBC programme, 1995]

See **GOVERNMENT, INSULTS, POLITICS**

POLITICS

ABBOTT, Diane (1953–)
Being an MP is the sort of job all working-class parents want for their children – clean, indoors and no heavy lifting.
[The Observer, 1994]

ADAMS, Douglas (1952–2001)
Anyone who is capable of getting themselves made President should on no account be allowed to do the job.
[The Hitch Hiker's Guide to the Galaxy (1979)]

ADAMS, Henry (1838-1918)
Politics, as a practice, whatever its
professions, has always been the systematic
organization of hatreds.
[*The Education of Henry Adams* (1918)]

ARENDT, Hannah (1906-1975)
Truthfulness has never been counted among
the political virtues, and lies have always been
regarded as justifiable tools in political
dealings.
[*Crises of the Republic* (1972)]

ARISTOTLE (384-322 BC)
Man is by nature a political animal.
[*Politics*]

ASTOR, Nancy (Viscountess) (1879-1964)
Women are young at politics, but they are old
at suffering; soon they will learn that through
politics they can prevent some kinds of
suffering.
[*My Two Countries* (1923)]

BARZAN, Gerald
You don't have to fool all the people all of the
time; you just have to fool enough to get
elected.
[In Lieberman, *3,500 Good Quotes for Speakers*
(1983)]

BIERCE, Ambrose (1842-c.1914)
Nepotism: Appointing your grandfather to
office for the good of the party.
[*The Enlarged Devil's Dictionary* (1961)]

BISMARCK, Prince Otto von (1815-1898)
Politics is the art of the possible.
[Remark, 1863]

BURCHILL, Julie (1960-)
Green politics, in the final analysis, is so
popular with the rich because it contains no
race or class analysis at all; politics with
everything but the glow of involvement taken
out.
[*Sex and Sensibility* (1992)]

CAMUS, Albert (1913-1960)
Politics and the fate of mankind are shaped
by men without ideals and without greatness.
Men who have greatness within them don't
concern themselves with politics.
[*Notebooks*, 1935-1942]

CLARK, Alan (1928-1999)
There are no true friends in politics. We are all
sharks circling and waiting, for traces of blood
to appear in the water.
[*Diary*, 1990]

DE GAULLE, Charles (1890-1970)
I have come to the conclusion that politics
are too serious a matter to be left to the
politicians.
[Attr.]

DISRAELI, Benjamin (1804-1881)
Damn your principles! Stick to your party.
[Attr.]

EINSTEIN, Albert (1879-1955)
An empty stomach is not a good political
adviser.
[*Cosmic Religion* (1931)]

FIELDS, W.C. (1880-1946)
Hell, I never vote for anybody. I always vote
against.
[In Taylor, *W. C. Fields: His Follies and Fortunes*
(1950)]

FISHER, H.A.L. (1856-1940)
Politics is the art of human happiness.
[*History of Europe* (1935)]

FROST, Robert (1874-1963)
I never dared be radical when young
For fear it would make me conservative when
old.
['Precaution' (1936)]
A liberal is a man too broadminded to take his
own side in a quarrel.
[Attr.]

GAITSKELL, Hugh (1906-1963)
All terrorists, at the invitation of the
Government, end up with drinks at the
Dorchester.
[Letter to *The Guardian*, 1977]

GALBRAITH, J.K. (1908-2006)
There are times in politics when you must be
on the right side and lose.
[*The Observer*, 1968]

HAVEL, Václav (1936-2011)
Ideology is a special way of relating to the
world. It offers human beings the illusion of
an identity, of dignity, and of morality, while
making it easier for them to part with it.
[*Living in Truth* (1987)]

HIGHTOWER, Jim (1933-)
Only things in the middle of the road are
yellow lines and dead armadillos.
[Attr.]

HITLER, Adolf (1889-1945)
What is essential is the formation of the
political will of the entire nation: that is the
starting point for political actions.
[Speech, 1932]

HORNE, Donald Richmond (1921–2005)
Politics is both fraud and vision.
[*The Legend of King O'Malley*]

JOHNSON, Samuel (1709–1784)
Politics are now nothing more than a means
of rising in the world.
[In Boswell, *The Life of Samuel Johnson* (1791)]

LA BRUYÈRE, Jean de (1645–1696)
Party loyalty brings the greatest of men down
to the petty level of the masses.
[*Les caractères ou les moeurs de ce siècle* (1688)]

MCCARTHY, Senator Eugene (1916–2005)
Being in politics is like being a football coach.
You have to be smart enough to understand
the game and dumb enough to think it's
important.
[Interview, 1968]

MACMILLAN, Harold (1894–1986)
(On the life of a Foreign Secretary)
Forever poised between a cliché and an
indiscretion.
[*Newsweek*, 1956]

MANDELA, Nelson (1918–)
The struggle is my life.
[Letter from underground, 1961]

MILLIGAN, Spike (1918–2002)
(On a pre-election poll)
One day the don't-knows will get in, and then
where will we be?
[Attr.]

NAPOLEON I (1769–1821)
(To Josephine in 1809 on divorcing her for
reasons of state)
I still love you, but in politics there is no heart,
only head.
[Attr.]

ORWELL, George (1903–1950)
No book is genuinely free from political bias.
The opinion that art should have nothing to
do with politics is itself a political attitude.
['Why I Write' (1946)]

PANKHURST, Emmeline (1858–1928)
The argument of the broken pane of glass is
the most valuable argument in modern politics.
[Attr.]

PARRIS, Matthew (1949–)
Being an MP feeds your vanity and starves
your self-respect.
[*The Times*, 1994]

PAXMAN, Jeremy (1950–)
(Interview with Henry Kissinger)
Didn't you feel a fraud accepting the Nobel
Peace Prize?
[BBC radio programme *Start the Week*, 1999]

POWELL, Enoch (1912–1998)
Above any other position of eminence, that of
Prime Minister is filled by fluke.
[*The Observer*, 1987]

RAWNSLEY, Andrew (1962–)
A British Prime Minister in command of a
parliamentary majority is an elected dictator
with vastly more domestic power than an
American President.
[*The Observer*, May 1999]

REAGAN, Ronald (1911–2004)
Politics is supposed to be the second oldest
profession. I have come to understand that it
bears a very close resemblance to the first.
[Remark at a conference, 1977]

SHAW, George Bernard (1856–1950)
He knows nothing; and he thinks he knows
everything. That points clearly to a political
career.
[*Major Barbara* (1907)]

SOMOZA, Anastasio (1925–1980)
You won the elections. But I won the count.
[*The Guardian*, 1977]

SOPER, Donald (1903–1998)
(On the quality of debate in the House of
Lords)
It is, I think, good evidence of life after death.
[*The Listener*, 1978]

STEVENSON, Robert Louis (1850–1894)
Politics is perhaps the only profession for
which no preparation is thought necessary.
[*Familiar Studies of Men and Books* (1882)]

STOPPARD, Tom (1937–)
The House of Lords, an illusion to which I
have never been able to subscribe –
reponsibility without power, the prerogative
of the eunuch throughout the ages.
[*Lord Malquist and Mr Moon* (1966)]

VALÉRY, Paul (1871–1945)
Politics is the art of preventing people from
becoming involved in affairs which concern
them.
[*As Such* 2 (1943)]

VIDAL, Gore (1925-2012)
Any American who is prepared to run for
President should automatically, by definition,
be disqualified from ever doing so.
[Attr.]

WILSON, Harold (1916-1995)
A week is a long time in politics.
[Remark, 1964]

ZAPPA, Frank (1940-1993)
Politics is the entertainment branch of
industry.
[Attr.]

See **COMMUNISM, DEMOCRACY,
DIPLOMACY, FASCISM, GOVERNMENT,
MONARCHY AND ROYALTY,
POLITICIANS, SOCIALISM**

PORNOGRAPHY

ALLEN, Woody (1935-)
Fielding Mellish: I once stole a pornographic
book that was printed in braille. I used to rub
the dirty parts.
[Film *Bananas*, (1971)]

CRISP, Quentin (1908-1999)
What is wrong with pornography is that it is a
successful attempt to sell sex for more than it
is worth.
[In Kettlehack (ed.), *The Wit and Wisdom of
Quentin Crisp*]

HUXLEY, Aldous (1894-1963)
Real orgies are never so exciting as
pornographic books.
[*Point Counter Point* (1928)]

LAWRENCE, D.H. (1885-1930)
Pornography is the attempt to insult sex, to
do dirt on it.
[*Phoenix* (1936)]

NICHOLSON, Jack (1937-)
(Explaining why he disconnected his home
computer from the Internet)
There's so much darn porn out there, I never
got out of the house.
[*The Times*, March 1999]

RUSSELL, Bertrand (1872-1970)
Obscenity is what happens to shock some
elderly and ignorant magistrate.
[*Look* magazine]

See **CENSORSHIP, INTERNET, SEX**

POVERTY

BAGEHOT, Walter (1826-1877)
Poverty is an anomaly to rich people. It is very
difficult to make out why people who want
dinner do not ring the bell.
[*Literary Studies* (1879)]

**THE BIBLE
(King James Version)**
The poor always ye have with you.
[*John*, 12:8]

COWPER, William (1731-1800)
(Of a burglar)
He found it inconvenient to be poor.
['Charity' (1782)]

CRABBE, George (1754-1832)
The murmuring poor, who will not fast in peace.
[*The Newspaper* (1785)]

FARQUHAR, George (1678-1707)
'Tis still my maxim, that there is no scandal
like rags, nor any crime so shameful as
poverty.
[*The Beaux' Stratagem* (1707)]

FRANCE, Anatole (1844-1924)
It is only the poor who pay cash, and that not
from virtue, but because they are refused credit.
[In J.R. Solly, *A Cynic's Breviary*]

GELDOF, Bob (1954-)
I'm not interested in the bloody system! Why
has he no food? Why is he starving to death?
[In Care, *Sayings of the Eighties* (1989)]

JUVENAL (c.60-130)
Rarely they rise by virtue's aid, who lie
Plung'd in the depths of helpless poverty.
[*Satires*]

MARX, Groucho (1895-1977)
Look at me: I worked my way up from nothing
to a state of extreme poverty.
[*Monkey Business*, film, 1931]

SHAW, George Bernard (1856-1950)
The greatest of our evils and the worst of our
crimes is poverty.
[*Major Barbara* (1907)]

TRACY, Spencer (1900-1967)
(Of leaner times in his life)
There were times my pants were so thin I
could sit on a dime and tell if it was heads or
tails.
[In Swindell, *Spencer Tracy*]

WILDE, Oscar (1854-1900)
We are often told that the poor are grateful for charity. Some of them are, no doubt, but the best amongst the poor are never grateful. They are ungrateful, discontented, disobedient, and rebellious. They are quite right to be so.
['The Soul of Man under Socialism' (1891)]

See **MONEY AND WEALTH**

POWER

ACTON, Lord (1834-1902)
Power tends to corrupt, and absolute power corrupts absolutely. Great men are almost always bad men ... There is no worse heresy than that the office sanctifies the holder of it.
[Letter to Bishop Mandell Creighton, 1887]

AMIS, Kingsley (1922-1995)
Generally, nobody behaves decently when they have power.
[*Radio Times*, 1992]

ANDREOTTI, Giulio (1919-2001)
Power wears down the man who doesn't have it.
[In Biagi, *The Good and the Bad* (1989)]

BURKE, Edmund (1729-1797)
Those who have been once intoxicated with power, and have derived any kind of emolument from it, even though but for one year, never can willingly abandon it.
[*Letter to a Member of the National Assembly* (1791)]

CLARE, Dr Anthony (1942-2007)
Apart from the occasional saint, it is difficult for people who have the smallest amount of power to be nice.
[In Care, *Sayings of the Eighties* (1989)]

GOERING, Hermann (1893-1946)
Guns will make us powerful; butter will only make us fat.
[Broadcast, 1936]

KISSINGER, Henry (1923-)
Power is the ultimate aphrodisiac.
[Attr.]

KUNDERA, Milan (1929-)
The struggle of man against power is the struggle of memory against forgetting.
[Attr.]

MALCOLM X (1925-1965)
Power never takes a back step - only in the face of more power.
[*Malcolm X Speaks*, 1965]

MAO TSE-TUNG (1893-1976)
Every Communist must grasp the truth. Political power grows out of the barrel of a gun.
[Speech, 1938]

STEVENSON, Adlai (1900-1965)
Power corrupts, but lack of power corrupts absolutely.
[*The Observer*, 1963]

TURENNE, Henri (Vicomte) (1611-1675)
God is always on the side of the big battalions.
[Attr.]

See **RESPONSIBILITY**

PRAISE

BIERCE, Ambrose (1842-c.1914)
Eulogy: Praise of a person who has either the advantages of wealth and power, or the consideration to be dead.
[*The Enlarged Devil's Dictionary* (1961)]

GAY, John (1685-1732)
Praising all alike, is praising none.
['A Letter to a Lady' (1714)]

LA ROCHEFOUCAULD (1613-1680)
Refusal of praise reveals a desire to be praised twice over.
[*Maximes* (1678)]

MARTIAL (c.AD 40-c.104)
They praise those works but they read something else.
[*Epigrammata*]

SMITH, Sydney (1771-1845)
Praise is the best diet for us, after all.
[In Holland, *A Memoir of the Reverend Sydney Smith* (1855)]

See **FLATTERY**

PREGNANCY

ANNE (the Princess Royal) (1950-)
It's a very boring time. I am not particularly maternal - it's an occupational hazard of being a wife.
[TV interview, quoted in the *Daily Express*, 1981]

LETTE, Kathy (1958-)
I used to rush to the mirror every morning to see if I had bloomed, but all I did was swell. My ankles looked like flesh-coloured flares and my breasts were so huge they needed their own postcode.
[*The Daily Telegraph*, May 1999]

NICHOLS, Peter (1927-)
'One advantage of being pregnant,' says a
wife in one of my television plays, 'you don't
have to worry about getting pregnant.'
[*Feeling You're Behind* (1984)]

PARKER, Dorothy (1893-1967)
(Telegram sent to Mary Sherwood after her
much-publicised pregnancy)
Dear Mary, We all knew you had it in you.
[In J. Keats, *You Might As Well Live*
(1970)]
(Said on going into hospital for an abortion)
It serves me right for putting all my eggs in
one bastard.
[Attr. in J. Keats, *You Might As Well Live* (1970)]
See **BIRTH, MOTHERS**

THE PRESENT

ARNOLD, Matthew (1822-1888)
This strange disease of modern life.
['The Scholar-Gipsy' (1853)]

CLARE, John (1793-1864)
The present is the funeral of the past,
And man the living sepulchre of life.
['The Past' (1845)]

EMERSON, Ralph Waldo (1803-1882)
Write it on your heart that every day is the
best day in the year. No man has learned
anything rightly until he knows that every day
is Doomsday.
[*Society and Solitude* (1870)]

FRANKLIN, Benjamin (1706-1790)
The golden age never was the present age.
[*Poor Richard's Almanac* (1750)]

HAMMARSKJÖLD, Dag (1905-1961)
Do not look back. And do not dream about
the future, either. It will neither give you back
the past, nor satisfy your other daydreams.
Your duty, your reward - your destiny - are
here and now.
[*Markings* (1965)]

HORACE (65-8 BC)
Carpe diem. Seize the day.
[*Odes*]

MCLUHAN, Marshall (1911-1980)
The present cannot be revealed to people
until it has become yesterday.
[In Marchand, *Marshall McLuhan* (1989)]

MALLARMÉ, Stéphane (1842-1898)
That virgin, vital, beautiful day: today.
[*Plusieurs sonnets* (1881)]

SHAKESPEARE, William (1564-1616)
Past and to come seems best; things present,
worst.
[*Henry IV, Part 2*, I.iii]
See **FUTURE, PAST, TIME**

PRIDE

**THE BIBLE
(King James Version)**
Pride goeth before destruction, and an
haughty spirit before a fall.
[*Proverbs*, 16:18]

COLERIDGE, Samuel Taylor (1772-1834)
And the Devil did grin, for his darling sin
Is pride that apes humility.
['The Devil's Thoughts' (1799)]

POPE, Alexander (1688-1744)
Pride, the never-failing vice of fools.
[*An Essay on Criticism* (1711)]

RENARD, Jules (1864-1910)
Be modest! It is the kind of pride least likely to
offend.
[*Journal*]
There is false modesty, but there is no false
pride.
[*Journal*]

SHAKESPEARE, William (1564-1616)
O world, how apt the poor are to be proud!
[*Twelfth Night*, III.i]

SHELLEY, Percy Bysshe (1792-1822)
But human pride
Is skilful to invent most serious names
To hide its ignorance.
[*Queen Mab* (1813)]
See **EGOISM, SELF, VANITY**

PRINCIPLES

ADLER, Alfred (1870-1937)
It is easier to fight for one's principles than to
live up to them.
[Attr.]

BALDWIN, Stanley (1867-1947)
I would rather be an opportunist and float
than go to the bottom with my principles
round my neck.
[Attr.]

LONG, Huey (1893-1935)
The time has come for all good men to rise
above principle.
[Attr.]

MACKENZIE, Sir Compton (1883–1972)
I don't believe in principles. Principles are only excuses for what we want to think or what we want to do.
[*The Adventures of Sylvia Scarlett* (1918)]

MAUGHAM, William Somerset (1874–1965)
You can't learn too soon that the most useful thing about a principle is that it can always be sacrificed to expediency.
[*The Circle* (1921)]

MELBOURNE, Lord (1779–1848)
Nobody ever did anything very foolish except from some strong principle.
[Attr.]

ROOSEVELT, Franklin Delano (1882–1945)
To stand upon the ramparts and die for our principles is heroic, but to sally forth to battle and win for our principles is something more than heroic.
[Speech, 1928]

SADE, Marquis de (1740–1814)
All universal moral principles are idle fancies.
[*The 120 Days of Sodom* (1784)]

TODD, Ron (1927–2005)
You don't have power if you surrender all your principles — you have office.
[Attr.]

See **MORALITY, VIRTUE**

PRISON

AITKEN, Jonathan (1942–)
I lived at Eton in the 1950s and know all about life in uncomfortable quarters.
[*The Times*, January 1999]

BOTTOMLEY, Horatio William (1860–1933)
(When spotted sewing mailbags during his imprisonment for misappropriation of funds)
Visitor: Ah, Bottomley, sewing? Bottomley: No, reaping.
[Attr.]

HAWTHORNE, Nathaniel (1804–1864)
The black flower of civilized society, a prison.
[*The Scarlet Letter* (1850)]

HOOGSTRATEN, Nicholas van (1945–)
When they put me away in 1968, it was nothing. When I was freed I was five times richer, a hundred times more intelligent and a thousand times more dangerous.
[*The Sunday Times*, July 2002]

LEVI, Primo (1919–1987)
(Of the Nazi concentration camps)
The worst survived — that is, the fittest; the best all died.
[*The Drowned and the Saved* (1988)]

LOVELACE, Richard (1618–1658)
Stone walls do not a prison make
Nor iron bars a cage;
Minds innocent and quiet take
That for an hermitage;
If I have freedom in my love,
And in my soul am free;
Angels alone, that soar above,
Enjoy such liberty.
['To Althea, From Prison' (1649)]

RALEIGH, Sir Walter (c.1552–1618)
But now close kept, as captives wonted are:
That food, that heat, that light I find no more;
Despair bolts up my doors, and I alone
Speak to dead walls, but those hear not my moan.
[Untitled poem]

THOREAU, Henry David (1817–1862)
Under a government which imprisons any unjustly, the true place for a just man is also a prison.
[*Civil Disobedience* (1849)]

WILDE, Oscar (1854–1900)
The vilest deeds like poison-weeds
Bloom well in prison-air;
It is only what is good in Man
That wastes and withers there.
[*The Ballad of Reading Gaol* (1898)]

See **CRIME, PUNISHMENT**

PROBLEMS

ADAMS, Scott (1957–)
There are very few personal problems that cannot be solved through a suitable application of high explosives.
[*The Dilbert Principle*]

ANONYMOUS
Inside every small problem is a large problem struggling to get out.

CLEAVER, Eldridge (1935–1998)
If you're not part of the solution, you're part of the problem.
[Attr.]

DOYLE, Sir Arthur Conan (1859–1930)
It is quite a three-pipe problem, and I beg that you won't speak to me for fifty minutes.
[*The Adventures of Sherlock Holmes* (1892)]

LOVELL, James (1928-)
(After the explosion on board Apollo XIII,
which put the crew in serious danger)
OK, Houston, we have had a problem here ...
Houston, we have a problem.
[Radio message, 11 April 1970]

PROGRESS

ANONYMOUS
We've made great medical progress in the last
generation. What used to be merely an itch is
now an allergy.

BENN, Tony (1925-)
It's the same each time with progress. First
they ignore you, then they say you're mad,
then dangerous, then there's a pause and
then you can't find anyone who disagrees
with you.
[*The Observer*, October 1991]

BORGES, Jorge Luis (1899-1986)
We have stopped believing in progress. What
progress that is!
[Ibarra, Borges et Borges]

BUTLER, Samuel (1835-1902)
All progress is based upon a universal innate
desire on the part of every organism to live
beyond its income.
[*The Note-Books of Samuel Butler* (1912)]

CLIFFORD, William Kingdon (1845-1879)
... scientific thought is not an accompaniment
or condition of human progress, but human
progress itself.
[*Aims and Instruments of Scientific Thought*
(1872)]

COMTE, Auguste (1798-1857)
Love our principle, order our foundation,
progress our goal.
[*Système de politique positive*]

DOUGLASS, Frederick (c.1818-1895)
If there is no struggle, there is no progress.
[Attr.]

ELLIS, Havelock (1859-1939)
What we call 'Progress' is the exchange of
one nuisance for another nuisance.
[Impressions and Comments (1914)]

FREUD, Sigmund (1856-1939)
What progress we are making. In the Middle
Ages they would have burned me. Now they
are content with burning my books.
[Letter, 1933]

GIBBON, Edward (1737-1794)
All that is human must retrograde if it does
not advance.
[*Decline and Fall of the Roman Empire*
(1776-88)]

HEGEL, Georg Wilhelm (1770-1831)
The history of the world is none other than
the progress of the consciousness of freedom.
[*Philosophy of History*]

HUBBARD, Elbert (1856-1915)
The world is moving so fast these days that
the man who says it can't be done is generally
interrupted by someone doing it.
[Attr.]

LEM, Stanislaw (1909-1966)
Is it progress if a cannibal uses knife and fork?
[*Unkempt Thoughts* (1962)]

LINDBERGH, Anne Morrow (1906-2001)
Why do progress and beauty have to be so
opposed?
[*Hour of Gold, Hour of Lead* (1973)]

SAINT-EXUPÉRY, Antoine de (1900-1944)
Man's 'progress' is but a gradual discovery
that his questions have no meaning.
[*The Wisdom of the Sands*]

SHAW, George Bernard (1856-1950)
The reasonable man adapts himself to the
world: the unreasonable one persists in trying
to adapt the world to himself. Therefore all
progress depends on the unreasonable man.
[*Man and Superman* (1903)]

THURBER, James (1894-1961)
Progress was all right; only it went on too
long.
[Attr.]

VIGNEAUD, Vincent de (1901-1978)
Nothing holds up the progress of science so
much as the right idea at the wrong time.
[*Most Secret War* (1978)]

See **CHANGE, TECHNOLOGY**

PROMISES

FROST, Robert (1874-1963)
The woods are lovely, dark and deep,
But I have promises to keep,
And miles to go before I sleep,
And miles to go before I sleep.
['Stopping by Woods on a Snowy Evening'
(1923)]

SERVICE, Robert W. (1874-1958)
A promise made is a debt unpaid.
['The Cremation of Sam McGee' (1907)]

SWIFT, Jonathan (1667–1745)
Promises and pie-crusts are made to be
broken, they say.
[*Polite Conversation* (1738)]

TWAIN, Mark (1835–1910)
To promise not to do a thing is the surest way
in the world to make a body want to go and
do that very thing.
[*The Adventures of Tom Sawyer* (1876)]

PROPERTY

DICKENS, Charles (1812–1870)
Get hold of portable property.
[*Great Expectations* (1861)]

DRUMMOND, Thomas (1797–1840)
Property has its duties as well as its rights.
[Letter, 1838]

EDGEWORTH, Maria (1767–1849)
Well! some people talk of morality, and some
of religion, but give me a little snug property.
[*The Absentee* (1812)]

EMERSON, Ralph Waldo (1803–1882)
A man builds a fine house; and now he has a
master, and a task for life; he is to furnish,
watch, show it, and keep it in repair, the rest
of his days.
[*Society and Solitude* (1870)]

INGERSOLL, Robert Greene (1833–1899)
Few rich men own their own property. The
property owns them.
[Address, 1896]

JAMES, Henry (1843–1916)
The black and merciless things that are
behind the great possessions.
[*The Ivory Tower* (1917)]

MACHIAVELLI (1469–1527)
Men sooner forget the death of their father
than the loss of their possessions.
[*The Prince* (1532)]

PROUDHON, Pierre-Joseph (1809–1865)
If I were asked to answer the following
question:'What is slavery?' and I replied in
one word, 'Murder!' my meaning would be
understood at once ... Why, then, to this
other question: 'What is property?'may I not
likewise answer 'Theft'?
[*Qu'est-ce que la propriété?* (1840)]

VANBRUGH, Sir John (1664–1726)
The want of a thing is perplexing enough, but
the possession of it is intolerable.
[*The Confederacy* (1705)]

WILDE, Oscar (1854–1900)
If property had simply pleasures, we could
stand it; but its duties make it unbearable. In
the interest of the rich we must get rid of it.
[*The Fortnightly Review*, 1891]

See **CAPITALISM, MONEY AND WEALTH**

PSYCHIATRY

ANONYMOUS
(Definition of a psychoanalyst)
A Jewish doctor who hates the sight of blood.
[In Leo Rosten, *The Joys of Yiddish* (1968)]

AUDEN, W.H. (1907–1973)
To us he is no more a person
Now but a climate of opinion.
[*In Memory of Sigmund Freud*]

CHASE, Alexander (1926–)
Psychiatry's chief contribution to philosophy
is the discovery that the toilet is the seat of
the soul.
[*Perspectives* (1966)]

GOLDWYN, Samuel (1882–1974)
Any man who goes to a psychiatrist should
have his head examined.
[In Zierold, *Moguls* (1969)]

STOCKWOOD, Mervyn (1913–1995)
A psychiatrist is a man who goes to the
Folies-Bergère and looks at the audience.
[*The Observer*, 1961]

SZASZ, Thomas (1920–2012)
Psychiatrists classify a person as neurotic if
he suffers from his problems in living, and a
psychotic if he makes others suffer.
[*The Second Sin* (1973)]

See **MADNESS**

PUBLISHING

AYER, A.J. (1910–1989)
If I had been someone not very clever, I would
have done an easier job like publishing. That's
the easiest job I can think of.
[Attr.]

CAMPBELL, Thomas (1777–1844)
Now Barabbas was a publisher.
[Attr. in Samuel Smiles, *A Publisher and his
Friends* (1891)]

CONNOLLY, Cyril (1903–1974)
As repressed sadists are supposed to become
policemen or butchers so those with irrational
fear of life become publishers.
[*Enemies of Promise* (1938)]

INGRAMS, Richard (1937–)
(Referring to his editorship of Private Eye)
My own motto is publish and be sued.
[BBC radio broadcast, 1977]

WELLINGTON (Duke of) (1769–1852)
(Reply to a threat of blackmail by Harriette
Wilson)
Publish and be damned.
[Attr.]

WILDE, Oscar (1854–1900)
No publisher should ever express an opinion
of the value of what he publishes. That is a
matter entirely for the literary critic to decide
... A publisher is simply a useful middle-man.
It is not for him to anticipate the verdict of
criticism.
[Letter in St James's Gazette, 1890]

See **BOOKS, EDITING**

PUNISHMENT

ARENDT, Hannah (1906–1975)
No punishment has ever possessed enough
power of deterrence to prevent the
commission of crimes.
[*Eichmann in Jerusalem: A Report on the
Banality of Evil* (1963)]

BENTHAM, Jeremy (1748–1832)
All punishment is mischief: all punishment in
itself is evil.
[*An Introduction to the Principles of Morals and
Legislation* (1789)]

HALIFAX, Lord (1633–1695)
Men are not hang'd for stealing Horses, but
that Horses may not be stolen.
['Of Punishment' (1750)]

HUBBARD, Elbert (1856–1915)
Men are not punished for their sins, but by
them.
[*A Thousand and One Epigrams* (1911)]

JOHNSON, Samuel (1709–1784)
The power of punishment is to silence, not to
confute.
[*Sermons* (1788)]
Depend upon it, Sir, when a man knows he is
to be hanged in a fortnight, it concentrates
his mind wonderfully.
[In Boswell, *The Life of Samuel Johnson* (1791)]

JUVENAL (c.60–130)
The chief punishment is this: that no guilty
man is acquitted in his own judgement.
[*Satires*]

KARR, Alphonse (1808–1890)
If we want to abolish the death penalty, let
our friends the murderers take the first step.
[*Les Guêpes* (1849)]

KEY, Ellen (1849–1926)
Corporal punishment is as humiliating for him
who gives it as for him who receives it; it is
ineffective besides. Neither shame nor
physical pain have any other effect than a
hardening one.
[*The Century of the Child* (1909)]

MAJOR, Sir John (1943–)
Society needs to condemn a little more and
understand a little less.
[*Mail on Sunday*, 1993]

MANN, Horace (1796–1859)
The object of punishment is prevention from
evil; it never can be made impulsive to good.
[*Lectures and Reports on Education* (1845)]

SHAKESPEARE, William (1564–1616)
Use every man after his desert, and who shall
scape whipping?
[*Hamlet*, II.ii]

STOWE, Harriet Beecher (1811–1896)
Whipping and abuse are like laudanum; you
have to double the dose as the sensibilities
decline.
[*Uncle Tom's Cabin* (1852)]

VIDAL, Gore (1925–2012)
(When asked for his views about corporal
punishment)
I'm all for bringing back the birch, but only
between consenting adults.
[TV interview with David Frost]

WILDE, Oscar (1854–1900)
A community is infinitely more brutalised by
the habitual employment of punishment than
it is by the occasional occurrence of crime.
['The Soul of Man under Socialism' (1891)]

See **CRIME, EDUCATION**

QUOTATIONS

CHURCHILL, Sir Winston (1874–1965)
It is a good thing for an uneducated man to
read books of quotations.
[*My Early Life* (1930)]

D'ISRAELI, Isaac (1766–1848)
The art of quotation requires more delicacy in
the practice than those conceive who can see
nothing more in a quotation than an extract.
[*Curiosities of Literature*]

EMERSON, Ralph Waldo (1803–1882)
We are as much informed of a writer's genius by what he selects as by what he originates.
[*Letters and Social Aims* (1875)]
Next to the originator of a good sentence is the first quoter of it.
[*Letters and Social Aims* (1875)]

**FOWLER, F.G. (1871–1918) and
FOWLER, H.W. (1858–1933)**
Pretentious quotations being the surest road to tedium.
[*The King's English*]

MONTAGUE, C.E. (1867–1928)
To be amused at what you read – that is the great spring of happy quotation.
[*A Writer's Notes on his Trade* (1930)]

PEARSON, Hesketh (1887–1964)
A widely-read man never quotes accurately ... Misquotation is the pride and privilege of the learned.
[*Common Misquotations* (1937)]

SHAW, George Bernard (1856–1950)
I often quote myself. It adds spice to the conversation.
[*Reader's Digest*, 1943]

STOPPARD, Tom (1937–)
It's better to be quotable than to be honest.
[*The Guardian*]

WILDE, Oscar (1854–1900)
Quotation is a serviceable substitute for wit.

WILLIAMS, Kenneth (1926–1988)
The nicest thing about quotes is that they give us a nodding acquaintance with the originator which is often socially impressive.
[*Acid Drops* (1980)]

YOUNG, Edward (1683–1765)
Some, for renown, on scraps of learning dote, And think they grow immortal as they quote.
[*Love of Fame, the Universal Passion* (1725–1728)]

RACISM

BIKO, Steve (1946–1977)
We wanted to remove him [the white man] from our table, strip the table of all the trappings put on it by him, decorate it in true African style, settle down and then ask him to join us if he liked.
[Speech, 1971]

BRODSKY, Joseph (1940–1996)
Racism? But isn't it only a form of misanthropy?
[*Less Than One* (1986)]

DE BLANK, Joost (1908–1968)
I suffer from an incurable disease – colour blindness.
[Attr.]

DISRAELI, Benjamin (1804–1881)
All is race; there is no other truth.
[*Tancred* (1847)]

EINSTEIN, Albert (1879–1955)
If my theory of relativity is proven successful, Germany will claim me as a German and France will declare that I am a citizen of the world. Should my theory prove untrue, France will say that I am a German and Germany will declare that I am a Jew.
[Address, c.1929]

FANON, Frantz (1925–1961)
For the black man there is only one destiny. And it is white.
[*Black Skin, White Masks*]

GORDIMER, Nadine (1923–)
The force of white men's wills, which dispensed and withdrew life, imprisoned and set free, fed or starved, like God himself.
[*Six Feet of the Country* (1956)]

HITLER, Adolf (1889–1945)
Whoever is not racially pure in this world is chaff.
[*Mein Kampf* (1925)]

KING, Martin Luther (1929–1968)
I want to be the white man's brother, not his brother-in-law.
[*New York Journal*, 1962]

LEE, Spike (1957–)
The only thing I like integrated is my coffee.
[*Malcolm X*, film, 1992]

MANDELA, Nelson (1918–)
I have fought against white domination, and I have fought against black domination. I have cherished the ideal of a democratic and free society in which all persons will live together in harmony and with equal opportunities. It is an ideal which I hope to live for and achieve. But, if needs be, it is an ideal for which I am prepared to die.
[Statement in the dock, 1964]

MILLER, Arthur (1915–2005)
If there weren't any anti-semitism, I wouldn't think of myself as Jewish.
[*The Observer*, 1995]

SHERIDAN, Philip Henry (1831–1888)
The only good Indian is a dead Indian.
[Attr.]

TUTU, Archbishop Desmond (1931–)
It is very difficult now to find anyone in South
Africa who ever supported apartheid.
[*The Observer*, 1994]

ZANGWILL, Israel (1864–1926)
The law of dislike for the unlike will always
prevail. And whereas the unlike is normally
situated at a safe distance, the Jews bring the
unlike into the heart of every milieu, and
must there defend a frontier line as large as
the world.
[Speech, 1911]

See **EQUALITY, FREEDOM, JUDAISM,
SLAVERY**

READING

CHANDLER, Raymond (1888–1959)
All men who read escape from something
else ... [they] must escape at times from the
deadly rhythm of their private thoughts.
[*Atlantic Monthly* (1944)]

DESCARTES, René (1596–1650)
The reading of all good books is like a
conversation with the finest men of past
centuries.
[*Discours de la Méthode* (1637)]

DISRAELI, Benjamin (1804–1881)
(His customary reply to those who sent him
unsolicited manuscripts)
Thank you for the manuscript; I shall lose no
time in reading it.
[Attr.]

EMERSON, Ralph Waldo (1803–1882)
Tis the good reader that makes the good
book.
[*Society and Solitude* (1870)]

FLAUBERT, Gustave (1821–1880)
Do not read, as children do, for the sake of
entertainment, or like the ambitious, for the
purpose of instruction. No, read in order to
live.
[Letter, 1857]

FRANKLIN, Benjamin (1706–1790)
(On being asked what condition of man he
considered the most pitiable)
A lonesome man on a rainy day who does not
know how to read.
[In Shriner, *Wit, Wisdom, and Foibles of
the Great*]

HAMERTON, P.G. (1834–1894)
The art of reading is to skip judiciously.
[*The Intellectual Life* (1873)]

HANDKE, Peter (1942–)
The most unthinking person of all: the one
who only flicks through every book.
[*The Weight of the World. A Diary* (1977)]

HELPS, Sir Arthur (1813–1875)
Reading is sometimes an ingenious device for
avoiding thought.
[*Friends in Council* (1849)]

JOHNSON, Samuel (1709–1784)
A man ought to read just as inclination leads
him; for what he reads as a task will do him
little good.
[In Boswell, *The Life of Samuel Johnson* (1791)]

ORTON, Joe (1933–1967)
Reading isn't an occupation we encourage
among police officers. We try to keep the
paper work down to a minimum.
[*Loot* (1967)]

RUSSELL, Bertrand (1872–1970)
There are two motives for reading a book:
one, that you enjoy it, the other that you can
boast about it.
[*The Conquest of Happiness* (1930)]

SMITH, Logan Pearsall (1865–1946)
People say that life is the thing, but I prefer
reading.
[*Afterthoughts* (1931)]

SMITH, Sydney (1771–1845)
Live always in the best company when you
read.
[In Lady Holland, *Memoir* (1855)]

STERNE, Laurence (1713–1768)
Digressions, incontestably, are the sunshine;
– they are the life, the soul of reading; – take
them out of this book for instance, – you
might as well take the book along with them.
[*Tristram Shandy*]

WILDE, Oscar (1854–1900)
I never travel without my diary. One should
always have something sensational to read in
the train.
[*The Importance of Being Earnest* (1895)]

See **BOOKS, CRITICISM, FICTION,
LITERATURE, WRITING**

REALISM

BACON, Francis (1561–1626)
We are much beholden to Machiavel and
others, that write what men do, and not what
they ought to do.
[*The Advancement of Learning* (1605)]

BURGESS, Anthony (1917–1993)
Reality is what I see, not what you see.
[*The Sunday Times Magazine*, 1983]

CONNOLLY, Cyril (1903–1974)
Everything is a dangerous drug to me except reality, which is unendurable.
[*The Unquiet Grave* (1944)]

DÜRRENMATT, Friedrich (1921–1990)
Whoever is faced with the paradoxical exposes himself to reality.
[*The Physicists* (1962)]

ELIOT, T.S. (1888–1965)
Human kind
Cannot bear very much reality.
[*Four Quartets* (1944)]

HEGEL, Georg Wilhelm (1770–1831)
What is rational is real, and what is real is rational.
[*Basis of Legal Philosophy* (1820)]

KHRUSHCHEV, Nikita (1894–1971)
If you cannot catch a bird of paradise, better take a wet hen.
[Attr.]

TWAIN, Mark (1835–1910)
Don't part with your illusions. When they are gone, you may still exist, but you have ceased to live.
[*Pudd'nhead Wilson's Calendar* (1894)]

RELIGION

ADDISON, Joseph (1672–1719)
We have in England a particular bashfulness in every thing that regards religion.
[*The Spectator*, 1712]

ARNOLD, Matthew (1822–1888)
The true meaning of religion is thus not simply morality, but morality touched by emotion.
[*Literature and Dogma* (1873)]

ASHFORD, Daisy (1881–1972)
Bernard always had a few prayers in the hall and some whiskey afterwards as he was rarther pious but Mr Salteena was not very addicted to prayers so he marched up to bed.
[*The Young Visiters* (1919)]

BARRIE, Sir J.M. (1860–1937)
One's religion is whatever he is most interested in, and yours is Success.
[*The Twelve-Pound Look*]

BEHAN, Brendan (1923–1964)
Pound notes are the best religion in the world.
[*The Wit of Brendan Behan* (1968)]

BELLOC, Hilaire (1870–1953)
(Suggested rider to the Ten Commandments)
Candidates should not attempt more than six of these.
[Attr.]

BRENAN, Gerald (1894–1987)
Religions are kept alive by heresies, which are really sudden explosions of faith. Dead religions do not produce them.
[*Thoughts in a Dry Season* (1978)]

BROWNE, Sir Thomas (1605–1682)
Persecution is a bad and indirect way to plant religion.
[*Religio Medici* (1643)]

BURKE, Edmund (1729–1797)
Nothing is so fatal to religion as indifference, which is, at least, half infidelity.
[Letter to William Smith, 1795]

BURTON, Robert (1577–1640)
One religion is as true as another.
[Anatomy of Melancholy (1621)]

BUTLER, Samuel (1835–1902)
To be at all is to be religious more or less.
[*The Note-Books of Samuel Butler* (1912)]

COLERIDGE, Samuel Taylor (1772–1834)
Time consecrates; and what is grey with age becomes religion
[Attr.]

COLTON, Charles Caleb (c.1780–1832)
Men will wrangle for religion; write for it; fight for it; anything but – live for it.
[*Lacon* (1820)]

DIX, George Eglington (1901–1952)
It is no accident that the symbol of a bishop is a crook, and the sign of an archbishop is a double-cross.
[Letter to *The Times*, 1977]

ELLIS, Havelock (1859–1939)
The whole religious complexion of the modern world is due to the absence from Jerusalem of a lunatic asylum.
[*Impressions and Comments* (1914)]

FREUD, Sigmund (1856–1939)
Religion is an illusion and it derives its strength from the fact that it falls in with our instinctual desires.
[*New Introductory Lectures on Psychoanalysis* (1933)]

HOPE, Bob (1903–2003)
I do benefits for all religions. I'd hate to blow the hereafter on a technicality.
[In Simon Rose, *Classic Film Guide* (1995)]

INGE, William Ralph (1860–1954)
To become a popular religion, it is only necessary for a superstition to enslave a philosophy.
[*Outspoken Essays*]

JERROLD, Douglas William (1803–1857)
Religion's in the heart, not in the knees.
[*The Devil's Ducat* {1830}]

MARLOWE, Christopher (1564–1593)
I count religion but a childish toy, And hold there is no sin but ignorance.
[*The Jew of Malta* (c.1592)]

MARX, Karl (1818–1883)
Religion ... is the opium of the people.
[*A Contribution to the Critique of Hegel's Philosophy of Right* (1844)]

MELBOURNE, Lord (1779–1848)
(On listening to an evangelical sermon)
Things have come to a pretty pass when religion is allowed to invade the sphere of private life.
[In Russell, *Collections and Recollections* (1898)]

MENCKEN, H.L. (1880–1956)
We must respect the other fellow's religion, but only in the sense and to the extent that we respect his theory that his wife is beautiful and his children smart.
[*Notebooks* (1956)]

O'CASEY, Sean (1880–1964)
There's no reason to bring religion into it. I think we ought to have as great a regard for religion as we can, so as to keep it out of as many things as possible.
[*The Plough and the Stars* (1926)]

SWIFT, Jonathan (1667–1745)
We have just enough religion to make us hate, but not enough to make us love one another.
[*Thoughts on Various Subjects* (1711)]

WEBB, Beatrice (1858–1943)
Religion is love; in no case is it logic.
[*My Apprenticeship* (1926)]

ZANGWILL, Israel (1864–1926)
Let us start a new religion with one commandment, 'Enjoy thyself'.
[*Children of the Ghetto* (1892)]

See **ATHEISM, BELIEF, CHRISTIANITY, CHURCH, DEVIL, GOD, HEAVEN, HELL, SUNDAY**

REPUTATION

BURNEY, Fanny (1752–1840)
Nothing is so delicate as the reputation of a woman; it is at once the most beautiful and most brittle of all human things.
[*Evelina* (1778)]

COLETTE (1873–1954)
Never wear artistic jewellery; it ruins a woman's reputation.
[*Gigi* (1944)]

ELIOT, George (1819–1880)
'Abroad', that large home of ruined reputations.
[*Felix Holr* (1866)]

MITCHELL, Margaret (1900–1949)
Until you've lost your reputation, you never realize what a burden it was or what freedom really is.
[*Gone with the Wind* (1936)]

SHAKESPEARE, William (1564–1616)
Good name in man and woman, dear my lord, Is the immediate jewel of their souls:
Who steals my purse steals trash; 'tis something, nothing;
'Twas mine,'tis his, and has been slave to thousands;
But he that filches from me my good name Robs me of that which not enriches him And makes me poor indeed.
[*Othello*, III.iii]

WASHINGTON, George (1732–1799)
Associate yourself with men of good quality if you esteem your own reputation; for 'tis better to be alone than in bad company.
[*Rules of Civility and Decent Behaviour*]

See **CELEBRITY, CHARACTER, FAME**

RESPONSIBILITY

SAINT-EXUPÉRY, Antoine de (1900–1944)
You become responsible, for ever, for what you have tamed. You are responsible for your rose.
[*The Little Prince* (1943), 21]

TRUMAN, Harry S. (1884–1972)
The buck stops here.
[Sign on his desk]

REVENGE

ATWOOD, Margaret (1939–)
An eye for an eye leads only to more blindness.
[*Cat's Eye* (1988)]

BACON, Francis (1561–1626)
Revenge is a kind of wild justice, which the more man's nature runs to, the more ought law to weed it out.

['Of Revenge' (1625)]

THE BIBLE
(King James Version)
Vengeance is mine; I will repay, saith the Lord.

[*Romans*, 12:19]

CYRANO DE BERGERAC, Savinien de (1619–1655)
The universe may perish, so long as I have my revenge.

[*La Mort d'Agrippine* (1654)]

FORD, John (c.1586–1639)
Revenge proves its own executioner.

[*The Broken Heart* (1633)]

MILTON, John (1608–1674)
Revenge, at first though sweet, Bitter ere long back on it self recoils.

[*Paradise Lost* (1667)]

SHAKESPEARE, William (1564–1616)
Let's make us med'cines of our great revenge
To cure this deadly grief.

[*Macbeth*, IV.iii]

REVOLUTION

BOULEZ, Pierre (1925–)
Revolutions are celebrated when they are no longer dangerous.

[*The Guardian*, 1989]

BRADSHAW, John (1602–1659)
Rebellion to tyrants is obedience to God.

[In Randall, *Life of Jefferson* (1865)]

CAMUS, Albert (1913–1960)
Every revolutionary ends as an oppressor or a heretic.

[*The Rebel* (1951)]

ENGELS, Friedrich (1820–1895)
The proletariat has nothing to lose but its chains in this revolution. It has a world to win. Workers of the world, unite!

[*The Communist Manifesto* (1848)]

ORWELL, George (1903–1950)
Nine times out of ten a revolutionary is merely a climber with a bomb in his pocket.

[*New English Weekly*, 1939]

REED, John (1887–1920)
(Of the October Revolution in Russia)
Ten Days that Shook the World.

[Title of book, 1919]

TALLEYRAND, Charles-Maurice de (1754–1838)
(Of the French Revolution)
He who has not lived during the years around 1789 cannot know what is meant by the joy of living.

[In M. Guizot, *Mémoires pour servir á l'histoire de mon temps* (1858)]

WELLINGTON (Duke of) (1769–1852)
Beginning reform is beginning revolution.

[In Mrs Arbuthnot's Journal, 1830]

RIDICULE

ALBEE, Edward (1928–)
I have a fine sense of the ridiculous, but no sense of humour.

[*Who's Afraid of Virginia Woolf?* (1962)]

HATTERSLEY, Roy (1932–)
In politics, being ridiculous is more damaging than being extreme.

[*The Observer*, 1996]

NAPOLEON I (1769–1821)
It is only one step from the sublime to the ridiculous.

[Attr.]

PAINE, Thomas (1737–1809)
The sublime and the ridiculous are often so nearly related, that it is difficult to class them separately. One step above the sublime, makes the ridiculous; and one step above the ridiculous, makes. the sublime again.

[*The Age of Reason* (1795)]

SCOTT, Sir Walter (1771–1832)
Ridicule often checks what is absurd, and fully as often smothers that which is noble.

[*Quentin Durward* (1823)]

See **CONTEMPT**

RIGHT AND WRONG

BUFFETT, Warren (1930–)
It is better to be approximately right than precisely wrong.

[*Fortune*, 1994]

CLAY, Henry (1777–1852)
I had rather be right than be President.

[Remark, 1839]

CONFUCIUS (c.550–c.478 BC)
To see what is right and not to do it is want of courage.

[*Analects*]

COWPER, William (1731-1800)
A noisy man is always in the right.
['Conversation' (1782)]

GOLDWYN, Samuel (1882-1974)
I am willing to admit that I may not always be right, but I am never wrong.
[Attr.]

JUNIUS (1769-1772)
It is not that you do wrong by design, but that you should never do right by mistake.
[*Letters* (1769-1771)]

LA CHAUSSÉE, Nivelle de (1692-1754)
When everyone is wrong, everyone is right.
[*La Gouvernante* (1747)]

SOLON (c.638-c.559 BC)
Wrongdoing can only be avoided if those who are not wronged feel the same indignation at it as those who are.
[Attr.]

See **GOOD AND EVIL, MORALITY, PRINCIPLES**

Rights

CONDORCET, Antoine-Nicolas de (1743-1794)
Either none of mankind possesses genuine rights, or everyone shares them equally; whoever votes against another's rights, whatever his religion, colour or sex, forswears his own.
[In Vansittart (ed.), *Voices of the Revolution* (1989)]

JEFFERSON, Thomas (1743-1826)
We hold these truths to be self-evident: that all men are created equal; that they are endowed by their Creator with certain unalienable rights; that among these are life, liberty, and the pursuit of happiness.
[Declaration of Independence, 1776]

JOHNSON, Samuel (1709-1784)
I have got no further than this: Every man has a right to utter what he thinks truth, and every other man has a right to knock him down for it. Martyrdom is the test.
[In Boswell, *The Life of Samuel Johnson* (1791)]

MAGNA CARTA (1215)
No free man shall be taken or imprisoned or dispossessed, or outlawed or exiled, or in any way destroyed, nor will we go upon him, nor will we send against him, except by the lawful judgement of his peers or by the law of the land.
[Clause 39]

PANKHURST, Emmeline (1858-1928)
Women had always fought for men, and for their children. Now they were ready to fight for their own human rights. Our militant movement was established.
[*My Own Story* (1914)]

UNIVERSAL DECLARATION OF HUMAN RIGHTS
All human beings are born free and equal in dignity and rights.
[Article 1]

VOLTAIRE (1694-1778)
I disapprove of what you say, but I will defend to the death your right to say it.
[Attr.]

See **EQUALITY, FEMINISM, FREEDOM, JUSTICE AND INJUSTICE**

School

CLARK, Lord Kenneth (1903-1983)
(On boarding schools)
This curious, and, to my mind, objectionable feature of English education was maintained solely in order that parents could get their children out of the house.
[*Another Part of the Wood* (1974)]

DAVIES, Robertson (1913-1995)
The most strenuous efforts of the most committed educationalists in the years since my boyhood have been quite unable to make a school into anything but a school, which is to say a jail with educational opportunities.
[*The Cunning Man* (1994)]

FIELDING, Henry (1707-1754)
Public schools are the nurseries of all vice and immorality.
[*Joseph Andrews* (1742)]

FORSTER, E.M. (1879-1970)
(Of public schoolboys)
They go forth into it [the world] with well-developed bodies, fairly developed minds, and undeveloped hearts.
[*Abinger Harvest* (1936)]

GREENE, Graham (1904-1991)
I had left civilisation behind and entered a savage country of strange customs and inexplicable cruelties: a country in which I was a foreigner and a suspect, quite literally a hunted creature, known to have dubious associates. Was not my father the headmaster? I was like the son of a quisling in a country under occupation.
[*A Sort of Life* (1971)]

LINDSAY, Sir David (c.1490–1555)
We think them verray naturall fules,
That lemis ouir mekle at the sculis.
['Complaynt to the King']

NEIL, A.S. (1883–1973)
'Casting Out Fear'ought to be the motto over
every school door.
[*The Problem Child* (1926)]

WELLINGTON (Duke of) (1769–1852)
The battle of Waterloo was won on the
playing fields of Eton.
[Attr.]

See **EDUCATION, KNOWLEDGE,
LEARNING, TEACHERS, WISDOM**

Science

ARCHIMEDES (c.287–212 BC)
Give me a place to stand, and I will move the
Earth.
[*On levers*]

AUDEN, W.H. (1907–1973)
The true men of action in our time, those
who transform the world, are not the
politicians and statesmen, but the scientists.
[*The Dyer's Hand* (1963)]

BRONOWSKI, Jacob (1908–1974)
Science has nothing to be ashamed of, even
in the ruins of Nagasaki.
[*Science and Human Values*]

BUSH, Vannevar (1890–1974)
To pursue science is not to disparage things
of the spirit.
[Speech, 1953]

CHOMSKY, Noam (1928–)
As soon as questions of will or decision or
reason or choice of action arise, human
science is at a loss.
[Television interview, 1978]

CLARKE, Sir Arthur C. (1917–2008)
Technology, sufficiently advanced, is
indistinguishable from magic.
[*The Times*, 1996]

CRONENBERG, David (1943–)
A virus is only doing its job.
[*Sunday Telegraph*, 1992]

DÜRRENMATT, Friedrich (1921–1990)
Our science has become terrible, our research
dangerous, our knowledge fatal.
[*The Physicists* (1962)]

EINSTEIN, Albert (1879–1955)
A theory can be proved by experiment; but no
path leads from experiment to the birth of a
theory.
[In Mackay, *The Harvest of a Quiet Eye*
(1977)]
When a man sits with a pretty girl for an hour,
it seems like a minute. But let him sit on a
hot stove for a minute – and it's longer than
any hour. That's relativity.
[Attr.]

HEISENBERG, Werner (1901–1976)
Natural science does not simply describe and
explain nature, it is part of the interplay
between nature and ourselves.
[Attr.]

HUXLEY, T.H. (1825–1895)
The great tragedy of Science – the slaying of a
beautiful hypothesis by an ugly fact.
[*British Association Annual Report* (1870)]

JEANS, Sir James Hopwood (1877–1946)
Science should leave off making
pronouncements: the river of knowledge has
too often turned back on itself.
[*The Mysterious Universe* (1930)]

NEWTON, Sir Isaac (1642–1727)
If I have seen further it is by standing on the
shoulders of giants.
[Letter to Robert Hooke, 1675–76]

OPPENHEIMER, J. Robert (1904–1967)
(On the consequences of the first atomic test)
The physicists have known sin; and this is a
knowledge which they cannot lose.
[Lecture, 1947]

PEACOCK, Thomas Love (1785–1866)
I almost think it is the ultimate destiny of
science to exterminate the human race.
[*Gryll Grange* (1861)]

POPPER, Sir Karl (1902–1994)
Science may be described as the art of
systematic oversimplification.
[*The Observer*, 1982]

PORTER, George (Baron) (1920–)
Should we force science down the throats of
those that have no taste for it? Is it our duty
to drag them kicking and screaming into the
twenty-first century? I am afraid that it is.
[Speech, 1986]

ROUX, Joseph (1834–1886)
Science is for those who learn; poetry, for
those who know.
[*Meditations of a Parish Priest* (1886)]

RUTHERFORD, Sir Ernest (1871–1937)
All science is either physics or stamp collecting.
[*Rutherford at Manchester* (1962)]

SAGAN, Carl (1934–1996)
The Universe is not obliged to conform to what we consider comfortable or plausible.
[*Pale Blue Dot* (1995)]

SANTAYANA, George (1863–1952)
If all the arts aspire to the condition of music, all the sciences aspire to the condition of mathematics.
[*The Observer*, 1928]

SZENT-GYÖRGYI, Albert von (1893–1986)
Discovery consists of seeing what everybody has seen and thinking what nobody has thought.
[In Good (ed.), *The Scientist Speculates* (1962)]

WINSTON, Robert (Baron) (1940–)
Science is 90% boredom.
[*The Sunday Times*, July 2001]

See **CULTURE, MATHEMATICS, NATURE, PROGRESS, TECHNOLOGY**

SCOTLAND

BARRIE, Sir J.M. (1860–1937)
There are few more impressive sights in the world than a Scotsman on the make.
[*What Every Woman Knows* (1908)]

BOORDE, Andrew (c.1490–1549)
The devellysche dysposicion of a Scottysh man, not to love nor favour an Englishe man.
[Letter to Thomas Cromwell, 1536]

BURNS, Robert (1759–1796)
My heart's in the Highlands, my heart is not here,
My heart's in the Highlands a-chasing the deer,
A-chasing the wild deer and following the roe –
My heart's in the Highlands, wherever I go!
['My Heart's in the Highlands' (1790)]

CONNERY, Sir Sean (1930–)
Scotland should be nothing less than equal with all the other nations of the world.
[*The Times*, May 1999]

EWART, Gavin (1916–1995)
The Irish are great talkers
Persuasive and disarming,
You can say lots and lots
Against the Scots –
But at least they're never charming!
[*The Complete Little Ones* (1986)]

GRAY, Muriel (1959–)
Of course I want political autonomy but not cultural autonomy. You just have to watch the Scottish Baftas to want to kill yourself.
[*Scotland on Sunday*, 1996]

JENKINS, Robin (1912–2005)
Football has taken the place of religion in Scotland.
[*A Would-Be Saint*]

JOHNSON, Samuel (1709–1784)
Oats. A grain, which in England is generally given to horses, but in Scotland supports the people.
[*A Dictionary of the English Language* (1755)]
Much may be made of a Scotchman, if he be caught young.
[In Boswell, *The Life of Samuel Johnson* (1791)]

KEILLOR, Garrison (1942–)
Lutherans are like Scottish people, only with less frivolity.
[*The Independent*, 1992]

KENNEDY, Charles (1959–)
(On being berated in Glasgow)
In a west-of-Scotland context that's a positively warm reception. If they love you they let you live.
[*The Sunday Times*, June 2001]

LAMB, Charles (1775–1834)
I have been trying all my life to like Scotchmen, and am obliged to desist from the experiment in despair.
['Imperfect Sympathies' (1823)]

LOCKIER, Francis (1667–1740)
In all my travels I have never met with any one Scotchman but what was a man of sense. I believe everybody of that country that has any, leaves it as fast as they can.
[In Spence, *Anecdotes* (1858)]

NASH, Ogden (1902–1971)
No McTavish
Was ever lavish.
['Genealogical Reflection' (1931)]

OGILVY, James (1663–1730)
(On signing the Act of Union)
Now there's an end of ane old song.
[Remark, 1707]

SALMOND, Alex (1955–)
There is not an anti-English bone in my body. I have forgotten more about English history than most Tory MPs ever learned.
[*The Observer*, 1998]

SCOTT, Sir Walter (1771–1832)
Still from the sire the son shall hear
Of the stern strife, and carnage drear,
Of Flodden's fatal field,
Where shiver'd was fair Scotland's spear,
And broken was her shield!
[*Marmion*]

WODEHOUSE, P.G. (1881–1975)
It is never difficult to distinguish between a
Scotsman with a grievance and a ray of
sunshine.
[*Blandings Castle and Elsewhere* (1935)]

The Sea

AESCHYLUS (525–456 BC)
The ceaseless twinkling laughter of the waves
of the sea.
[*Prometheus Bound*]

BYRON, Lord (1788–1824)
Dark-heaving – boundless, endless, and
sublime,
The image of eternity.
[*Childe Harold's Pilgrimage* (1818)]

CHOPIN, Kate (1851–1904)
The voice of the sea speaks to the soul. The
touch of the sea is sensuous, enfolding the
body in its soft, close embrace.
[*The Awakening* (1899)]

COLERIDGE, Samuel Taylor (1772–1834)
Water, water, every where,
And all the boards did shrink;
Water, water, every where
Nor any drop to drink.
['The Rime of the Ancient Mariner' (1798)]

CUNNINGHAM, Allan (1784–1842)
A wet sheet and a flowing sea,
A wind that follows fast
And fills the white and rustling sail
And bends the gallant mast ...
['A Wet Sheet and a Flowing Sea' (1825)]

DICKENS, Charles (1812–1870)
I want to know what it says ... The sea, Floy,
what it is that it keeps on saying?
[*Dombey and Son* (1848)]

DONNE, John (1572–1631)
The sea is as deepe in a calme as in a storme.
[*Sermons*]

FLECKER, James Elroy (1884–1915)
The dragon-green, the luminous, the dark,
the serpent-haunted sea.
[*The Golden Journey to Samarkand* (1913)]

JOYCE, James (1882–1941)
The snotgreen sea. The scrotumtightening sea.
[*Ulysses* (1922)]

MASEFIELD, John (1878–1967)
I must go down to the seas again, to the
lonely sea and the sky,
And all I ask is a tall ship and a star to steer
her by.
['Sea Fever' (1902)]

RIMBAUD, Arthur (1854–1891)
I have bathed in the Poem
Of the Sea, steeped in stars, milky,
Devouring the green azures.
['Le Bâteau ivre' (1870)]

ROSSETTI, Dante Gabriel (1828–1882)
The sea hath no king but God alone.
['The White Ship']

WHITING, William (1825–1878)
Eternal Father, strong to save,
Whose arm hath bound the restless wave, ...
O hear us when we cry to Thee
For those in peril on the sea.
[Hymn, 1869]

The Seasons

ADAMS, Richard (1920–)
Many human beings say that they enjoy the
winter, but what they really enjoy is feeling
proof against it.
[*Watership Down* (1974)]

COLERIDGE, Samuel Taylor (1772–1834)
Summer has set in with its usual severity.
[*Letters of Charles Lamb* (1888)]

HOLMES, Oliver Wendell (1809–1894)
For him in vain the envious seasons roll
Who bears eternal summer in his soul.
['The Old Player' (1861)]

SANTAYANA, George (1863–1952)
To be interested in the changing seasons is,
in this middling zone, a happier state of mind
than to be hopelessly in love with spring.
[*Little Essays* (1920)]

SHAKESPEARE, William (1564–1616)
At Christmas I no more desire a rose
Than wish a snow in May's new fangled shows;
But like of each thing that in season grows.
[*Love's Labour's Lost*, I.i]

WALPOLE, Horace (1717–1797)
The way to ensure summer in England is to have
it framed and glazed in a comfortable room.
[Letter to William Cole, 1774]

See **WEATHER**

SECRETS

ACTON, Lord (1834-1902)
Everything secret degenerates ... nothing is
safe that does not show how it can bear
discussion and publicity.
[Attr.]

CLARK, Alan (1928-1999)
(On being asked whether he had any
embarrassing skeletons in the cupboard)
Dear boy, I can hardly close the door.
[*The Observer*, 1998]

CONGREVE, William (1670-1729)
I know that's a secret, for it's whispered
everywhere.
[*Love for Love* (1695)]

DRYDEN, John (1631-1700)
For secrets are edged tools,
And must be kept from children and from
fools.
[*Sir Martin Mar-All* (1667)]

FRANKLIN, Benjamin (1706-1790)
Three may keep a secret, if two of them are
dead.
[*Poor Richard's Almanac* (1735)]

FRANKS, Oliver (Baron) (1905-1992)
It is a secret in the Oxford sense: you may tell
it to only one person at a time.
[*Sunday Telegraph*, 1977]

FROST, Robert (1874-1963)
We dance round in a ring and suppose,
But the Secret sits in the middle and knows.
['The Secret Sits' (1942)]

See **GOSSIP**

SELF

ARNOLD, Matthew (1822-1888)
Resolve to be thyself; and know, that he,
Who finds himself, loses his misery!
['Self-Dependence' (1852)]

AURELIUS, Marcus (121-180)
This whatever this is that I am is flesh and
spirit, and the ruling part.
[*Meditations*]

BRONTË, Emily (1818-1848)
He is more myself than I am.
[*Wuthering Heights* (1847)]

BURNS, Robert (1759-1796)
O wad some Power the giftie gie us
To see oursels as ithers see us!
['To a Louse' (1786)]

EMERSON, Ralph Waldo (1803-1882)
All sensible people are selfish, and nature is
tugging at every contract to make the terms
of it fair.
[*Conduct of Life* (1860)]

HUXLEY, Aldous (1894-1963)
There's only one corner of the universe you
can be certain of improving, and that's your
own self.
[*Time Must Have a Stop* (1944)]

JOAD, C.E.M. (1891-1953)
Whenever I look inside myself I am afraid.
[*The Observer*, 1942]

KEMPIS, Thomas á (c.1380-1471)
The humble knowledge of thyself is a surer
way to God than the deepest search after
learning.
[*De Imitatione Christi* (1892)]

LA ROCHEFOUCAULD (1613-1680)
Self-love is the greatest flatterer of all.
[*Maximes* (1678)]
Self-interest speaks every kind of language,
and plays every role, even that of
disinterestedness.
[*Maximes* (1678)]

MOLIÈRE (1622-1673)
We should look long and carefully at
ourselves before we consider judging others.
[*Le Misanthrope* (1666)]

MONTAIGNE, Michel de (1533-1592)
The greatest thing in the world is to know
how to belong to oneself.
[*Essais* (1580)]

PASCAL, Blaise (1623-1662)
Self is hateful.
[*Pensées* (1670)]

POWELL, Anthony (1905-2000)
He fell in love with himself at first sight and it
is a passion to which he has always remained
faithful. Self-love seems so often unrequited.
[*The Acceptance World* (1955)]

SHAKESPEARE, William (1564-1616)
This above all - to thine own self be true,
And it must follow, as the night the day,
Thou canst not then be false to any man.
[*Hamlet*, I.iii]

SHAW, George Bernard (1856-1950)
It is easy - terribly easy - to shake a man's
faith in himself. To take advantage of that to
break a man's spirit is devil's work.
[*Candida* (1898)]

TOLSTOY, Leo (1828–1910)
I am always with myself, and it is I who am
my own tormentor.
[*Memoirs of a Madman* (1943)]

WILDE, Oscar (1854–1900)
Other people are quite dreadful. The only
possible society is oneself.
[*An Ideal Husband* (1895)]

See **APPEARANCE, PRIDE, VANITY**

SEPARATION

BAYLY, Thomas Haynes (1797–1839)
Absence makes the heart grow fonder,
Isle of Beauty, Fare thee well!
['Isle of Beauty', song, 1830]

BRENNAN, Christopher (1870–1932)
I am shut out of mine own heart because my
love is far from me.
['I Am Shut Out of Mine Own Heart' (1914)]

BUSSY-RABUTIN, Comte de (1618–1693)
Absence is to love what the wind is to fire; it
extinguishes the small, it kindles the great.
[*Histoire Amoureuse des Gaules* (1665)]

COPE, Wendy (1945–)
The day he moved out was terrible –
That evening she went through hell.
His absence wasn't a problem
But the corkscrew had gone as well.
['Loss' (1992)]

ELIOT, George (1819–1880)
In every parting there is an image of death.
[*Scenes of Clerical Life* (1858)]

KEATS, John (1795–1821)
I wish you could invent some means to make
me at all happy without you. Every hour I am
more and more concentrated in you; every
thing else tastes like chaff in my Mouth.
[Letter to Fanny Brawne, 1820]

SHAKESPEARE, William (1564–1616)
Parting is such sweet sorrow
That I shall say good night till it be morrow.
[*Romeo and Juliet*, II.ii]

See **ABSENCE**

SEX

ALLEN, Woody (1935–)
Hey, don't knock masturbation! It's sex with
someone I love.
[*Annie Hall*, film, 1977]

BANKHEAD, Tallulah (1903–1968)
(To an admirer)
I'll come and make love to you at five o'clock.
If I'm late start without me.
[In Morgan, *Somerset Maugham* (1980)]

BURCHILL, Julie (1960–)
Sex, on the whole, was meant to be short,
nasty and brutish. If what you want is
cuddling, you should buy a puppy.
[*Sex and Sensibility* (1992)]

CAMPBELL, Mrs Patrick (1865–1940)
I don't mind where people make love, so long
as they don't do it in the street and frighten
the horses.
[Attr.]

CHANDLER, Raymond (1888–1959)
She gave me a smile I could feel in my hip
pocket.
[*Farewell, My Lovely* (1940)]

CHESTERFIELD, Lord (1694–1773)
The pleasure is momentary, the position
ridiculous, and the expense damnable.
[Attr.]

COMFORT, Alex (1920–2000)
A woman who has the divine gift of lechery
will always make a superlative partner.
[Attr.]

DONNE, John (1572–1631)
Licence my roving hands, and let them go,
Before, behind, between, above, below.
O my America! my new-found-land,
My kingdom, safeliest when with one man
mann'd.
['To His Mistress Going to Bed' (c.1595)]

DURRELL, Lawrence (1912–1990)
No more about sex, it's too boring.
[*Tunc* (1968)]

DWORKIN, Andrea (1946–2005)
Seduction is often difficult to distinguish from
rape. In seduction, the rapist often bothers to
buy a bottle of wine.
[*The Independent*, 1992]

EKLAND, Britt (1942–)
I say I don't sleep with married men, but what
I mean is that I don't sleep with happily
married men.
[Attr.]

EPHRON, Nora (1941–2012)
Women need a reason to have sex. Men need
a place.
[*When Harry Met Sally*, film, 1989]

FLYNT, Larry (1942–)
(Defending President Bill Clinton)
People always lie about sex – to get sex,
during sex, after sex, about sex.
[*The Times*, January 1999]

GREER, Germaine (1939–)
No sex is better than bad sex.
[Attr.]

GWYN, Nell (1650–1687)
(On prostitution)
As for me, it is my profession, I do not
pretend to anything better.
[In Miles, *The Women's History of the World*
(1988)]

HALL, Jerry (1956–)
(On her divorce from Mick Jagger)
I feel sorry for Mick. Y'know sexual
promiscuity just leads to chaos.
[*The Sunday Times*, June 2000]

HILLINGDON, Lady Alice (1857–1940)
I am happy now that Charles calls on my
bedchamber less frequently than of old. As it
is, I now endure but two calls a week and
when I hear his steps outside my door I lie
down on my bed, close my eyes, open my
legs and think of England.
[*Journal* (1912)]

HUXLEY, Aldous (1894–1963)
'Bed,' as the Italian proverb succinctly puts it,
'is the poor man's opera.'
[*Heaven and Hell* (1956)]

KRISTOFFERSON, Kris (1936–)
Never go to bed with anyone crazier than
yourself.
[*The Observer*, 1999]

LAWRENCE, D.H. (1885–1930)
It's all this cold-hearted fucking that is death
and idiocy.
[*Lady Chatterley's Lover* (1928)]

LONGFORD, Lord (1905–2001)
No sex without responsibility.
[*The Observer*, 1954]

MACLAINE, Shirley (1934–)
The more sex becomes a non-issue in
people's lives, the happier they are.
[Attr.]

MIKES, George (1912–1987)
Continental people have sex life; the English
have hot-water bottles.
[*How to be an Alien* (1946)]

MILLER, Henry (1891–1980)
Sex is one of the nine reasons for reincarnation
... The other eight are unimportant.
[Big Sur and the Oranges of
Hieronymus Bosch]

MUGGERIDGE, Malcolm (1903–1990)
The orgasm has replaced the Cross as the
focus of longing and the image of fulfilment.
[*The Most of Malcolm Muggeridge* (1966)]

NASH, Ogden (1902–1971)
Home is heaven and orgies are vile
But you need an orgy, once in a while.
['Home, Sweet Home' (1935)]

NEWBOLD, H.L. (1890–1971)
Sex is between the ears as well as between
the legs.
[Mega-Nutrients for Your Nerves]

SHAKESPEARE, William (1564–1616)
Is it not strange that desire should so many
years outlive performance?
[*Henry IV, Part 2*, II.iv]

THURBER, James (1894–1961)
(On being accosted at a party by a drunk
woman who claimed she would like to have a
baby by him)
Surely you don't mean by unartificial
insemination!
[Attr.]

VIDAL, Gore (1925–2012)
(On being asked if his first sexual experience
had been heterosexual or homosexual)
I was too polite to ask.
[*Forum*, 1987]

VOLTAIRE (1694–1778)
It is one of the superstitions of the human
mind to have imagined that virginity could be
a virtue.
['The Leningrad Notebooks' (c.1735–1750)]

WELDON, Fay (1931–)
Reading about sex in yesterday's novels is like
watching people smoke in old films.
[*The Guardian*, December 1989]

See **ADULTERY, CONTRACEPTION,
PORNOGRAPHY**

SHOWBUSINESS

ALLEN, Woody (1935–)
Showbusiness is dog eat dog. It's worse than
dog eat dog. It's dog doesn't return other
dog's phone calls.
[*Crimes and Misdemeanours*, film, 1989]

ANONYMOUS
Can't act, can't sing, slightly bald. Can dance
a little.
[Hollywood executive on Fred Astaire's first
screen test]

BROOKS, Mel (1926–)
That's it, baby, if you've got it, flaunt it.
[*The Producers*, film, 1968]

CHASEN, Dave (1926–)
Bogart's a helluva nice guy until 11.30 p.m.
After that he thinks he's Bogart.
[In Halliwell, *The Filmgoer's Book of Quotes*
(1973)]

CHER (1946–)
Mother told me a couple of years ago,
'Sweetheart, settle down and marry a rich
man.' I said, 'Mom, I am a rich man.'
[*The Observer Review*, 1995]

COCHRAN, Charles B. (1872–1951)
I still prefer a good juggler to a bad Hamlet.
[*The Observer*, 1943]

DAVIS, Bette (1908–1989)
(Of a starlet)
I see – she's the original good time that was
had by all.
[In Halliwell, *Filmgoer's Book of Quotes* (1973)]

DAVIS, Sammy (Junior) (1925–1990)
Being a star has made it possible for me to
get insulted in places where the average
Negro could never hope to get insulted.
[*Yes I can* (1965)]

GARBO, Greta (1905–1990)
I never said, 'I want to be alone.' I only said, 'I
want to be let alone.' There is all the
difference.
[In Colombo, *Wit and Wisdom of the
Moviemakers*]

GARLAND, Judy (1922–1969)
I was born at the age of twelve on a
Metro-Goldwyn-Mayer lot.
[*The Observer*, 1951]

GOLDWYN, Samuel (1882–1974)
Directors [are] always biting the hand that
lays the golden egg.
[In Zierold, *Moguls* (1969)]
I'll give you a definite maybe.
[In Colombo, *Wit and Wisdom of the
Moviemakers*]
In two words: im possible.
[Attr.; in Zierold, *Moguls* (1969)]
What we want is a story that starts with an
earthquake and works its way up to a climax.
[Attr.]

GRABLE, Betty (1916–1973)
There are two reasons why I'm in show
business, and I'm standing on both of them.
[Attr.]

GRADE, Lew (1906–1994)
All my shows are great. Some of them are
bad. But they are all great.
[*The Observer*, 1975]

HILL, Benny (1924–1992)
That's what show business is – sincere
insincerity.
[*The Observer*, June 1977]

LEVANT, Oscar (1906–1972)
Strip the phony tinsel off Hollywood and you'll
find the real tinsel underneath.
[In Halliwell, *Filmgoer's Book of Quotes* (1973)]

REED, Rex (1938–)
Cannes is where you lie on the beach and
stare at the stars – or vice versa.
[Attr.]

SHAW, George Bernard (1856–1950)
The trouble, Mr Goldwyn, is that you are only
interested in art and I am only interested in
money.
[In Johnson, *The Great Goldwyn* (1937)]

THOMAS, Irene (1920-2001)
It was the kind of show where the girls are
not auditioned – just measured.
[Attr.]

TRACY, Spencer (1900–1967)
(Explaining what he looked for in a script)
Days off.

WELLES, Orson (1915–1985)
I began at the top and I've been working my
way down ever since.
[In Colombo, *Wit and Wisdom of the
Moviemakers*]

See **CELEBRITY, CINEMA, FAME,
HOLLYWOOD**

SILENCE

AUSTEN, Jane (1775–1817)
From politics, it was an easy step to silence.
[*Northanger Abbey* (1818)]

BACON, Francis (1561–1626)
Silence is the virtue of fools.
[*Of the Dignity and Advancement of Learning*
(1623)]

HOLMES, Oliver Wendell (1809–1894)
And silence, like a poultice, comes
To heal the blows of sound.
['The Music-Grinders' (1836)]

JONSON, Ben (1572–1637)
Calumnies are answered best with silence.
[*Volpone* (1607)]

LA ROCHEFOUCAULD (1613–1680)
Silence is the safest policy for the man who
distrusts himself.
[*Maximes* (1678)]

LINCOLN, Abraham (1809–1865)
Better to remain silent and be thought a fool
than to speak out and remove all doubt.
[Attr.]

MANDELSTAM, Nadezhda (1899–1980)
If nothing else is left, one must scream.
Silence is the real crime against humanity.
[*Hope Against Hope* (1970)]

ROSSETTI, Christina (1830–1894)
Silence more musical than any song.
['Rest' (1862)]

TUPPER, Martin (1810–1889)
Well-timed silence hath more eloquence than
speech.
[*Proverbial Philosophy* (1838)]

WITTGENSTEIN, Ludwig (1889–1951)
What can be said at all can be said clearly;
and whereof one cannot speak, thereon one
must keep silent.
[*Tractatus Logico-Philosophicus* (1922)]

See **CONVERSATION**

SIN

AUDEN, W.H. (1907–1973)
All sin tends to be addictive, and the terminal
point of addiction is what is called damnation.
[*A Certain World* (1970)]

**THE BIBLE
(King James Version)**
Be sure your sin will find you out.
[*Numbers*, 32:23]
He that is without sin among you, let him
first cast a stone.
[*John*, 8:7]
The wages of sin is death.
[*Romans*, 6:23]

BULGAKOV, Mikhail (1891–1940)
Cowardice is, without a doubt, one of the
greatest sins.
[*The Master and Margarita* (1967)]

BUNYAN, John (1628–1688)
One leak will sink a ship, and one sin will
destroy a sinner.
[*The Pilgrim's Progress* (1678)]

COOLIDGE, Calvin (1872–1933)
(On being asked what had been said by a
clergyman who preached on sin)
He said he was against it.
[Attr.]

COWLEY, Abraham (1618–1667)
Lukewarmness I account a sin
As great in love as in religion.
['The Request' (1647)]

EDDY, Mary Baker (1821–1910)
Sin brought death, and death will disappear
with the disappearance of sin.
[*Science and Health* (1875)]

JUVENAL (c.60–130)
Count it the greatest sin to put life before
honour, and for the sake of life to lose the
reasons for living.
[*Satires*]

SHAKESPEARE, William (1564–1616)
Plate sin with gold,
And the strong lance of justice hurtless breaks;
Arm it in rags, a pigmy's straw does pierce it.
[*King Lear*, IV.vi]
Few love to hear the sins they love to act.
[*Pericles, Prince of Tyre*, I.i]
Nothing emboldens sin so much as mercy.
[*Timon of Athens*, III.v]

THOMAS, Dylan (1914–1953)
You just wait, I'll sin till I blow up!
[*Under Milk Wood* (1954)]

WILDE, Oscar (1854–1900)
There is no sin except stupidity.
[*Intentions* (1891), 'The Critic as Artist']

See **EVIL**

SLAVERY

GANDHI (1869–1948)
The moment the slave resolves that he will no
longer be a slave, his fetters fall. He frees
himself and shows the way to others.
Freedom and slavery are mental states.
[*Non-Violence in Peace and War* (1949)]

GILL, Eric (1882–1940)
That state is a state of Slavery in which a man
does what he likes to do in his spare time and
his working time that which is required of him.
['Slavery and Freedom' (1929)]

JOHNSON, Samuel (1709–1784)
How is it that we hear the loudest yelps for liberty among the drivers of negroes?
[*Taxation No Tyranny* (1775)]

LINCOLN, Abraham (1809–1865)
In giving freedom to the slave, we assure freedom to the free – honourable alike in what we give and what we preserve.
[Speech, 1862]

STANTON, Elizabeth Cady (1815–1902)
The prolonged slavery of woman is the darkest page in human history.
[In Anthony and Gage, *History of Woman Suffrage* (1881)]

WEDGWOOD, Josiah (1730–1795)
Am I not a man and a brother?
[Motto adopted by Anti-Slavery Society]

See **RACISM**

SLEEP

BROWNE, Sir Thomas (1605–1682)
Sleep is a death, O make me try,
By sleeping what it is to die.
And as gently lay my head
On my grave, as now my bed.
[*Religio Medici* (1643)]

BURGESS, Anthony (1917–1993)
Laugh and the world laughs with you; snore and you sleep alone.
[*Inside Mr. Enderby* (1963)]

DICKENS, Charles (1812–1870)
It would make any one go to sleep, that bedstead would, whether they wanted to or not.
[*The Pickwick Papers* (1837)]

FIELDS, W.C. (1880–1946)
The best cure for insomnia is to get a lot of sleep.
[Attr.]

GOLDING, William (1911–1993)
Sleep is when all the unsorted stuff comes flying out as from a dustbin upset in a high wind.
[*Pincher Martin* (1956)]

HENRI IV (1553–1610)
Great eaters and great sleepers are not capable of doing anything great.
[Attr.]

NIETZSCHE, Friedrich Wilhelm (1844–1900)
Sleeping is no mean art: it is necessary to stay awake for it all day.
[*Thus Spake Zarathustra* (1884)]

SHAKESPEARE, William (1564–1616)
Methought I heard a voice cry 'Sleep no more; Macbeth does murder sleep' – the innocent sleep,
Sleep that knits up the ravell'd sleave of care,
The death of each day's life, sore labour's bath,
Balm of hurt minds, great nature's second course,
Chief nourisher in life's feast.
[*Macbeth*, II.ii]

SOUTHEY, Robert (1774–1843)
Thou hast been call'd, O Sleep! the friend of Woe,
But 'tis the happy who have called thee so.
[*The Curse of Kehama* (1810)]

THOMAS, Dylan (1914–1953)
Sleeping as quiet as death, side by wrinkled side, toothless, salt and brown, like two old kippers in a box.
[*Under Milk Wood* (1954)]

See **BED, DEATH, DREAMS**

SMOKING

CALVERLEY, C.S. (1831–1884)
How they who use fusees All grow by slow degrees Brainless as chimpanzees, Meagre as lizards: Go mad, and beat their wives; Plunge (after shocking lives) Razors and carving knives Into their gizzards.
['Ode to Tobacco' (1861)]

ELIZABETH I (1533–1603)
(To Sir Walter Raleigh)
I have known many persons who turned their gold into smoke, but you are the first to turn smoke into gold.
[In Chamberlin, *The Sayings of Queen Elizabeth* (1923)]

HELPS, Sir Arthur (1813–1875)
What a blessing this smoking is! perhaps the greatest that we owe to the discovery of America.
[*Friends in Council* (1859)]

JAMES VI (OF SCOTLAND AND I OF ENGLAND) (1566–1625)
A custom loathesome to the eye, hateful to the nose, harmful to the brain, dangerous to the lungs, and in the black, stinking fume thereof, nearest resembling the horrible Stygian smoke of the pit that is bottomless.
[*A Counterblast to Tobacco* (1604)]

KIPLING, Rudyard (1865–1936)
And a woman is only a woman, but a good cigar is a Smoke.
['The Betrothed' (1886)]

NAPOLEON III (1808–1873)
(On being asked to ban smoking)
This vice brings in one hundred million francs in taxes every year. I will certainly forbid it at once – as soon as you can name a virtue that brings in as much revenue.
[In Hoffmeister, *Anekdotenschatz*]

SATIE, Erik (1866–1925)
'My doctor has always told me to smoke. He explains himself thus: 'Smoke, my friend. If you don't, someone else will smoke in your place.'
[*Mémoires d'un amnésique* (1924)]

TWAIN, Mark (1835–1910)
(Saying how easy it is to give up smoking)
I've done it a hundred times!
[Attr.]

WILDE, Oscar (1854–1900)
A cigarette is the perfect type of a perfect pleasure. It is exquisite, and it leaves one unsatisfied. What more can one want?
[*The Picture of Dorian Gray* (1891)]

SNOBBERY

LYNES, J. Russel (1910–1991)
The true snob never rests: there is always a higher goal to attain, and there are, by the same token, always more and more people to look down upon.

THACKERAY, William Makepeace (1811–1863)
He who meanly admires mean things is a Snob.
[*The Book of Snobs* (1848)]

USTINOV, Sir Peter (1921–2004)
Laughter would be bereaved if snobbery died.
[*The Observer*, March 1955]

WILDE, Oscar (1854–1900)
Never speak disrespectfully of Society, Algernon. Only people who can't get into it do that.
[*The Importance of Being Earnest* (1895)]

See **ARISTOCRACY, CLASS**

SOCIALISM

BENNETT, Alan (1934–)
Why is it always the intelligent people who are socialists?
[*Forty Years On* (1969)]

BEVAN, Aneurin (1897–1960)
The language of priorities is the religion of Socialism.
[Attr.]

DURANT, Will (1885–1982)
There is nothing in Socialism that a little age or a little money will not cure.
[Attr.]

ORWELL, George (1903–1950)
As with the Christian religion, the worst advertisement for Socialism is its adherents.
[*The Road to Wigan Pier* (1937)]

STOPPARD, Tom (1937–)
Socialists treat their servants with respect and then wonder why they vote Conservative.
[*Lord Malquist and Mr Moon* (1966)]

THATCHER, Margaret (1925–2013)
State socialism is totally alien to the British character.
[*The Times*, 1983]

WARREN, Earl (1891–1974)
Many people consider the things which government does for them to be social progress, but they consider the things government does for others as socialism.
[*Peter's Quotations*]

See **COMMUNISM**

SOCIETY

ARISTOTLE (384–322 BC)
A person who cannot live in society, or does not need to because he is self-sufficient, is either a beast or a god.
[*Politics*]

AURELIUS, Marcus (121–180)
What is not good for the beehive, cannot be good for the bees.
[*Meditations*]

BACON, Francis (1561–1626)
Man seeketh in society comfort, use, and protection.
[*The Advancement of Learning* (1605)]

CICERO (106–43 BC)
What times! What manners!
[In Catilinam]

CLAUDEL, Paul (1868–1955)
The only living societies are those which are animated by inequality and injustice.
[*Conversations dans le Loir-et-Cher*]

COUNIHAN, Noel Jack (1913–1986)
In human society the warmth is mainly at the
bottom.
[*Age*, 1986]

GALBRAITH, J.K. (1908–2006)
In the affluent society, no sharp distinction
can be made between luxuries and
necessaries.
[*The Affluent Society* (1958)]

SPINOZA, Baruch (1632–1677)
Man is a social animal.
[*Ethics* (1677)]

THATCHER, Margaret (1925–2013)
There is no such thing as society. There are
individual men and women and there are
families.
[Attr.]

WILDE, Oscar (1854–1900)
(Of society)
To be in it is merely a bore. But to be out of it
simply a tragedy.
[*A Woman of No Importance* (1893)]

See **HUMANITY AND HUMAN NATURE,
PEOPLE**

SOLITUDE

BACON, Francis (1561–1626)
It had been hard for him that spake it to have
put more truth and untruth together, in a few
words, than in that speech: 'Whosoever is
delighted in solitude is either a wild beast,
or a god.'
['Of Friendship' (1625)]

GIBBON, Edward (1737–1794)
I was never less alone than when by myself.
[*Memoirs of My Life and Writings* (1796)]

MONTAIGNE, Michel de (1533–1592)
We should keep for ourselves a little back
shop, all our own, untouched by others, in
which we establish our true freedom and
chief place of seclusion and solitude.
[*Essais* (1580)]

ROSTAND, Jean (1894–1977)
To be an adult is to be alone.
[*Thoughts of a Biologist* (1939)]

SARTON, May (1912–1995)
Loneliness is the poverty of self; solitude is
the richness of self.
[*Mrs Stevens Hears the Mermaids Singing*
(1993)]

SASSOON, Siegfried (1886–1967)
Alone ... The word is life endured and known.
It is the stillness where our spirits walk
And all but inmost faith is overthrown.
[*The Heart's Journey* (1928)]

SCHOPENHAUER, Arthur (1788–1860)
Solitude is the fate of all outstanding minds: it
will at times be deplored; but it will always be
chosen as the lesser of two evils.
['Aphorisms for Wisdom' (1851)]

THOREAU, Henry David (1817–1862)
I never found the companion that was so
companionable as solitude.
[*Walden* (1854)]

See **LONELINESS**

THE SOUL

**THE BIBLE
(King James Version)**
What is a man profited, if he shall gain the
whole world, and lose his own soul?
[*Matthew*, 16:26]

CRABBE, George (1754–1832)
It is the soul that sees; the outward eyes
Present the object, but the mind descries.
[*The Lover's Journey*]

KEATS, John (1795–1821)
A man should have the fine point of his soul
taken off to become fit for this world.
[Letter to J.H. Reynolds, 1817]

LEWIS, Wyndham (1882–1957)
The soul started at the knee-cap and ended at
the navel.
[*The Apes of Gods* (1930)]

LUCRETIUS (c.95–55 BC)
What has this bugbear death to frighten man
If souls can die as well as bodies can?
[*De Rerum Natura*]

MEREDITH, George (1828–1909)
There is nothing the body suffers the soul
may not profit by.
[*Diana of the Crossways* (1885)]

SMITH, Logan Pearsall (1865–1946)
Most people sell their souls, and live with a
good conscience on the proceeds.
[*Afterthoughts* (1931)]

STERNE, Laurence (1713–1768)
I am positive I have a soul; nor can all the
books with which materialists have pestered
the world ever convince me to the contrary.
[*A Sentimental Journey* (1768)]

WEBSTER, John (c.1580–c.1625)
My soul, like to a ship in a black storm,
Is driven, I know not whither.
[*The White Devil* (1612)]

See **IMMORTALITY**

SPACE

ADDISON, Joseph (1672–1719)
The spacious firmament on high,
With all the blue ethereal sky,
And spangled heavens, a shining frame,
Their great Original proclaim.
[*The Spectator*, 1712]

ALFONSO X (1221–1284)
(On the Ptolemaic system of astronomy)
If the Lord Almighty had consulted me before
embarking upon Creation, I should have
recommended something simpler.
[Attr.]

ARMSTRONG, Neil (1930–2012)
(On stepping on to the moon)
That's one small step for a man, one giant
leap for mankind.
[*New York Times*, (1969)]

**THE BIBLE
(King James Version)**
The heavens declare the glory of God; and the
firmament sheweth his handywork.
[*Psalms*, 19:1]

BYRON, Lord (1788–1824)
Ye stars! which are the poetry of heaven!
[*Childe Harold's Pilgrimage* (1812–18)]

FROST, Robert (1874–1963)
They cannot scare me with their empty
spaces
Between stars – on stars where no human
race is.
I have it in me so much nearer home
To scare myself with my own desert places.
['Desert Places' (1936)]

FULLER, Richard Buckminster (1895–1983)
I am a passenger on the spaceship, Earth.
[*Operating Manual for Spaceship Earth* (1969)]

HOLMES, Rev. John H. (1879–1964)
This universe is not hostile, nor yet is it
friendly. It is simply indifferent.
[*A Sensible Man's View of Religion* (1932)]

HOPKINS, Gerard Manley (1844–1889)
Look at the stars! look, look up at the skies!
Oh look at all the fire-folk sitting in the air!
The bright boroughs, the circle-citadels there!
['The Starlight Night' (1877)]

VIDAL, Gore (1925–2012)
The astronauts! ... Rotarians in outer space.
[*Two Sisters* (1970)]

VIRGIL (70–19 BC)
And when the rising sun has first breathed on
us with his panting horses, over there the
glowing evening-star is lighting his late
lamps.
[*Georgics*]

See **SCIENCE, STARS, TECHNOLOGY,
UNIVERSE**

SPORT AND GAMES

ALI, Muhammad (1942–)
Float like a butterfly, sting like a bee.
[Catchphrase]

ALLISON, Malcolm (1927–2010)
Professional football is no longer a game. It's
a war. And it brings out the same primitive
instincts that go back thousands of years.
[*The Observer*, March 1973]

ATKINSON, Ron (1939–)
He dribbles a lot and the opposition don't like
it – you can see it over their faces.
[Sky Sports]

I never comment on referees and I'm not
going to break the habit of a lifetime for that
prat.
[Sky Sports]

BARDOT, Brigitte (1934–)
(On the 1998 World Cup, hosted by France)
It's a pity to see Paris, the world capital of
thinking, devoting so much interest to a game
played with feet.
[*The Scotsman*, June 1998]

BARNES, Simon (1951–)
Sport is something that does not matter, but
is performed as if it did. In that contradiction
lies its beauty.
[*The Spectator*, 1996]

BENNETT, Alan (1934–)
If you think squash is a competitive activity,
try flower arrangement.
[*Talking Heads* (1988)]

BEST, George (1946-2005)
(On being named Footballer of the Century)
It's a pleasure to be standing up here. It's a
pleasure to be standing up.
[Speech, 1999]

BROWN, Rita Mae (1944-)
Sport strips away personality, letting the
white bone of character shine through.
[Sudden Death (1983)]

BYRON, H.J. (1834-1884)
Life's too short for chess.
[Our Boys]

CANTERBURY, Tom
The trouble with referees is that they just
don't care which side wins.
[The Guardian, 1980]

CLARK, Alan (1928-2000)
(On football hooligans)
A compliment to the English martial spirit.
[The Times, 1998]

COLEMAN, David (1926-)
That's the fastest time ever run – but it's not
as fast as the world record.
[In Fantoni, Private Eye's Colemanballs (1986)]

CONNOLLY, Billy (1942-)
I love fishing. It's like transcendental
meditation with a punchline.
[Gullible's Travels (1982)]

CONNORS, Jimmy (1952-)
New Yorkers love it when you spill your guts
out there. Spill your guts at Wimbledon and
they make you stop and clean it up.
[The Guardian, 1984]

COWPER, William (1731-1800)
(Of hunting)
Detested sport,
That owes its pleasures to another's pain.
[The Task (1785)]

DEMPSEY, Jack (1895-1983)
Kill the other guy before he kills you.
[Motto]

DUROCHER, Leo (1905-1991)
(Remark at a practice ground, 1946)
Nice guys finish last.
[Attr.]

EUBANK, Chris (1966-)
Any boxer who says he loves boxing is either a
liar or a fool. I'm not looking for glory ... I'm
looking for money. I'm looking for readies.
[The Times, 1993]

FORD, Henry (1863-1947)
Exercise is bunk. If you are healthy, you don't
need it: if you are sick, you shouldn't take it.
[Attr.]

GRACE, W.G. (1848-1915)
(Refusing to leave the crease after being
bowled first ball in front of a large crowd)
They came to see me bat not to see you bowl.
[Attr.]

HEMINGWAY, Ernest (1898-1961)
Bullfighting is the only art in which the artist
is in danger of death and in which the degree
of brilliance in the performance is left to the
fighter's honour.
[Death in the Afternoon (1932)]

HICKSON, Paul
(Headline describing Celtic's 3-1 defeat by
Inverness Caledonian Thistle)
Super Caley Go Ballistic, Celtic Are Atrocious.
[The Sun, February 2000]

HOPPER, Denis (1936-2010)
If you survive your drug days, you have golf
ahead of you. That is, if you have any brain
left at all.
[The Sunday Times, March 2001]

HORNBY, Nick (1957-)
The natural state of the football fan is bitter
disappointment, no matter what the score.
[Fever Pitch (1992)]

HUMPHRIES, Barry (1934-)
Sport is a loathsome and dangerous pursuit.
[Sydney Morning Herald, 1982]

INGHAM, Sir Bernard (1932-)
Blood sport is brought to its ultimate
refinement in the gossip columns.
[Remark, 1986]

JERROLD, Douglas William (1803-1857)
The only athletic sport I ever mastered was
backgammon.
[In W. Jerrold, Douglas Jerrold (1914)]

JOHNSON, Boris (1964-)
(At the end of the Beijing Olympics, in
anticipation of the 2012 London Olympics)
I say to the Chinese and I say to the world –
ping pong is coming home!
[The Independent, 2008]

KING, Ty
Giles: I just think it's rather odd that a nation
that prides itself on its virility should feel
compelled to strap on forty pounds of
protective gear just in order to play rugby.
[Buffy the Vampire Slayer, TV series, 1998]

LAMB, Charles (1775-1834)
Man is a gaming animal. He must always be trying to get the better in something or other.
['Mrs Battle's Opinions on Whist' (1823)]

LOUIS, Joe (1914-1981)
(Referring to the speed of an opponent, Billy Conn)
He can run, but he can't hide.
[Attr.]

MARADONA, Diego (1960-)
(On his controversial goal against England in the 1986 World Cup)
The goal was scored a little bit by the hand of God, another bit by head of Maradona.
[*The Guardian*, July 1986]

MOURIE, Graham (1952-)
Nobody ever beats Wales at rugby, they just score more points.
[In Keating, *Caught by Keating*]

NAVRATILOVA, Martina (1956-)
The moment of victory is much too short to live for that and nothing else.
[*The Guardian*, June 1989]

O'ROURKE, P.J. (1947-)
The sport of skiing consists of wearing three thousand dollars' worth of clothes and equipment and driving two hundred miles in the snow in order to stand around at a bar and get drunk.
[*Modern Manners* (1984)]

ORWELL, George (1903-1950)
Serious sport has nothing to do with fair play. It is bound up with hatred, jealousy, boastfulness, disregard for all rules and sadistic pleasure in witnessing violence; in other words it is war minus the shooting.
[*Shooting an Elephant* (1950)]

PALMER, Arnold (1929-)
The more I practise the luckier I get.
[Attr.]

PAXMAN, Jeremy (1950-)
Internationally, football has become a substitute for war.
[*The Sunday Times*, June 2000]

PELÉ (1940-)
Football? It's the beautiful game.
[Attr.]

RICE, Grantland (1880-1954)
For when the One Great Scorer comes to mark against your name,
He marks - not that you won or lost - but how you played the Game.
['Alumnus Football' (1941)]

SHANKLY, Bill (1914-1981)
Some people think football is a matter of life and death. I don't like that attitude. I can assure them it is much more serious than that.
[Remark on BBC TV, 1981]

SMITH, Delia (1941-)
(On her appointment as a director of Norwich City football club)
Football and cookery are the two most important subjects in the country.
[*The Observer*, February 1997]

STUBBES, Philip (c.1555-1610)
Football ... causeth fighting, brawling, contention, quarrel picking, murder, homicide and great effusion of blood, as daily experience teacheth.
[*Anatomy of Abuses* (1583)]

TWAIN, Mark (1835-1910)
Golf is a good walk spoiled.
[Attr.]

TYSON, Mike (1966-)
(On boxing)
I'm in the hurt business.
[*The Independent on Sunday*, 2000]

WALTON, Izaak (1593-1683)
As no man is born an artist, so no man is born an angler.
[*The Compleat Angler* (1653)]

WILDE, Oscar (1854-1900)
The English country gentleman galloping after a fox - the unspeakable in full pursuit of the uneatable.
[*A Woman of No Importance* (1893)]

WODEHOUSE, P.G. (1881-1975)
The least thing upset him on the links. He missed short putts because of the uproar of the butterflies in the adjoining meadows.
[*The Clicking of Cuthbert* (1922)]

THE STATE

BURKE, Edmund (1729-1797)
A state without the means of some change is without the means of its conservation.
[*Reflections on the Revolution in France* (1790)]

ENGELS, Friedrich (1820–1895)
The state is not abolished, it dies away.
[*Anti-Dühring* (1878)]

LANDOR, Walter Savage (1775–1864)
States, like men, have their growth, their manhood, their decrepitude, their decay.
[Imaginary Conversations (1876)]

LENIN, V.I. (1870–1924)
So long as the state exists there is no freedom. When there is freedom there will be no state.
[*The State and Revolution* (1917)]

LOUIS XIV (1638–1715)
I am the State.
[Attr.]

MILL, John Stuart (1806–1873)
The worth of a State, in the long run, is the worth of the individuals composing it.
[*On Liberty* (1859)]

PLATO (c.429–347 BC)
Our object in the establishment of the state is the greatest happiness of the whole, and not that of any one class.
[*Republic*]

STALIN, Joseph (1879–1953)
The state is a machine in the hands of the ruling class for suppressing the resistance of its class enemies.
[*Foundations of Leninism* (1924)]

TEMPLE, William (1881–1944)
In place of the conception of the Power-State we are led to that of the Welfare-State.
[*Citizen and Churchman* (1941)]

See **DEMOCRACY, GOVERNMENT**

Statistics

AUDEN, W.H. (1907–1973)
Out of the air a voice without a face
Proved by statistics that some cause was just
In tones as dry and level as the place.
[*The Shield of Achilles* (1955)]

BELLOC, Hilaire (1870–1953)
Statistics are the triumph of the quantitative method, and the quantitative method is the victory of sterility and death.
[*The Silence of the Sea*]

CARLYLE, Thomas (1795–1881)
A witty statesman said, you might prove anything by figures.
[*Chartism* (1839)]

DISRAELI, Benjamin (1804–1881)
There are three kinds of lies: lies, damned lies and statistics.
[Attr.]

NIGHTINGALE, Florence (1820–1910)
To understand God's thoughts we must study statistics, for these are the measure of his purpose.
[Attr.]

STOUT, Rex Todhunter (1886–1975)
There are two kinds of statistics, the kind you look up and the kind you make up.
[*Death of a Doxy*]

Stupidity

DICKENS, Charles (1812–1870)
He'd be sharper than a serpent's tooth, if he wasn't as dull as ditch water.
[*Our Mutual Friend* (1866)]

MARX, Groucho (1895–1977)
You've got the brain of a four-year-old boy, and I bet he was glad to get rid of it.
[*Horse Feathers*, film, 1932]

MUIR, Frank (1920–1998)
I've examined your son's head, Mr Glum, and there's nothing there.
[*Take it from Here*, with Dennis Norden, 1957]

O'ROURKE, P.J. (1947–)
Earnestness is just stupidity sent to college.
[Attr. in *The Observer*, 1996]

WILDE, Oscar (1854–1900)
There is no sin except stupidity.
[*Intentions* (1891), 'The Critic as Artist']

See **FOOLISHNESS**

Style

BLAIR, Tony (1953–)
Is there anyone in the real world who believes I dress as if I have a style consultant?
[*The Sunday Times*, June 2001]

BUFFON, Comte de (1707–1788)
These things [subject matter] are external to the man; style is the essence of man.
['Discours sur le Style' (1753)]

CAMUS, Albert (1913–1960)
Style, like sheer silk, too often hides eczema.
[*The Fall* (1956)]

RENARD, Jules (1864–1910)
Poor style reflects imperfect thought.
[*Journal*, 1898]

WILDE, Oscar (1854–1900)
In matters of grave importance, style, not sincerity, is the vital thing.
[*The Importance of Being Earnest* (1895)]

See **FASHION, TASTE**

SUCCESS

ADAMS, Joey (1911–1999)
Rockefeller once explained the secret of success. 'Get up early, work late – and strike oil.'

BROWNING, Robert (1812–1889)
A minute's success pays the failure of years.
['Apollo and the Fates' (1887)]

CAGNEY, James (1904–1986)
Made it, Ma! Top of the world!
[*White Heat*, film, 1949]

DICKINSON, Emily (1830–1886)
Success is counted sweetest
By those who ne'er succeed.
To comprehend a nectar
Requires sorest need.
['Success is counted sweetest' (c.1859)]

LA ROCHEFOUCAULD (1613–1680)
To succeed in the world we do all we can to appear successful.
[*Maximes* (1678)]

LEHMAN, Ernest (1920–2005)
Sweet Smell of Success.
[Title of novel and film, 1957]

LERNER, Alan Jay (1918–1986)
You write a hit the same way you write a flop.
[Attr.]

RUSSELL, Rosalind (1911–1976)
Success is a public affair. Failure is a private funeral.
[*Life Is a Banquet* (1977)]

VIDAL, Gore (1925–2012)
It is not enough to succeed. Others must fail.
[In Irvine, *Antipanegyric for Tom Driberg* (1976)]

VIRGIL (70–19 BC)
To these success gives heart: they can because they think they can.
[*Aeneid*]

See **FAILURE, VICTORY**

SUFFERING

AUSTEN, Jane (1775–1817)
One does not love a place the less for having suffered in it, unless it has all been suffering, nothing but suffering.
[*Persuasion* (1818)]

BACON, Francis (1561–1626)
It is a miserable state of mind to have few things to desire and many things to fear.
['Of Empire' (1625)]

BOETHIUS (c.475–524)
At every blow of fate, the worst kind of misfortune is to have been happy.
[*De Consolatione Philosophiae* (c.522–524)]

BONO, Edward de (1933–)
Unhappiness is best defined as the difference between our talents and our expectations.
[*The Observer*, 1977]

BROWNING, Elizabeth Barrett (1806–1861)
For frequent tears have run
The colours from my life.
[*Sonnets from the Portuguese* (1850)]

CHAUCER, Geoffrey (c.1340–1400)
For of fortunes sharpe adversitee
The worste kynde of infortune is this,
A man to han ben in prosperitee,
And it remembren, whan it passed is.
[*Troilus and Criseyde*]

GAY, John (1685–1732)
A moment of time may make us unhappy forever.
[*The Beggar's Opera* (1728)]

HAZLITT, William (1778–1830)
The least pain in our little finger gives us more concern and uneasiness, than the destruction of millions of our fellow-beings.
[*Edinburgh Review*, 1829]

HEMINGWAY, Ernest (1898–1961)
The world breaks everyone and afterward many are strong at the broken places.
[*A Farewell to Arms* (1929)]

HOGG, James (1770–1835)
How often does the evening cup of joy lead to sorrow in the morning!
[Attr.]

JOHNSON, Samuel (1709–1784)
There is no wisdom in useless and hopeless sorrow.
[Letter to Mrs. Thrale, 1781]

KEMPIS, Thomas á (c.1380–1471)
If you bear the cross willingly, it will bear you.
[*De Imitatione Christi* (1892)]

LA ROCHEFOUCAULD (1613–1680)
One is never as unhappy as one thinks, or as happy as one hopes to be.
[*Maximes* (1664)]

LOWELL, James Russell (1819–1891)
The misfortunes hardest to bear are those which never come.
['Democracy' (1887)]

MONTAIGNE, Michel de (1533–1592)
A man who fears suffering is already suffering from what he fears.
[*Essais* (1580)]

NIETZSCHE, Friedrich Wilhelm (1844–1900)
What actually fills you with indignation as regards suffering is not suffering in itself but the pointlessness of suffering.
[*On the Genealogy of Morals* (1881)]

SAKI (1870–1916)
He's simply got the instinct for being unhappy highly developed.
[*The Chronicles of Clovis* (1911)]

SHAKESPEARE, William (1564–1616)
When sorrows come, they come not single spies,
But in battalions.
[*Hamlet*, IV.v]
Misery acquaints a man with strange bedfellows.
[*The Tempest*, II.ii]

SHAW, George Bernard (1856–1950)
The secret of being miserable is to have leisure to bother about whether you are happy or not.
[*Misalliance* (1914)]

SINATRA, Frank (1915–1998)
I'm for anything that can get you through the night, be it prayer, tranquillizers or a bottle of Jack Daniels.
[Attr. in *The Herald*, 1998]

VERLAINE, Paul (1844–1896)
Tears fall in my heart as rain falls on the city.
[*Romances sans paroles* (1874)]

WHITTIER, John Greenleaf (1807–1892)
For all sad words of tongue or pen,
The saddest are these: 'It might have been!'.
['Maud Muller' (1854)]

WILDE, Oscar (1854–1900)
Where there is sorrow, there is holy ground.
[*De Profundis* (1897)]

See **DESPAIR**

SUICIDE

GREER, Germaine (1939–)
Suicide is an act of narcissistic manipulation and deep hostility.
[*The Observer Review*, 1995]

NIETZSCHE, Friedrich Wilhelm (1844–1900)
The thought of suicide is a great comfort: it's a good way of getting through many a bad night.
[*Beyond Good and Evil* (1886)]

PARKER, Dorothy (1893–1967)
Razors pain you;
Rivers are damp;
Acids stain you;
And drugs cause cramp.
Guns aren't lawful;
Nooses give;
Gas smells awful;
You might as well live.
['Résumé' (1937)]

TENNYSON, Alfred (Lord) (1809–1892)
Nor at all can tell
Whether I mean this day to end myself,
Or lend an ear to Plato where he says,
That men like soldiers may not quit the post
Allotted by the Gods.
['Lucretius' (1868)]

See **DEATH**

SUNDAY

ADDISON, Joseph (1672–1719)
Sunday clears away the rust of the whole week.
[*The Spectator*, July 1711, 112]

CAREY, Henry (c.1687–1743)
Of all the days that's in the week
I dearly love but one day –
And that's the day that comes betwixt
A Saturday and Monday.
['Sally in our Alley' (1729)]

DE QUINCEY, Thomas (1785–1859)
It was a Sunday afternoon, wet and cheerless: and a duller spectacle this earth of ours has not to show than a rainy Sunday in London.
[*Confessions of an English Opium Eater* (1822)]

RHYS, Jean (1894–1979)
The feeling of Sunday is the same everywhere, heavy, melancholy, standing still. Like when they say, 'As it was in the beginning, is now, and ever shall be, world without end.'
[*Voyage in the Dark* (1934)]

SWIFT, Jonathan (1667–1745)
I always love to begin a journey on Sundays, because I shall have the prayers of the church, to preserve all that travel by land, or by water.
[*Polite Conversation* (1738)]

SUPERSTITION

BACON, Francis (1561–1626)
There is a superstition in avoiding superstition.
['Of Superstition' (1625)]

BARRIE, Sir J.M. (1860–1937)
Every time a child says 'I don't believe in fairies,' there is a little fairy somewhere that falls down dead.
[*Peter Pan* (1904)]

BOHR, Niels Henrik David (1885–1962)
(Explaining why he had a horseshoe on his wall)
Of course I don't believe in it. But I understand that it brings you luck whether you believe in it or not.
[Attr.]

BROWNE, Sir Thomas (1605–1682)
For my part, I have ever believed, and do now know, that there are witches.
[*Religio Medici* (1643)]

BURKE, Edmund (1729–1797)
Superstition is the religion of feeble minds.
[*Reflections on the Revolution in France* (1790)]

GOETHE (1749–1832)
Superstition is the poetry of life.
['Literature and Language' (1823)]

JOHNSON, Samuel (1709–1784)
(Of ghosts)
All argument is against it; but all belief is for it.
[In Boswell, *The Life of Samuel Johnson* (1791)]

TALENT

BRONTË, Anne (1820–1849)
All our talents increase in the using, and every faculty, both good and bad, strengthens by exercise.
[*The Tenant of Wildfell Hall* (1848)]

DEGAS, Edgar (1834–1917)
Everybody has talent at twenty-five. The difficult thing is to have it at fifty.
[In Gammell, *The Shop-Talk of Edgar Degas* (1961)]

LERNER, Alan Jay (1918–1986)
Back home everyone said I didn't have any talent. They might be saying the same thing over here, but it sounds better in French.
[*An American in Paris*, film, 1951]

See **GENIUS**

TASTE

ADAMS, Henry (1838–1918)
Every one carries his own inch-rule of taste, and amuses himself by applying it, triumphantly, wherever he travels.
[*The Education of Henry Adams* (1918)]

BENNETT, Arnold (1867–1931)
Good taste is better than bad taste, but bad taste is better than no taste.
[*The Observer*, 1930]

FITZGERALD, Edward (1809–1883)
Taste is the feminine of genius.
[Letter to J.R. Lowell, 1877]

HUXLEY, Aldous (1894–1963)
The aristocratic pleasure of displeasing is not the only delight that bad taste can yield. One can love a certain kind of vulgarity for its own sake.
[*Vulgarity in Literature* (1930)]

REYNOLDS, Sir Joshua (1723–1792)
Taste does not come by chance: it is a long and laborious task to acquire it.
[In Northcote, *Life of Sir Joshua Reynolds* (1818)]

VALÉRY, Paul (1871–1945)
Taste is created from a thousand distastes.
[*Unsaid Things*]

TAXES

BURKE, Edmund (1729–1797)
To tax and to please, no more than to love and to be wise, is not given to men.
[*Speech on American Taxation* (1774)]

CAPONE, Al (1899–1947)
(Objecting to the US government claiming unpaid back tax)
They can't collect legal taxes from illegal money.
[In Kobler, *Capone* (1971)]

DICKENS, Charles (1812–1870)
'It was as true,' said Mr Barkis, '... as taxes is. And nothing's truer than them.'
[*David Copperfield* (1850)]

FRANKLIN, Benjamin (1706–1790)
But in this world nothing can be said to be certain, except death and taxes.
[Letter to Jean Baptiste Le Roy, 1789]

HELMSLEY, Leona (1920–2007)
(Hotel tycoon during her trial for tax evasion)
We don't pay taxes. Only the little people pay taxes.
[Remark, 1989]

JOHNSON, Samuel (1709–1784)
Excise. A hateful tax levied upon commodities.
[*A Dictionary of the English Language* (1755)]

MANDELSON, Peter (1953–)
We are intensely relaxed about people getting filthy rich as long as they pay their taxes.
[Speech to conference of computing executives, 1998]

OTIS, James (1725–1783)
Taxation without representation is tyranny.
[Attr.]

ROGERS, Will (1879–1935)
Income tax has made more liars out of American people than golf.
[*The Illiterate Digest* (1924)]

SHAW, George Bernard (1856–1950)
A government which robs Peter to pay Paul can always depend on the support of Paul.
[*Everybody's Political What's What* (1944)]

SMITH, Adam (1723–1790)
There is no art which one government sooner learns of another than that of draining money from the pockets of the people.
[*Wealth of Nations* (1776)]

Tea

ADDISON, Joseph (1672–1719)
The infusion of a China plant sweetened with the pith of an Indian cane.
[*The Spectator*, 1711]

ARMOUR, G.D. (1864–1949)
Look here, Steward, if this is coffee, I want tea; but if this is tea, then I wish for coffee.
[*Punch*, cartoon caption, July 1902]

CHESTERTON, G.K. (1874–1936)
Tea, although an Oriental,
Is a gentleman at least;
Cocoa is a cad and coward,
Cocoa is a vulgar beast.
[*The Flying Inn* (1914)]

COBBETT, William (1762–1835)
Resolve to free yourselves from the slavery of the tea and coffee and other slop-kettle.
[*Advice to Young Men* (1829)]

GLADSTONE, William (1809–1898)
The domestic use of tea is a powerful champion able to encounter alcoholic drink in a fair field and throw it in a fair fight.
[Budget Speech, 1882]

PINERO, Sir Arthur Wing (1855–1934)
While there's tea there's hope.
[*The Second Mrs Tanqueray* (1893)]

SMITH, Sydney (1771–1845)
Thank God for tea! What would the world do without tea? How did it exist? I am glad I was not born before tea.
[Attr.]

Teachers

AUDEN, W.H. (1907–1973)
A professor is one who talks in someone else's sleep.
[Attr.]

BERLIOZ, Hector (1803–1869)
Time is a great teacher, but unfortunately it kills all its pupils.
[Attr.]

CARLYLE, Thomas (1795–1881)
It were better to perish than to continue schoolmastering.
[In Wilson, *Carlyle Till Marriage* (1923)]

CHURCHILL, Sir Winston (1874–1965)
Headmasters have powers at their disposal with which Prime Ministers have never yet been invested.
[*My Early Life* (1930)]

MONTESSORI, Maria (1870–1952)
We teachers can only help the work going on, as servants wait upon a master.
[*The Absorbent Mind*]

SHAW, George Bernard (1856–1950)
He who can, does. He who cannot, teaches.
[*Man and Superman* (1903)]

TROLLOPE, Anthony (1815–1882)
(Of his headmaster)
He must have known me had he seen me as he was wont to see me, for he was in the habit of flogging me constantly. Perhaps he did not recognize me by my face.
[*Autobiography* (1883)]

WAUGH, Evelyn (1903–1966)
We schoolmasters must temper discretion with deceit.
[*Decline and Fall* (1928)]

WILDE, Oscar (1854–1900)
Everybody who is incapable of learning has taken to teaching.
['The Decay of Lying' (1889)]

YEATMAN, Robert Julian (1897–1968)
For every person wishing to teach there are thirty not wanting to be taught.
[*And Now All This* (1932)]

See **EDUCATION, LEARNING, SCHOOL, UNIVERSITY**

TECHNOLOGY

AULETTA, Ken (1942–)
The digital revolution is almost as disruptive to the traditional media business as electricity was to the candle business.
[*The New Yorker*, 2011]

CARLYLE, Thomas (1795–1881)
Man is a tool-using animal.
[*Sartor Resartus* (1834)]

CLARKE, Sir Arthur C. (1917–2008)
Any sufficiently advanced technology is indistringuisable from magic.
[*Technology and the Future*]

FEYNMAN, Richard (1918–1988)
For a successful technology, reality must take precedence over public relations, for nature cannot be fooled.
[Rogers Commission Report on the Space Shuttle Challenger Accident, 1986]

FRISCH, Max (1911–1991)
Technology is the knack of so arranging the world that we do not experience it.
[In Rollo May, *The Cry for Myth*]

HARRINGTON, Michael (1928–1989)
If there is a technological advance without a social advance, there is, almost automatically, an increase in human misery.
[*The Other America* (1962)]

RILKE, Rainer Maria (1875–1926)
The machine threatens all achievement.
[*The Sonnets to Orpheus* (1923)]

VERNE, Jules (1828–1905)
Captain Nemo: I wonder if you are familiar with utensils, Mr. Land? Ned Land: I'm indifferent to 'em.
[*20,000 Leagues Under the Sea*, film, 1954]

See **COMPUTERS, INTERNET, PROGRESS, SCIENCE**

TELEVISION

ALLEN, Woody (1935–)
Life doesn't imitate art. It imitates bad television.
[*Husbands and Wives*, film, 1992]

ANONYMOUS
The human race is faced with a cruel choice: work or daytime television.

BAKEWELL, Joan (Baroness) (1933–)
The BBC is full of men appointing men who remind them of themselves when young, so you get the same backgrounds, the same education, and the same programmes.
[*The Observer*, 1993]

BARNES, Clive (1927–2008)
Television is the first truly democratic culture – the first culture available to everybody and entirely governed by what the people want. The most terrifying thing is what people do want.

BIRT, John (1944–)
There is a bias in television journalism. It is not against any particular party or point of view – it is a bias against understanding.
[*The Times*, 1975]

COREN, Alan (1938–2007)
Television is more interesting than people. If it were not, we should have people standing in the corners of our rooms.
[Attr.]

COWARD, Sir Noël (1899–1973)
Television is for appearing on, not looking at.
[Attr.]

DEBRAY, Régis (1942–)
The darkest spot in modern society is a small luminous screen.
[*Teachers, Writers, Celebrities*]

ECO, Umberto (1932–)
Television doesn't present, as an ideal to aspire to, the superman but the everyman. Television puts forward, as an ideal, the absolutely average man.
[*Diario Minimo*]

FORD, Anna (1943–)
Let's face it, there are no plain women on television.
[*The Observer*, 1979]

FROST, Sir David (1939-)
Television is an invention that permits you to be entertained in your living room by people you wouldn't have in your home.
[Remark, 1971]

GOLDWYN, Samuel (1882-1974)
Television has raised writing to a new low.
[Attr.]

HITCHCOCK, Alfred (1899-1980)
Television has brought murder back into the home – where it belongs.
[The Observer, 1965]

JAMES, Clive (1939-)
Television is simultaneously blamed, often by the same people, for worsening the world and for being powerless to change it.
[Glued to the Box (1983)]

KOVACS, Ernie (1919-1962)
Television – a medium. So called because it is neither rare nor well-done.
[Attr.]

LANDERS, Ann (1918-2002)
Television has proved that people will look at anything rather than each other.

MCLUHAN, Marshall (1911-1980)
Television brought the brutality of war into the comfort of the living room. Vietnam was lost in the living rooms of America – not on the battle fields of Vietnam.
[Montreal Gazette, 1975]

MARX, Groucho (1895-1977)
I find television very educating. Every time somebody turns on the set, I go into the other room and read a book.

PAGLIA, Camille (1947-)
Television is actually closer to reality than anything in books. The madness of TV is the madness of human life.
[Sex, Art, and American Culture (1992)]
Television? The word is half Latin and half Greek. No good can come of it.
[Attr.]

SEINFELD, Jerry (1955-)
Men don't care what's on TV. They only care what else is on TV.
[Attr.]

TRUSS, Lynne (1955-)
Abuse is the currency of all reality shows.
[Talk to the Hand (2005)]

WELLES, Orson (1915-1985)
I hate television. I hate it as much as peanuts. But I can't stop eating peanuts.
[New York Herald Tribune, 1956]

WILDER, Billy (1906-2002)
It used to be that we in film were the lowest form of art. Now we have something to look down on.
[In A. Madsen, Billy Wilder (1968)]

See **MEDIA**

TEMPTATION

ANONYMOUS
The trouble with resisting temptation is it may never come your way again.

BECKFORD, William (1760-1844)
I am not over-fond of resisting temptation.
[Vathek (1787)]

DRYDEN, John (1631-1700)
Thou strong seducer, opportunity!
[The Conquest of Granada (1670)]

JERROLD, Douglas William (1803-1857)
Honest bread is very well – it's the butter that makes the temptation.
[The Cat's Paw (1930)]

SHAW, George Bernard (1856-1950)
I never resist temptation, because I have found that things that are bad for me do not tempt me.
[The Apple Cart (1930)]

WILDE, Oscar (1854-1900)
I couldn't help it. I can resist everything except temptation.
[Lady Windermere's Fan (1892)]

THEATRE

ADAMOV, Arthur (1908-1970)
The reason why Absurdist plays take place in No Man's Land with only two characters is primarily financial.
[Attr.]

ADDISON, Joseph (1672-1719)
A perfect tragedy is the noblest production of human nature.
[The Spectator, 1711]

AGATE, James (1877-1947)
Long experience has taught me that in England nobody goes to the theatre unless he or she has bronchitis.
[Attr.]

ARISTOTLE (384-322 BC)
The plot is the first principle and, as it were, the soul of tragedy; character comes second.
[*Poetics*]

ASKEY, Arthur (1900-1982)
Pantomimes – the smell of oranges and wee-wee.
[Attr.]

BANKHEAD, Tallulah (1903-1968)
It's one of the tragic ironies of the theatre that only one man in it can count on steady work – the night watchman.
[*Tallulah* (1952)]

BERNARD, Tristan (1866-1947)
In the theatre the audience want to be surprised – but by things that they expect.
[Attr.]

BROOKS, Mel (1926-)
Tragedy is if I cut my finger. Comedy is if you walk into an open sewer and die.
[*The New Yorker*, 1978]

BYRON, Lord (1788-1824)
All tragedies are finish'd by a death,
All comedies are ended by a marriage.
[*Don Juan* (1824)]

COOK, Peter (1937-1995)
You know, I go to the theatre to be entertained ... I don't want to see plays about rape, sodomy and drug addiction ... I can get all that at home.
[*The Observer*, cartoon caption, 1962]

CRAIG, Sir Gordon (1872-1966)
Farce is the essential theatre. Farce refined becomes high comedy: farce brutalized becomes tragedy.
[Attr.]

CRISP, Quentin (1908-1999)
(Description of his touring show)
going about the country preaching to the perverted.
[*The Times*, 1999]

HITCHCOCK, Alfred (1899-1980)
What is drama but life with the dull bits cut out?
[*The Observer*, 1960]

HUXLEY, Aldous (1894-1963)
We participate in a tragedy; at a comedy we only look.
[*The Devils of Loudun* (1952)]

KEMBLE, John Philip (1757-1823)
(Said during a play which was continually interrupted by a crying child)
Ladies and gentlemen, unless the play is stopped, the child cannot possibly go on.
[Attr.]

PETER, John
Political theatre is by definition subversive: anything else is only propaganda.
[Review, *Sunday Times*, 1998]

PINTER, Harold (1930-2008)
I've never regarded myself as the one authority on my plays just because I wrote the damned things.
[*The Observer*, 1993]

SHAW, George Bernard (1856-1950)
You don't expect me to know what to say about a play when I don't know who the author is, do you? ... If it's by a good author, it's a good play, naturally. That stands to reason.
[*Fanny's First Play* (1911)]
(Responding to a solitary boo amongst the mid-act applause at the first performance of Arms and the Man in 1894)
I quite agree with you, sir, but what can two do against so many?
[*Oxford Book of Literary Anecdotes*]

STOPPARD, Tom (1937-)
The bad end unhappily, the good unluckily. That is what tragedy means.
[*Rosencrantz and Guildenstern Are Dead* (1967)]

See **ACTING, ACTORS, CENSORSHIP, CRITICISM, LITERATURE**

THOUGHT

BIERCE, Ambrose (1842-c.1914)
Brain: An apparatus with which we think that we think.
[*The Cynic's World Book* (1906)]

CONFUCIUS (c.550-c.478 BC)
Learning without thought is labour lost; thought without learning is perilous.
[*Analects*]

DESCARTES, René (1596-1650)
I think, therefore I am.
[*Discours de la Méthode* (1637)]

EMERSON, Ralph Waldo (1803-1882)
Beware when the great God lets loose a thinker on this planet. Then all things are at risk.
['Circles' (1841)]

GOETHE (1749–1832)
Everything worth thinking has already been thought, our concern must only be to try to think it through again.
['Thought and Action' (1829)]

HAZLITT, William (1778–1830)
The most fluent talkers or most plausible reasoners are not always the justest thinkers.
[*Atlas* (1830)]

JAMES, William (1842–1910)
A great many people think they are thinking when they are merely rearranging their prejudices.
[Attr.]

LUTHER, Martin (1483–1546)
Thoughts are not subject to duty.
[*On Worldly Authority* (1523)]

NEWTON, Sir Isaac (1642–1727)
If I have done the public any service, it is due to patient thought.
[Letter to Dr Bentley, 1713]

REITH, Lord (1889–1971)
You can't think rationally on an empty stomach, and a whole lot of people can't do it on a full one either.
[Attr.]

RUSKIN, John (1819–1900)
The purest and most thoughtful minds are those which love colour the most.
[*The Stones of Venice* (1853)]

RUSSELL, Bertrand (1872–1970)
Many people would sooner die than think. In fact they do.
[In Flew, *Thinking about Thinking* (1975)]

SARTRE, Jean-Paul (1905–1980)
My thought is me: that is why I cannot stop. I exist by what I think ... and I can't prevent myself from thinking.
[*Nausea* (1938)]

SHAKESPEARE, William (1564–1616)
There is nothing either good or bad, but thinking makes it so.
[*Hamlet*, II.ii]

SHELLEY, Percy Bysshe (1792–1822)
A single word even may be a spark of inextinguishable thought.
[*A Defence of Poetry* (1821)]

VALÉRY, Paul (1871–1945)
A gloss on Descartes: Sometimes I think: and sometimes I am.
[*The Faber Book of Aphorisms* (1962)]

VOLTAIRE (1694–1778)
People use thought only to justify their injustices, and they use words only to disguise their thoughts.
[*Dialogues* (1763)]

See **BELIEF, IDEAS, INTELLECTUALS, INTELLIGENCE, MIND, PHILOSOPHY**

TIME

AURELIUS, Marcus (121–180)
Time is like a river made up of the things which happen, and its current is strong; no sooner does anything appear than it is carried away, and another comes in its place, and will be carried away too.
[*Meditations*]

BACON, Francis (1561–1626)
He that will not apply new remedies, must expect new evils; for time is the greatest innovator.
['Of Innovations' (1625)]

**THE BIBLE
(King James Version)**
To every thing there is a season, and a time to every purpose under the heaven.
[*Ecclesiastes*, 3:1–8]

BOUCICAULT, Dion (1822–1890)
Men talk of killing time, while time quietly kills them.
[*London Assurance* (1841)]

COWARD, Sir Noël (1899–1973)
Time is the reef upon which all our frail mystic ships are wrecked.
[*Blithe Spirit* (1941)]

DISRAELI, Benjamin (1804–1881)
Time is the great physician.
[*Henrietta Temple* (1837)]

DOBSON, Henry Austin (1840–1921)
Time goes, you say? Ah no!
Alas, Time stays, we go.
['The Paradox of Time' (1877)]

EMERSON, Ralph Waldo (1803–1882)
A day is a miniature eternity.
[*Journals*]

FRAME, Janet (1924–2004)
There is no past present or future. Using tenses to divide time is like making chalk marks on water.
[*Faces in the Water* (1961)]

MCLUHAN, Marshall (1911–1980)
For tribal man space was the uncontrollable mystery. For technological man it is time that occupies the same role.
[*The Mechanical Bridge* (1951)]

MARX, Groucho (1895–1977)
Time wounds all heels.
[Attr.]

MAXWELL, Gavin (1914–1969)
Yet while there is time, there is the certainty of return.
[*Ring of Bright Water* (1960)]

PERICLES (c.495–429)
Wait for that wisest of counsellors, Time.
[In Plutarch, *Life*]

ROGERS, Will (1879–1935)
Half our life is spent trying to find something to do with the time we have rushed through life trying to save.
[*New York Times*, 1930]

SHAKESPEARE, William (1564–1616)
I wasted time, and now doth time waste me.
[*Richard II*, V.v]

STOPPARD, Tom (1937–)
Eternity's a terrible thought. I mean, where's it all going to end?
[*Rosencrantz and Guildenstern Are Dead* (1967)]

THOMAS, Dylan (1914–1953)
Oh as I was young and easy in the mercy of his means,
Time held me green and dying
Though I sang in my chains like the sea.
['Fern Hill' (1946)]

WATTS, Isaac (1674–1748)
Time, like an ever-rolling stream,
Bears all its sons away;
They fly forgotten, as a dream
Dies at the opening day.
[*The Psalms of David Imitated* (1719)]

YOUNG, Edward (1683–1765)
Procrastination is the Thief of Time.
[*Night-Thoughts on Life, Death and Immortality* (1742–1746)]

See **CHANGE, FUTURE, LIFE, PAST, PRESENT**

THE BIBLE
(King James Version)
For ye suffer fools gladly, seeing ye yourselves are wise.
[*Paul*, 3:67]

BROWNE, Sir Thomas (1605–1682)
No man can justly censure or condemn another, because indeed no man truly knows another.
[*Religio Medici* (1643)]

BURKE, Edmund (1729–1797)
There is, however, a limit at which forbearance ceases to be a virtue.
[*Observations on 'The Present State of the Nation'* (1769)]

SADE, Marquis de (1740–1814)
Tolerance is the virtue of the weak.
[*La nouvelle Justine* (1797)]

STAËL, Mme de (1766–1817)
Understanding everything makes one very tolerant.
[*Corinne* (1807)]

TROLLOPE, Anthony (1815–1882)
It is because we put up with bad things that hotel-keepers continue to give them to us.
[*Orley Farm* (1862)]

ARISTOTLE (384–322 BC)
(Of the dramatic form of tragedy)
A whole is that which has a beginnings middle, and an end.
[*Poetics*]

AUSTEN, Jane (1775–1817)
One of Edward's Mistresses was Jane Shore, who has had a play written about her, but it is a tragedy and therefore not worth reading.
[*The History of England* (1791)]

CHAUCER, Geoffrey (c.1340–1400)
Tragedie is to seyn a certeyn storie,
As olde bookes maken us memorie,
Of hym that stood in greet prosperitee
And is yfallen out of heigh degree
Into myserie, and endeth wrecchedly.
[*The Canterbury Tales* (1387)]

FYFE, Alistair (1961–)
(On the obscurity of Glasgow architect Alexander 'Greek' Thomson compared with Charles Rennie Mackintosh)
Thomson was guilty of not having enough tragedy in his life.
[*The Guardian*, June 1999]

SCOTT, Sir Walter (1771–1832)
The play-bill, which is said to have announced the tragedy of Hamlet, the character of the Prince of Denmark being left out.
[*The Talisman* (1825)]

TRANSLATION

BORROW, George (1803–1881)
Translation is at best an echo.
[Lavengro (1851)]

CAMPBELL, Roy (1901–1957)
Translations (like wives) are seldom strictly faithful if they are in the least attractive.
[Poetry Review, 1949]

DENHAM, Sir John (1615–1669)
Such is our pride, our folly, or our fate,
That few, but such as cannot write, translate.
['To Richard Fanshaw' (1648)]

FROST, Robert (1874–1963)
Poetry is what is lost in translation.
[In Untermeyer, Robert Frost: a Backward Look (1964)]

JOHNSON, Samuel (1709–1784)
A translator is to be like his author; it is not his business to excel him.
[Attr.]

TRAVEL

ARNOLD, Matthew (1822–1888)
A wanderer is man from his birth.
He was born in a ship
On the breast of the river of Time.
['The Future']

BOONE, Daniel (1734–1820)
(Reply on being asked if he had ever been lost)
I can't say I was ever lost, but I was bewildered once for three days.
[Attr.]

BRIEN, Alan (1925–2008)
I have done almost every human activity inside a taxi which does not require main drainage.
[Punch, 1972]

CHESTERTON, G.K. (1874–1936)
Chesterton taught me this: the only way to be sure of catching a train is to miss the one before it.
[In P. Daninos, Vacances à tous prix (1958)]

CLARKSON, Jeremy (1960–)
To argue that a car is simply a means of conveyance is like arguing that Blenheim Palace is simply a house.
[Sunday Times, 1999]

COLERIDGE, Samuel Taylor (1772–1834)
From whatever place I write you will expect that part of my 'Travels' will consist of excursions in my own mind.
[Satyrane's Letters (1809)]

COWPER, William (1731–1800)
How much a dunce that has been sent to roam
Excels a dunce that has been kept at home.
['The Progress of Error' (1782)]

DIDION, Joan (1934–)
Certain places seem to exist mainly because someone has written about them.
[The White Album (1979)]

DREW, Elizabeth (1887–1965)
Too often travel, instead of broadening the mind, merely lengthens the conversation.
[The Literature of Gossip (1964)]

ELIOT, T.S. (1888–1965)
The first condition of understanding a foreign country is to smell it.
[Attr.]

EMERSON, Ralph Waldo (1803–1882)
Travelling is a fool's paradise. Our first journeys discover to us the indifference of places.
['Self-Reliance' (1841)]

GEORGE VI (1895–1952)
Abroad is bloody.
[In Auden, A Certain World (1970)]

JOHNSON, Amy (1903–1941)
Had I been a man I might have explored the Poles or climbed Mount Everest, but as it was my spirit found an outlet in the air...
[In Margot Asquith (ed.), Myself When Young]

JOHNSON, Samuel (1709–1784)
The grand object of travelling is to see the shores of the Mediterranean.
[In Boswell, The Life of Samuel Johnson (1791)]

KILVERT, Francis (1840–1879)
Of all noxious animals, too, the most noxious is a tourist. And of all tourists, the most vulgar, ill-bred, offensive and loathsome is the British tourist.
[Diary, 1870]

KIPLING, Rudyard (1865–1936)
Down to Gehenna or up to the Throne,
He travels the fastest who travels alone.
['The Winners' (1888)]

MACAULAY, Dame Rose (1881–1958)
The great and recurrent question about abroad is, is it worth getting there?
[Attr.]

MARX BROTHERS
Captain Jeffrey Spaulding: You are going Uruguay, and I'm going my way.
[Film Animal Crackers, 1930]

MCLUHAN, Marshall (1911–1980)
The car has become the carapace, the protective and aggressive shell, of urban and suburban man.
[*Understanding Media* (1964)]

MOORE, George (1852–1933)
A man travels the world over in search of what he needs and returns home to find it.
[*The Brook Kerith* (1916)]

SACKVILLE-WEST, Vita (1892–1962)
Travel is the most private of pleasures. There is no greater bore than the travel bore. We do not in the least want to hear what he has seen in Hong-Kong.
[*Passenger to Tehran* (1926)]

SANTAYANA, George (1863–1952)
(On being asked why he always travelled third class)
Because there's no fourth class.
[In Thomas, *Living Biographies of the Great Philosophers*]

SCOTT, Captain Robert (1868–1912)
(Of the South Pole)
Great God! this is an awful place.
[*Journal*, 1912]

STARK, Dame Freya (1893–1993)
The beckoning counts, and not the clicking latch behind you.
[*Sunday Telegraph*, 1993]

STERNE, Laurence (1713–1768)
A man should know something of his own country too, before he goes abroad.
[*Tristram Shandy* (1767)]

STEVENSON, Robert Louis (1850–1894)
To travel hopefully is a better thing than to arrive, and the true success is to labour.
[*Virginibus Puerisque* (1881)]
But all that I could think of, in the darkness and the cold,
Was that I was leaving home and my folks were growing old.
['Christmas at Sea' (1890)]
There's nothing under Heav'n so blue
That's fairly worth the travelling to.
['A Song of the Road' (1896)]

VIZINCZEY, Stephen (1933–)
I was told I am a true cosmopolitan. I am unhappy everywhere.
[*The Guardian*, 1968]

See **FOREIGNERS**

TRUST

ANONYMOUS
Trust in Allah, but tie your camel.
[Old Muslim Proverb]

CAINE, Sir Michael (1933–)
Never trust anyone who wears a beard, a bow tie, two-toned shoes, sandals or sunglasses.
[*The Times*, 1992; quoting his father]

CAMUS, Albert (1913–1960)
It is very true that we seldom confide in those who are better than ourselves.
[*The Fall* (1956)]

CHRISTIE, Dame Agatha (1890–1976)
Where large sums of money are concerned, it is advisable to trust nobody.
[*Endless Night* (1967)]

FIELDING, Henry (1707–1754)
Never trust the man who hath reason to suspect that you know that he hath injured you.
[*Jonathan Wild* (1743)]

JEFFERSON, Thomas (1743–1826)
When a man assumes a public trust, he should consider himself as public property.
[Remark, 1807]

PITT, William (1708–1778)
I cannot give them my confidence; pardon me, gentlemen, confidence is a plant of slow growth in an aged bosom: youth is the season of credulity.
[Speech, 1766]

RUBIN, Jerry (1936–1994)
Don't trust anyone over thirty.
[In S.B. Flexner, *Listening to America*]

SHERIDAN, Richard Brinsley (1751–1816)
There is no trusting appearances.
[*The School for Scandal* (1777)]

WILLIAMS, Tennessee (1911–1983)
We have to distrust each other. It's our only defence against betrayal.
[*Camino Real* (1953)]

TRUTH

ADLER, Alfred (1870–1937)
The truth is often a terrible weapon of aggression. It is possible to lie, and even to murder, for the truth.
[*Problems of Neurosis* (1929)]

AGAR, Herbert Sebastian (1897–1980)
The truth which makes men free is for the most part the truth which men prefer not to hear.
[*A Time for Greatness* (1942)]

ANGELOU, Maya (1928-)
There's a world of difference between truth and facts. Facts can obscure truth.
[*I Know Why the Caged Bird Sings* (1970)]

ARNOLD, Matthew (1822-1888)
Truth sits upon the lips of dying men.
['Sohrab and Rustum' (1853)]

BACON, Francis (1561-1626)
What a man had rather were true he more readily believes.
[*The New Organon* (1620)]

BALDWIN, Stanley (1867-1947)
A platitude is simply a truth repeated until people get tired of hearing it.
[Attr.]

BERKELEY, Bishop George (1685-1753)
Truth is the cry of all, but the game of the few.
[*Siris* (1744)]

THE BIBLE
(King James Version)
Great is Truth, and mighty above all things.
[*Apocrypha, I Esdras*, 4:41]
And ye shall know the truth, and the truth shall make you free.
[*John*, 8:32]

BLAKE, William (1757-1827)
A truth thats told with bad intent
Beats all the Lies you can invent.
['Auguries of Innocence' (c.1803)]

BOLINGBROKE, Henry (1678-1751)
Plain truth will influence half a score of men at most in a nation, or an age, while mystery will lead millions by the nose.
[Letter, 1721]

BOWEN, Elizabeth (1899-1973)
Nobody speaks the truth when there's something they must have.
[*The House in Paris* (1935)]

BRAQUE, Georges (1882-1963)
Truth exists; only lies are invented.
[*Day and Night, Notebooks* (1952)]

CHAUCER, Geoffrey (c.1340-1400)
Trouthe is the hyeste thyng that man may kepe.
[*The Canterbury Tales* (1387)]

COWPER, William (1731-1800)
And diff'ring judgments serve but to declare
That truth lies somewhere, if we knew but where.
['Hope' (1782)]

DARLING, Charles (1849-1936)
Much truth is spoken, that more may be concealed.
[*Scintillae Juris* (1877)]

DOYLE, Sir Arthur Conan (1859-1930)
It is an old maxim of mine that when you have excluded the impossible, whatever remains, however improbable, must be the truth.
['The Beryl Coronet' (1892)]

DRYDEN, John (1631-1700)
I never saw any good that came of telling truth.
[*Amphitryon* (1690)]

FRAME, Janet (1924-2004)
In an age of explanation one can always choose varieties of truth.
[*Living in the Maniototo* (1979)]

HELLMAN, Lillian (1905-1984)
Cynicism is an unpleasant way of saying the truth.
[*The Little Foxes* (1939)]

IBSEN, Henrik (1828-1906)
A man should never have his best trousers on when he goes out to battle for freedom and truth.
[*An Enemy of the People* (1882)]

JEROME, Jerome K. (1859-1927)
It is always the best policy to speak the truth, unless of course you are an exceptionally good liar.
[In *The Idler*, 1892]

JOHNSON, Samuel (1709-1784)
(On sceptics)
Truth, Sir, is a cow which will yield such people no more milk, and so they are gone to milk the bull.
[In Boswell, *The Life of Samuel Johnson* (1791)]

LEACOCK, Stephen (1869-1944)
A half truth in argument, like a half brick, carries better.
[In Flesch, *The Book of Unusual Quotations*]

NIXON, Richard (1913-1994)
Let us begin by committing ourselves to the truth, to see it like it is and to tell it like it is, to find the truth, to speak the truth and live with the truth. That's what we'll do.
[Nomination acceptance speech, 1968]

PROUST, Marcel (1871-1922)
A truth which is clearly understood can no longer be written with sincerity.
['Senancour c'est moi']

SAMUEL, Lord (1870–1963)
A truism is on that account none the less true.
[*A Book of Quotations* (1947)]

SHAW, George Bernard (1856–1950)
All great truths begin as blasphemies.
[*Annojanska* (1919)]

TWAIN, Mark (1835–1910)
When in doubt, tell the truth.
[*Pudd'nhead Wilson's New Calendar*]

WILDE, Oscar (1854–1900)
If one tells the truth, one is sure, sooner or later, to be found out.
[*The Chameleon*, 1894]

WRIGHT, Frank Lloyd (1869–1959)
The truth is more important than the facts.
[In Simcox, *Treasury of Quotations*]

ZOLA, Emile (1840–1902)
(Article on the Dreyfus affair)
Truth is on the move and nothing can stop it.
[In *La Vérité en marche* (1901)]

See **ERROR, FACTS, HONESTY, LIES**

TYRANNY

ARENDT, Hannah (1906–1975)
Under conditions of tyranny it is far easier to act than to think.
[In Auden, *A Certain World* (1970)]

BROWNING, Robert (1812–1889)
Oppression makes the wise man mad.
[*Luria* (1846)]

BURKE, Edmund (1729–1797)
Bad laws are the worst sort of tyranny.
[*Speech at Bristol* (1780)]

DEFOE, Daniel (c.1661–1731)
Nature has left this tincture in the blood,
That all men would be tyrants if they could.
['The Kentish Petition' (1713)]

HERRICK, Robert (1591–1674)
'Twixt Kings & Tyrants there's this difference known;
Kings seek their Subjects good: Tyrants their owne.
[*Hesperides* (1648)]

MANDELA, Nelson (1918–)
Never, never and never again shall it be that this beautiful land will again experience the oppression of one by another and suffer the indignity of being the skunk of the world.
[Inauguration speech, 1994]

MILL, John Stuart (1806–1873)
Whatever crushes individuality is despotism, by whatever name it may be called.
[*On Liberty* (1859)]

PITT, William (1708–1778)
Where law ends, there tyranny begins.
[Speech, 1770]

See **CENSORSHIP**

UNCERTAINTY

BARNFIELD, Richard (1574–1627)
Nothing more certain than incertainties;
Fortune is full of fresh variety:
Constant in nothing but inconstancy.
[*The Affectionate Shepherd* (1594)]

BISSELL, Claude T. (1916–2000)
I prefer complexity to certainty, cheerful mysteries to sullen facts.
[Address, University of Toronto, 1969]

DRABBLE, Margaret (Dame) (1939–)
When nothing is sure, everything is possible.
[*The Middle Ground* (1980)]

RUMSFELD, Donald (1932–)
(Addressing the absence of evidence linking Iraq with the supply of weapons of mass destruction to terrorists)
There are known knowns; there are things we know that we don't know. There are known unknowns; that is to say, there are things that we know we don't know. But there are also unknown unknowns – there are things we do not know we don't know.
[press conference, 2002]

See **DOUBT, INDECISION**

UNIVERSITY

BATESON, Mary Catherine (1939–)
Most higher education is devoted to affirming the traditions and origins of an existing elite and transmitting them to new members.
[*Composing a Life* (1989)]

FRY, Stephen (1957–)
The competitive spirit is an ethos which it is the business of universities ... to subdue and neutralise.
[*Paperweight* (1992)]

MCLUHAN, Marshall (1911–1980)
The reason universities are so full of knowledge is that the students come with so much and they leave with so little.
[*Antigonish Review*, 1988]

MELVILLE, Herman (1819–1891)
A whale ship was my Yale College and my Harvard.
                                                    [*Moby Dick* (1851)]

NABOKOV, Vladimir (1899–1977)
Like so many ageing college people, Pnin had long ceased to notice the existence of students on the campus.
                                                    [*Pnin* (1957)]

OZICK, Cynthia (1928–)
It is the function of a liberal university not to give the right answers, but to ask the right questions.
                                    ['Women and Creativity' (1969)]

SPOONER, William (1844–1930)
Sir, you have tasted two whole worms; you have hissed all my mystery lectures and have been caught fighting a liar in the quad; you will leave Oxford by the town drain.
                                                                [Attr.]

See **EDUCATION, KNOWLEDGE, LEARNING, SCHOOL, TEACHERS**

VANITY

**THE BIBLE
(King James Version)**
Vanity of vanities, saith the Preacher, vanity of vanities; all is vanity.
                                            [*Ecclesiastes*, 1:2]

COWLEY, Hannah (1743–1809)
Vanity, like murder, will out.
                            [*The Belle's Stratagem* (1780)]

PARRIS, Matthew (1949–)
Being an MP feeds your vanity and starves your self-respect.
                            [*The Times*, February 1994]

STEVENSON, Robert Louis (1850–1894)
Vanity dies hard; in some obstinate cases it outlives the man.
                                            [*Prince Otto*]

See **APPEARANCE, PRIDE, SELF**

VEGETARIANISM

BROWN, A. Whitney
I am not a vegetarian because I love animals; I am a vegetarian because I hate plants.

CAMPBELL, Mrs Patrick (1865–1940)
(To Bernard Shaw, a vegetarian)
Some day you'll eat a pork chop, Joey, and then God help all women.
                    [In Woollcott, *While Rome Burns* (1934)]

DAVIS, Miles (1926–1991)
(On vegetarianism)
I figure if horses can eat green shit and be strong and run like motherfuckers, why shouldn't I?
            [In Ian Carr, *Miles Davis: a Critical Biography*
                                                        (1982)]

LANG, K.D. (1961–)
If you knew how meat was made, you'd probably lose your lunch. I'm from cattle country. That's why I became a vegetarian.

OBIS, Paul
(Founder of Vegetarian Times on his decision to start eating meat, 1997)
Twenty-two years of tofu is a lot of time.

See **DINING, FOOD**

VICTORY

CHURCHILL, Sir Winston (1874–1965)
You ask, what is our aim? I can answer that in one word: victory at all costs, victory in spite of all terror, victory however long and hard the road may be; for without victory there is no survival.
                [Speech, House of Commons, May 1940]

DUVALL, Robert (1931–)
(As Colonel Killgore in Apocalypse Now, 1977)
I love the smell of Napalm in the morning ... smells like victory.

KENNEDY, John F. (1917–1963)
Victory has a thousand fathers but defeat is an orphan.
                                                            [Attr.]

KHRUSHCHEV, Nikita (1894–1971)
(Of The Cuban missile crisis)
People talk about who won and who lost. Human reason won. Mankind won.
                                            [*The Observer*, 1962]

MACARTHUR, Douglas (1880–1964)
In war there is no substitute for victory.
                                    [Speech to Congress, 1951]

NELSON, Lord (1758–1805)
(At the Battle of the Nile, 1798)
Victory is not a name strong enough for such a scene.
            [In Robert Southey, *The Life of Nelson* (1860)]

SOUTHEY, Robert (1774–1843)
'And everybody praised the Duke,
Who this great fight did win.'
'But what good came of it at last?'
Quoth little Peterkin.
'Why that I cannot tell,' said he,
'But 'twas a famous victory.'
['The Battle of Blenheim' (1798)]

See **SUCCESS, WAR**

VIOLENCE

ADIE, Kate (1945–)
I have never been attracted to any kind of violence. I even refused to join the Girl Guides because they wore uniforms.
[*The Sunday Times*, 2001]

ALI, Muhammad (1942–)
Fighting is not the answer to frustration and hate. It is a sport, not a philosophy of life.
[Interview, *TV Guide* magazine, 1999]

ASCHERSON, Neal (1932–)
Rioting is at least as English as thatched cottages and honey still for tea.
[*The Observer*, 1985]

ASIMOV, Isaac (1920–1992)
Violence is the last refuge of the incompetent.
[*Foundation* (1951)]

BRIEN, Alan (1925–2008)
Violence is the repartee of the illiterate.
[*Punch*, 1973]

BRIGHT, John (1811–1889)
Force is not a remedy.
[Speech, 1880]

BRONOWSKI, Jacob (1908–1974)
The wish to hurt, the momentary intoxication with pain, is the loophole through which the pervert climbs into the minds of ordinary men.
[*The Face of Violence* (1954)]

HORACE (65–8 BC)
Brute force without judgement collapses under its own weight.
[*Odes*]

INGE, William Ralph (1860–1954)
A man may build himself a throne of bayonets, but he cannot sit upon it.
[*Philosophy of Plotinus* (1923)]

KING, Martin Luther (1929–1968)
A riot is at bottom the language of the unheard.
[*Chaos or Community* (1967)]

KORAN
Let there be no violence in religion.
[Chapter 2]

MACKENZIE, Sir Compton (1883–1972)
There is little to choose morally between beating up a man physically and beating him up mentally.
[*On Moral Courage* (1962)]

MILTON, John (1608–1674)
Who overcomes
By force, hath overcome but half his foe.
[*Paradise Lost* (1667)]

UNAMUNO, Miguel de (1864–1936)
(Of Franco's supporters)
To conquer is not to convince.
[Speech, 1936]

See **CRUELTY, FORCE, WAR, WEAPONS**

VIRTUE

ARISTOTLE (384–322 BC)
Moral virtues we acquire through practice like the arts.
[*Nicomachean Ethics*]

BACON, Francis (1561–1626)
Virtue is like a rich stone, best plain set.
['Of Beauty' (1625)]

BAGEHOT, Walter (1826–1877)
Nothing is more unpleasant than a virtuous person with a mean mind.
[*Literary Studies* (1879)]

BROWNE, Sir Thomas (1605–1682)
There is no road or ready way to virtue.
[*Religio Medici* (1643)]

COLETTE (1873–1954)
My virtue's still far too small, I don't trot it out and about yet.
[*Claudine at School* (1900)]

CONFUCIUS (c.550–c.478 BC)
To be able to practise five things everywhere under heaven constitutes perfect virtue ... gravity, generosity of soul, sincerity, earnestness, and kindness.
[*Analects*]

FLETCHER, John (1579–1625)
'Tis virtue, and not birth that makes us noble:
Great actions speak great minds, and such should govern.
[*The Prophetess* (1647)]

GOLDSMITH, Oliver (c.1728–1774)
The virtue which requires to be ever guarded, is scarce worth the sentinel.
[*The Vicar of Wakefield* (1766)]

HAZLITT, William (1778–1830)
The greatest offence against virtue is to speak ill of it.
[*London Weekly Review*, 1828]

JUVENAL (c.60–130)
The one and only true nobility is virtue.
[*Satires*]

LA ROCHEFOUCAULD (1613–1680)
Greater virtues are needed to sustain good fortune than bad.
[*Maximes* (1678)]

MILTON, John (1608–1674)
Most men admire
Vertue, who follow not her lore.
[*Paradise Regained* (1671)]

MOLIÈRE (1622–1673)
Virtue, in this world, should be accommodating.
[*Le Misanthrope* (1666)]

MONTAIGNE, Michel de (1533–1592)
Virtue shuns ease as a companion. It needs a rough and thorny path.
[*Essais* (1580)]

SHAKESPEARE, William (1564–1616)
Dost thou think, because thou art virtuous, there shall be no more cakes and ale?
[*Twelfth Night*, II.iii]

SKINNER, Cornelia Otis (1901–1979)
Woman's virtue is man's greatest invention.
[Attr.]

WASHINGTON, George (1732–1799)
Few men have virtue to withstand the highest bidder.
[*Moral Maxims*]

WHITE, Patrick (1912–1990)
Virtue is ... frequently in the nature of an iceberg, the other parts of it submerged.
[*The Tree of Man* (1955)]

See **GOOD AND EVIL, GOODNESS, MORALITY, PRINCIPLES, VICE**

WAR

ACHESON, Dean (1893–1971)
(Of the Vietnam war)
It is worse than immoral, it's a mistake.
[Quoted on Alistair Cooke's radio programme *Letter from America*]

ANONYMOUS
Friendly fire isn't.
[American officer on the town of Ben Tre, Vietnam, during the Tet offensive, 1968]
To save the town, it became necessary to destroy it.

AUSTEN, Jane (1775–1817)
(Of the Battle of Albuera in 1811)
How horrible it is to have so many people killed! – And what a blessing that one cares for none of them!
[Letter to Cassandra Austen, 1811]

BARUCH, Bernard M. (1870–1965)
Let us not be deceived – we are today in the midst of a cold war.
[Speech, 1947]

BELLOC, Hilaire (1870–1953)
Whatever happens, we have got The Maxim Gun, and they have not.
[*Modern Traveller* (1898)]

BENNETT, Alan (1934–)
I have never understood this liking for war. It panders to instincts already catered for within the scope of any respectable domestic establishment.
[*Forty Years On* (1969)]

**THE BIBLE
(King James Version)**
All they that take the sword shall perish with the sword.
[*Matthew*, 26:52]

BORGES, Jorge Luis (1899–1986)
(On the Falklands War of 1982)
The Falklands thing was a fight between two bald men over a comb.
[*Time*, 1983]

BOSQUET, Pierre François Joseph (1810–1861)
(Remark on witnessing the suicidal Charge of the Light Brigade, 1854)
It is magnificent, but it is not war.
[Attr.]

BRADLEY, Omar Nelson (1893–1981)
(On a proposal to carry the Korean war into China)
The wrong war, at the wrong place, at the wrong time, and with the wrong enemy.
[Senate inquiry, 1951]

BUSH, George W. (1946–)
In time, perhaps, we will mark the memory of September 11 in stone and metal, something we can show children as yet unborn to help them understand what happened on this minute and on this day. But for those of us who lived through these events, the only marker we'll ever need is the tick of a clock at the 46th minute of the eighth hour of the 11th day.
[Speech, 11 December 2001]

CHRISTIE, Dame Agatha (1890–1976)
One is left with the horrible feeling now that war settles nothing; that to win a war is as disastrous as to lose one!
[*An Autobiography* (1977)]

CHURCHILL, Sir Winston (1874–1965)
(On RAF pilots in the Battle of Britain)
Never in the field of human conflict was so much owed by so many to so few.
[Speech, 1940]

CICERO (106–43 BC)
The sinews of war, unlimited money.
[*Philippic*]

CLAUSEWITZ, Karl von (1780–1831)
War is nothing but a continuation of politics by other means.
[*On War* (1834)]

ELLIS, Havelock (1859–1939)
In many a war it has been the vanquished, not the victor, who has carried off the finest spoils.
[*The Soul of Spain* (1908)]

ERASMUS (c.1466–1536)
War is sweet to those who do not fight.
[*Adagia* (1500)]

GOLDWATER, Barry (1909–1998)
You've got to forget about this civilian. Whenever you drop bombs, you're going to hit civilians.
[Speech, 1967]

HAIG, Douglas (1861–1928)
Every position must be held to the last man: there must be no retirement. With our backs to the wall, and believing in the justice of our cause, each one of us must fight on to the end.
[Order to British forces on the Western Front, 1918]

HANRAHAN, Brian (1949–2010)
(Reporting the British attack on Port Stanley airport, during the Falklands war)
I'm not allowed to say how many planes joined the raid but I counted them all out and I counted them all back.
[BBC report, 1 May 1982]

HARKIN, Thomas (1939–)
The Gulf War was like teenage sex. We got in too soon and we got out too soon.
[*Independent on Sunday*, 1991]

HIROHITO, Emperor (1901–1989)
The war situation has developed not necessarily to Japan's advantage.
[Announcing Japan's surrender, 15 August 1945]

HITLER, Adolf (1889–1945)
(Said in 1939)
In starting and waging a war it is not right that matters, but victory.
[In Shirer, *The Rise and Fall of the Third Reich* (1960)]

HOBBES, Thomas (1588–1679)
Force, and fraud, are in war the two cardinal virtues.
[*Leviathan* (1651)]

HOOVER, Herbert (1874–1964)
Older men declare war. But it is youth that must fight and die.
[Speech, 1944]

JOHNSON, Hiram (1866–1945)
The first casualty when war comes is truth.
[Speech, US Senate, 1917]

LEBED, Alexander (1950–2002)
He who laughs last is the one who shot first.
[Attr.]

LEE, Robert E. (1807–1870)
It is well that war is so terrible – we would grow too fond of it.
[Remark after the Battle of Fredericksburg, 1862]

LLOYD GEORGE, David (1863–1945)
(Referring to the popular opinion that World War I would be the last major war)
This war, like the next war, is a war to end war.
[Attr.]

MACDONALD, Ramsay (1866–1937)
We hear war called murder. It is not: it is suicide.
[*The Observer*, 1930]

MCNAMARA, Robert (1916–2009)
I don't object to it's being called 'McNamara's War' ... It is a very important war and I am pleased to be identified with it and do whatever I can to win it.
[*New York Times*, April 1964]
(Speech on the twentieth anniversary of the American withdrawal from Vietnam)
We were wrong. We were terribly wrong.
[*Daily Telegraph*, April 1995]

MEIR, Golda (1898–1978)
A leader who doesn't hesitate before he sends his nation into battle is not fit to be a leader.
[I. and M. Shenker, *As Good as Golda* (1943)]

MONTAGUE, C.E. (1867–1928)
War hath no fury like a non-combatant.
[*Disenchantment* (1922)]

OWEN, Wilfred (1893–1918)
What passing-bells for these who die as cattle?
Only the monstrous anger of the guns.
Only the stuttering rifles' rapid rattle
Can patter out their hasty orisons.
['Anthem for Doomed Youth' (1917)]

PYRRHUS (319–272 BC)
(After a hard-won battle)
If we are victorious against the Romans in
one more battle we shall be utterly ruined.
[In Plutarch, *Lives*]

ROOSEVELT, Franklin Delano (1882–1945)
More than an end to war, we want an end to
the beginnings of all wars.
[Speech, 1945]

SANDBURG, Carl (1878–1967)
Sometime they'll give a war and nobody will
come.
[*The People, Yes* (1936)]

SCHWARTZKOPF, Norman (1934–2012)
(Describing Saddam Hussein of Iraq, 1991)
He is neither a strategist nor is he schooled in
the operational arts, nor is he a tactician, nor
is he a general. Other than that he's a great
military man.

SHAKESPEARE, William (1564–1616)
Once more unto the breach, dear friends,
once more;
Or close the wall up with our English dead.
In peace there's nothing so becomes a man
As modest stillness and humility;
But when the blast of war blows in our ears,
Then imitate the action of the tiger:
Stiffen the sinews, summon up the blood.
Disguise fair nature with hard-favour'd rage;
Then lend the eye a terrible aspect.
[*Henry V*, III.i]

SHERMAN, William Tecumseh (1820–1891)
There is many a boy here today who looks on
war as all glory, but, boys, it is all hell.
[Speech, 1880]

SPOCK, Dr Benjamin (1903–1998)
To win in Vietnam, we will have to
exterminate a nation.
[*Dr Spock on Vietnam* (1968)]

UREY, Harold (1893–1981)
The next war will be fought with atom bombs
and the one after that with spears.
[*The Observer*, 1946]

WELLINGTON (Duke of) (1769–1852)
(Refusing permission to shoot at Napoleon
during the Battle of Waterloo)
It is not the business of generals to shoot one
another.
[Attr.]

WILDE, Oscar (1854–1900)
As long as war is regarded as wicked it will
always have its fascination. When it is looked
upon as vulgar, it will cease to be popular.
[*The Critic as Artist* (1890)]

WILSON, Woodrow (1856–1924)
Once lead this people into war and they'll
forget there ever was such a thing as tolerance.
[In Dos Passos, *Mr Wilson's War* (1917)]

See **ARMY, NUCLEAR WEAPONS,
PATRIOTISM, SACRIFICE, VICTORY**

THE WEATHER

AUSTEN, Jane (1775–1817)
What dreadful hot weather we have! It keeps
me in a continual state of inelegance.
[Letter, 1796]

CHEKHOV, Anton (1860–1904)
He who doesn't notice whether it is winter or
summer is happy. I think that if I were in
Moscow, I wouldn't notice what the weather
was like.
[*The Three Sisters* (1901)]

ELLIS, George (1753–1815)
Snowy, Flowy, Blowy,
Showery, Flowery, Bowery,
Hoppy, Croppy, Droppy,
Breezy, Sneezy, Freezy.
['The Twelve Months']

JOHNSON, Samuel (1709–1784)
When two Englishmen meet, their first talk is
of the weather.
[*The Idler* (1758–1760)]

LODGE, David (1935–)
The British, he thought, must be gluttons for
satire: even the weather forecast seemed to
be some kind of spoof, predicting every
possible combination of weather for the next
twenty-four hours without actually
committing itself to anything specific.
[*Changing Places* (1975)]

MACAULAY, Dame Rose (1881–1958)
Owing to the weather, English social life must
always have largely occurred either indoors,
or, when out of doors, in active motion.
['Life Among The English' (1942)]

POUND, Ezra (1885–1972)
Winter is icumમen in,
Lhude sing Goddamn,
Raineth drop and staineth slop,
And how the wind doth ramm!
Sing: Goddamn.

['Ancient Music' (1916)]

RUSKIN, John (1819–1900)
There is really no such thing as bad weather,
only different kinds of good weather.

[Attr.]

TWAIN, Mark (1835–1910)
Everybody talks about the weather but
nobody does anything about it.

[Attr.]

See **SEASONS**

WISDOM

AESCHYLUS (525–456 BC)
It is a fine thing even for an old man to learn
wisdom.

[*Fragments*]

ARISTOPHANES (c.445–385 BC)
One may learn wisdom even from one's
enemies.

[*Birds*]

BACON, Francis (1561–1626)
A wise man will make more opportunities
than he finds.

['Of Ceremonies and Respects' (1625)]

**THE BIBLE
(King James Version)**
Wisdom is the principal thing; therefore get
wisdom: and with all thy getting get
understanding.

[*Proverbs*, 4:7]

CHESTERFIELD, Lord (1694–1773)
Be wiser than other people if you can; but do
not tell them so.

[Letter to his son, 1745]

COWPER, William (1731–1800)
Knowledge is proud that he has learn'd so
much;
Wisdom is humble that he knows no more.

[*The Task* (1785)]

EMERSON, Ralph Waldo (1803–1882)
Now that is the wisdom of a man, in every
instance of his labor, to hitch his wagon to a
star, and see his chore done by the gods
themselves.

[*Society and Solitude* (1870)]

HORACE (65–8 BC)
To have made a beginning is half of the
business; dare to be wise.

[*Epistles*]

HUTCHESON, Francis (1694–1746)
Wisdom denotes the pursuing of the best
ends by the best means.

[*An Inquiry into the Original of our Ideas of
Beauty and Virtue* (1725)]

LÉVI-STRAUSS, Claude (1908–2009)
The wise man is not the man who gives the
right answers; he is the one who asks the
right questions.

[*The Raw and the Cooked*]

PLATO (c.429–347 BC)
That man is wisest who, like Socrates, has
realized that in truth his wisdom is worth
nothing.

[The Apology of Socrates]

QUARLES, Francis (1592–1644)
Be wisely worldly, not worldly wise.

[*Emblems* (1635)]

ROOSEVELT, Theodore (1858–1919)
Nine-tenths of wisdom is being wise in time.

[Speech, 1917]

SMOLLETT, Tobias (1721–1771)
Some folks are wise, and some are otherwise.

[*The Adventures of Roderick Random* (1748)]

SWIFT, Jonathan (1667–1745)
No wise man ever wished to be younger.

[*Thoughts on Various Subjects* (1711)]

SZASZ, Thomas (1920–2012)
The stupid neither forgive nor forget; the
naive forgive and forget; the wise forgive but
do not forget.

[*The Second Sin* (1973)]

See **INTELLIGENCE, KNOWLEDGE, WIT**

WIT

JOHNSON, Samuel (1709–1784)
(Of Lord Chesterfield)
This man I thought had been a Lord among
wits; but, I find, he is only a wit among Lords.

[In Boswell, *The Life of Samuel Johnson* (1791)]

MAHAFFY, Sir John Pentland (1839–1919)
My dear Oscar, you are not clever enough for
us in Dublin. You had better run over to
Oxford.

[In H. Montgomery Hyde, *Oscar Wilde:
A Biography* (1975)]

MAUGHAM, William Somerset (1874-1965)
Impropriety is the soul of wit.
[*The Moon and Sixpence* (1919)]

POPE, Alexander (1688-1744)
Some have at first for Wits, then Poets pass'd,
Turned Critics next, and proved plain fools at last.
[*An Essay on Criticism* (1711)]

RUSSELL, Lord John (1792-1878)
A proverb is one man's wit and all men's wisdom.
[In R.J. Mackintosh, *Sir James Mackintosh* (1835)]

SKELTON, Robin (1925-1997)
Anything said off the cuff has usually been written on it first.
[Attr.]

STERNE, Laurence (1713-1768)
An ounce of a man's own wit is worth a ton of other people's.
[*Tristram Shandy* (1759-1767)]

See **WISDOM**

WOMEN

ARNOLD, Matthew (1822-1888)
With women the heart argues, not the mind.
[*Merope* (1858)]

AUSTEN, Jane (1775-1817)
Next to being married, a girl likes to be crossed in love a little now and then.
[*Pride and Prejudice* (1813)]
In nine cases out of ten, a woman had better show more affection than she feels.
[Letter]

BACALL, Lauren (1924-)
I'm not a member of the weaker sex.
[In Simon Rose, *Classic Film Guide* (1995)]

BEAUVOIR, Simone de (1908-1986)
One is not born a woman: one becomes a woman.
[*The Second Sex* (1950)]

BEERBOHM, Sir Max (1872-1956)
Most women are not so young as they are painted.
[*The Works of Max Beerbohm* (1896)]

BUTLER, Samuel (1835-1902)
Brigands demand your money or your life; women require both.
[Attr.]

BYRON, Lord (1788-1824)
There is something to me very softening in the presence of a woman,- some strange influence, even if one is not in love with them - which I cannot at all account for, having no very high opinion of the sex.
[*Journal*, 1814]

CATULLUS (84-c.54 BC)
But what a woman says to her eager lover, she ought to write in the wind and the running water.
[*Carmina*]

CERVANTES, Miguel de (1547-1616)
An honest woman and a broken leg should be at home; and for a decent maiden, working is her holiday.
[*Don Quixote* (1615)]

CHANDLER, Raymond (1888-1959)
It was a blonde. A blonde to make a bishop kick a hole in a stained glass window.
[*Farewell, My Lovely* (1940)]

CHAUCER, Geoffrey (c.1340-1400)
What is bettre than wisedoom? Womman. And what is bettre than a good womman? Nothyng.
[*The Canterbury Tales* (1387)]

CHEKHOV, Anton (1860-1904)
Women don't forgive failure.
[*The Seagull* (1896)]

COWARD, Sir Noël (1899-1973)
Certain women should be struck regularly, like gongs.
[*Private Lives* (1930)]

COWLEY, Hannah (1743-1809)
But what is woman?-only one of Nature's agreeable blunders.
[*Who's the Dupe?* (1779)]

DELANEY, Shelagh (1939-2011)
Women never have young minds. They are born three thousand years old.
[*A Taste of Honey* (1959)]

DYSON, Sir James (1947-)
I don't operate rationally. I think just like a woman.
[*The Times*, February 1999]

EKLAND, Britt (1942-)
As a single woman with a child, I would love to have a wife.
[*The Independent*, 1994]

ELIOT, George (1819–1880)
I should like to know what is the proper function of women, if it is not to make reasons for husbands to stay at home, and still stronger reasons for bachelors to go out.
[*The Mill on the Floss* (1860)]

FRAYN, Michael (1933–)
No woman so naked as one you can see to be naked underneath her clothes.
[*Constructions*]

FREUD, Sigmund (1856–1939)
The great question ... which I have not been able to answer, despite my thirty years of research into the feminine soul, is 'What does a woman want?'.
[In Robb, *Psychiatry in American Life*]

GORMAN, Theresa (1931–)
The Conservative establishment has always treated women as nannies, grannies and fannies.
[*The Observer*, 1998]

GRANVILLE, George (1666–1735)
Of all the plagues with which the world is curst,
Of every ill, a woman is the worst.
[*The British Enchanters*]

HARMAN, Sir Jeremiah (1930–)
I've always thought there were only three kinds of women: wives, whores and mistresses.
[*Daily Mail*, 1996]

IRVING, Washington (1783–1859)
A woman's whole life is a history of the affections.
[*The Sketch Book* (1820)]

JOHNSON, Samuel (1709–1784)
Sir, a woman's preaching is like a dog's walking on his hinder legs. It is not done well; but you are surprised to find it done at all.
[In Boswell, *The Life of Samuel Johnson* (1791)]

LERNER, Alan Jay (1918–1986)
There is no greater fan of the opposite sex than me, and I have the bills to prove it.
[Attr.]

MAILER, Norman (1923–2007)
You don't know a woman until you've met her in court.
[*The Observer*, 1983]

MAUGHAM, William Somerset (1874–1965)
A woman will always sacrifice herself if you give her the opportunity. It is her favourite form of self-indulgence.
[*The Circle* (1921)]

MENCKEN, H.L. (1880–1956)
When women kiss, it always reminds me of prize-fighters shaking hands.
[Attr.]

MILTON, John (1608–1674)
... nothing lovelier can be found In Woman, than to studie household good, And good works in her Husband to promote.
[*Paradise Lost* (1667)]

MORISSETTE, Alanis (1974–)
I want to walk through life instead of being dragged through it.
[Attr.]

NASH, Ogden (1902–1971)
Women would rather be right than reasonable.
['Frailty, Thy Name is a Misnomer' (1942)]

NIETZSCHE, Friedrich Wilhelm (1844–1900)
Everything to do with women is a mystery, and everything to do with women has one solution: it's called pregnancy.
[*Thus Spake Zarathustra* (1884)]

NIN, Anais (1903–1977)
Women (and I, in this Diary) have never separated sex from feeling, from love of the whole man.
[*Delta of Venus* (1977)]

PAGLIA, Camille (1947–)
There is no female Mozart because there is no female Jack the Ripper.
[Attr. in *The Observer*, 1996]

RACINE, Jean (1639–1699)
She wavers, she hesitates; in a word, she is a woman.
[*Athalie* (1691)]

ROWLAND, Helen (1875–1950)
It takes a woman twenty years to make a man of her son, and another woman twenty minutes to make a fool of him.
[*Reflections of a Bachelor Girl* (1909)]

RUBINSTEIN, Helena (c.1872–1965)
There are no ugly women, only lazy ones.
[*My Life for Beauty* (1965)]

SCHOPENHAUER, Arthur (1788–1860)
One needs only to see the way she is built to realise that woman is not intended for great mental labour.

[Attr.]

SHAKESPEARE, William (1564–1616)
Frailty, thy name is woman!

[*Hamlet*, I.ii]

She's beautiful, and therefore to be woo'd;
She is a woman, therefore to be won.

[*Henry VI, Part 1*, V.iii]

SOUTHEY, Robert (1774–1843)
What will not woman, gentle woman, dare,
When strong affection stirs her spirit up?

[*Madoc* (1805)]

STEINEM, Gloria (1934–)
One day, an army of grey-haired women may quietly take over the earth.

[*Outrageous Acts and Everyday Rebellions* (1984)]

VANBRUGH, Sir John (1664–1726)
Once a woman has given you her heart you can never get rid of the rest of her.

[*The Relapse, or Virtue in Danger* (1696)]

WOLFF, Charlotte (1904–1986)
Women have always been the guardians of wisdom and humanity which makes them natural, but usually secret, rulers. The time has come for them to rule openly, but together with and not against men.

[*Bisexuality: A Study*]

WYNNE-TYSON, Esme (1898–1972)
Scheherazade is the classical example of a woman saving her head by using it.

[Attr.]

See **FEMINISM, MEN AND WOMEN**

Words

AESCHYLUS (525–456 BC)
Words are physic to the distempered mind.

[*Prometheus Bound*]

ASHDOWN, Paddy (Baron) (1941–)
Lord, make my words sweet and reasonable. Some day I may have to eat them.

[*The Observer*, 1998]

CONFUCIUS (c.550–c.478 BC)
Without knowing the force of words, it is impossible to know men.

[*Analects*]

EMERSON, Ralph Waldo (1803–1882)
Words are also actions, and actions are a kind of words.

['The Poet' (1844)]

HARDY, Thomas (1840–1928)
Dialect words – those terrible marks of the beast to the truly genteel.

[*The Mayor of Casterbridge* (1886)]

HOBBES, Thomas (1588–1679)
Words are wise men's counters, they do but reckon by them; but they are the money of fools.

[*Leviathan* (1651)]

HUXLEY, Aldous (1894–1963)
Thanks to words, we have been able to rise above the brutes; and thanks to words, we have often sunk to the level of the demons.

[*Adonis and the Alphabet* (1956)]

KIPLING, Rudyard (1865–1936)
Words are, of course, the most powerful drug used by mankind.

[Speech, 1923]

POPE, Alexander (1688–1744)
Words are like leaves; and where they most abound,
Much fruit of sense beneath is rarely found.

[*An Essay on Criticism* (1711)]

SHAKESPEARE, William (1564–1616)
But words are words: I never yet did hear
That the bruis'd heart was pierced through the ear.

[*Othello*, I.iii]

SPENCER, Herbert (1820–1903)
How often misused words generate misleading thoughts.

[*Principles of Ethics* (1879)]

See **CONVERSATION, LANGUAGE**

Work

ACHESON, Dean (1893–1971)
(On leaving his post as US Secretary of State, 1952)
I will undoubtedly have to seek what is happily known as gainful employment, which I am glad to say does not describe holding public office.

[Attr.]

BACON, Francis (1909–1993)
How can I take an interest in my work when I don't like it?

[Attr.]

BALDWIN, James (1924–1987)
The price one pays for pursuing any profession or calling is an intimate knowledge of its ugly side.
[*Nobody Knows My Name* (1961)]

BENCHLEY, Robert (1889–1945)
I do most of my work sitting down; that's where I shine.
[Attr.]

THE BIBLE
(King James Version)
The labourer is worthy of his hire.
[*Luke*, 10:7]
If any would not work, neither should he eat.
[*II Thessalonians*, 3:10]

BURNS, Robert (1759–1796)
We labour soon, we labour late,
To feed the titled knave, man,
And a' the comfort we're to get,
Is that ayont the grave, man.
['The Tree of Liberty' (1838)]

BUTLER, Samuel (1835–1902)
Every man's work, whether it be literature or music or pictures or architecture or anything else, is always a portrait of himself.
[*The Way of All Flesh* (1903)]

CARLYLE, Thomas (1795–1881)
Work is the grand cure of all the maladies and miseries that ever beset mankind.
[Speech, 1886]

CLARKE, John (fl.1639)
He that would thrive
Must rise at five;
He that hath thriven
May lie till seven.
[*Paraemiologia Anglo-Latina* (1639)]

COLERIDGE, Samuel Taylor (1772–1834)
Work without hope draws nectar in a sieve,
And hope without an object cannot live.
['Work Without Hope' (1828)]

COLLINGWOOD, Robin George (1889–1943)
Perfect freedom is reserved for the man who lives by his own work and in that work does what he wants to do.
[*Speculum Mentis* (1924)]

COWARD, Sir Noël (1899–1973)
Work is much more fun than fun.
[*The Observer*, 1963]

CURIE, Marie (1867–1934)
One never notices what has been done; one can only see what remains to be done ...
[Letter to her brother, 1894]

GEORGE, Henry (1839–1897)
The man who gives me employment, which I must have or suffer, that man is my master, let me call him what I will.
[*Social Problems* (1884)]

JEROME, Jerome K. (1859–1927)
I like work; it fascinates me. I can sit and look at it for hours. I love to keep it by me: the idea of getting rid of it nearly breaks my heart.
[*Three Men in a Boat* (1889)]

KATZENBERG, Jeffrey (1951–)
If you don't show up for work on Saturday, don't bother coming in on Sunday.
[Attr.]

LARKIN, Philip (1922–1985)
Why should I let the toad work
Squat on my life?
Can't I use my wit as a pitchfork
And drive the brute off?
['Toads' (1955)]

PARKINSON, C. Northcote (1909–1993)
Work expands so as to fill the time available for its completion.
[Parkinson's Law (1958)]

PETER, Laurence J. (1919–1990)
In a hierarchy every employee tends to rise to his level of incompetence.
[*The Peter Principle – Why Things Always Go Wrong* (1969)]

REAGAN, Ronald (1911–2004)
They say hard work never hurt anybody, but I figure why take the chance.
[Attr.]

RHODES, Zandra (1940–)
I was lucky to always have a work ethic. Relationships end, men fail, but your work will never let you down.
[*The Observer*, 1998]

ROOSEVELT, Theodore (1858–1919)
No man needs sympathy because he has to work ... Far and away the best prize that life offers is the chance to work hard at work worth doing.
[Address, 1903]

ROWLAND, Helen (1875–1950)
When you see what some girls marry, you realize how they must hate to work for a living.
[*Reflections of a Bachelor Girl* (1909)]

RUSSELL, Bertrand (1872–1970)
One of the symptoms of approaching nervous breakdowns is the belief that one's work is terribly important. If I were a medical man, I should prescribe a holiday to any patient who considered his work important.
[Attr.]

SHAKESPEARE, William (1564–1616)
The labour we delight in physics pain.
[*Macbeth*, II.iii]

STANTON, Elizabeth Cady (1815–1902)
Woman has been the great unpaid laborer of the world.
[In Anthony and Gage, *History of Woman Suffrage* (1881)]

TEBBITT, Norman (1931–)
(Of his father who had grown up during the 1930s)
He didn't riot. He got on his bike and looked for work and he kept looking till he found it.
[Speech, 1981]

VOLTAIRE (1694–1778)
Work keeps away those three great evils: boredom, vice, and poverty.
[*Candide* (1759)]

WATTS, Isaac (1674–1748)
In works of labour, or of skill,
I would be busy too;
For Satan finds some mischief still
For idle hands to do.
['Against Idleness and Mischief' (1715)]

WHITEHORN, Katherine (1926–)
The best careers advice to give to the young is 'Find out what you like doing best and get someone to pay you for doing it.'
[*The Observer*, 1975]

WILDE, Oscar (1854–1900)
Work is the curse of the drinking classes.
[In Pearson, *Life of Oscar Wilde* (1946)]

YEATS, W.B. (1865–1939)
The intellect of man is forced to choose
Perfection of the life, or of the work.
['The Choice' (1933)]

The World

BALFOUR, A.J. (1848–1930)
This is a singularly ill-contrived world, but not so ill-contrived as all that.
[Attr.]

BRONOWSKI, Jacob (1908–1974)
The world is made of people who never quite get into the first team and who just miss the prizes at the flower show.
[*The Face of Violence* (1954)]

BROWNE, Sir Thomas (1605–1682)
For the world, I count it not an inn, but an hospital, and a place, not to live, but to die in.
[*Religio Medici* (1643)]

DICKINSON, Emily (1830–1886)
How much can come
And much can go,
And yet abide the World!
['There came a Wind' (c.1883)]

DIDEROT, Denis (1713–1784)
What a fine comedy this world would be if one did not play a part in it!
[Letters to Sophie Volland]

FIRBANK, Ronald (1886–1926)
The world is disgracefully managed, one hardly knows to whom to complain.
[*Vainglory* (1915)]

HAZLITT, William (1778–1830)
If the world were good for nothing else, it is a fine subject for speculation.
[*Characteristics* (1823)]

HEMINGWAY, Ernest (1898–1961)
The world is a fine place and worth the fighting for.
[*For Whom the Bell Tolls* (1940)]

KAFKA, Franz (1883–1924)
In the struggle between you and the world, support the world.
[*Reflections on Sin, Sorrow, Hope and the True Way* (1953)]

MARQUIS, Don (1878–1937)
Ours is a world where people don't know what they want and are willing to go through hell to get it.
[In *Treasury of Humorous Quotations*]

OPPENHEIMER, J. Robert (1904–1967)
The optimist thinks that this is the best of all possible worlds and the pessimist knows it.
[*Bulletin of Atomic Scientists*, 1951]

SARTRE, Jean-Paul (1905–1980)
The world can survive very well without literature. But it can survive even more easily without man.
[*Situations*]

SHAKESPEARE, William (1564–1616)

How many goodly creatures are there here!
How beauteous mankind is! O brave new
world
That has such people in't!

[*The Tempest*, V.i]

SMOLLETT, Tobias (1721–1771)

I consider the world as made for me, not me
for the world: it is my maxim therefore to
enjoy it while I can, and let futurity shift for
itself.

[*The Adventures of Roderick Random* (1748)]

WALPOLE, Horace (1717–1797)

This world is a comedy to those that think,
and a tragedy to those that feel.

[Letter to Anne, Countess of Upper Ossory,
1776]

WHEDON, Joss (1964–)

Spike: Truth is, I like this world. You got dog
racing, Manchester United, Love Boat, and
you got people.

[*Buffy the Vampire Slayer*, TV series, 1998]

WRITERS

AUDEN, W.H. (1907–1973)

No poet or novelist wishes he were the only
one who ever lived, but most of them wish
they were the only one alive, and quite a
number fondly believe their wish has been
granted.

[*The Dyer's Hand* (1963)]

AUSTEN, Jane (1775–1817)

I think I may boast myself to be, with all
possible vanity, the most unlearned and
uninformed female who ever dared to be an
authoress.

[Letter to James Stanier Clarke, 1815]

BAGEHOT, Walter (1826–1877)

Writers, like teeth, are divided into incisors
and grinders.

['The First Edinburgh Reviewers' (1858)]

BEAUVOIR, Simone de (1908–1986)

Writers who stand out, as long as they are not
dead, are always scandalous.

[*The Second Sex* (1950)]

BENNETT, Alan (1934–)

We were put to Dickens as children but it
never quite took. That unremitting humanity
soon had me cheesed off.

[*The Old Country* (1978)]

BERNARD, Jeffrey (1932–1997)

Writers as a rule don't make fighters,
although I would hate to have to square up to
Taki or Andrea Dworkin.

[*The Spectator*, 1992]

BROWNE, Coral (1913–1991)

(To a Hollywood writer who had criticized the
work of Alan Bennett)
Listen, dear, you couldn't write fuck on a
dusty Venetian blind.

[*The Sunday Times Magazine*, 1984]

CHATEAUBRIAND, François-René (1768–1848)

The original writer is not the one who refrains
from imitating others, but the one who can
be imitated by none.

[*The Beauties of Christianity* (1802)]

CONNOLLY, Cyril (1903–1974)

Better to write for yourself and have no
public, than write for the public and have no
self.

[In Pritchett (ed.), *Turnstile One*]

DIDION, Joan (1934–)

Writers are always selling somebody out.

[*Slouching Towards Bethlehem* (1968)]

EMERSON, Ralph Waldo (1803–1882)

Talent alone cannot make a writer. There
must be a man behind the book.

['Goethe; or, the Writer' (1850)]

FAULKNER, William (1897–1962)

The writer's only responsibility is to his art ...
If a writer has to rob his mother, he will not
hesitate; the 'Ode on a Grecian Urn' is worth
any number of old ladies.

[*Paris Review*, 1956]

FROST, Robert (1874–1963)

No tears in the writer, no tears in the reader.

[*Collected Poems* (1939)]

GORDIMER, Nadine (1923–)

The tension between standing apart and
being fully involved; that is what makes a
writer.

[*Selected Stories* (1975)]

HILL, Reginald (1936–2012)

(When asked in America why all the great
crime writers of the 1920s were female)
Because the men were all dead.

HOBBES, Thomas (1588–1679)
The praise of ancient authors, proceeds not from the reverence of the dead, but from the competition, and mutual envy of the living.
[*Leviathan* (1651)]

JOHNSON, Samuel (1709–1784)
The greatest part of a writer's time is spent in reading, in order to write: a man will turn over half a library to make one book.
[In Boswell, *The Life of Samuel Johnson* (1791)]

JOSEPH, Michael (1897–1958)
Authors are easy to get on with – if you're fond of children.
[*The Observer*, 1949]

KOESTLER, Arthur (1905–1983)
A writer's ambition should be ... to trade a hundred contemporary readers for ten readers in ten years' time and for one reader in a hundred years' time.
[*New York Times Book Review*, 1951]

LAMB, Lady Caroline (1785–1828)
(Of Byron)
Mad, bad, and dangerous to know.
[*Journal*, 1812]

LANDOR, Walter Savage (1775–1864)
Clear writers, like clear fountains, do not seem so deep as they are; the turbid look the most profound.
[*Imaginary Conversations* (1824)]

MACDIARMID, Hugh (1892–1978)
Our principal writers have nearly all been fortunate in escaping regular education.
[*The Observer*, 1953]

MACMANUS, Michael (1888–1951)
But my work is undistinguished
And my royalties are lean
Because I never am obscure
And not at all obscene.
['An Author's Lament']

SARTRE, Jean-Paul (1905–1980)
The writer, a free man addressing free men, has only one subject – freedom.
[*What Is Literature?*]

SINGER, Isaac Bashevis (1904–1991)
When I was a little boy they called me a liar but now that I am a grown up they call me a writer.
[*The Observer*, 1983]

SOLZHENITSYN, Alexander (1918–2008)
No regime has ever loved great writers, only minor ones.
[*The First Circle* (1968)]

VIDAL, Gore (1925–2012)
American writers want to be not good but great; and so are neither.
[*Two Sisters* (1970)]

YEATS, W.B. (1865–1939)
It's not a writer's business to hold opinions.
[Attr.]

See **CRITICISM, POETS, WRITING**

WRITING

ANONYMOUS
Inspiration is the act of drawing up a chair to the writing desk.

AUSTEN, Jane (1775–1817)
Let other pens dwell on guilt and misery.
[*Mansfield Park* (1814)]

BOILEAU-DESPRÉAUX, Nicolas (1636–1711)
He who does not know how to limit himself does not know how to write.
[*L'Art Poétique* (1674)]

BULWER-LYTTON, Edward (1803–1873)
Beneath the rule of men entirely great
The pen is mightier than the sword.
[*Richelieu* (1839)]

BURCHILL, Julie (1960–)
Writing is more than anything a compulsion, like some people wash their hands thirty times a day for fear of awful consequences if they do not. It pays a whole lot better than this type of compulsion, but it is no more heroic.
[*Sex and Sensibility* (1992)]

CAPOTE, Truman (1924–1984)
(Referring to the Beat novelists)
That isn't writing at all, it's typing.
[*New Republic*, February 1959]

CARLYLE, Thomas (1795–1881)
After two weeks of blotching and blaring I have produced two clear papers.
[Attr.]

CARTLAND, Barbara (1901–2000)
(On the publication of her 217th book)
As long as the plots keep arriving from outer space, I'll go on with my virgins.
[*New Yorker*, August 1976]

ELIOT, T.S. (1888–1965)
(On his ideal of writing)
The common word exact without vulgarity, the formal word precise but not pedantic, the complete consort dancing together.
[*Sunday Telegraph*, 1993]

FROST, Robert (1874–1963)
Writing free verse is like playing tennis with the net down.

[Address, 1935]

GORKY, Maxim (1868–1936)
You must write for children just as you do for adults, only better.

[Attr.]

HEMINGWAY, Ernest (1898–1961)
Prose is architecture, not interior decoration, and the Baroque is over.

[*Death in the Afternoon* (1932)]

JOHNSON, Samuel (1709–1784)
The only end of writing is to enable the readers better to enjoy life, or better to endure it.

[*Works* (1787)]

No man but a blockhead ever wrote, except for money.

[In Boswell, *The Life of Samuel Johnson* (1791)]

LYNES, J. Russel (1910–1991)
Every journalist has a novel in him, which is an excellent place for it.

MANSFIELD, Katherine (1888–1923)
Better to write twaddle, anything, than nothing at all.

[Attr.]

MURDOCH, Iris (1919–1999)
Writing is like getting married. One should never commit oneself until one is amazed at one's luck.

[*The Black Prince* (1989)]

ORWELL, George (1903–1950)
Good prose is like a window pane.

['Why I Write' (1946)]

PASCAL, Blaise (1623–1662)
The last thing one finds out when constructing a work is what to put first.

[*Pensées* (1670)]

RENARD, Jules (1864–1910)
The profession of letters is, after all, the only one in which one can make no money without being ridiculous.

[*Journal*]

SIMENON, Georges (1903–1989)
Writing is not a profession but a vocation of unhappiness.

[*Writers at Work* (1958)]

STOPPARD, Tom (1937–)
You can only write about what bites you.

[*The Observer*, 1984]

TROLLOPE, Anthony (1815–1882)
Three hours a day will produce as much as a man ought to write.

[*Autobiography* (1883)]

WRIGHT, Frank Lloyd (1869–1959)
I'm all in favor of keeping dangerous weapons out of the hands of fools. Let's start with typewriters.

See **BOOKS, CRITICISM, FICTION, LITERATURE, POETRY, READING, WRITERS**

YOUTH

ASQUITH, Herbert (1852–1928)
Youth would be an ideal state if it came a little later in life.

[*The Observer*, 1923]

CRISP, Quentin (1908–1999)
The young always have the same problem – how to rebel and conform at the same time. They have now solved this by defying their parents and copying one another.

[*The Naked Civil Servant* (1968)]

DISRAELI, Benjamin (1804–1881)
Youth is a blunder; Manhood a struggle; Old Age a regret.

[*Coningsby* (1844)]

GAY, John (1685–1732)
Youth's the season made for joys,
Love is then our duty.

[*The Beggar's Opera* (1728)]

JOHNSON, Samuel (1709–1784)
Young men have more virtue than old men; they have more generous sentiments in every respect.

[In Boswell, *The Life of Samuel Johnson* (1791)]

PARSONS, Tony (1953–)
Funky royals, coked-out old men and streaking BA stewardesses make me nostalgic for an age when people knew youth was just a stage you passed through, like acne.

[*The Observer*, May 1999]

PORTER, Hal (1911–1984)
How ruthless and hard and vile and right the young are.

[*The Watcher on the Cast-Iron Balcony* (1963)]

SHAW, George Bernard (1856–1950)
Youth, which is forgiven everything, forgives
itself nothing: age, which forgives itself
everything, is forgiven nothing.
> [*Man and Superman* (1903)]

It's all that the young can do for the old, to
shock them and keep them up to date.
> [*Fanny's First Play* (1911)]

WILDE, Oscar (1854–1900)
The old-fashioned respect for the young is
fast dying out.
> [*The Importance of Being Earnest* (1895)]

WILSON, Woodrow (1856–1924)
Generally young men are regarded as radicals.
This is a popular misconception. The most
conservative persons I ever met are college
undergraduates.
> [Speech, 1905]

See **AGE, CHILDREN**

INDEX